Quilted Quisine

A Collection of Recipes
from the Paoli Memorial
Hospital Auxiliary

The Cover

The committee thanks Betty Ann Flynn of Flynn Photography for photographing the quilts on the cover. She also provided valuable assistance and professional expertise.

We also thank Ted Regan and Conrad Vogel, of N W Ayer advertising agency, who designed our front and back covers.

The name "Quilted Quisine" was created by Linda Glovach.

This cookbook is a collection of our favorite recipes, which are not necessarily original recipes.

Published by: Favorite Recipes® Press
P. O. Box 305142
Nashville, Tennessee 37230

Library of Congress Number: 92-11047
ISBN: 0-87197-337-5

Printed in the United States of America
First Printing: 1992 10,000 copies

Contents

* *on recipe titles denotes Quick and Easy preparation.*

Paoli Memorial Hospital Auxiliary

In 1968 the Paoli Memorial Hospital opened its doors in its present location in Chester County, Pennsylvania. From the beginning, the Auxiliary, an enthusiastic and talented group of women, has been an extremely active and supportive arm of the hospital, most notably through fund raising, volunteer service and public relations.

The Auxiliary manages three on-site businesses: the Coffee Shop, the Gift Shop, and the Palm Tree Thrift Shop. Its members sponsor many special events: the Radnor Hunt International Three-Day Event, the Festival of Trees, the Charity Ball, the Needlework Show and a Golf Tournament, and now proudly presents ***Quilted Quisine***.

All the monies raised through these activities are contributed to the hospital. At this time the Auxiliary is committed to a 1.5 million dollar pledge for the hospital's new Cancer Center which is affiliated with the Fox Chase Cancer Center. In consideration of the Auxiliary's major contribution, the Board of Directors voted to name the center "The Cancer Center of Paoili Memorial Hospital Auxiliary." The Auxiliary is proud to be part of this state of art treatment center which will give the hospital a better opporutunity to serve the community.

Paoili Memorial Hospital is a voluntary non-profit community hospital and member of the Main Line Health Family of Hospitals, which also includes Lankenau Hospital, Bryn Mawr Hospital and Bryn Mawr Rehabilitation Hospital.

Acknowledgements

Cookbook Committee

Kathleen Papariello - Chairman
Mary Moller - Co-Chairman
Sue Brewer - Chairman 1990-1991

Louisa McDonald
Auxiliary President

Marina Armstrong
Gerry Baumgardner
Barbara Borst
Marie Cuthbertson
Janet Davis
Helen DeHaven
Millie Gill
Annetta Hesch
Suie Kennedy
Molly Markle
Peggy Mason
Suzan McCorry
Patricia McOsker
Kay Miller
Maureen Mulhall

Elva Musslewhite
Cookbook Advisor

Louise Phiel
Helen Pierce
Pat Reeser
Maree Regan
Rosellen Sandquist
Karen Schilgen
Kathy Schwartz
Marj Singmaster
Mary Alice Spane
Janet Stalder
Betty Tinley
Janet Tily
Mary Vitray
Ruth Watson
Betsy Yamarick

The objective of the Committee was to create a community cookbook, one to be used and enjoyed by cooks of all ages. We are grateful to all who helped, especially the evaluators, testers and tasters. We also thank those who submitted their favorite recipes. Due to duplication and publishing limitations we regret all recipes are not included.

Chester County

Chester County is one of the three original counties—the other two were Bucks County and Philadelphia County—in Pennsylvania. It originally included the present-day Delaware County, Lancaster County, most of Berks County, and the other counties to the west and northwest.

Less than three months after William Penn received his charter for "Pennsilvania" from Charles II, a group of seventeen Welsh Quakers purchased 40,000 acres in the new colony. This "Welsh Tract," or barony, as it was sometimes called, included a large part of the eastern section of Chester County, and many of the early settlers there were from Wales as well as England. In the early 18th century a number of Scotch-Irish emigrated to the southern part of the county, and two decades later there were a number of German and Swiss arrivals. Thus, almost from its beginning, the new colony, including Chester County, was populated by peoples from different countries, each bringing their own customs, traditions and heritage that together have enriched our culture.

In fulfilling Penn's dream of freedom of worship and each person's right to worship in accordance with his or her conscience, the new colony also experienced a diversity of religion. By the first quarter of the 18th century, there were already established congregations of Friends, Baptists, Presbyterians, and Anglicans (now known as Episcopalians), with congregations of Lutherans, Mennonites, Amish, and other sects soon to follow. The routes of many early roads were laid out especially to accommodate people going to church or meeting at their meeting houses.

Other roads were built so that the colonial farmer could get to the nearby grist mills established on the banks of the principal streams in the area, to have their grain ground into flour, "middlins," used for mush or in making sausage, and feed for their livestock. In the early 18th century, the mill was often the local gathering place to exchange news, post notices, or occasionally, for a vendue or public sale. There are still today many towns and villages in Chester County that take their name from an early mill at that place.

Market roads were also needed, and laid out, to provide a means by which the farmer could transport his surplus production and grain to sell them in the larger towns.

These early roads, on which travel was often quite difficult—mud and ruts in the springtime, dust in the summer, and in the winter frozen ruts and ice, not to mention stumps and boulders—soon created a need for inns and taverns along the way. The particular reasons given in petitions to the Court for a license to operate a "publick house" or "house of entertainment" are sometimes rather amusing. In a number of instances the petitioner or would-be innkeeper pointed out that his house was conveniently located along the road and many weary travelers would stop by for rest and refreshment, but that "being but a poor man" he could not afford the burden of supplying their wants as a courtesy. In another case it was pointed out that the petitioner, being lame and incapable of *hard labor and "also having two ancient helpless women (to wit his own mother and mother-in-law) beside his wife and children to maintain,"* was therefore seeking the license to operate a tavern.

The taverns replaced the mill as the meeting place for the community, and as other businesses—a blacksmith shop, a wheelright, perhaps a cooper, and others serving the traveling public—were established nearby it became the center of a small village or hamlet. This, too, is reflected in the names of many of the older communities throughout the county, from Paoli to Compassville to Chatham, each taking its name from the old inn or tavern that was its beginning.

The many inns and taverns also contributed to the tradition of good eating. Hearty meals were prepared for the burly wagoners or drovers stopping by—the taverns where the innkeeper was German or Pennsylvania Dutch were, according to some observers, particularly noteworthy in this respect—while at inns catering to stagecoach passengers in the early 19th century the menus were more elaborate.

It is a part of our heritage that is being continued in this cookbook. While most of the recipes are more contemporary—although some have probably been handed down from mother to daughter over several generations—they carry on the tradition of good eating in Chester County.

Robert M. Goshorn

The Quilts

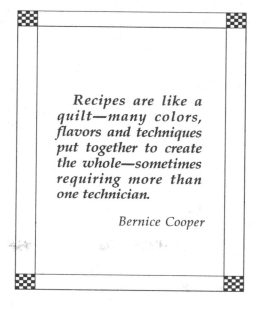

Recipes are like a quilt—many colors, flavors and techniques put together to create the whole—sometimes requiring more than one technician.

Bernice Cooper

The quilts pictured on the cover of *Quilted Quisine* are on permanent display in the lobby of Paoli Memorial Hospital. They symbolize the cooperation, dedication and commitment of the Auxiliary to the Hospital.

The idea of creating the quilts originated in 1985 during the hospital expansion, a project to which the Auxiliary contributed over a million dollars. The quilts were designed and hand sewn by Auxilians, volunteers and interested members of the community. The quilt shown on the front cover depicts historic landmarks of Chester County; the one on the back cover represents logos and activities significant to the Auxiliary.

Main Line Selections

Paoli Local

Main Line Selections

A collection of recipes from restaurants along the Main Line and beyond.

Auberge Restaurant
Bloomingdale's
Buckley's Tavern
Café 100
Jimmy Duffy's
Feastivities, Inc.
Al E. Gators Restaurant
Gators Restaurant
The General Warren Inne
General Wayne Inn
The Greenhouse
The Grille at Chesterbrook
The Guard House
The Healthy Gourmet
Hu-Nan
La Fourchette Restaurant
The Lamb Tavern
The Mile Post Inn Restaurant
Mendenhall Inn
Natural Cuisine Restaurant
Passerelle Restaurant
Jean Passo of Antoinette's Day Spa
The Pepper Mill Cafe
Pace One Restaurant
Queen of Hearts
Quissett Restaurant
The Strafford Inn
Taquet Restaurant at the Wayne Hotel
Tanner's Restaurant at the Great Valley Hilton
The Terrace at Greenhill
Yangming Restaurant
The White Horse Restaurant at the Sheraton Inn

The ribbon marks recipes from the WINNER'S CHOICE, sponsored by the Main Line Health Family of Hospitals. These menu items of participating restaurants are approved by registered dieticians based on U.S. Dietary and American Heart Association guidelines.

MAIN LINE SELECTIONS

Roasted Sea Bass with Orange-Basil Sauce

Auberge Restaurant
Wayne, Pennsylvania

5 sprigs of fresh basil
1/2 cup 100% virgin olive oil
5 tablespoons flour
5 tablespoons cornstarch
Salt and pepper to taste
2 8-ounce sea bass filets, scaled, skin on
1/2 cup thawed frozen orange juice concentrate

Cut off and reserve top 1 1/2 inches of basil leaves; chop remaining leaves and stems. Combine chopped basil with 1/2 cup oil in bowl. Let stand at room temperature for 24 hours. Strain, crushing basil with back of spoon; set aside. Mix flour, cornstarch, salt and pepper in shallow dish. Coat fleshy side of fish with flour mixture. Heat 1/4 cup basil-oil in ovenproof sauté pan over high heat. Sear floured side of fish in hot basil-oil. Drain sauté pan; turn fish. Bake at 400 degrees for 5 minutes. Heat orange juice concentrate in saucepan until reduced by 1/4. Add remaining strained oil in steady stream, whisking constantly. Chop 3 of reserved basil tops. Add to sauce. Spoon onto serving plates. Pat fish with paper towel to remove excess cooking oil. Place fish in sauce. Garnish with remaining basil leaves and chopped tomato.
Yield: 2 servings.

Black Forest Pork Medallions

Bloomingdale's
King of Prussia, Pennsylvania

8 pork medallions
Salt and pepper to taste
2 tablespoons oil
1/4 cup beef stock
1 17-ounce can pitted dark sweet cherries
1/2 teaspoon nutmeg
1/2 teaspoon ground cloves
1/2 teaspoon marjoram
2 tablespoons lemon juice
2 teaspoons cornstarch
1 teaspoon Bovril
1/2 cup chopped walnuts

Pound pork to 1/4-inch thickness with meat mallet; season with salt and pepper. Heat oil to sizzling point in heavy skillet. Brown pork on both sides in oil; drain skillet. Add beef stock. Cook until pork is tender and stock is reduced by 1/2; keep warm. Drain cherries, reserving syrup. Combine reserved syrup with nutmeg, cloves and marjoram in saucepan; mix well. Add mixture of lemon juice and cornstarch. Simmer until thickened, stirring constantly. Stir in Bovril. Cook over low heat for 5 to 10 minutes. Stir in cherries and walnuts. Cook until heated through. Place pork on serving plates. Spoon cherry sauce over pork. Garnish with parsley. **Yield:** 4 servings.

Thai Beef Salad

Buckley's Tavern
Centerville, Delaware

2 tablespoons Thai fish sauce
1/4 cup fresh lime juice
1 tablespoon sugar
2/3 teaspoon minced garlic
Dried red chili powder to taste
6 ounces beef eye of round, trimmed
1 cup cooked cappellini
2 cups torn lettuce
4 tomato slices
1/4 cup sliced cucumber

Combine fish sauce, lime juice, sugar, garlic and chili powder in bowl; mix until sugar is completely dissolved. Cut beef into thin slices. Grill until done to taste. Spoon pasta into bed of lettuce on serving plates. Fan beef slices over pasta. Top with tomato and cucumber slices. Spoon dressing over salads. Look for fish sauce and dried red chili powder at Asian markets. **Yield:** 2 servings. Each serving has 423 Calories; 11 gr. Fat (23% of total calories); 80 mg. Cholesterol; and 187 mg. Sodium.

Apple and Walnut-Stuffed Pork Chops

Café 100
Exton, Pennsylvania

1 stalk celery, finely chopped
1/2 small onion, finely chopped
2 tablespoons butter
1 Macintosh apple, peeled, chopped into 1/2-inch pieces
2 to 3 tablespoons chicken stock
1 1/2 tablespoons brown sugar
1 1/4 cups coarse bread crumbs
Cinnamon, salt and pepper to taste
2 tablespoons chopped walnuts
4 8-ounce double-thick pork chops with pockets
2 tablespoons oil
1/2 cup bourbon
1 teaspoon minced shallots
1 cup heavy cream
2 tablespoons molasses
1/4 cup chopped walnuts

Sauté celery and onion in butter in sauté pan over low heat for 5 minutes or until tender. Add apple. Cook until apple is tender. Stir in chicken stock, brown sugar, bread crumbs, cinnamon, salt, pepper and 2 tablespoons walnuts. Cool to room temperature. Season pork chops with salt and pepper. Spoon stuffing mixture into pockets in pork chops. Brown on both sides in oil in ovenproof sauté pan. Bake at 350 degrees for 1 hour or until well done. Cook bourbon in saucepan until reduced by 2/3. Add shallots and cream. Cook until reduced by 1/2. Stir in molasses and 1/4 cup walnuts. Season with salt and pepper. Serve immediately with pork chops. This recipe was featured in *Ford Times Magazine* in December of 1990. **Yield:** 4 servings.

Devils on Horseback

Jimmy Duffy's
Daylesford, Pennsylvania

1 1/2 cups flour
1/2 cup yellow cornmeal
1 1/2 teaspoons baking powder
2 eggs, slightly beaten
1 1/4 cups beer
18 thin slices smoked bacon, cut into halves crosswise
36 freshly shucked oysters
4 cups peanut oil

Mix flour, cornmeal and baking powder in medium bowl; make well in center. Add eggs and beer; whisk until smooth. Chill, covered, for 2 hours to overnight. Cook bacon in several portions in large skillet over medium heat for 4 minutes or just until bacon begins to brown, turning frequently. Drain and cool bacon. Wrap around oysters; secure with wooden picks. Heat oil in deep fryer, wok or large skillet for 10 minutes or to 350 degrees. Stir chilled batter. Dip oysters a few at a time into batter. Fry in oil for 4 minutes or until golden brown and crisp; drain well. Serve immediately with lemon wedges. **Yield:** 6 servings.

Saffron Pasta Salad

Feastivities, Inc.
Berwyn, Pennsylvania

1/4 ounce sun-dried tomatoes
1 ounce wine
4 ounces uncooked wagon wheel pasta
1/4 teaspoon turmeric
4 ounces uncooked tortellini
1 1/2 ounces chopped green bell pepper
1 1/4 ounces julienned carrot
1 1/2 ounces chopped zucchini
2 1/2 ounces chopped summer squash
3 ounces chopped cauliflower
1 ounce raisins
1 1/2 ounces chopped onion
4 ounces chopped artichoke hearts
Saffron to taste
1/8 teaspoon salt
1/4 teaspoon pepper
1/2 cup Italian salad dressing

Soften tomatoes in wine for several minutes. Cook wagon wheel pasta using package directions, adding turmeric to water. Cook tortellini using package directions. Drain and rinse pasta under cold water. Combine with tortellini, tomatoes, green pepper, carrot, zucchini, summer squash, cauliflower, raisins, onion, artichoke hearts, saffron, salt, pepper and salad dressing; mix lightly. Chill for several hours to blend flavors. **Yield:** 6 servings.

Shrimp Salad

Feastivities, Inc.
Berwyn, Pennsylvania

1 1/2 pounds medium shrimp, cooked
3 ounces snow peas
3 ounces chopped celery
1 ounce julienned carrot
2 1/2 ounces cashews
1/2 cup mayonnaise
1 teaspoon Dijon mustard
1/4 teaspoon pepper

Drain shrimp well and pat dry. Combine with snow peas, celery, carrot, cashews, mayonnaise, mustard and pepper in large bowl; mix well. Serve with croissants. May prepare in advance, adding cashews at serving time. **Yield:** 6 servings.

Choose low-cholesterol foods. Lowering blood cholesterol by 15 percent reduces coronary risk by 30 percent.

Vegetable Basket with Yogurt-Dill Dressing

Al E. Gators Restaurant
Haverford, Pennsylvania

1/3 cup plain low-fat yogurt
2 2/3 tablespoons light mayonnaise
2 teaspoons chopped fresh dill
1 leaf kale
6 celery sticks
6 carrot sticks
5 bite-sized broccoli flowerets
5 bite-sized caulifloweretts
4 cherry tomatoes

Combine yogurt, mayonnaise and dill in small serving bowl; mix well. Place in 1 corner of basket. Place kale next to dressing. Arrange carrots and celery in center of other end of basket. Arrange broccoli and cauliflower on either side of carrots and celery. Place 1 tomato on top of each group of vegetables. **Yield:** 2 servings. Each serving has 174 Calories; 4.7 gr. Fat (24% of total calories); 3 mg. Cholesterol; and 215 mg. Sodium.

Honey-Roasted Chicken

Gators Restaurant
Devon, Pennsylvania

1/4 cup chopped Spanish onion
1 clove of garlic, crushed
1 tablespoon dry mustard
1 cup sugar
3/4 teaspoon each thyme, basil and oregano
3/4 teaspoon white pepper
1/2 cup cider vinegar
1/4 cup honey
3/4 cup oil
1 2 1/2 to 3-pound roasting chicken

Combine onion, garlic, dry mustard, sugar, thyme, basil, oregano, white pepper, vinegar and honey in blender container; process until onion is puréed. Add oil very gradually, processing until smooth; batter will be consistency of thin mayonnaise. Rinse chicken and pat dry. Dip in batter, coating well; drain excess batter. Place in roasting pan. Roast at 375 degrees for 1 hour. **Yield:** 4 servings.

Ask the waiter to describe how a dish is prepared and eliminate extra fat in the preparation. Order sauces and dressings on the side.

Lobster and Scallop Terrine

The General Warren Inne
Malvern, Pennsylvania

1 pound sea scallops
1 cup heavy cream
2 egg whites
6 to 8 ounces chopped uncooked lobster
Salt and pepper to taste
2 tablespoons mixed fresh parsley, tarragon, chives or basil
1 cup heavy cream
Red Pepper Sauce (below)

Purée scallops in food processor. Add 1 cup cream and egg whites gradually, processing until smooth. Combine with lobster, salt, pepper and fresh herbs in large bowl; mix well. Whip 1 cup cream in small mixer bowl until soft peaks form. Fold into scallop mixture. Spoon into greased 4x9-inch terrine mold or 5x9-inch loaf pan. Cover with greased foil or baking parchment. Place in baking pan. Add boiling water halfway up side of pan. Bake at 275 degrees for 1½ hours or until edges of terrine pull away from sides of pan and center is firm to touch. Cool for 45 minutes. Unmold onto serving plate. Serve with Red Pepper Sauce. **Yield:** 8 servings.

Red Pepper Sauce

1 8-ounce red bell pepper, chopped
1 tablespoon chopped shallot or onion
1 clove of garlic, sliced
1 tablespoon butter
½ cup dry white wine
½ cup chicken stock, fish stock or bouillon
1 cup heavy cream
Salt and pepper to taste

Sauté bell pepper, shallots and garlic in butter in heavy 2-quart saucepan until tender but not brown. Stir in wine and stock. Bring to a boil; reduce heat. Simmer for 15 minutes. Add cream. Cook until reduced by ½. Purée in food processor. Season with salt and pepper. Serve warm or chilled with fish, meat, vegetables and pasta. **Yield:** 2 cups.

Snack on crudités, fruit or unbuttered popcorn before eating out so you can make wiser menu choices.

White Chocolate Mousse with Fruit Purée

The General Warren Inne
Malvern, Pennsylvania

1 pint fresh strawberries or raspberries
2 tablespoons sugar
1 tablespoon cherry brandy, strawberry brandy or raspberry liqueur
1/2 cup sugar
1/2 cup water
3 egg whites
1 cup whipping cream
8 ounces white chocolate, finely chopped
8 Almond Tulips (below)

Combine strawberries with 2 tablespoons sugar in food processor or blender container. Process until smooth. Press through fine sieve. Combine strained purée with brandy; set aside. Combine 1/2 cup sugar and water in small saucepan. Cook over medium-high heat to 250 degrees on candy thermometer or until mixture is syrupy and amber-colored. Beat egg whites in small mixer bowl until soft peaks form. Add hot syrup gradually, beating constantly for 5 minutes or until cool. Beat whipping cream in large mixer bowl until soft peaks form. Fold in egg white mixture and chocolate. Spoon into Almond Tulips. Top with fruit purée. **Yield:** 8 servings.

Almond Tulips

1 cup sugar
1 cup ground blanched almonds
1/4 cup flour
4 eggs

Combine sugar, almonds, flour and eggs in mixer bowl; beat until smooth. Spoon by scant 1/4 cupfuls 7 inches apart onto greased cookie sheet; spread into 5-inch circles. Bake at 400 degrees for 6 to 8 minutes or until edges are light brown. Remove immediately to place over large glasses. Let stand until cool. Store in airtight container. May recrisp soggy cookies by reheating at 300 degrees for 3 to 4 minutes, reshaping on glass and cooling until crisp. **Yield:** 10 almond tulips.

Limiting portion size can allow a taste of "forbidden treats." Share your dessert with a companion.

Seafood Mousse with Cucumber Concasse

General Wayne Inn
Merion Station, Pennsylvania

1 egg white
2 ounces shrimp
1 teaspoon chopped scallion
1/2 teaspoon sesame oil
Pepper to taste
2 5-ounce flounder filets
3 ounces water
1 large cucumber
1/2 teaspoon chopped garlic
1 teaspoon chopped fresh dill
1 tablespoon olive oil

Beat egg white in mixer bowl until stiff peaks form. Fold in shrimp, scallion, sesame oil and pepper. Cut each fish filet into 2 pieces. Arrange 2 pieces in baking dish. Spoon shrimp mixture on top. Cut remaining 2 pieces fish into halves lengthwise. Arrange over shrimp mixture, allowing shrimp mixture to show through center. Add 3 ounces water. Bake at 375 degrees for 10 to 13 minutes or until fish flakes easily. Peel and seed cucumber; cut into 1/2-inch cubes. Sauté cucumber, garlic, dill and pepper in olive oil in saucepan until heated through. Place fish on serving plates. Spoon cucumber concasse around fish. Serve with angel hair pasta and fresh asparagus. **Yield:** 2 servings. Each serving has 364 Calories; 11.3 gr. Fat (28% of total calories); 141 mg Cholesterol; and 206 mg. Sodium.

Roasted Tomato and Red Pepper Sauce

The Greenhouse
Radnor, Pennsylvania

6 plum tomatoes
1 red bell pepper
Juice of 1 lemon
1 teaspoon Worcestershire sauce
4 cloves of garlic, slow roasted
Salt and pepper to taste

Roast tomatoes and bell pepper on grill or over open gas flame until skins are black. Cool to room temperature. Remove and discard skins and seed, reserving any juices. Combine tomatoes and bell pepper with lemon juice, Worcestershire sauce, garlic, salt and pepper in food processor container. Process until smooth. Serve with grilled fish or chicken. **Yield:** 4 cups.

Salmon Calypso

The Grille at Chesterbrook
Wayne, Pennsylvania

1 papaya
1 mango
1 red bell pepper
1/4 cup raisins
Juice of 1 lemon
2 peppercorns
2 stalks celery, coarsely chopped
1 small white onion, coarsely chopped
1 cup white wine
4 8-ounce salmon filets

Peel, seed and julienne papaya, mango and bell pepper. Combine with raisins and lemon juice in bowl; mix well. Chill in refrigerator for 3 to 4 hours. Add peppercorns, celery, onion and wine to saucepan filled 3/4 of the way with water. Bring to a boil. Add salmon. Poach for 10 to 12 minutes or until fish flakes easily. Remove fish to serving platter. Top with fruit mixture. Serve with steamed rice and green vegetable. **Yield:** 4 servings. Each serving has 523 calories, 10.3 gr. Fat (18% of total calories); 120 mg. Cholesterol; and 135 mg. Sodium.

Sea Scallops with Ginger

The Guard House
Gladwyne, Pennsylvania

1 teaspoon chopped garlic
1 teaspoon chopped shallot
1 1/4 tablespoons chopped crystallized ginger
1 tomato, chopped, seeded
2 ounces dry vermouth
2 pounds sea scallops

Combine garlic, shallot, ginger, tomato and wine in baking dish; mix well. Place scallops over top. Bake at 425 degrees for 5 to 8 minutes or until scallops are cooked through. Serve with rice and steamed fresh vegetable. **Yield:** 4 servings. Each serving has 405 Calories, 1 gr. Fat (2% of total calories); 80 mg. Cholesterol; and 535 mg. Sodium.

Make lighter food choices during the day to enjoy dining out without guilt.

Italian Vegetable Stir-Fry

The Healthy Gourmet
West Chester, Pennsylvania

2 tablespoons pine nuts
1 tablespoon olive oil
1/2 cup onion ring halves
1 cup green bell pepper strips
1 cup red bell pepper strips
1 1/2 tablespoons chopped garlic
1 cup chopped tomato
1/2 cup chopped parsley
1 teaspoon dried rosemary
1 teaspoon dried basil or 1/4 cup chopped fresh basil
1/2 cup cannellini or white kidney beans, rinsed, drained
1 cup tomato sauce

Toast pine nuts in wok or large skillet over medium heat for 2 minutes or until light brown, stirring frequently; remove and reserve. Increase heat to high; add olive oil. Stir-fry onion, green pepper and red pepper in hot oil for 5 minutes or until light brown. Add garlic, tomato, parsley, rosemary and basil. Stir-fry for several minutes. Reduce heat to low. Add cannellini, pine nuts and tomato sauce. Simmer, covered, for 5 minutes. Serve over hot cooked pasta with crusty whole-grain bread. Garnish with freshly ground pepper and Parmesan cheese. May omit tomato sauce if preferred. **Yield:** 2 servings.

Turkey Bok Choy

The Healthy Gourmet
West Chester, Pennsylvania

10 ounces fresh turkey breast
2 teaspoons cornstarch
2 tablespoons orange juice
1 1/2 to 2 tablespoons reduced-sodium soy sauce
2 teaspoons apple juice concentrate or honey
2 cloves of garlic, crushed
1/2 cup sliced onions or scallions
2 to 3 teaspoons canola oil
1 pound mushrooms, thickly sliced
1 cup bean sprouts
1 head bok choy, stems and leaves chopped separately
2 to 3 tablespoons stock
2 tablespoons sunflower seed, toasted

Freeze turkey for 30 to 45 minutes. Cut into slivers. Combine with next 4 ingredients in bowl; mix well. Sauté garlic and onions in oil in large wok or skillet; discard garlic. Drain turkey, reserving sauce. Add turkey to oil in wok. Stir-fry until no longer pink. Add mushrooms, bean sprouts and bok choy stems. Stir-fry until coated well. Add stock. Steam, covered, for 2 to 3 minutes. Add bok choy leaves; make well in center. Stir reserved sauce into well. Cook until thickened, stirring constantly. Reduce heat. Cook, covered, for several minutes. Sprinkle with sunflower seed. Serve with rice. May substitute pork tenderloin, beef top round or chicken breast filets for turkey. **Yield:** 2 to 3 servings.

Mixed Vegetables

Hu-Nan
Ardmore, Pennsylvania

1 slice gingerroot, grated
2 cloves of garlic, minced
1/2 cup chopped scallions
1/2 cup chopped Chinese cabbage
1/2 cup chopped carrot
1 tablespoon peanut oil
1/2 cup bamboo shoots
1/2 cup snow peas
1/2 cup baby corn
1 teaspoon sugar
Salt and pepper to taste
2 tablespoons cornstarch
4 ounces chicken broth
2 to 4 drops of sesame oil
2 cups steamed rice

Stir-fry first 5 ingredients in peanut oil in wok until tender-crisp. Add bamboo shoots, snow peas and corn. Stir-fry for several minutes. Add sugar, salt, pepper and mixture of cornstarch and chicken broth. Cook until thickened, stirring constantly. Sprinkle with sesame oil. Serve over steamed rice. **Yield:** 2 servings. Each serving has 221 Calories; 8 gr. Fat (30% of total calories); 0 mg. Cholesterol; and 326 mg. Sodium.

Snapper Provençal

La Fourchette Restaurant
Wayne, Pennsylvania

1 small onion
12 plum tomatoes, cut into quarters
1 cup white wine
2 cloves of garlic, minced
2 bay leaves
1 pound eggplant, chopped
1 pound zucchini, chopped
1 red bell pepper, chopped
4 shallots, minced
2 cloves of garlic, minced
1 tablespoon olive oil
1 tablespoon chopped fresh rosemary
Salt and pepper to taste
4 6-ounce red snapper filets
Flour
1/2 tablespoon peanut oil

Cut onion into halves and slice. Combine with tomatoes, wine, 2 cloves of garlic and bay leaves in 4-quart saucepan. Cook for 20 minutes over medium heat or until tomatoes are tender and liquid is reduced to 1/4 cup; discard bay leaves. Purée in blender; strain. Set coulis aside. Sauté eggplant, zucchini, bell pepper, shallots and 2 cloves of garlic in olive oil in sauté pan for 3 to 5 minutes or until tender-crisp. Add 1/2 cup tomato coulis. Cook for 3 minutes longer. Add rosemary, salt and pepper. Coat fish with flour. Heat peanut oil in medium skillet over medium heat until hot but not smoking. Add fish. Cook for 3 minutes; turn fish. Cook for 2 minutes longer. Spoon ratatouille onto serving plates. Place fish on plates and surround with remaining tomato coulis. Garnish with sprigs of rosemary. **Yield:** 4 servings.

Chicken and Tomato-Caper Vinaigrette

The Lamb Tavern
Springfield, Pennsylvania

2 tomatoes, peeled, seeded, chopped
2 teaspoons capers
6 black olives, chopped
1 teaspoon minced garlic
1 teaspoon minced shallot
2 tablespoons olive oil
1 tablespoon balsamic vinegar
2 teaspoons mixed fresh basil, oregano, rosemary and thyme
Salt and pepper to taste
2 6-ounce boneless chicken breast halves
2 cups cooked fettucini
8 ounces steamed fresh vegetables

Combine tomatoes, capers, olives, garlic, shallot, olive oil, vinegar and seasonings in bowl. Rinse chicken; pat dry. Add to marinade, coating well. Marinate in refrigerator for 2 hours. Drain, reserving marinade. Grill until cooked through. Heat reserved marinade in saucepan until heated through. Serve with chicken. Serve with fresh vegetable and fettucini tossed with olive oil and fresh herbs. Garnish with scallion flower and radish rose. **Yield:** 2 servings. Each serving has 509 Calories; 157 gr. Fat (28% of total calories); 146 mg. Cholesterol; and 223 mg. Sodium.

Veal Français with Lemon-Caper Sauce

The Mile Post Inn Restaurant
Strafford, Pennsylvania

1 4-ounce veal cutlet
2 eggs
Chopped parsley to taste
1 teaspoon grated cheese
Salt and pepper to taste
2 tablespoons oil
1/4 cup flour
8 capers
1 teaspoon chopped shallot
1 tablespoon butter
2 ounces white wine
1 tablespoon lemon juice
3 tablespoons butter

Pound veal with meat mallet. Whisk eggs with parsley, cheese, salt and pepper in bowl. Heat oil in skillet preheated to 375 degrees. Coat veal with flour; dip into egg mixture. Sauté in hot oil in skillet until golden brown on both sides. Remove and drain on paper towel. Sauté capers and shallot in 1 tablespoon butter in skillet. Add wine, stirring to deglaze skillet. Cook until most of liquid has evaporated. Add lemon juice and remaining 3 tablespoons butter. Serve over veal. **Yield:** 1 serving.

Mile Post Steak

The Mile Post Inn Restaurant
Strafford, Pennsylvania

3 2-ounce tenderloin filets
1/4 cup cracked peppercorns
2 tablespoons oil
1 tablespoon Dijon mustard
2 ounces white wine
1/4 cup beef stock

Coat filets with cracked pepper. Heat oil in skillet preheated to 375 degrees. Sauté steak in oil until brown and crisp; turn. Add mustard, wine and beef stock. Cook until liquid is reduced to desired consistency.
Yield: 1 serving.

Tortellini Carbonara

Mendenhall Inn
Mendenhall, Pennsylvania

15 spinach tortellini
15 cheese tortellini
2 slices bacon, finely chopped
1 shallot, finely chopped
1/2 green bell pepper, finely chopped
1/2 red bell pepper, finely chopped
1/2 yellow bell pepper, chopped into medium pieces
1 clove of garlic, finely chopped
10 ounces heavy cream
1 1/2 handfuls freshly grated Parmesan cheese
Garlic powder and white pepper to taste
3 sprigs of parsley, finely chopped

Cook pasta *al dente*; drain and rinse. Render bacon in sauté pan until light brown. Add shallot, bell peppers and garlic. Sauté for several minutes. Add tortellini, cream and cheese. Cook until sauce is reduced by 1/2. Add garlic powder and white pepper; garnish with parsley.
Yield: 4 first-course or 2 main-course servings.

For every teaspoon of salt eliminated from a recipe, the sodium will be reduced by 2,000 milligrams.

New Mexico Baked Corn

Natural Cuisine Restaurant
Downingtown, Pennsylvania

2 eggs, beaten, or egg substitute to equal 2 eggs
2 17-ounce cans no salt-added cream-style corn
3/4 cup cornmeal
1/2 teaspoon baking powder
3 7-ounce cans chopped green chilies, drained, rinsed
3 tablespoons low-calorie margarine
1 1/2 cups shredded low-salt sharp cheese
1 teaspoon garlic powder
1 teaspoon red chili powder
1 teaspoon jalapeño powder
Freshly ground pepper to taste

Combine eggs, corn, cornmeal, baking powder, green chilies, margarine, cheese and seasonings in mixer bowl; mix well. Spoon into 2-quart baking dish sprayed with nonstick cooking spray. Bake at 375 degrees for 45 minutes; reduce oven temperature to 325 degrees. Bake for 30 to 45 minutes longer or until golden brown. Serve as side dish. May bake in advance and reheat in microwave. **Yield:** 6 to 8 servings.

Chili with a Twist

Natural Cuisine Restaurant
Downingtown, Pennsylvania

1 pound ground turkey
1 pound ground veal
1/2 cup Tequila
1 tablespoon light olive oil
1 large onion, chopped
1 large carrot, shredded
2 stalks celery, finely chopped
3 cloves of garlic, minced
5 or 6 roasted green chilies, chopped, or 2 tablespoons green chili powder
2 15-ounce cans pinto or cranberry beans, rinsed, drained
1 13-ounce can low-salt tomatoes or 4 tomatoes, peeled, seeded, chopped
1 can light beer
5 to 6 cups water
1/4 cup hot red chili powder
1/4 cup medium red chili powder
2 teaspoons jalapeño powder
1 teaspoon oregano
2 teaspoons cumin
1 teaspoon marjoram
3 tablespoons chopped fresh parsley
Freshly ground pepper to taste

Brown ground turkey and ground veal in stockpot, stirring until crumbly. Add Tequila. Simmer for 3 to 5 minutes. Remove to bowl with slotted spoon. Add olive oil to drippings in stockpot. Add onion, carrot, celery and garlic. Sauté for 2 to 3 minutes or until tender. Return browned meat to stockpot; mix well. Add remaining ingredients; simmer for 2 to 3 hours. Garnish servings with shredded low-salt Cheddar cheese and sliced scallions. Serve with warmed flour tortillas. **Yield:** 8 servings.

Caramelized Rice Flan with Dried Cherries

Passerelle Restaurant
Radnor, Pennsylvania

1 cup water
1/4 cup (heaping) uncooked rice
2 cups milk
Grated zest of 2 oranges
1 egg
2 egg yolks
1/3 cup sugar
1 1/3 cups heavy cream
2/3 cup dried cherries
Brown sugar

Bring water to a boil in saucepan. Add rice. Bring to a boil; remove from heat. Drain rice and rinse under cold water. Bring milk and orange zest to a boil in ovenproof pan. Stir in blanched rice. Bring to a boil. Bake, covered, at 325 degrees until milk is absorbed and rice is tender. Whisk egg, egg yolks and sugar in bowl. Whisk in cream. Stir in rice and cherries. Spoon into 9-inch baking dish or individual ramekins. Place in large pan of water. Bake at 250 degrees until custard is almost set. Chill in refrigerator. Cover top of custard with brown sugar. Broil until sugar caramelizes. **Yield:** 4 servings.

Salmon on Snow Pea-Belgian Endive Salad

Passerelle Restaurant
Radnor, Pennsylvania

2 tablespoons Dijon mustard
2 tablespoons red wine vinegar
Salt and pepper to taste
1/2 cup extra-virgin olive oil
1 pound snow peas
1 head Belgian endive
1 head radicchio, torn
1 bunch dill, chopped
4 5-ounce salmon medallions, skinned
1 tablespoon olive oil
1/4 cup sherry vinegar
3 tablespoons butter

Whisk mustard, red wine vinegar, salt and pepper together in bowl. Whisk in 1/2 cup olive oil gradually; set aside. Trim ends of snow peas. Blanch in boiling salted water for 1 minute or until tender-crisp. Rinse in cold water. Separate leaves of endive; cut into halves lengthwise. Toss with snow peas, radicchio, dill and salad dressing in bowl. Season with salt and pepper. Spoon onto individual serving plates. Sauté salmon in 1 tablespoon olive oil in skillet for 1 1/2 minutes on each side or until fish flakes easily. Place salmon on salads; drain skillet. Add sherry vinegar to skillet, stirring to deglaze. Whisk in butter until smooth. Spoon over salmon. May omit deglazing step to eliminate butter from recipe. **Yield:** 4 servings.

Mushroom and Roasted Red Pepper Soup

Jean Passo of Antoinette's Day Spa
Paoli, Pennsylvania

1 ounce dried mushrooms
1 cup boiling water
1 onion, minced
2 cloves of garlic, minced
1/4 cup olive oil
12 ounces roasted red bell peppers, cut into 1/4-inch pieces
2 stalks celery, cut into 1/4-inch slices
1 cup chopped carrots
1 pound mushrooms, sliced
1/4 cup flour
4 cups hot chicken stock
4 cups hot beef stock
1 bay leaf
1 teaspoon chervil
1/2 teaspoon rosemary
1/2 teaspoon thyme
Salt and pepper to taste

Soak dried mushrooms in boiling water in bowl for 30 minutes. Drain and reserve liquid. Chop mushrooms; set aside. Sauté onion and garlic in olive oil in skillet until tender. Add red peppers, celery, carrots and mushrooms. Cook for 15 minutes. Sprinkle flour over vegetables; mix until absorbed. Add hot stock gradually. Add remaining ingredients and reserved mushrooms. Simmer for 30 minutes: **Yield:** 8 to 10 servings.

Oriental Salad

The Pepper Mill Cafe
Ardmore, Pennsylvania

3 cups mixed red leaf lettuce, arugula and watercress
2 ounces boneless chicken breast, sliced
2 ounces beef filet mignon, trimmed, thinly sliced
4 medium shrimp, peeled, deveined
1 ounce each julienned red and green bell peppers
2 ounces mushrooms, sliced
1 ounce snow peas
1 ounce julienned zucchini
1 ounce julienned carrot
2 ounces olive oil
1 ounce red wine or balsamic vinegar
1 teaspoon light soy sauce
1 teaspoon fresh gingerroot, crushed
1 clove of garlic, crushed
1 teaspoon curry powder
1 cup water
2 slices whole grain bread

Place salad greens on individual plates. Rinse chicken and pat dry. Mix with next 14 ingredients and water in large sauté pan. Cook over high heat for 5 to 8 minutes or until liquid is reduced by 1/2, stirring frequently. Spoon salad and sauce onto prepared plates. Serve with whole wheat bread. **Yield:** 2 servings. Each serving has 348 Calories; 11 gr Fat (30% of total calories); 113 mg. Cholesterol; and 600 mg. Sodium.

New England Pudding

Pace One Restaurant
Thornton, Pennsylvania

1 6½-pound can pineapple chunks, drained
8 red apples, chopped
2½ cups packed brown sugar
3 cups chopped walnuts
7 eggs
4 cups sugar
4 cups flour
3 cups melted butter

Spread pineapple and apples in shallow 15x14-inch baking pan. Sprinkle with brown sugar and walnuts. Beat eggs in large mixer bowl. Beat in sugar. Add flour alternately with melted butter, mixing well after each addition. Pour over fruit in pan. Bake at 350 degrees for 1 to 1½ hours or until brown. **Yield:** 25 servings.

Swordfish with Creole Sauce

Queen of Hearts
Paoli, Pennsylvania

6 4-ounce swordfish steaks, trimmed
6 tablespoons lemon juice
6 tablespoons white wine
⅓ teaspoon Old Bay seasoning
Salt to taste
¾ teaspoon cracked pepper
Creole Sauce (below)

Place fish in baking dish lightly sprayed with nonstick cooking spray. Combine lemon juice, wine, Old Bay seasoning, salt and pepper in small bowl; mix well. Drizzle over fish. Bake at 375 degrees for 15 minutes. Serve with Creole Sauce. **Yield:** 6 servings.

Creole Sauce

3 ounces tomato juice
2 ounces chopped tomatoes, seeded
1 tablespoon chopped red onion
Chopped garlic to taste
2 tablespoons chopped green bell pepper
½ teaspoon chopped fresh parsley
1/16 teaspoon Tabasco sauce
Thyme to taste
⅛ teaspoon chili powder
½ teaspoon chopped coriander
Salt and pepper to taste

Combine tomato juice, tomatoes, onion, garlic, green pepper, parsley, Tabasco sauce, thyme, chili powder, coriander, salt and pepper in small saucepan. Bring to a boil; reduce heat. Simmer for 10 minutes; keep warm. **Yield:** 6 servings.

Fruited Rice Salad

Queen of Hearts
Paoli, Pennsylvania

1 cup cooked rice
1/4 cup seedless grapes
1/2 cup chopped orange sections
Grated zest of 1 orange
1/2 cup julienned carrot
1/4 cup chopped celery
1/4 cup chopped parsley
2 tablespoons chopped walnuts, toasted
1 teaspoon orange juice concentrate
1 teaspoon white wine vinegar
1 teaspoon canola oil
1 1/2 teaspoons lemon juice
1/8 teaspoon Tabasco sauce
1/8 teaspoon thyme
1/16 teaspoon nutmeg
1/2 teaspoon pepper

Combine rice, grapes, oranges, orange zest, carrot, celery, parsley and toasted walnuts in large bowl; mix well. Add orange juice concentrate, vinegar, oil, lemon juice, Tabasco sauce, thyme, nutmeg and pepper; mix gently. Chill until serving time. **Yield:** eight 1/2-cup servings. Each serving has 58 Calories; 1.7 gr. Fat (25% of total calories); 0 mg. Cholesterol; and 4 mg. Sodium.

Salmon-Potato Cakes with Dill-Yogurt Cream

Quissett Restaurant
Haverford, Pennsylvania

3 cups low-fat yogurt, well drained
1/2 bunch dill, chopped
1 teaspoon lemon juice
1 teaspoon grated lemon zest
Cayenne pepper and white pepper to taste
4 Idaho potatoes, cooked, peeled
9 ounces cooked salmon
2 egg whites, beaten
1 tablespoon low-fat yogurt
1/2 bunch scallions, finely chopped
1/2 bunch dill, chopped
1 1/2 tablespoons olive oil

Combine 3 cups yogurt, 1/2 bunch dill, lemon juice, lemon zest, cayenne pepper and white pepper in bowl; mix well. Set aside. Mash potatoes in bowl. Chop salmon in food processor. Add to potatoes. Add egg whites, 1 tablespoon yogurt, scallions, 1/2 bunch dill and white pepper; mix well. Shape into 8 large or 16 small patties. Brown on both sides in olive oil in skillet. Serve with yogurt sauce. **Yield:** 4 main-dish servings or 8 appetizer servings. Each main-dish serving has 395 Calories; 12 gr. Fat (28 % of total calories); 56 mg. Cholesterol; and 193 mg. Sodium.

Marinated Chicken Breasts

The Strafford Inn
Strafford, Pennsylvania

2 6-ounce boneless chicken breast halves
2 teaspoons olive oil
1 clove of garlic, minced
Juice of 1/2 lemon
Rosemary and oregano to taste

Rinse chicken and pat dry. Combine with olive oil, garlic, lemon juice, rosemary and oregano in bowl; mix to coat well. Marinate in refrigerator for 4 to 5 hours. Drain, reserving marinade. Grill or broil chicken for 2 to 3 minutes on each side or until brown. Place in baking dish; pour reserved marinade over top. Bake at 375 degrees for 20 minutes. Serve with steamed rice and vegetable. **Yield:** 2 servings. Each serving has 383 Calories; 8 gr. Fat (19% of total calories); 146 mg. Cholesterol; and 172 mg. Sodium.

Escalope of Salmon with Black Olives

Taquet Restaurant at the Wayne Hotel
Wayne, Pennsylvania

4 6-ounce salmon filets
3 tablespoons olive oil
Grated rind of 1 lemon
1 clove of garlic, minced
4 black olives, sliced
1 cup consommé
Coriander, salt and pepper to taste
2 ounces butter

Sauté salmon in olive oil in skillet until fish flakes easily. Add lemon rind, garlic and black olives. Cook for 30 seconds. Stir in consommé, coriander, salt and pepper. Place salmon on serving plates. Whisk butter into cooking liquids in skillet. Cook just until heated through. Spoon over salmon. **Yield:** 4 servings.

Unsaturated fat (which is liquid at room temperature) can actually lower cholesterol levels when used in moderation. Sources of unsaturated fat are safflower, sunflower, corn, soybean, olive, peanut and canola oils.

Banana-Walnut Bread Pudding

Tanner's Restaurant at the Great Valley Hilton
Malvern, Pennsylvania

1 loaf stale French bread
1 quart milk
4 eggs
1 cup sugar
1/2 teaspoon vanilla extract
1/2 teaspoon cinnamon
2 bananas, sliced
1/2 cup chopped walnuts
3/4 cup butter
1 1/2 cups confectioners' sugar
2 eggs, beaten
Whiskey to taste

Crumble bread into milk in bowl; mix well. Let stand for 1 hour. Combine 4 eggs, sugar, vanilla and cinnamon in mixer bowl; mix well. Add to bread mixture. Add bananas and walnuts; mix well. Spoon into buttered 9x13-inch baking pan. Bake at 325 degrees for 1 hour or until wooden pick inserted in center comes out clean. Melt butter in double boiler. Add confectioners' sugar. Cook until bubbly, stirring to dissolve sugar. Add 2 eggs; mix well. Cook for 30 seconds; remove from heat. Stir until mixture cools. Stir in whiskey. Serve over pudding. **Yield:** 15 servings. This recipe is a specialty of Executive Chef Sam Kenyon.

Chicken Sautéed with Mushrooms and Spinach

Tanner's Restaurant at the Great Valley Hilton
Malvern, Pennsylvania

2 boneless chicken breast halves
1/2 teaspoon olive oil
1/3 cup white wine
Juice of 1/2 lemon
1/2 cup chicken broth
1/2 cup sliced mushrooms
6 ounces fresh spinach

Rinse chicken and pat dry. Brush lightly with olive oil. Place in preheated sauté pan over high heat. Sear well on both sides. Remove chicken to baking pan. Bake at 350 degrees for 7 to 8 minutes or until cooked through. Stir wine into hot sauté pan. Cook over high heat until alcohol has evaporated. Add lemon juice. Cook until reduced by 1/3. Stir in chicken broth, mushrooms and spinach. Cook until spinach wilts, tossing lightly. Place chicken on serving plates. Serve with spinach mixture. May also serve rice or potatoes and steamed fresh vegetables. **Yield:** 2 servings. This recipe is a specialty of Executive Chef Sam Kenyon.

Sesame Chicken

The Terrace at Greenhill
Wilmington, Delaware

4 6-ounce boneless chicken breast halves
3 tablespoons unsweetened pineapple juice
1 tablespoon honey
1 tablespoon sesame seed, toasted
1/4 teaspoon sage, crushed
4 slices fresh pineapple

Rinse chicken and pat dry. Place on rack in broiler pan sprayed with nonstick cooking spray. Combine pineapple juice, honey, sesame seed and sage in small bowl; mix well. Brush on chicken. Broil 8 inches from heat source for 25 minutes, basting with honey mixture frequently. Turn chicken. Broil for 15 minutes longer or until tender. Brush pineapple slices with remaining honey mixture. Place on rack in broiler pan. Broil for 5 minutes. Place chicken on serving platter. Cut pineapple slices into halves; arrange on chicken. **Yield:** 4 servings. Each serving has 240 calories; 4.8 gr. Fat (18% of total calories); 181 mg. Cholesterol; and 70 mg. Sodium.

Capellini and Shrimp

Yangming Restaurant
Bryn Mawr, Pennsylvania

24 medium uncooked shrimp, peeled
2 teaspoons chopped garlic
1 teaspoon chopped fresh basil
2 teaspoons sugar
1 tablespoon sesame paste
2 teaspoons soy sauce
2 teaspoons vegetable oil
4 cups cooked capellini

Combine shrimp, garlic, basil, sugar, sesame paste and soy sauce in bowl. Sauté in oil in sauté pan over medium heat just until shrimp are cooked through; do not overcook. Serve over pasta. **Yield:** 4 servings. Each serving has 295 Calories; 5 gr. Fat (16% of total calories); 150 mg. Cholesterol; and 238 mg. Sodium.

Try to reduce fat consumption to under 30 percent of total calories consumed each day. Each gram of fat contains 9 calories.

Glazed Ham with Cranberry-Pear Chutney

The White Horse Restaurant at the Sheraton Inn
Frazer, Pennsylvania

6 ounces honey
3 tablespoons Dijon mustard
1 10 to 12-pound semiboneless ham
1 6-ounce jar Major Grey's chutney
6 pears, peeled, chopped
8 ounces fresh cranberries
Juice of 1 orange
Juice of 1 lemon
1 teaspoon grated orange zest
1 teaspoon grated lemon zest
3 ounces Grand Marnier

Combine honey and mustard in bowl; mix well. Spread on ham; place in baking pan. Bake at 350 degrees for 3½ hours, basting occasionally. Combine chutney, pears, cranberries, orange juice, lemon juice, orange zest, lemon zest and Grand Marnier in saucepan. Simmer for several minutes. Place ham on serving platter. Add water to pan ham was baked in, stirring to deglaze pan. Stir into sauce. Simmer for 10 minutes. Serve with ham. **Yield:** 6 to 8 servings.

Le Filet de Dinde "Façon du Chef"

The White Horse Restaurant at the Sheraton Inn
Frazer, Pennsylvania

4 ounces chopped carrot
4 ounces chopped onion
4 ounces chopped green bell pepper
4 ounces chopped red bell pepper
4 ounces chopped yellow bell pepper
2 teaspoons olive oil
2 ounces bread crumbs
1 egg white
½ teaspoon poultry seasoning
¼ teaspoon thyme
Salt and pepper to taste
4 3-ounce turkey breast medallions
4 cups chicken stock
½ cup white wine

Sauté carrot, onion and bell peppers in olive oil in sauté pan. Cool slightly. Add bread crumbs, egg white, poultry seasoning, thyme, salt and pepper; mix well. Spoon onto 2 turkey medallions; top with remaining medallions. Tie with butchers' twine. Place in saucepan with chicken stock and wine. Braise until turkey is cooked through. Remove turkey to platter. Cook stock until reduced to ½ cup. Spoon sauce onto serving plates. Slice turkey; arrange in sauce. **Yield:** 2 servings. Each serving has 314 Calories; 10 gr. Fat (30% of total calories); 61 mg. Cholesterol; and 600 mg. Sodium.

Wine List

Wine has been romanticized throughout the ages. Poets and philosophers have exalted it; artists have been inspired by it; and authors have written countless volumes explaining it. In an effort to de-mystify the pairings of wines and food, Americans have "married" fish and fowl to white wines and red wine to meat. This is not a rule—only a guideline—for no one, not even the greatest wine connoisseur, can tell you what wine is the perfect companion for a certain food. Only your own palate can do that. The following list, then, is a guide to recommended wines. Try them with favorite foods, and let your taste determine whether the relationship will be casual, serious, or a true "marriage."

Chardonnay

A dry white wine with a versatile taste that holds up to most seafood, poultry and is also good served chilled as a cocktail.

Chateau Montelena ■ Estancia Monterey County
Meridian ■ Louis Latour
Groth ■ Fetzer Sundial
Columbia Crest ■ Chateau St. Michelle
Louis Jadot ■ Clos Du Bois
Chateau St. Jean ■ Stag's Leap
Franciscan ■ Beringer
Kendall Jackson ■ Rodney Strong Chalk Hill

Cabernet Sauvignon

A full-bodied red wine that goes well with red meat. Serve at room temperature after allowing 20 to 30 minutes to breathe.

B. V. Georges de Latour Private Reserve
Robert Mondavi, Private Reserve ■ Caymus ■ Arrowood
Kenwood ■ Groth ■ Meridian
Opus ■ Heitz Cellars—Martha's Vineyard
Duckhorn ■ Stag's Leap
Silverado ■ Guenoc ■ Clos Du Bois
Chateau Souverain ■ Liberty School

Recommended Table Wines

La Vielle Ferme—Côtes du Ventoux
Chateau du Moulin—Bordeaux
Louis Jadot—Beaujolais Villages
Melini Borghi D'elsa—Chianti
Chateau Olivier— Bordeaux
Concha y Toro—Cabernet Merlot
Chateau de Beaucastel—Chateau neuf Du Pape
Chateau La Gurgue—Bordeaux
Beringer—White Zinfandel
Lungarotti—Pinot Grigio
Moreau Chablis—1er cru Vaillons
Marqués de Riscal—Rioja
Mouton Cadet—Red or White Bordeaux
Louis Latour—Pouilly Fuissé

Recommended Sparkling Wines

Domaine Ste Michelle—Brut
Iron Horse—Brut
Cordorniu—Blanc de Blanc
Moet & Chandon White Star
Scharffenberger—Blanc de Blanc
Pol Roger—Brut N.V.
Domaine Chandon—Brut
Veuve Clicquot—Brut
G. H. Mumm Cordon Rouge—Brut

Appetizers

Diamond Rock School

Festival of Trees Cocktail Gala

Chilled Fresh Salmon with Herb Mayonnaise
page 50

Caviar-Topped Avocado Supreme
page 37

Water Chestnut Meatballs in Cherry Sauce
page 54

Sun-Dried Tomato Bites
page 60

Roasted Pepper Dip with French Bread
page 63

Smoked Turkey with Gingerbread Muffins
page 60

Cranberry-Glazed Brie
page 64

Fresh Strawberry Dip
page 253

Eggnog Refrigerator Cake
page 262

APPETIZERS

Caviar-Topped Avocado Supreme

"A very attractive presentation"

1 envelope unflavored gelatin
1/4 cup cold water
4 hard-boiled eggs, chopped
1/2 cup mayonnaise
6 green onions, finely chopped
1 teaspoon Dijon mustard
1 teaspoon drained, chopped green chilies
Dash of Tabasco sauce
Dash of white pepper
2 medium avocados, mashed
6 green onions, finely chopped
2 tablespoons fresh lime juice
2 tablespoons mayonnaise
1 tablespoon drained, chopped green chilies
1/2 teaspoon salt
2 drops of Tabasco sauce
Black pepper to taste
2 cups sour cream
1/4 teaspoon onion powder
1 2-ounce jar red caviar, rinsed, drained

Soften gelatin in cold water in saucepan. Heat until gelatin is dissolved, stirring constantly. Oil bottom and sides of 7-inch springform pan. Combine next 7 ingredients with 1 tablespoon gelatin in bowl; mix well. Spread in springform pan. Mix avocados, 6 green onions, lime juice, 2 tablespoons mayonnaise, 1 tablespoon green chilies, salt, 2 drops of Tabasco sauce, black pepper and 1 tablespoon gelatin in bowl. Spread over egg layer. Combine sour cream, onion powder and remaining 2 tablespoons gelatin in bowl; mix well. Spread over avocado layer. Chill, covered with plastic wrap, until set. Remove side of pan. Place on serving dish. Arrange caviar in 1-inch border around edge. Garnish in middle with thin lemon slice. Serve with party rye bread, melba toast or crackers. **Yield:** 20 servings.

Approx Per Serving: Cal 158; Prot 4; Carbo 4 g; Fiber 2 g; T Fat 15 g; 83% Calories from Fat; Chol 73 mg; Sod 170 mg.

Teriyaki Beef Nuggets*

"Nice to serve ahead of fish entrée"

12 ounces boneless sirloin steak
1 8-ounce can water chestnuts
1 tablespoon sugar
1 teaspoon dried minced onion
1 clove of garlic, minced
1/4 teaspoon ginger
1/4 cup soy sauce

Cut steak into 1/2x3/4-inch strips. Cut water chestnuts into halves. Wrap steak around water chestnut halves; secure with wooden pick. Place in shallow dish. Mix remaining ingredients in bowl. Pour over steak. Marinate in refrigerator for several hours. Place on broiler pan. Cook 5 to 8 inches from heat source for 3 to 4 minutes or until done to taste. **Yield:** 10 servings.

Approx Per Serving: Cal 65; Prot 7; Carbo 5 g; Fiber 1 g; T Fat 2 g; 27% Calories from Fat; Chol 19 mg; Sod 424 mg.

Cold Filet of Beef Appetizer

"A favorite at tailgate and cocktail parties"

1 carrot, chopped
1 stalk celery, chopped
1 medium onion, chopped
2 tablespoons butter
1 2-pound whole filet mignon
Salt to taste
Black pepper to taste
1 teaspoon chopped parsley
1/4 cup butter
8 ounces bacon, chopped
1 clove of garlic, minced
1 cup sour cream
1 tablespoon grated onion
1 tablespoon chopped chives
1 teaspoon horseradish
1/4 teaspoon tarragon
1/4 teaspoon dillweed
White pepper to taste

Sauté carrot, celery and onion in 2 tablespoons butter in small roasting pan until soft. Sprinkle filet with salt, black pepper and parsley. Place over vegetables in roasting pan; dot with 1/4 cup butter. Bake in preheated 500-degree oven for 20 to 25 minutes or until done to taste. Cool in pan for 1 hour. Place filet on platter. Strain and reserve 2 tablespoons pan drippings. Cut V-shape trough 1-inch deep down center of entire filet. Cut bottom point from V-shape so it is flattened to use as lid. Sauté bacon with garlic in skillet until bacon is crisp; drain on paper towels. Mix reserved pan drippings, salt to taste and remaining ingredients in bowl. Spoon into trough in filet; cover with filet lid. Chill, covered with foil, until serving time. Cut gently into 1/2-inch slices; place on serving platter. Garnish with parsley. **Yield:** 10 servings.

Approx Per Serving: Cal 304; Prot 20; Carbo 3 g; Fiber 1 g; T Fat 23 g; 69% Calories from Fat; Chol 102 mg; Sod 241 mg.

Cheese Puffs

"May be made ahead and chilled until ready to bake."

8 ounces soft cream cheese
2 eggs
2 teaspoons lemon juice
2 teaspoons frozen chives
Dash of pepper
4 ounces white Cheddar cheese, shredded
8 slices crisp-fried bacon, crumbled
8 frozen patty shells, thawed
1/4 cup milk

Mix first 5 ingredients in bowl. Stir in cheese and bacon. Chill, covered, in refrigerator. Roll each patty shell into 4x8-inch rectangle on floured surface; cut into 2-inch squares. Top each square with 1 rounded teaspoonful cream cheese mixture; brush edges of square with milk. Fold into triangle enclosing filling; press edges to seal. Place on ungreased baking . Place in preheated 450-degree oven. Reduce temperature to 400 degrees. Bake for 12 to 15 minutes or until brown. **Yield:** 64 servings.

Approx Per Serving: Cal 58; Prot 2; Carbo 2 g; Fiber <1 g; T Fat 4 g; 67% Calories from Fat; Chol 13 mg; Sod 65 mg.

Cheese-Filled Miniature Strudels

"Fun to make if you like phyllo"

3 large onions, thinly sliced
3 tablespoons unsalted butter
6 ounces cream cheese, softened
1 1/2 cups shredded Swiss cheese
1 teaspoon caraway seed
1/2 teaspoon salt
16 sheets phyllo dough
1/2 cup melted unsalted butter

Sauté onions in 3 tablespoons butter in skillet for 20 minutes or until soft and golden brown. Cool to lukewarm. Combine onions, cream cheese, Swiss cheese, caraway seed and salt in bowl; mix well. Unroll phyllo dough; cover with damp towel. Layer 4 sheets of phyllo dough together, brushing each with melted butter. Spoon 1/4 of the cheese mixture onto short side of phyllo dough, making 1-inch wide strip of filling. Roll dough tightly to enclose filling; tuck ends under. Place on plastic wrap. Score top of roll crosswise about 1/4-inch deep and 1 inch apart. Brush with melted butter. Seal in plastic wrap. Repeat with remaining phyllo dough and filling, making 4 rolls. Freeze for up to 3 months. Remove plastic wrap; place strudels on ungreased baking sheet. Bake at 400 degrees for 15 to 20 minutes or until golden brown. Cut into servings along scored markings. **Yield:** 48 servings.

Approx Per Serving: Cal 64; Prot 2; Carbo 6 g; Fiber <1 g; T Fat 4 g; 53% Calories from Fat; Chol 12 mg; Sod 68 mg.

Chicken and Bacon Bits

4 boneless chicken breast halves
10 slices bacon, cut into thirds
1 egg
1 cup flour
1 tablespoon cornstarch
1 tablespoon sugar
2 teaspoons salt
1½ teaspoons baking powder
½ cup milk
½ cup water
Oil for frying
1 cup apricot preserves
½ cup orange juice
1 tablespoon Dijon mustard

Rinse chicken; cut into 30 small pieces. Wrap chicken in bacon; secure with wooden pick. Beat egg in mixer bowl. Add flour, cornstarch, sugar, salt and baking powder in order listed, beating until smooth after each addition. Add milk and water; mix well. Pour oil to 2-inch depth in deep saucepan. Heat to 375 degrees. Dip chicken rolls into batter. Fry several rolls at a time in hot oil until brown. Drain on paper towels. Combine preserves, orange juice and mustard in bowl; mix well. Serve sauce with chicken rolls. **Yield:** 30 servings.

Approx Per Serving: Cal 85; Prot 5; Carbo 12 g; Fiber <1 g; T Fat 2 g; 20% Calories from Fat; Chol 19 mg; Sod 212 mg. Nutritional information does not include oil for frying.

Sesame Chicken with Dipping Sauce

6 boneless chicken breast halves
1 1-inch piece of fresh ginger, peeled, thinly sliced
2 cloves of garlic, minced
Pinch of cayenne pepper
1 teaspoon chili powder
½ cup white wine
¼ cup soy sauce
2 tablespoons sesame oil
½ cup flour
3 tablespoons black sesame seed
3 tablespoons white sesame seed
3 tablespoons butter
1 cup apricot preserves
2 teaspoons minced fresh ginger
1 teaspoon Dijon mustard
1 tablespoon rice wine vinegar

Rinse chicken; cut into 1-inch cubes. Combine sliced ginger, garlic, cayenne pepper, chili powder, white wine, soy sauce and sesame oil in bowl; mix well. Place chicken in shallow dish; pour in ginger mixture. Marinate, covered, in refrigerator for 30 minutes to overnight; drain. Combine flour and sesame seed in plastic bag. Add chicken; shake to coat. Sauté chicken in butter in skillet for 3 to 4 minutes or until golden brown and cooked through. Combine preserves, minced ginger, mustard and vinegar in bowl; mix well. Place wooden pick in each piece of chicken. Serve with sauce. **Yield:** 40 servings.

Approx Per Serving: Cal 74; Prot 5; Carbo 7 g; Fiber <1 g; T Fat 3 g; 35% Calories from Fat; Chol 13 mg; Sod 123 mg.

Chicken Chutney Puffs

1/3 cup margarine
3/4 cup water
3/4 cup flour
1/4 teaspoon salt
3 eggs
5 ounces cream cheese, softened
2 5-ounce cans chunk white chicken
1/2 cup finely chopped chutney
1/4 teaspoon curry powder
1/2 cup chopped walnuts

Bring margarine and water to a rolling boil in saucepan. Stir in flour and salt quickly. Cook over low heat until mixture leaves side of pan, stirring constantly. Remove from heat. Add eggs 1 at a time, beating well after each addition. Drop by teaspoonfuls onto greased baking sheet. Bake at 400 degrees for 30 minutes. Remove to wire rack to cool. Split into halves; remove soft center. Combine cream cheese, chicken, chutney and curry powder in bowl; mix well. Stir in walnuts. Spoon about 1/2 teaspoonful mixture into each pastry puff. **Yield:** 35 servings.

Approx Per Serving: Cal 70; Prot 3; Carbo 3 g; Fiber <1 g; T Fat 5 g; 62% Calories from Fat; Chol 23 mg; Sod 102 mg.

Mini-Chilies Rellenos

"Serve with salsa or taco sauce."

2 4-ounce cans whole green chilies, drained
1 8-ounce can whole pimentos, drained
8 ounces Monterey Jack cheese with jalapeño peppers
8 ounces sharp Cheddar cheese
2 cups unbleached flour
1 tablespoon cumin
2 teaspoons salt
2 cups beer
Oil for deep frying

Cut green chilies and pimentos into 1/2-inch wide strips. Cut Monterey Jack cheese and Cheddar cheese into 1/2-inch cubes. Wrap green chili strips around Cheddar cheese; secure with wooden picks. Wrap pimento strips around Monterey Jack cheese; secure with wooden picks. Place on tray. Chill, wrapped, in refrigerator for several hours. Combine flour, cumin and salt in bowl; mix well. Add beer; mix well. Let stand at room temperature for 1 hour. Heat 1 inch oil in large skillet to 400 degrees. Dip cheese cubes into beer batter; drop several at a time immediately into hot oil. Fry until light golden brown, turning once. Drain on paper towels. These may be prepared up to 3 hours before serving and reheated in preheated 375-degree oven for 5 minutes. **Yield:** 48 servings.

Approx Per Serving: Cal 62; Prot 3; Carbo 5 g; Fiber <1 g; T Fat 3 g; 46% Calories from Fat; Chol 9 mg; Sod 178 mg. Nutritional information does not include oil for deep frying.

Bacon 'n Cheese on Rye

1 cup finely grated Swiss cheese
1/4 cup crumbled, crisp-fried bacon
1 4-ounce can chopped ripe olives, drained
1/4 cup minced green onions
1 teaspoon Worcestershire sauce
1/4 cup mayonnaise
30 pieces of party rye bread

Mix cheese, bacon, olives, green onions, Worcestershire sauce and mayonnaise in bowl. Spread on party rye. Place on baking sheet. Bake at 375 degrees for 10 to 15 minutes or until brown. **Yield:** 30 servings.

Approx Per Serving: Cal 53; Prot 2; Carbo 4 g; Fiber <1 g; T Fat 4 g; 61% Calories from Fat; Chol 5 mg; Sod 107 mg.

Bermuda Triangles*

"May be frozen after baking and reheated."

1 cup Hellman's mayonnaise
3 bunches scallions, finely chopped
4 cups shredded sharp Cheddar cheese
12 English muffins, split

Combine mayonnaise, scallions and cheese in bowl; mix well. Spread thickly on muffin halves. Cut each half into quarters. Place on baking sheet. Broil for 10 minutes. Serve hot. **Yield:** 96 servings.

Approx Per Serving: Cal 54; Prot 2; Carbo 4 g; Fiber <1 g; T Fat 4 g; 67% Calories from Fat; Chol 6 mg; Sod 90 mg.

Spinach Squares

"These freeze well in plastic bags."

6 tablespoons butter
3 eggs
1 cup flour
1 cup milk
1/2 teaspoon salt
1 teaspoon baking powder
1 pound Monterey Jack cheese, shredded
4 cups chopped fresh spinach

Melt butter in 9x13-inch baking pan. Beat eggs in bowl. Add flour, milk, salt and baking powder; mix well. Add cheese and spinach; mix well. Spread in prepared pan. Bake at 350 degrees for 35 minutes. Cool for 30 minutes before serving. Cut into squares. **Yield:** 24 servings.

Approx Per Serving: Cal 133; Prot 7; Carbo 5 g; Fiber <1 g; T Fat 10 g; 65% Calories from Fat; Chol 53 mg; Sod 204 mg.

Empañadas de Picadillo

"These can be served hot or at room temperature."

1 pound lean ground beef
1 teaspoon butter
1 large clove of garlic, minced
1/2 cup tomato purée
1/2 cup seedless raisins
1/4 cup sherry
2 teaspoons cinnamon
1 teaspoon each salt and cumin
Pinch of cloves
1 teaspoon chili powder
2 tablespoons vinegar
2 teaspoons sugar
1/2 cup slivered almonds
1 17-ounce package frozen puff pastry, thawed
1 egg
1 tablespoon water

Brown ground beef in butter in skillet, stirring until crumbly; drain. Add garlic, tomato purée, raisins, sherry, cinnamon, salt, cumin, cloves, chili powder, vinegar and sugar; mix well. Cook over medium heat for 20 minutes or until most of liquid is absorbed, stirring frequently. Stir in almonds. Cool to room temperature. Roll each pastry sheet into 12x15-inch rectangle on floured surface. Cut each into 15 squares. Place 2 teaspoonfuls filling on each piece. Brush edges of pastry with mixture of egg and water; fold into triangles. Press edges to seal; place on ungreased baking sheet. Bake at 400 degrees for 15 to 20 minutes or until golden brown. May substitute 1 package pie crust mix for puff pastry. May freeze and bake while frozen at 400 degrees for 7 to 8 minutes. **Yield:** 30 servings.

Approx Per Serving: Cal 130; Prot 5; Carbo 9 g; Fiber 1 g; T Fat 8 g; 57% Calories from Fat; Chol 17 mg; Sod 161 mg.

Jalapeño Squares

"Very tasty and different"

2 4-ounce cans chopped green chilies, drained
16 ounces extra sharp Cheddar cheese, shredded
1 1/2 cups Italian-seasoned bread crumbs
5 eggs, beaten
1/2 teaspoon salt
1/2 teaspoon cumin
1/2 teaspoon chili powder
1 teaspoon oregano
1 cup milk

Layer chilies and mixture of cheese and bread crumbs in greased 9x13-inch baking dish. Combine eggs, salt, cumin, chili powder, oregano and milk in bowl; mix well. Pour over layers, spreading to cover. Bake at 375 degrees for 50 to 60 minutes or until set. Cool at room temperature for 10 minutes. Cut into squares. Serve warm. **Yield:** 50 servings.

Approx Per Serving: Cal 60; Prot 3; Carbo 3 g; Fiber <1 g; T Fat 4 g; 58% Calories from Fat; Chol 32 mg; Sod 141 mg.

Deep-Fried Mozzarella with Creole Sauce

"You can use marinara sauce to save time."

8 ounces mozzarella cheese
1/2 cup flour
Salt and pepper to taste
2 eggs
1 cup milk
2 cups cracker meal
3 medium onions, chopped
1/4 cup bacon drippings
10 ripe tomatoes, chopped
4 stalks celery, chopped
2 green bell peppers, chopped
1 tablespoon oregano
Hot sauce to taste
1 tablespoon chopped parsley
1 tablespoon liquid smoke
Oil for deep frying

Cut cheese into bite-sized pieces. Mix flour with salt and pepper in bowl. Mix eggs with milk in bowl. Dip cheese in flour mixture; dip in egg mixture. Roll in cracker meal to coat. Place on rack on baking sheet. Chill, covered, for up to 4 hours. Sauté onions in bacon drippings in large skillet until soft. Add tomatoes 1 at a time, stirring constantly. Add celery, green peppers, oregano, salt, pepper, hot sauce, parsley and liquid smoke. Cook over high heat for 4 to 5 minutes or until vegetables are tender, stirring constantly. Deep-fry cheese cubes several at a time in 400-degree oil until golden brown; drain on paper towels. Place on serving plate; drizzle with hot creole sauce. Serve hot. Creole sauce may be made several days ahead and refrigerated or frozen; reheat over low heat to serve. **Yield:** 20 servings.

Approx Per Serving: Cal 142; Prot 5; Carbo 15 g; Fiber 2 g; T Fat 7 g; 45% Calories from Fat; Chol 51 mg; Sod 204 mg. Nutritional information does not include oil for deep frying.

Chadds Ford Mushrooms

"Self-fulfilling mushrooms!"

2 pounds mushrooms
1 large onion, finely chopped
1 teaspoon lemon juice
1/2 cup margarine
2 tablespoons flour
1/2 cup milk or half and half
Salt and pepper to taste

Wash and dry mushrooms. Cut off stems; finely chop. Sauté mushroom stems and onion with lemon juice in margarine in skillet for 3 minutes or until tender. Add flour, stirring to mix well. Add milk. Cook until thickened, stirring constantly. Add salt and pepper; mix well. Fill mushroom caps; place on greased baking sheet. Bake at 350 degrees for 15 to 20 minutes or until light brown. **Yield:** 16 servings.

Approx Per Serving: Cal 77; Prot 2; Carbo 5 g; Fiber 1 g; T Fat 6 g; 69% Calories from Fat; Chol 1 mg; Sod 73 mg.

Grandma's Mushrooms*

"Every Christmas day Grandma served these mushrooms. You had to watch closely because they disappeared quickly."

3 eggs
1 tablespoon chopped parsley
1 clove of garlic, minced
Salt and pepper to taste
1/2 cup grated locatelli or Romano cheese
3 pounds mushrooms, stems removed

Combine first 6 ingredients in bowl; mix well. Spoon into mushroom caps; place on foil-lined baking sheet. Bake at 350 degrees for 40 minutes or until brown. **Yield:** 36 servings.

Approx Per Serving: Cal 22; Prot 2; Carbo 2 g; Fiber 1 g; T Fat 1 g; 39% Calories from Fat; Chol 19 mg; Sod 26 mg.

Fried Pasta Crisps

8 ounces fresh small tortellini or ravioli
Oil for frying
1/3 cup grated locatelli cheese
1 teaspoon basil
1/4 teaspoon cayenne pepper
Pinch of garlic salt
1 cup marinara sauce

Fry pasta in 1/2-inch deep 350-degree oil in 10-inch skillet for 2 to 3 minutes or until crisp and golden; drain on paper towel. Keep warm in 200-degree oven. Combine cheese and seasonings in paper bag. Add warm pasta; shake to coat. Serve with marinara sauce for dipping. **Yield:** 35 servings.

Approx Per Serving: Cal 162; Prot 14; Carbo 4 g; Fiber 0 g; T Fat 10 g; 54% Calories from Fat; Chol 26 mg; Sod 630 mg. Nutritional information does not include oil for frying.

Pepperoni Bread*

1 can Pillsbury crusty French loaf
8 ounces sliced provolone cheese
4 ounces 3-inch slices pepperoni

Unroll dough on baking sheet. Layer 2 rows of cheese across long side, overlapping edges slightly. Layer 3 rows of pepperoni over cheese, overlapping edges slightly. Roll to enclose filling; press edges to seal. Place on baking sheet. Bake at 350 degrees for 30 minutes or until brown. Cool on wire rack for 25 minutes. Cut into 1-inch slices. **Yield:** 15 servings.

Approx Per Serving: Cal 143; Prot 7; Carbo 10 g; Fiber 0 g; T Fat 8 g; 52% Calories from Fat; Chol 13 mg; Sod 390 mg.

Roasted Pepper Antipasto

"This is a variation of a more elaborate antipasto."

2 7-ounce jars roasted red peppers, drained
1 4-ounce jar button mushrooms, drained
1 6-ounce can pitted black olives, drained
1 medium onion, thinly sliced
2 cloves of garlic, minced
2 to 3 tablespoons olive oil
Salt, pepper and oregano to taste

Clean red peppers of any blackened areas. Remove skin; cut red peppers into 1-inch pieces. Cut mushrooms and black olives into halves. Combine red peppers, mushrooms, black olives, onion, garlic, olive oil, salt, pepper and oregano in bowl; mix well. Chill in refrigerator. Let stand at room temperature for 1 hour before serving. Serve with Italian bread. **Yield:** 8 servings.

Approx Per Serving: Cal 103; Prot 1; Carbo 6 g; Fiber 2 g; T Fat 10 g; 77% Calories from Fat; Chol 0 mg; Sod 223 mg.

Italian-Style Pickled Vegetables

"Nice change!"

12 carrots, julienne-style
Flowerets of 1 small head cauliflower
1 cup olive oil
1/2 cup wine vinegar
2 teaspoons salt
3/4 teaspoon pepper
1 1/2 teaspoons oregano
1 teaspoon basil
3 cloves of garlic, cut into halves

Cook carrots and cauliflower in a small amount of boiling water for 7 to 10 minutes or until tender-crisp; drain. Pour into shallow dish. Combine olive oil, vinegar, salt, pepper, oregano, basil and garlic in saucepan. Bring to a boil, stirring occasionally. Pour over vegetables. Marinate, covered, in refrigerator for 24 hours or longer. Drain before serving. **Yield:** 20 servings.

Approx Per Serving: Cal 119; Prot 1; Carbo 6 g; Fiber 2 g; T Fat 11 g; 79% Calories from Fat; Chol 0 mg; Sod 230 mg.

Potato Skins

"These do a disappearing act."

4 potatoes
1/2 cup shredded Cheddar cheese
8 slices crisp-fried bacon, crumbled
2 green chili peppers, cut into thin strips

Scrub potatoes; dry. Bake potatoes at 350 degrees for 1 hour. Cut into halves. Scoop out centers and reserve for another purpose. Combine cheese, bacon and pepper strips in bowl; mix well. Spoon into potato skins. The filling will be very thin. Place on broiler pan. Broil for 5 minutes. **Yield:** 8 servings.

Approx Per Serving: Cal 127; Prot 5; Carbo 15 g; Fiber 1 g; T Fat 6 g; 38% Calories from Fat; Chol 13 mg; Sod 152 mg.

Mexican Quesadillas

2 cloves of garlic, minced
2 tablespoons vegetable oil
1/2 cup chopped green bell pepper
1 1/2 cups drained, canned peeled tomatoes
3 to 5 tablespoons canned, chopped peeled green chili peppers
1/4 teaspoon salt
Dash of freshly ground pepper
12 ounces Monterey Jack or white Cheddar cheese, shredded
12 large flour tortillas
1/2 cup vegetable oil

Sauté garlic lightly in 2 tablespoons hot oil in skillet. Add green pepper. Sauté for 3 to 5 minutes. Stir in tomatoes, crushing with spoon. Add 3 tablespoons chili peppers, salt and pepper. Simmer for 20 minutes, stirring frequently. Sprinkle cheese in center of each tortilla. Top each with 1 tablespoon tomato sauce and chili peppers. Fold in half; secure with wooden pick. Lay quesadillas on oiled baking sheet. Brush each with oil. Bake at 375 degrees for 6 to 7 minutes or until brown. Cut each into 4 wedges. Serve hot. May cover lightly and reheat in 375-degree oven with door ajar until crisp. **Yield:** 48 servings.

Approx Per Serving: Cal 96; Prot 3; Carbo 8 g; Fiber 1 g; T Fat 6 g; 55% Calories from Fat; Chol 6 mg; Sod 121 mg.

Party Italian Sausage*

"Time saving for a large party"

2 pounds sweet Italian sausage
1 30-ounce jar spaghetti sauce

Place sausage in baking dish. Bake at 325 degrees for 30 minutes or until cooked through. Cool slightly. Cut into 1-inch pieces. Place in chafing dish. Heat spaghetti sauce in saucepan. Pour over sausage. Serve with wooden picks. **Yield:** 25 servings.

Approx Per Serving: Cal 25; Prot 1; Carbo 1 g; Fiber <1 g; T Fat 1 g; 62% Calories from Fat; Chol 4 mg; Sod 97 mg.

Sausage and Spinach in Phyllo

18 13x17-inch sheets frozen phyllo dough
1 pound bulk pork sausage
1/2 cup chopped onion
2 10-ounce packages frozen chopped spinach
4 ounces feta cheese, crumbled
1/2 cup grated Parmesan cheese
1 teaspoon oregano
1/2 cup melted margarine

Thaw phyllo dough using package directions; cover with damp towel. Brown sausage with onion in skillet, stirring frequently; drain. Cook spinach using package directions; drain. Combine sausage, spinach, feta cheese, Parmesan cheese and oregano in bowl; mix well. Remove 1 sheet phyllo dough from under damp towel. Place on ungreased baking sheet; brush with melted margarine. Repeat with 5 sheets of phyllo dough. Spread 1/3 of the sausage mixture along long side of dough to within 2 inches of long edge. Roll carefully from sausage-covered edge to enclose filling. Repeat with remaining ingredients to make 2 more rolls. Place rolls on baking sheet; brush with remaining melted margarine. Score tops crosswise at 1-inch intervals, cutting through just to filling. Bake at 350 degrees for 25 to 30 minutes or until brown. Serve warm. **Yield:** 36 servings.

Approx Per Serving: Cal 94; Prot 4; Carbo 8 g; Fiber 1 g; T Fat 5 g; 51% Calories from Fat; Chol 8 mg; Sod 214 mg.

Spray phyllo with butter-flavored nonstick vegetable spray instead of brushing with butter to lower fat content.

Linda's Seafood Pie

"You can skip dinner after this hearty treat."

1 8-count can crescent rolls
1 pound shrimp or crab meat
1 to 2 tablespoons butter
Pepper and garlic powder to taste
3 tablespoons white wine
2 eggs, beaten
1 tablespoon grated Parmesan cheese
2 cups mozzarella or Monterey Jack cheese cubes

Unroll crescent roll dough. Press into 9-inch pie plate to form pie shell, pressing edges and perforations to seal. Sauté shrimp in butter in skillet. Remove from heat. Sprinkle with pepper and garlic powder. Add wine. Combine eggs, Parmesan cheese and mozzarella cheese in bowl; mix well. Stir in shrimp mixture. Pour into prepared pie plate. Bake at 350 degrees for 45 to 60 minutes or until golden brown. **Yield:** 10 servings.

Approx Per Serving: Cal 221; Prot 15; Carbo 9 g; Fiber 0 g; T Fat 13 g; 55% Calories from Fat; Chol 138 mg; Sod 393 mg.

Clam Broth Puffs

"An auxiliary favorite"

4 6-ounce cans minced clams
1/2 cup margarine
1 cup flour
4 eggs
16 ounces cream cheese, softened
6 drops of Tabasco sauce
1 teaspoon seasoned salt

Drain clams, reserving 1 cup clam broth. Bring margarine and broth to a boil in saucepan. Add flour quickly, stirring until mixture leaves side of pan and forms a ball. Remove to mixer bowl. Add eggs 1 at a time, beating well after each addition until thick dough is formed. Place dough by level teaspoonfuls 1-inch apart on ungreased baking sheet. Bake at 400 degrees for 25 minutes. Cool slightly. Cut into halves; remove soft centers. Combine clams and cream cheese in bowl; mix well. Add Tabasco sauce and seasoned salt; mix well. Spoon into puffs; replace tops. Reheat in preheated 350-degree oven for 15 minutes. May be frozen after puffs are filled. **Yield:** 48 servings.

Approx Per Serving: Cal 87; Prot 5; Carbo 3 g; Fiber <1 g; T Fat 6 g; 62% Calories from Fat; Chol 38 mg; Sod 110 mg.

Crab-Filled Mushrooms*

"Healthy choice"

24 2-inch mushrooms
1/4 cup light process cream cheese product
1 tablespoon grated Parmesan cheese
2 tablespoons plain nonfat yogurt
2 tablespoons fresh lemon juice
1/8 teaspoon red pepper
8 ounces fresh lump crab meat, drained
1/4 cup minced red bell pepper
2 tablespoons minced green onions

Wash mushrooms; dry. Cut off stems. Combine cream cheese product, Parmesan cheese, yogurt, lemon juice and red pepper in bowl; mix well. Fold in crab meat, red pepper and green onions. Spoon 1 tablespoonful mixture into each mushroom cap; place in 9x13-inch baking dish. Bake at 350 degrees for 20 minutes. Serve warm. **Yield:** 24 servings.

Approx Per Serving: Cal 22; Prot 3; Carbo 1 g; Fiber <1 g; T Fat 1 g; 29% Calories from Fat; Chol 11 mg; Sod 45 mg.

Chilled Fresh Salmon with Herb Mayonnaise

"This deserves a round of applause."

2 pounds fresh salmon
Salt and pepper to taste
1 cup wine vinegar
1 medium onion, sliced
2 celery stalks with leaves, cut into halves
2 cloves of garlic, minced
2 cups mayonnaise
10 fresh parsley sprigs, finely chopped
2 fresh green scallions, finely chopped
1 5-ounce can chopped pimentos, drained
8 ounces fresh peas, cooked
1 teaspoon oregano

Place salmon in shallow saucepan; cover with water. Add salt, pepper, vinegar, onion and celery. Simmer for 30 to 40 minutes or until salmon flakes easily; drain. Cool slightly; remove bones. Place salmon on serving dish. Combine garlic, mayonnaise, parsley, scallions, pimentos, peas and oregano in mixer bowl; mix well. Spoon over top of salmon. Serve with party rye bread. May substitute canned peas for fresh.
Yield: 30 servings.

Approx Per Serving: Cal 145; Prot 6; Carbo 3 g; Fiber 1 g; T Fat 12 g; 77% Calories from Fat; Chol 21 mg; Sod 103 mg.

Pickled Scallops

"Scallops are a very good and low calorie appetizer."

30 (about 1 pound) bay scallops
3 to 4 tablespoons butter
1 cup vinegar
1 1/2 tablespoons bell pepper flakes
4 teaspoons instant minced onion
1/2 teaspoon whole allspice
2 teaspoons sugar
1 1/2 teaspoons salt
1/8 teaspoon garlic powder
1 whole hot red pepper

Wash scallops; pat dry. Sauté in butter in skillet for 2 to 3 minutes. Place in shallow dish. Combine vinegar, pepper flakes, minced onion, allspice, sugar, salt and garlic powder in saucepan. Bring to a boil. Boil for 1 minute, stirring occasionally. Break hot red pepper into halves. Add to hot mixture. Pour over scallops. Marinate, covered, in refrigerator for 24 hours. Drain. Serve with wooden picks. **Yield:** 30 servings.

Approx Per Serving: Cal 30; Prot 3; Carbo 1 g; Fiber <1 g; T Fat 2 g; 47% Calories from Fat; Chol 9 mg; Sod 144 mg.

Seviche de Acapulco

"Serve with plain taco chips."

1 1/2 pounds uncooked mild-flavored fish filets or scallops
1 cup lemon or lime juice
2 canned green chilies, seeded, chopped
1/2 cup minced onion
2 large tomatoes, peeled, seeded, chopped
1 teaspoon salt
1/4 teaspoon oregano
1/4 cup olive oil

Cut fish into small, thin pieces; place in shallow dish. Pour in lemon juice. Marinate, covered, in refrigerator for 2 hours. Combine green chilies, onion, tomatoes, salt, oregano and olive oil in bowl; mix well. Stir in fish and marinade. Chill in refrigerator. Spoon into chilled cocktail or sherbet glasses. Garnish with avocado slices, green chili strips, pimento strips or chopped parsley. **Yield:** 12 servings.

Approx Per Serving: Cal 107; Prot 11; Carbo 4 g; Fiber 1 g; T Fat 5 g; 44% Calories from Fat; Chol 31 mg; Sod 228 mg.

Bleu Cheese-Stuffed Shrimp

3 ounces cream cheese, softened
1 ounce bleu cheese, crumbled
1 teaspoon finely chopped green onions
1/2 teaspoon prepared mustard
24 jumbo shrimp, cooked, peeled
3/4 cup chopped fresh parsley

Combine first 4 ingredients in bowl; mix well. Cut slit into back of shrimp. Stuff with a small amount of mixture. Roll shrimp in parsley to coat. Chill, covered, in refrigerator for 1 to 4 hours. Serve on silver tray garnished with lemon and sprigs of fresh dill. **Yield:** 24 servings.

Approx Per Serving: Cal 39; Prot 5; Carbo <1 g; Fiber <1 g; T Fat 2 g; 43% Calories from Fat; Chol 48 mg; Sod 79 mg.

Shrimp Wrapped in Snow Peas

3 onions, thinly sliced
1 1/4 cups corn oil
3 tablespoons cloves
3 tablespoons capers
3 tablespoons celery seed
1 tablespoon garlic salt
2 1/2 pounds large shrimp, cooked, peeled
20 snow peas

Combine onions, oil, cloves, capers, celery seed and garlic salt in bowl; mix well. Place shrimp in shallow dish. Pour in marinade. Marinate, covered, in refrigerator for 2 to 3 days. Drain shrimp. Remove strings from snow peas. Blanch in boiling water for 30 seconds; drain. Chill in iced water; drain. Cut snow peas into halves lengthwise. Wrap snow pea half around each shrimp; fasten with wooden pick. Place on serving dish. Serve chilled. **Yield:** 20 servings.

Approx Per Serving: Cal 180; Prot 10; Carbo 3 g; Fiber 1 g; T Fat 14 g; 71% Calories from Fat; Chol 89 mg; Sod 410 mg.

Artichokes Iced with Caviar*

2 8-ounce cans artichoke hearts, drained, chopped
8 ounces cream cheese, softened
1 to 2 tablespoons mayonnaise
2 tablespoons sour cream
1/2 cup finely chopped onion
2 2-ounce jars black caviar, drained

Shape artichokes into mound on large serving plate. Spread mixture of next 4 ingredients over artichokes; sprinkle with caviar. Garnish with fresh parsley. Serve with butter-flavored crackers. **Yield:** 16 servings.

Approx Per Serving: Cal 95; Prot 3; Carbo 3 g; Fiber <1 g; T Fat 8 g; 75% Calories from Fat; Chol 58 mg; Sod 230 mg.

Swordfish on Spits

"Great to use the grill for before dinner as well as during!"

3 pounds swordfish or tuna
1 teaspoon paprika
2 tablespoons fresh lemon juice
1 tablespoon olive oil
1 clove of garlic, minced
1/4 teaspoon oregano
5 bay leaves
2 teaspoons olive oil
Juice of 1 lemon
1/4 teaspoon oregano
Salt and pepper to taste

Remove skin from fish; cut into 1-inch cubes. Place in shallow dish. Combine paprika, 2 tablespoons lemon juice, 1 tablespoon olive oil, garlic, 1/4 teaspoon oregano and bay leaves in bowl; mix well. Pour over fish. Marinate, covered, in refrigerator for 12 to 24 hours. Drain fish. Arrange on bamboo skewers. Broil 3 inches from heat source for 3 minutes or until brown on both sides. Process remaining 2 teaspoons olive oil, juice of 1 lemon, 1/4 teaspoon oregano, salt and pepper in blender until well mixed. Pour into bowl. Serve with fish.
Yield: 24 servings.

Approx Per Serving: Cal 80; Prot 12; Carbo <1 g; Fiber <1 g; T Fat 3 g; 38% Calories from Fat; Chol 23 mg; Sod 52 mg.

Taco Tarts

"This gets a thumbs up."

1 11-ounce can corn bread twists
8 ounces lean ground beef
1 4-ounce jar taco sauce
1/2 teaspoon chili powder
1/4 teaspoon cumin
Garlic powder to taste
1/3 cup canned refried beans
2 to 3 ounces shredded Cheddar cheese

Divide corn bread twists into 24 pieces. Press into 24 miniature muffin cups. Bake at 375 degrees for 10 to 12 minutes or until light brown. Remove to wire rack. Cool for 2 to 3 minutes. Brown ground beef in skillet, stirring until crumbly; drain. Add taco sauce, chili powder, cumin, garlic powder and beans; mix well. Spoon about 1 teaspoonful ground beef mixture into each muffin cup; sprinkle with cheese. Place on baking sheet. Bake at 375 degrees for 10 minutes. **Yield:** 24 servings.

Approx Per Serving: Cal 86; Prot 4; Carbo 7 g; Fiber <1 g; T Fat 5 g; 54% Calories from Fat; Chol 10 mg; Sod 177 mg.

Tomatoes Stuffed with 'Chokes and Hearts*

"Good summertime fare"

1 16-ounce can artichoke hearts, drained
1 16-ounce can hearts of palm, drained
Juice of 1 lemon
1/4 cup tarragon vinegar
1/3 cup olive oil
1/4 cup chopped fresh dill
1/4 cup chopped Italian flat-leaf parsley
Freshly ground pepper to taste
60 cherry tomatoes

Process artichoke hearts and hearts of palm in food processor until coarsely chopped. Blend lemon juice, vinegar and olive oil in mixer bowl. Add dill, parsley and pepper; mix well. Stir in artichoke hearts and hearts of palm. Scoop out centers of cherry tomatoes. Fill with mixture. **Yield:** 60 servings.

Approx Per Serving: Cal 20; Prot <1; Carbo 2 g; Fiber <1 g; T Fat 1 g; 61% Calories from Fat; Chol 0 mg; Sod 59 mg.

Water Chestnut Meatballs in Cherry Sauce

"Serve in chafing dish."

2 cups soft bread crumbs
1/2 cup (about) milk
1 tablespoon soy sauce
1/2 teaspoon garlic salt
1/4 teaspoon onion powder
1 cup drained, finely chopped water chestnuts
8 ounces lean ground beef
8 ounces hot pork sausage
1 21-ounce can cherry pie filling
1/4 cup white wine vinegar
1/4 cup steak sauce
1/3 cup sherry
2 tablespoons brown sugar
2 tablespoons soy sauce

Combine bread crumbs, milk, 1 tablespoon soy sauce, garlic salt and onion powder in bowl; mix well. Add water chestnuts, ground beef and sausage; mix well. Shape into small meatballs. Place in large baking pan. Bake at 350 degrees for 20 minutes; drain. Combine pie filling, vinegar, steak sauce, sherry, brown sugar and 2 tablespoons soy sauce in double boiler; mix well. Heat to serving temperature over boiling water. Add meatballs. Heat thoroughly. Pour into chafing dish. **Yield:** 50 servings.

Approx Per Serving: Cal 43; Prot 2; Carbo 6 g; Fiber <1 g; T Fat 1 g; 31% Calories from Fat; Chol 5 mg; Sod 127 mg.

Yaki-Mondu

"Korean fried won tons are a favorite of my family. This recipe was taught to me by our Korean maid while I was in Seoul, Korea."

1½ pounds extra-lean ground beef
½ to ⅔ cup chopped fresh chives
1 teaspoon salt
Pepper to taste
5 cloves of garlic, minced
½ teaspoon ginger
¼ cup sesame oil
¼ cup vegetable oil
½ teaspoon MSG
1 egg, beaten
1 14-ounce package Gyoza won ton wrappers
Oil for deep-frying
½ cup soy sauce
2 tablespoons sesame oil
1 tablespoon toasted sesame seed

Combine ground beef, chives, salt, pepper, garlic, ginger, ¼ cup sesame oil, ¼ cup vegetable oil, MSG and egg in bowl; mix well. Place about 1 teaspoonful in center of each won ton wrapper. Moisten edges with water. Fold over filling into triangle, pressing edges to seal. Deep-fry in very hot oil until golden brown; drain. Combine remaining ½ cup soy sauce, 2 tablespoons sesame oil and sesame seed in bowl; mix well. Pour into bowl. Serve with fried won tons. May also serve with Duck sauce. **Yield:** 60 servings.

Approx Per Serving: Cal 47; Prot 2; Carbo <1 g; Fiber <1 g; T Fat 4 g; 77% Calories from Fat; Chol 11 mg; Sod 216 mg. Nutritional information does not include oil for deep frying.

Zucchini Pizza Squares

4 eggs, beaten
½ cup oil
1 cup baking mix (Bisquick)
3 cups grated zucchini
½ cup finely chopped green bell pepper
½ cup finely chopped onion
½ cup shredded mozzarella cheese
½ cup grated Parmesan cheese
1 cup finely chopped pepperoni
½ teaspoon oregano
2 teaspoons chopped parsley
Salt and garlic powder to taste

Combine eggs, oil and baking mix in bowl; mix well. Add zucchini, green pepper, onion, mozzarella cheese, Parmesan cheese, pepperoni, oregano, parsley, salt and garlic powder; mix well. Spoon into well greased 9x13-inch baking dish. Bake at 350 degrees for 40 to 45 minutes. Cool slightly. Cut into squares. **Yield:** 32 servings.

Approx Per Serving: Cal 108; Prot 4; Carbo 4 g; Fiber <1 g; T Fat 9 g; 72% Calories from Fat; Chol 31 mg; Sod 234 mg.

Chicken Almond Rolls

"Save these for company!"

1 cup chopped cooked chicken
1 cup mayonnaise
1 small onion, finely chopped
3/4 cup shredded Monterey Jack cheese
1/3 cup finely chopped almonds
1/4 cup chopped parsley
2 teaspoons lemon juice
2 teaspoons curry powder
1/4 teaspoon salt
1/4 teaspoon pepper
18 slices whole wheat bread
1/4 cup melted butter
1 or 2 teaspoons dill

Combine chicken, mayonnaise, onion, cheese, almonds, parsley, lemon juice, curry powder, salt and pepper in large bowl; mix well. Chill, covered, for 30 minutes. Trim crusts from bread; flatten with rolling pin. Place 2 scant tablespoons filling in center of each slice. Roll to enclose filling. Cut into halves; secure with wooden picks. Arrange on lightly buttered baking sheet; sprinkle with dill. Bake at 375 degrees for 15 minutes. May freeze rolls before baking if desired and increase baking temperature to 400 degrees. **Yield:** 36 servings.

Approx Per Serving: Cal 115; Prot 4; Carbo 7 g; Fiber 1 g; T Fat 8 g; 64% Calories from Fat; Chol 13 mg; Sod 167 mg.

Chicken Nachos

"Great to make ahead!"

1 whole chicken breast, cooked, chopped
12 ounces cream cheese, softened
2 jalapeño peppers, seeded, minced
3 tablespoons chopped red onion
2 cloves of garlic, minced
1 teaspoon chili powder
1 1/2 cups shredded Monterey Jack cheese
Salt and pepper to taste
6 pita bread rounds, split, cut into quarters

Combine chicken, cream cheese, peppers, onion, garlic, chili powder, Monterey Jack cheese, salt and pepper in bowl; mix well. Spread on pita bread. Freeze on baking sheets. Remove to plastic bags to store in freezer. Arrange on baking sheets; do not thaw. Bake at 375 degrees for 5 to 7 minutes or until bubbly. **Yield:** 48 servings.

Approx Per Serving: Cal 65; Prot 3; Carbo 5 g; Fiber <1 g; T Fat 4 g; 52% Calories from Fat; Chol 14 mg; Sod 85 mg.

Eggplant and Gorgonzola Crostini

1 eggplant, peeled, cubed
1 teaspoon salt
3 tablespoons olive oil
1 tablespoon minced garlic
1 tablespoon dried basil
Pepper to taste
1/2 cup prepared pesto sauce
1 8-ounce loaf Italian bread, sliced
4 ounces provolone cheese, shredded
2 ounces Gorgonzola cheese, crumbled

Spread eggplant on paper towel. Sprinkle with salt. Let stand for 30 minutes to drain. Pat dry with paper towels. Heat oil in large heavy skillet over medium-high heat. Add eggplant, garlic and dried basil. Sauté for 8 to 10 minutes or until eggplant is tender and lightly browned. Sprinkle with pepper. Spread 1 1/2 teaspoons pesto sauce over one side of each bread slice. Top with 1 tablespoon eggplant mixture, 1 tablespoon provolone cheese and 1/2 tablespoon Gorgonzola cheese. Arrange on baking sheet. Broil for 3 to 4 minutes or until cheese melts. Garnish with fresh basil leaves. **Yield:** 16 servings.

Approx Per Serving: Cal 146; Prot 5; Carbo 11 g; Fiber 1 g; T Fat 9 g; 58% Calories from Fat; Chol 8 mg; Sod 405 mg.

Martini Bait

"This scallop mixture keeps for a week in the refrigerator, so you can make them as needed for spur-of-the-moment entertaining."

3 tablespoons unsalted butter
1 pound bay scallops, cut into quarters
2 teaspoons minced lemon zest
3 cloves of garlic, minced
3 tablespoons chopped fresh dill or basil
2 cups shredded Swiss cheese
2 1/4 cups mayonnaise
Freshly ground pepper to taste
36 slices white bread
Paprika to taste

Melt butter in skillet over medium-high heat. Add scallops, lemon zest and garlic. Cook for 2 to 3 minutes or just until scallops are cooked through, stirring constantly. Add dill. Cook for 30 minutes longer. Let stand until cool. Add cheese, mayonnaise and pepper, stirring well. Chill, covered, until ready to use. Cut four 1-inch rounds from each bread slice. Arrange on baking sheet. Toast lightly. Top with 1 heaping teaspoon scallop mixture; sprinkle with paprika. Broil 5 inches from heat source for 2 to 3 minutes or until puffed and golden. Serve hot.
Yield: 144 servings.

Approx Per Serving: Cal 54; Prot 2; Carbo 4 g; Fiber <1 g; T Fat 4 g; 61% Calories from Fat; Chol 5 mg; Sod 65 mg.

Newport Beach Party Bread*

1 long thin loaf Italian bread
1 tablespoon butter, softened
1 cup mayonnaise
1/2 cup grated Romano cheese
1/2 cup finely chopped green onions
1/4 to 1/2 teaspoon Tabasco sauce
Paprika to taste

Slice bread lengthwise; butter lightly. Place on baking sheet. Bake at 300 degrees for 5 minutes. Combine next 4 ingredients in bowl; mix well. Spread over bread. Sprinkle with paprika. Broil for 2 to 3 minutes or until lightly browned. Cut into 1-inch slices to serve. **Yield:** 20 servings.

Approx Per Serving: Cal 157; Prot 3; Carbo 13 g; Fiber <1 g; T Fat 10 g; 58% Calories from Fat; Chol 10 mg; Sod 239 mg.

Sausage Pizzas

1 pound sausage
8 ounces mushrooms, sliced
1 onion, chopped
1 tomato, chopped
1/2 teaspoon oregano
1/8 teaspoon salt
1/8 teaspoon pepper
12 ounces sharp Cheddar cheese, shredded
1 loaf party rye bread

Brown sausage in electric skillet, stirring until crumbly. Remove with slotted spoon; drain on paper towels. Sauté mushrooms and onion in drippings in skillet; drain. Mix in tomato, oregano, salt, pepper and sausage. Remove from heat. Stir in cheese. Spoon onto party bread. Arrange on baking sheet. Bake at 375 for 15 minutes. **Yield:** 32 servings.

Approx Per Serving: Cal 90; Prot 5; Carbo 4 g; Fiber 1 g; T Fat 6 g; 59% Calories from Fat; Chol 17 mg; Sod 211 mg.

Little Russian Reubens*

1 12-ounce can corned beef
1 7-ounce can sauerkraut, drained
6 ounces Swiss cheese, shredded
1 tomato, chopped
3/4 cup (or more) Russian salad dressing
1 loaf party pumpernickel bread

Crumble corned beef into bowl, discarding fat. Add sauerkraut, cheese and tomato; mix well. Add enough salad dressing to bind; mix lightly. Spread on bread; place on baking sheet. Bake at 325 degrees for 15 minutes. **Yield:** 40 servings.

Approx Per Serving: Cal 76; Prot 4; Carbo 4 g; Fiber <1 g; T Fat 5 g; 59% Calories from Fat; Chol 14 mg; Sod 201 mg.

Party Deli Sandwiches

1 8-ounce bottle of Russian salad dressing
18 slices firm rye bread
12 slices ham
6 slices Swiss cheese
12 slices deli turkey
1 cup coleslaw, drained

Spread salad dressing on 1 side of 6 bread slices. Arrange dressing side up on tray. Top each piece of bread with 2 ham slices and 1 cheese slice. Spread salad dressing on both sides of 6 bread slices. Place on cheese slice. Add 2 turkey slices to each bread slice and spread with coleslaw. Spread dressing on 1 side of each remaining bread slice. Place dressing side down on sandwiches. Cut each sandwich into halves; cut each half into 3 pieces. Secure with wooden picks. **Yield:** 36 servings.

Approx Per Serving: Cal 126; Prot 8; Carbo 9 g; Fiber <1 g; T Fat 7 g; 47% Calories from Fat; Chol 21 mg; Sod 285 mg.

Tortilla Crisps*

4 flour tortillas
1/4 cup butter, softened
Garlic salt to taste
1/2 cup shredded Monterey Jack cheese
1/2 cup shredded sharp Cheddar cheese
3 tablespoons chopped green chilies

Spread tortillas with butter. Sprinkle with garlic salt, cheeses and green chilies. Place on baking sheet. Bake at 400 degrees for 5 to 6 minutes or until hot and bubbly. Cut into wedges. Serve with salsa. **Yield:** 24 servings.

Approx Per Serving: Cal 53; Prot 2; Carbo 3 g; Fiber <1 g; T Fat 4 g; 63% Calories from Fat; Chol 10 mg; Sod 66 mg.

Shrimp Puffs

24 cooked shrimp, deveined
2 egg whites
1/2 cup grated Parmesan cheese
1/4 teaspoon paprika
Red pepper to taste
1/4 teaspoon salt
1 cup mayonnaise
48 Melba rounds

Cut shrimp into halves. Beat egg whites in mixer bowl until stiff peaks form. Fold in cheese, paprika, red pepper, salt and mayonnaise. Spoon onto Melba rounds. Top each with shrimp half. Arrange on baking sheet. Broil until light brown. Serve hot. **Yield:** 48 servings.

Approx Per Serving: Cal 68; Prot 4; Carbo 4 g; Fiber <1 g; T Fat 4 g; 55% Calories from Fat; Chol 25 mg; Sod 124 mg.

Sun-Dried Tomato Bites*

12 ounces montrachet cheese
1/4 cup light sour cream
1/2 teaspoon thyme
1/2 teaspoon rosemary
1 French bread baguette, sliced
2 cloves of garlic
1/4 cup olive oil
9 oil-pack sun-dried tomatoes, drained, coarsely chopped
Freshly ground pepper

Combine cheese with sour cream in bowl; mix until smooth. Add thyme and rosemary. Arrange bread on baking sheet. Crush garlic in olive oil in bowl. Brush on bread. Toast in preheated 425-degree oven until light brown. Spread with cheese mixture. Top with tomatoes and pepper. Bake for 3 minutes or until cheese melts. **Yield:** 20 servings.

Approx Per Serving: Cal 32; Prot 1; Carbo 2 g; Fiber <1 g; T Fat 2 g; 60% Calories from Fat; Chol 4 mg; Sod 32 mg.

Tuna Melts*

1 7-ounce can water-pack white tuna
1 teaspoon lemon juice
6 ounces Swiss cheese, shredded
2 tablespoons chopped onion
1/3 cup mayonnaise
1/4 teaspoon curry powder
1 can butterflake rolls

Combine first 6 ingredients in bowl; mix well. Separate each roll into 3 layers; place on baking sheet. Spread with tuna mixture. Bake at 375 degrees for 15 minutes or until golden brown. **Yield:** 36 servings.

Approx Per Serving: Cal 88; Prot 5; Carbo 5 g; Fiber <1 g; T Fat 5 g; 53% Calories from Fat; Chol 13 mg; Sod 117 mg.

Smoked Turkey with Gingerbread Muffins

2 1/2 cups flour
1/2 cup sugar
1 1/2 teaspoons baking soda
1 teaspoon cinnamon
1 teaspoon ginger
1/2 teaspoon ground cloves
2 teaspoons grated lemon rind
1 egg
1 cup light molasses
1/2 cup shortening
1 1/2 pounds thinly sliced smoked turkey breast

Beat first 10 ingredients in large mixer bowl at low speed for 2 minutes. Spoon into greased and floured miniature muffin cups. Bake at 375 degrees for 10 minutes or until muffins test done. Fill with turkey. Serve with chutney, marmalade and cranberry sauce. **Yield:** 36 servings.

Approx Per Serving: Cal 112; Prot 5; Carbo 15 g; Fiber <1 g; T Fat 4 g; 30% Calories from Fat; Chol 15 mg; Sod 176 mg.

Clam and Artichoke Dip

4 7-ounce cans chopped clams
2 12-ounce cans artichoke hearts, drained
6 tablespoons margarine
1 onion, chopped
6 tablespoons flour
2 cups whipping cream
1 cup grated provolone cheese
1/8 teaspoon Tabasco sauce
Dash of paprika

Drain half the clams, reserving 1 cup juice. Chop half the artichokes. Mix with drained clams; set aside. Purée remaining artichokes and clams in food processor. Melt margarine in skillet. Sauté onion until soft. Stir in flour. Add cream gradually, stirring constantly. Stir in reserved clam juice. Cook for 5 to 7 minutes or until thickened, stirring frequently. Stir in clam mixture and puréed mixture. Simmer for 5 minutes. Add cheese and Tabasco sauce; mix well. Spoon into 2-quart casserole. Sprinkle with paprika. Bake at 325 degrees for 20 minutes. **Yield:** 48 servings.

Approx Per Serving: Cal 90; Prot 5; Carbo 3 g; Fiber <1 g; T Fat 6 g; 62% Calories from Fat; Chol 26 mg; Sod 106 mg.

Hot Cheeses, Raisins and Almond Dip*

8 ounces each mild Cheddar, sharp Cheddar and Monterey Jack cheese, shredded
2 cups yogurt
2 jalapeño peppers, chopped
1/2 cup raisins
1/2 cup toasted almonds
1/2 teaspoon ground cumin

Layer cheeses, yogurt, peppers, raisins and almonds 1/2 at a time in 10-inch pie plate. Sprinkle with cumin. Bake at 375 degrees for 30 minutes or until lightly browned and bubbly. **Yield:** 50 servings.

Approx Per Serving: Cal 72; Prot 4; Carbo 2 g; Fiber <1 g; T Fat 5 g; 66% Calories from Fat; Chol 15 mg; Sod 85 mg.

Loie's Ginger Dip*

1 8-ounce can water chestnuts
2 tablespoons crystallized ginger
1/4 cup grated onion
1 cup mayonnaise
1 cup sour cream
1/4 cup chopped fresh parsley
1 tablespoon soy sauce
1/8 teaspoon Tabasco sauce

Drain and finely chop water chestnuts. Mince ginger. Combine water chestnuts, ginger and remaining ingredients in bowl; mix well. Chill, covered, for 24 to 48 hours. **Yield:** 48 servings.

Approx Per Serving: Cal 48; Prot <1; Carbo 2 g; Fiber <1 g; T Fat 5 g; 85% Calories from Fat; Chol 5 mg; Sod 51 mg.

Great Guacamole Dip*

1 avocado, peeled, seeded
1 tablespoon lemon juice
2 tablespoons chopped green chilies
1/2 cup chopped tomato
2 tablespoons mayonnaise
1 teaspoon salt
1/8 teaspoon garlic powder
4 drops of hot pepper sauce

Purée avocado with lemon juice in blender. Combine with green chilies, tomato, mayonnaise, salt, garlic powder and hot pepper sauce in bowl; mix well. Chill, covered, for 1 hour. **Yield:** 24 servings.

Approx Per Serving: Cal 23; Prot <1; Carbo 1 g; Fiber 1 g; T Fat 2 g; 80% Calories from Fat; Chol 1 mg; Sod 97 mg.

Humble Hummus Dip

"Serve as a spread or a dip with wedges of pita bread."

1 15-ounce can garbanzo beans
1/2 cup sesame seed
1 clove of garlic, chopped
3 tablespoons lemon juice
1 teaspoon salt

Drain beans, reserving liquid. Combine liquid with sesame seed and garlic in blender container. Process at high speed until well mixed. Add beans, lemon juice and salt. Process at high speed until of uniform consistency, scraping sides of blender container occasionally. Spoon into serving dish. Garnish with parsley. **Yield:** 30 servings.

Approx Per Serving: Cal 32; Prot 1; Carbo 4 g; Fiber <1 g; T Fat 2 g; 41% Calories from Fat; Chol 0 mg; Sod 114 mg.

Luxurious Lobster Dip

"Delicious!"

16 ounces cream cheese
1 12-ounce can lobster
1/3 cup (or more) dry white wine
1 teaspoon dry mustard
1/3 cup mayonnaise
1 teaspoon horseradish
1/2 teaspoon onion salt
1/8 teaspoon garlic powder

Mix all ingredients in 2-quart saucepan. Cook over medium heat until heated through, adding additional wine to thin if needed. Spoon into chafing dish. Serve with plain crackers. **Yield:** 65 servings.

Approx Per Serving: Cal 38; Prot 2; Carbo <1 g; Fiber 0 g; T Fat 3 g; 80% Calories from Fat; Chol 12 mg; Sod 63 mg.

Roasted Pepper Dip

"Serve with toasted French bread rounds or mild crackers."

16 ounces cream cheese, softened
1/2 cup mayonnaise
2 tablespoons horseradish
Salt and white pepper to taste
1 teaspoon tarragon
1 4-ounce jar chopped roasted peppers, drained

Process first 6 ingredients in blender container until thoroughly blended. Stir in peppers. Process until blended. Spoon into serving dish. Chill for several hours. **Yield:** 48 servings.

Approx Per Serving: Cal 50; Prot 1; Carbo <1 g; Fiber <1 g; T Fat 5 g; 90% Calories from Fat; Chol 12 mg; Sod 42 mg.

Prairie Fire*

"A hot Tex-Mex dip in more ways than one!"

4 cups refried beans
1 cup butter
4 to 6 canned jalapeño peppers, chopped
1 tablespoon jalapeño liquid
8 ounces provolone cheese, grated
2 tablespoons minced onion
1 tablespoon chopped garlic

Combine all ingredients in top of double boiler. Cook until cheese is melted and mixture is well blended, stirring frequently. Serve with tortilla chips. **Yield:** 100 servings.

Approx Per Serving: Cal 36; Prot 1; Carbo 2 g; Fiber 1 g; T Fat 3 g; 64% Calories from Fat; Chol 7 mg; Sod 95 mg.

Smoked Salmon Dip*

"An extravagant beginning!"

4 ounces smoked salmon
1/4 cup chopped onion
8 ounces cream cheese, softened
1/2 teaspoon fresh lemon juice
1/4 teaspoon pepper
1 tablespoon milk
1 teaspoon sliced scallions
3 teaspoons red caviar, drained
Scallion greens to taste

Combine first 7 ingredients in blender container. Process until smooth. Fold in 2 teaspoons caviar. Chill, covered, for 2 hours or longer. Top with remaining 1 teaspoon caviar and scallion greens. **Yield:** 30 servings.

Approx Per Serving: Cal 33; Prot 1; Carbo <1 g; Fiber <1 g; T Fat 3 g; 79% Calories from Fat; Chol 12 mg; Sod 60 mg.

Canadian Brie*

1 8-ounce baby Brie
1 cup chopped walnuts
2 tablespoons butter
1/4 cup packed brown sugar
1/2 teaspoon cinnamon
1 to 2 tablespoons maple syrup

Place cheese on ovenproof platter. Sauté walnuts in butter in skillet until slightly browned. Stir in brown sugar and cinnamon. Add syrup gradually, stirring just until moistened. Pour over cheese. Bake at 300 degrees for 10 minutes or until softened. Serve immediately with unsalted crackers. **Yield:** 48 servings.

Approx Per Serving: Cal 63; Prot 3; Carbo 2 g; Fiber <1 g; T Fat 5 g; 69% Calories from Fat; Chol 12 mg; Sod 70 mg.

Cranberry-Glazed Brie

1 16-ounce Brie
3 cups cranberries
3/4 cup packed brown sugar
1/3 cup currants
1/3 cup water
1/8 teaspoon dry mustard
1/8 teaspoon ground allspice
1/8 teaspoon ground cardamom
1/8 teaspoon ground cloves
1/8 teaspoon ground ginger

Cut circle in top of Brie, leaving 1/2-inch border. Place in 8-inch ceramic baking dish. Combine remaining ingredients in heavy non-aluminum saucepan. Cook over medium heat for 5 minutes or until berries pop, stirring frequently. Spread over cheese. Chill, covered, until baking time. Let stand at room temperature until softened. Bake at 300 degrees for 12 minutes. **Yield:** 100 servings.

Approx Per Serving: Cal 26; Prot 1; Carbo 2 g; Fiber <1 g; T Fat 1 g; 47% Calories from Fat; Chol 5 mg; Sod 32 mg.

Kelly's Brie with Sun-Dried Tomatoes*

1 16-ounce Brie, chilled
4 oil-packed sun-dried tomatoes
2 tablespoons minced fresh parsley
2 cloves of garlic, mashed
2 tablespoons freshly grated Parmesan cheese
1 teaspoon crumbled dried basil

Remove rind from Brie with sharp knife. Place on serving plate. Drain tomatoes, reserving 1 tablespoon oil; mince. Combine with remaining ingredients in bowl; mix well. Stir in reserved oil. Spread over Brie. Let stand for 1 hour. Serve with crackers. **Yield:** 65 servings.

Approx Per Serving: Cal 27; Prot 2; Carbo <1 g; Fiber <1 g; T Fat 2 g; 72% Calories from Fat; Chol 7 mg; Sod 47 mg.

Burgundy Cheese Spread

"Unusual and delicious"

2½ cups sharp white Cheddar cheese
⅓ cup grated red onion
½ cup chopped walnuts
2 to 3 tablespoons mayonnaise
½ teaspoon Tabasco sauce
1 cup raspberry preserves

Combine cheese, onion, walnuts, mayonnaise and Tabasco sauce in bowl; mix well. Spoon into shallow mold. Chill until firm. Unmold onto serving plate. Spread with preserves. Serve with Triscuits. May substitute strawberry preserves or jam for raspberry. **Yield:** 50 servings.

Approx Per Serving: Cal 54; Prot 2; Carbo 5 g; Fiber <1 g; T Fat 3 g; 53% Calories from Fat; Chol 6 mg; Sod 41 mg.

Cheese and Horseradish Spread*

"Try this and you'll use it often!"

8 ounces whipped cream cheese, softened
¼ cup horseradish
5 or 6 drops of Tabasco sauce

Combine cream cheese, horseradish and Tabasco sauce in bowl; mix well. Chill for several hours. Serve with Triscuits. **Yield:** 20 servings.

Approx Per Serving: Cal 41; Prot 1; Carbo 1 g; Fiber <1 g; T Fat 4 g; 86% Calories from Fat; Chol 12 mg; Sod 37 mg.

Chutney Cheese Spread*

"Best new spread I've found in years."

8 ounces cream cheese, softened
1 cup grated Cheddar cheese
1 teaspoon garlic powder
1 teaspoon curry powder
1 tablespoon sherry
1 8-ounce jar chopped chutney
¾ cup sliced scallions

Combine cream cheese, Cheddar cheese, garlic powder, curry powder and sherry in bowl; mix well. Spread in 9-inch pie plate. Top with chutney. Sprinkle with scallions. Serve with crackers. **Yield:** 48 servings.

Approx Per Serving: Cal 31; Prot 1; Carbo 1 g; Fiber <1 g; T Fat 2 g; 70% Calories from Fat; Chol 8 mg; Sod 56 mg.

Grate Kas*

"An old German recipe"

1 cup butter, softened
1/2 cone sapsago cheese, grated
3 ounces cream cheese, softened
1/2 cup chopped chives

Cream butter in mixer bowl until light and fluffy. Add cheeses; mix well. Stir in chives. Serve at room temperature on party rye bread. **Yield:** 30 servings.

Approx Per Serving: Cal 85; Prot 2; Carbo <1 g; Fiber 0 g; T Fat 8 g; 88% Calories from Fat; Chol 24 mg; Sod 100 mg.

Corned Beef Mold

1 envelope unflavored gelatin
1/2 cup cold water
1 cup boiling water
1 cup mayonnaise
1 15-ounce can corned beef, finely chopped
1 medium onion, grated
3 tablespoons horseradish
Salt and pepper to taste
Worcestershire sauce to taste
1/8 teaspoon garlic (optional)

Soften gelatin in cold water. Add boiling water; stir until dissolved. Add mayonnaise and corned beef; mix well. Stir in remaining ingredients. Spoon into salad mold. Chill until firm. Unmold onto serving plate. Garnish with parsley. Serve with party rye bread. **Yield:** 50 servings.

Approx Per Serving: Cal 54; Prot 2; Carbo <1 g; Fiber <1 g; T Fat 5 g; 79% Calories from Fat; Chol 10 mg; Sod 111 mg.

Mexican Dip*

"There's always a can of chili on my shelf, and it always comes in handy for this quick dip."

1 15-ounce can chili without beans
1 16-ounce can refried beans
12 ounces extra-sharp Cheddar cheese, grated
1 tablespoon chili powder
1/2 teaspoon garlic powder
1/2 teaspoon ground cumin

Combine chili, beans and cheese in large saucepan. Cook until heated through, stirring occasionally. Add chili powder, garlic powder and cumin; mix well. Serve with plain taco chips. **Yield:** 80 servings.

Approx Per Serving: Cal 31; Prot 2; Carbo 2 g; Fiber 1 g; T Fat 2 g; 53% Calories from Fat; Chol 5 mg; Sod 80 mg.

Bleu Cheese Pâté

"People who dislike liver pâté will enjoy this one."

8 ounces cream cheese, softened
2/3 cup liverwurst
1/2 cup bleu cheese
2 tablespoons dry sherry
4 ounces water chestnuts, chopped
2 slices crisp-fried bacon, crumbled
2 tablespoons minced onion
2 tablespoons chopped green olives
1 hard-boiled egg, sieved

Combine cream cheese, liverwurst, bleu cheese and sherry in food processor container. Process until blended. Add water chestnuts, bacon, onion and olives; mix well. Spoon into lightly oiled 3-cup mold. Chill, covered, overnight. Unmold onto bed of lettuce. Top with egg. Serve with crackers. **Yield:** 50 servings.

Approx Per Serving: Cal 37; Prot 1; Carbo 1 g; Fiber <1 g; T Fat 3 g; 77% Calories from Fat; Chol 15 mg; Sod 58 mg.

Chester County Pâté

"Try adding 1/2 cup pistachios before chilling."

3/4 cup butter
1 large onion, finely chopped
1 pound chicken livers, cut into 1-inch pieces
1/4 cup brandy
Salt and pepper to taste
1/4 teaspoon thyme
1/4 cup whipping cream
1 hard-boiled egg, sieved

Melt butter in heavy skillet. Add onion and livers. Sauté until onion is tender and livers are cooked through. Increase heat to high. Stir in brandy. Reduce heat. Cook for 5 minutes, stirring frequently. Stir in salt, pepper, and thyme. Cool for several minutes. Purée in blender, adding cream slowly. Pour into serving dish. Chill until serving time. Top with egg. Serve with plain crackers or toast points. **Yield:** 50 servings.

Approx Per Serving: Cal 42; Prot 2; Carbo 1 g; Fiber <1 g; T Fat 4 g; 78% Calories from Fat; Chol 48 mg; Sod 28 mg.

Freeze unsliced bread until almost frozen and slice into paper-thin fancy shapes for party sandwiches.

Smoked Salmon Pâté

"Serve on crackers or pumpernickel bread."

1/4 pound smoked salmon, chopped
16 ounces cream cheese, softened
2 tablespoons minced onion
1/4 cup chopped fresh dill
3 tablespoons lemon juice
3/4 teaspoon Tabasco sauce

Combine all ingredients in bowl; mix well. Spoon into serving dish. Chill, covered, for 2 hours or longer. Garnish with additional chopped dill and dill sprigs. **Yield:** 10 servings.

Approx Per Serving: Cal 184; Prot 7; Carbo 2 g; Fiber <1 g; T Fat 17 g; 82% Calories from Fat; Chol 59 mg; Sod 143 mg.

Tasty Tuna Pâté*

1 7-ounce can water-pack tuna, drained
3 ounces small canned shrimp, mashed
6 slices crisp-fried bacon, crumbled
1/4 cup minced fresh mushrooms
3 tablespoons mayonnaise
3 tablespoons sour cream
2 teaspoons lemon juice
1/4 teaspoon salt
Tabasco sauce to taste

Combine tuna, shrimp, bacon and mushrooms in bowl; mix well. Add remaining ingredients; mix well. Garnish with sliced black olives. Serve with bland crackers. **Yield:** 30 servings.

Approx Per Serving: Cal 32; Prot 3; Carbo <1 g; Fiber <1 g; T Fat 2 g; 59% Calories from Fat; Chol 12 mg; Sod 77 mg.

Smoky Salmon Spread*

1 7-ounce can sockeye salmon
8 ounces cream cheese with chives, softened
1 tablespoon lemon juice
2 tablespoons snipped parsley
2 teaspoons horseradish
1/4 teaspoon liquid smoke
Salt and pepper to taste
1/4 cup chopped pecans

Drain and rinse salmon. Combine with cream cheese, lemon juice, parsley, horseradish, liquid smoke, salt and pepper in bowl; mix well. Shape into large ball. Roll in pecans. **Yield:** 30 servings.

Approx Per Serving: Cal 44; Prot 2; Carbo <1 g; Fiber <1 g; T Fat 4 g; 78% Calories from Fat; Chol 11 mg; Sod 58 mg.

Soups & Salads

Longwood Gardens

Needlework Show Luncheon

Caldo Verde (Green Soup)
page 76

Spring Salad with Raspberry Vinaigrette
page 84

Chicken Crêpes or Creamy Crab Soufflé
pages 171 or 199

Snow Peas with Basil
page 231

Fresh Blueberry Muffins
116

Peaches Chablis
page 252

Almond Lace Cookies
page 268

SOUPS

White Bean Soup with Sun-Dried Tomatoes and Pasta

"This is a different kind of pasta e fagioli."

1 cup dried white beans
1/4 cup olive oil
2 cups chopped yellow onions
2 medium carrots, peeled, chopped
4 cloves of garlic, minced
1/2 cup chopped fennel
3/4 teaspoon dried red pepper flakes
2 bay leaves
8 cups chicken broth
4 ounces uncooked ziti, penne, bowtie or shell pasta
1/2 cup finely chopped oil-pack sun-dried tomatoes, drained
1/4 cup finely chopped fresh parsley

Combine beans with enough water to cover by 3 inches in large saucepan. Bring to a boil; remove from heat. Let stand, covered, for 1 hour. Drain well. Heat olive oil in heavy saucepan over medium heat. Add onions, carrots, garlic, fennel, pepper flakes and bay leaves. Reduce heat to low. Cook, covered, for 15 minutes or until onions are tender, stirring occasionally. Add beans and 7 cups chicken broth. Bring to a boil. Simmer, partially covered, for 1 1/4 hours or until beans are tender. Add pasta and tomatoes. Simmer, partially covered, for 15 minutes or until pasta is tender, adding enough remaining chicken broth if needed for desired consistency. Stir in parsley; discard bay leaves. Ladle into soup bowls. Garnish with freshly grated Parmesan cheese. **Yield:** 4 servings.

Approx Per Serving: Cal 531; Prot 26 g; Carbo 67 g; Fiber 5 g; T Fat 18 g; 30% Calories from Fat; Chol 2 mg; Sod 1575 mg. Nutritional information includes entire amount of chicken broth.

Basque Bean Soup

2 whole boneless chicken breasts
8 ounces pepperoni, chopped
1 or 2 large leeks, chopped
2 large cloves of garlic, chopped
3 tablespoons olive oil
4 or 5 medium carrots, sliced
3 cups shredded cabbage
1 14-ounce can kidney beans
1 14-ounce can chick peas
1 14-ounce can cannoli beans
2 10-ounce cans tomatoes with green chilies
1 teaspoon thyme
1 teaspoon salt
1/2 teaspoon pepper

Rinse chicken and pat dry; cut into cubes. Brown chicken, pepperoni, leeks and garlic in olive oil in Dutch oven, stirring frequently. Add carrots. Cook for 3 minutes. Add cabbage. Cook for 2 minutes. Stir in beans, tomatoes and chilies, thyme, salt and pepper. Bake, covered, at 325 degrees for 30 to 45 minutes. Bake, uncovered, for 30 minutes longer, stirring occasionally. **Yield:** 6 servings.

Approx Per Serving: Cal 551; Prot 29 g; Carbo 52 g; Fiber 14 g; T Fat 26 g; 42% Calories from Fat; Chol 37 mg; Sod 2218 mg.

Autumn Bisque Soup

"Wonderful"

1 pound butternut squash
2 tart apples
1 medium onion, chopped
2 slices white bread, crusts trimmed, cubed
4 cups chicken broth
1/4 teaspoon rosemary
1/4 teaspoon marjoram
1 1/2 teaspoons salt
1/4 teaspoon pepper
2 egg yolks, slightly beaten
1/4 cup whipping cream

Peel, seed and chop squash and apples. Combine with onion, bread cubes, chicken broth, rosemary, marjoram, salt and pepper in large saucepan. Bring to a boil; reduce heat. Simmer for 35 minutes or until squash and apples are tender. Cool to lukewarm. Process in several batches in blender or food processor until smooth. Return to saucepan. Reheat over low heat. Beat egg yolks and cream in small bowl. Add a small amount of hot soup to egg yolks; stir egg yolks into hot soup. Simmer just until heated through; do not boil. Garnish with apple slices and fresh rosemary sprig. May chill after puréeing and reheat with egg yolks at serving time. **Yield:** 6 servings.

Approx Per Serving: Cal 167; Prot 6 g; Carbo 21 g; Fiber 4 g; T Fat 7 g; 37% Calories from Fat; Chol 85 mg; Sod 1108 mg.

Cream of Cauliflower Soup

1 small bay leaf
1 teaspoon tarragon
1/2 teaspoon peppercorns
1/2 cup chopped onion
2 tablespoons oil
1 cup chopped celery
1/2 cup finely shredded carrot
Flowerets of 1 head cauliflower
2 tablespoons minced parsley
6 cups chicken broth
1/4 cup butter
1/2 cup flour
2 cups milk
1 cup half and half
2 teaspoons salt
1 cup sour cream, at room temperature

Tie bay leaf, tarragon and peppercorns in 3 layers of cheesecloth. Sauté onion in oil in saucepan for 5 minutes. Add celery and carrot. Cook for 2 minutes. Stir in cauliflower and 1 tablespoon parsley. Simmer, covered, for 15 minutes, stirring occasionally. Add chicken broth and seasonings in cheesecloth. Bring to a boil over medium heat; reduce heat. Simmer, covered, for 5 minutes. Melt butter in heavy saucepan. Stir in flour. Whisk in milk gradually. Cook until thickened and smooth, whisking constantly. Stir in half and half. Stir white sauce into simmering soup. Add salt. Simmer for 15 minutes or until cauliflower is tender. Remove cheesecloth bag. Stir 1/3 cup hot soup into sour cream; stir sour cream into hot soup. Sprinkle with remaining 1 tablespoon parsley. **Yield:** 10 servings.

Approx Per Serving: Cal 238; Prot 8 g; Carbo 17 g; Fiber 2 g; T Fat 18 g; 63% Calories from Fat; Chol 39 mg; Sod 991 mg.

Chicken and Andouille Gumbo

"This soup offers a taste of Cajun cooking. If you can't find andouille, use smoky link sausage."

1/2 cup flour
1/2 cup oil
2 cups chopped onions
1 cup chopped celery
1 cup chopped green bell pepper
1 or 2 cloves of garlic, chopped
2 cups chopped cooked chicken
12 ounces andouille (ham sausage), sliced
4 cups chicken stock
Salt to taste
1 cup chopped green onions

Blend flour into hot oil in saucepan over medium heat. Cook until roux is browned to taste. Add onions, celery, green pepper and garlic. Cook until vegetables are tender, stirring frequently. Stir in chicken, sausage, chicken stock and salt. Simmer for 1 hour or until of desired consistency. Stir in green onions. Simmer for 10 minutes. Serve over mounds of rice in serving bowls. Garnish with 1/4 to 1/2 teaspoon filé powder if desired. May serve with sherry. **Yield:** 8 servings.

Approx Per Serving: Cal 336; Prot 19 g; Carbo 12 g; Fiber 2 g; T Fat 24 g; 63% Calories from Fat; Chol 45 mg; Sod 733 mg.

Clam and Chicken Bisque

"This soup is better reheated the second day."

2 whole chicken breasts
3 cups (or more) water
4 cups clam juice
3/4 cup chopped celery
1 medium onion, chopped
1 bay leaf
6 tablespoons flour
1/2 cup butter
2 cups chopped canned clams
1 1/2 cups half and half
Salt and pepper to taste

Rinse chicken and pat dry. Cook in water in saucepan until tender. Drain, reserving 3 cups chicken broth. Chop chicken. Combine reserved broth with clam juice, celery, onion and bay leaf in saucepan. Simmer for 30 minutes. Discard bay leaf. Blend flour into butter in large saucepan. Cook until roux is browned to taste. Stir in broth mixture, chicken, clams, half and half, salt and pepper. Cook until thickened and heated through, stirring frequently. **Yield:** 8 servings.

Approx Per Serving: Cal 277; Prot 18 g; Carbo 9 g; Fiber 1 g; T Fat 20 g; 62% Calories from Fat; Chol 100 mg; Sod 426 mg.

Great Manhattan Clam Chowder*

1 1/2 cups chopped onions
3 tablespoons corn oil
1 1/2 cups shredded carrots
1 cup chopped celery
2 cups shredded cabbage
2 cups thinly sliced leek bulbs
2 cloves of garlic, crushed
2 29-ounce cans Italian tomatoes
4 7-ounce cans clams
2 cups (about) water
3 or 4 teaspoons thyme
1 tablespoon salt
1 teaspoon pepper
6 medium potatoes, shredded

Sauté onions in oil in heavy saucepan over medium heat for 5 minutes. Add carrots, celery, cabbage, leeks and garlic. Cook over low heat for 5 to 7 minutes or until tender. Add tomatoes. Drain clams, reserving liquid. Add reserved liquid, water, thyme, salt and pepper to soup. Bring to a boil; reduce heat. Simmer for 15 to 20 minutes. Add potatoes and clams. Simmer for 1 hour. **Yield:** 10 servings.

Approx Per Serving: Cal 231; Prot 11 g; Carbo 37 g; Fiber 5 g; T Fat 10 g; 33% Calories from Fat; Chol 50 mg; Sod 968 mg.

Easy Crab Soup*

3 10-ounce cans cream of asparagus soup
2 cups half and half
1/3 cup sherry
1 pound lump crab meat

Cook undiluted soup in saucepan until heated through. Blend in half and half, sherry and crab meat. Simmer for 1 hour. **Yield:** 6 servings.

Approx Per Serving: Cal 296; Prot 20 g; Carbo 16 g; Fiber 1 g; T Fat 15 g; 49% Calories from Fat; Chol 111 mg; Sod 246 mg.

Lemon Crab Soup*

"This soup is both so easy and so good."

1 teaspoon minced garlic
2 green onions, chopped
4 cups chicken broth
1 cup cooked rice
2 tablespoons fresh lemon juice
6 ounces crab meat
1/8 teaspoon white pepper

Combine garlic, green onions and 2 tablespoons chicken broth in 2 1/2-quart glass dish. Microwave, covered, on High for 1 to 2 minutes or until tender. Stir in rice, lemon juice, crab meat, pepper and remaining chicken broth. Microwave, tightly covered, on High for 3 to 4 minutes or until heated through. **Yield:** 4 servings.

Approx Per Serving: Cal 143; Prot 15 g; Carbo 15 g; Fiber <1 g; T Fat 2 g; 15% Calories from Fat; Chol 44 mg; Sod 895 mg.

Mary Larchar's Crab Soup*

1 pound crab meat
3/4 cup (or more) sherry
2 10-ounce cans tomato bisque or soup
1 1/4 cups milk
10 tablespoons cream

Marinate crab meat in sherry in bowl for 3 hours. Drain, reserving marinade. Add enough additional sherry if necessary to measure 3/4 cup. Combine tomato bisque, milk and cream in saucepan. Add sherry and crab meat. Cook until heated through. Serve hot with lemon slice garnish. **Yield:** 4 servings.

Approx Per Serving: Cal 481; Prot 29 g; Carbo 3 g; Fiber <1 g; T Fat 21 g; 39% Calories from Fat; Chol 180 mg; Sod 1522 mg.

Caldo Verde (Green Soup)

"This recipe is typical of Portuguese cuisine, which is different from that of Spain."

1 large yellow onion, minced
1 large clove of garlic, minced
3 tablespoons olive oil
6 large potatoes, thinly sliced
2 quarts cold water
6 ounces chorizo, thinly sliced
2 teaspoons salt
1/4 teaspoon pepper
1 pound kale or turnip greens, trimmed, thinly sliced
1 tablespoon olive oil

Sauté onion and garlic in 3 tablespoons olive oil in large saucepan until light brown. Add potatoes. Sauté for 2 to 3 minutes or until light brown. Add water. Simmer, covered, over medium heat for 20 to 25 minutes or until potatoes are tender. Fry sausage in medium skillet over low heat for 10 to 12 minutes, stirring frequently; drain. Mash potatoes in saucepan. Add salt and pepper. Simmer for 5 minutes. Add sausage and kale. Simmer for 5 minutes or until kale is tender-crisp. Stir in remaining 1 tablespoon olive oil. Ladle into large soup bowls. Serve with hard bread. Roll 6 or 8 leaves of kale into firm roll and slice crosswise for this recipe. **Yield:** 8 servings.

Approx Per Serving: Cal 297; Prot 8 g; Carbo 46 g; Fiber 7 g; T Fat 11 g; 31% Calories from Fat; Chol 8 mg; Sod 699 mg.

Italian Wedding Soup

"Don't wait for a wedding to try this recipe."

1 1/2 pounds chicken
1 large onion, chopped
8 cups water
Salt and pepper to taste
12 ounces lean ground beef
1/4 cup grated onion
1/2 cup dry bread crumbs
2 eggs
1 tablespoon chopped parsley
2 10-ounce packages frozen chopped spinach
3 eggs
1/2 cup grated Parmesan cheese

Rinse chicken and pat dry. Combine with chopped onion, water, salt and pepper in large saucepan. Cook until chicken is tender. Combine ground beef, grated onion, bread crumbs, 2 eggs, parsley, salt and pepper in bowl; mix well. Shape into small meatballs. Remove chicken from broth. Chop chicken, discarding skin and bones. Return chicken to broth. Add meatballs and spinach. Simmer for 15 minutes. Beat 3 eggs with cheese in bowl. Drizzle into soup. Cook just until heated through. May add small pasta if desired. **Yield:** 8 servings.

Approx Per Serving: Cal 299; Prot 30 g; Carbo 12 g; Fiber 3 g; T Fat 15 g; 45% Calories from Fat; Chol 203 mg; Sod 327 mg.

Onion Soup Gratinée

15 slices French bread, cut to fit soup bowls
5 pounds sweet Spanish onions, thinly sliced
1/4 cup unsalted butter
2 tablespoons sugar
2 tablespoons flour
2 quarts beef stock
1 750-milliliter bottle of dry red wine
Salt and white pepper to taste
8 ounces Gruyère cheese, sliced
8 ounces mozzarella cheese, coarsely shredded
4 ounces Parmesan cheese, grated
4 ounces French bread crumbs

Toast French bread. Let stand at room temperature until very crisp. Sauté onions in butter in large stockpot over medium heat until golden brown. Stir in sugar and flour. Cook until smooth, stirring constantly. Add beef stock. Simmer for 3 hours. Add wine, salt and white pepper. Simmer for 3 hours, adding 2 to 4 cups water if needed for desired consistency. Ladle into ovenproof soup bowls. Top with toasted bread. Top each serving with 1 slice Gruyère cheese, mozzarella cheese, Parmesan cheese and bread crumbs. Place on baking sheet. Broil until golden brown. Serve immediately. May add 1/2 teaspoon Cognac to each serving. May stir 1 or 2 egg yolks into warm soup. **Yield:** 15 servings.

Approx Per Serving: Cal 392; Prot 18 g; Carbo 37 g; Fiber 3 g; T Fat 16 g; 36% Calories from Fat; Chol 43 mg; Sod 918 mg.

Evergreen Soup

"This is a classic soup."

1 pound mixed dried green and yellow split peas
5 cups chicken stock
1 ham bone
2 stalks celery, chopped
2 sprigs parsley, chopped
1/4 teaspoon thyme
1 bay leaf
1/2 cup chopped carrot
1/2 cup chopped onion
2 large leeks, sliced
2 tablespoons oil
1 cup chopped spinach
1 10-ounce package frozen peas
Salt, cayenne pepper and black pepper to taste

Bring dried peas and chicken stock to a boil in saucepan. Add ham bone, celery, parsley, thyme and bay leaf. Simmer for 45 minutes. Sauté carrot, onion and leeks in oil in saucepan for 5 minutes. Add spinach. Stir into soup. Add frozen peas, salt, cayenne pepper and black pepper. Cook until heated through. Remove ham bone and bay leaf. Process 2 cups soup in blender until smooth. Return to saucepan. Cook until heated through. May substitute 2 ham hocks for ham bone. **Yield:** 6 servings.

Approx Per Serving: Cal 428; Prot 29 g; Carbo 60 g; Fiber 15 g; T Fat 9 g; 18% Calories from Fat; Chol 8 mg; Sod 879 mg.

Split Pea Soup with Dark Rum

"This is a hearty soup with the added flavor of rum."

1 pound dried split peas
4 ounces bacon
1/4 cup oil
2 medium onions, chopped
4 carrots, chopped
1 tablespoon minced garlic
2 cups crushed tomatoes with juice
3 quarts chicken stock
1 pound smoked ham, minced
1/4 cup dark rum
Juice of 1 lemon
1 bay leaf
1/2 teaspoon crushed peppercorns
Salt and pepper to taste

Combine peas with boiling water to cover in bowl. Let stand for 4 hours to overnight; drain. Fry bacon in oil in saucepan until light brown. Remove bacon with slotted spoon; crumble. Add onions and carrots to drippings in saucepan. Sauté until onions are transparent. Add garlic. Sauté for 1 minute. Add bacon, tomatoes, chicken stock, ham, rum, lemon juice, bay leaf, peppercorns, salt and pepper. Simmer, covered, for 2 hours or until peas are tender, stirring occasionally and adding water if needed for desired consistency. Discard bay leaf. **Yield:** 12 servings.

Approx Per Serving: Cal 322; Prot 26 g; Carbo 30 g; Fiber 7 g; T Fat 10 g; 29% Calories from Fat; Chol 24 mg; Sod 1340 mg.

Sherried Shrimp Soup

"Serve this soup with a salad as a main dish or as an appetizer course."

5 tablespoons finely chopped onion
1/4 cup butter
3 tablespoons flour
3 1/2 cups half and half
1/4 cup dry sherry
1 1/2 pounds cooked shrimp, finely chopped
1 teaspoon salt
1/2 teaspoon white pepper
2 tablespoons finely chopped parsley

Sauté onion in butter in large saucepan over low heat until tender but not brown. Stir in flour. Cook for 2 to 3 minutes. Add half and half; mix well. Bring to a simmer, stirring constantly. Stir in sherry, shrimp, salt and white pepper. Simmer for 3 to 5 minutes or until heated through. Serve in warm soup bowls; top with parsley. **Yield:** 6 servings.

Approx Per Serving: Cal 393; Prot 29 g; Carbo 10 g; Fiber <1 g; T Fat 25 g; 60% Calories from Fat; Chol 294 mg; Sod 733 mg.

Provençale Summer Soup

"A special soup for a special dinner party"

1/2 cup chopped leeks
2 tablespoons olive oil
1 potato, chopped
1 cup lima beans
8 ounces cut fresh green beans
1 small zucchini, chopped
2 tomatoes, chopped
6 cups chicken broth
1/4 cup uncooked shell pasta
3 cloves of garlic, crushed
1 tomato, chopped
2 tablespoons grated Parmesan cheese
3 tablespoons olive oil

Sauté leeks lightly in 2 tablespoons olive oil in large saucepan. Add potato, lima beans, green beans, zucchini, 2 tomatoes and chicken broth. Add water if needed to cover vegetables. Simmer for 10 minutes or until vegetables are tender. Stir in pasta. Cook for 10 minutes or until pasta is tender. Combine garlic, 1 tomato, cheese and 3 tablespoons olive oil in blender or food processor container; process until smooth. Spoon into soup bowls. Ladle soup into prepared bowls; mix gently.
Yield: 6 servings.

Approx Per Serving: Cal 313; Prot 14 g; Carbo 35 g; Fiber 12 g; T Fat 14 g; 38% Calories from Fat; Chol 2 mg; Sod 824 mg.

Tortilla Soup

"Texas-style soup is spicy but good."

1 onion, chopped
1 jalapeño pepper, chopped
2 cloves of garlic, minced
1 10-ounce can tomatoes with green chilies
4 cups chicken stock
1 10-ounce can tomato soup
1 teaspoon cumin
2 teaspoons Worcestershire sauce
1 teaspoon (or more) chili powder
Salt and pepper to taste
1/2 teaspoon lemon pepper
4 corn tortillas
1 tablespoon oil
1 avocado, chopped
1 cup shredded Monterey Jack cheese

Mix onion, jalapeño pepper, garlic and tomatoes in large saucepan. Cook for several minutes. Add chicken stock, soup, cumin, Worcestershire sauce, chili powder, salt, pepper and lemon pepper; mix well. Simmer for 45 minutes. Soften tortillas in oil in skillet. Tear into bite-sized pieces. Add to soup. Simmer for 10 to 20 minutes. Place avocado and cheese in 6 soup bowls. Ladle soup into bowls. Garnish with sour cream. May substitute beef stock for chicken stock. **Yield:** 6 servings.

Approx Per Serving: Cal 266; Prot 12 g; Carbo 23 g; Fiber 6 g; T Fat 16 g; 51% Calories from Fat; Chol 18 mg; Sod 1157 mg.

Sherried Wild Rice Soup

"This has a pleasant nutty flavor."

2/3 cup uncooked wild rice
2 cups water
1/2 teaspoon salt
2 medium leeks
2 or 3 large mushrooms, chopped
1/2 cup butter
1/2 cup flour
2 quarts chicken broth
1 cup light cream
3 tablespoons dry sherry
Salt and pepper to taste

Rinse wild rice. Combine with water and 1/2 teaspoon salt in heavy saucepan. Simmer, covered, for 45 minutes or just until tender. Fluff with fork. Simmer, uncovered, for 5 minutes longer; drain. Chop leek bulbs and part of stems. Sauté leeks and mushrooms in butter in large saucepan for 3 minutes or just until tender. Stir in flour with wooden spoon. Cook for 1 minute. Add chicken broth gradually, stirring to mix well. Stir in rice. Cook until thickened, whisking constantly. Whisk in cream and sherry. Cook just until heated through; do not boil. Season with salt and pepper to taste. Garnish servings with minced parsley.
Yield: 8 servings.

Approx Per Serving: Cal 327; Prot 9 g; Carbo 22 g; Fiber 1 g; T Fat 22 g; 62% Calories from Fat; Chol 65 mg; Sod 1023 mg.

Cold Avocado Soup

"Also good served hot"

2 avocados, chopped
1/2 cup whipping cream
1 teaspoon curry powder
Salt and freshly ground pepper to taste
2 cups chicken stock
2 teaspoons lemon juice
Cayenne pepper to taste

Reserve a small portion of avocado for garnish. Combine remaining avocado with cream, curry powder, salt and pepper in blender container; process until smooth. Bring chicken stock and lemon juice to a boil in saucepan. Stir a small amount into avocado mixture; stir avocado mixture into hot soup. Cook just until heated through. Add cayenne pepper and adjust seasonings. Chill until serving time if desired. Ladle into soup bowls. Garnish with reserved avocado and parsley.
Yield: 6 servings.

Approx Per Serving: Cal 190; Prot 3 g; Carbo 6 g; Fiber 6 g; T Fat 18 g; 81% Calories from Fat; Chol 28 mg; Sod 273 mg.

Chilled Blueberry Soup

$1\frac{1}{2}$ tablespoons cornstarch
3 tablespoons lemon juice
$1\frac{1}{2}$ cups water
$1\frac{1}{2}$ cups mountain cherry juice
$\frac{1}{2}$ cup sugar
$\frac{1}{4}$ teaspoon cinnamon
$\frac{1}{8}$ teaspoon nutmeg
2 cups fresh blueberries
1 tablespoon cornstarch
2 tablespoons water
$\frac{1}{2}$ cup plain yogurt
$\frac{1}{4}$ cup sweet Marsala

Combine $1\frac{1}{2}$ tablespoons cornstarch, lemon juice, $1\frac{1}{2}$ cups water, cherry juice, sugar, cinnamon, nutmeg and blueberries in large saucepan. Cook over medium heat for 15 to 20 minutes or until slightly thickened and clear. Blend 1 tablespoon cornstarch with 2 tablespoons water in small bowl. Stir into soup. Cook for 2 minutes longer. Cool to room temperature. Combine with yogurt in blender container; process until smooth. Stir in wine. Chill until serving time. Spoon into serving bowls. Garnish with sweetened yogurt and mint leaves. May substitute dark rum for Marsala or cranberry juice for cherry juice. **Yield:** 4 servings.

Approx Per Serving: Cal 251; Prot 2 g; Carbo 57 g; Fiber 3 g; T Fat 1 g; 5% Calories from Fat; Chol 4 mg; Sod 25 mg.

Shrimp Gazpacho

2 tablespoons olive oil
2 tablespoons red wine vinegar
2 tablespoons lemon juice
2 cloves of garlic, chopped
8 ounces large shrimp, cooked, peeled, deveined
6 large plum tomatoes, seeded, chopped
1 green bell pepper, chopped
1 red bell pepper, chopped
$\frac{1}{2}$ large cucumber, peeled, seeded, chopped
1 bunch green onions, chopped
$\frac{1}{2}$ bunch cilantro, chopped
1 large jalapeño pepper, minced
$4\frac{1}{2}$ cups tomato juice, chilled
Salt and pepper to taste

Combine olive oil, vinegar, lemon juice and garlic in medium bowl; mix well. Add shrimp. Marinate in refrigerator for 1 to 2 hours. Combine tomatoes, bell peppers, cucumber, green onions, cilantro and jalapeño pepper in large bowl. Stir in tomato juice and shrimp mixture. Season with salt and pepper. Chill, covered, for up to 6 hours. Garnish with lemon wedges. **Yield:** 6 servings.

Approx Per Serving: Cal 146; Prot 10 g; Carbo 18 g; Fiber 5 g; T Fat 5 g; 30% Calories from Fat; Chol 59 mg; Sod 745 mg.

SALADS

Bing Cherry and Raspberry Salad

1 16-ounce can pitted dark sweet cherries
½ cup currant jelly
1 6-ounce package red raspberry gelatin
1 10-ounce package frozen raspberries, thawed
½ cup sherry
¼ cup lemon juice

Drain cherries, reserving juice. Add enough water to reserved cherry juice to measure 2 cups. Combine ½ cup juice mixture with jelly in saucepan. Heat until jelly melts. Stir in remaining 1½ cups cherry juice. Bring to a boil. Stir in gelatin until dissolved; remove from heat. Drain raspberries, reserving juice. Add reserved raspberry juice to gelatin mixture with sherry and lemon juice; mix well. Chill until partially set. Fold in raspberries and cherries. Spoon into 6-cup mold or 9x9-inch dish. Chill until set. **Yield:** 9 servings.

Approx Per Serving: Cal 205; Prot 2 g; Carbo 48 g; Fiber 2 g; T Fat <1 g; 1% Calories from Fat; Chol 0 mg; Sod 67 mg.

Steep fresh herbs such as tarragon, basil or oregano in vinegar for several weeks for herb vinegar.

Candied Cranberry-Orange Lettuce Salad

2 cups fresh cranberries
1 cup sugar
2 heads Boston lettuce, torn
1 11-ounce can mandarin oranges, drained
Orange and Poppy Seed Dressing (page 101)
Freshly ground pepper to taste

Spread cranberries in shallow baking dish; sprinkle with sugar. Cover tightly with foil. Bake at 350 degrees for 1 hour, stirring occasionally. Cool to room temperature. Chill for up to 2 days. Toss lettuce with oranges and salad dressing in bowl. Season with pepper. Spoon onto serving plates. Sprinkle with cranberries. **Yield:** 8 servings.

Approx Per Serving: Cal 333; Prot 1 g; Carbo 40 g; Fiber 1 g; T Fat 21 g; 54% Calories from Fat; Chol 0 mg; Sod 6 mg.

Cranberry and Apple Relish*

2 pounds cranberries, coarsely chopped
4 cups chopped peeled apples
2 cups sugar
2 cups orange marmalade
2 cups chopped walnuts, toasted

Combine all ingredients in bowl; mix well. Spoon into glass jar with lid. Store in refrigerator for up to 1 month. **Yield:** 48 (1-tablespoon) servings.

Approx Per Serving: Cal 114; Prot 1 g; Carbo 22 g; Fiber 1 g; T Fat 3 g; 23% Calories from Fat; Chol 0 mg; Sod 4 mg.

Tuxedo Fruit Bowl

1/3 cup sugar
1/3 cup water
1 tablespoon lemon juice
1/8 teaspoon anise flavoring
1 cup chopped apple
1 cup grape halves
1 cup chopped pears
1 cup chopped cantaloupe
1 cup chopped honeydew melon
1 cup sliced peaches
1 cup orange sections
1 cup sliced banana

Mix sugar and water in 1-cup glass measure. Microwave on High for 5 to 6 minutes or until mixture boils for several minutes and thickens slightly, stirring once. Cool to room temperature. Stir in lemon juice and flavoring. Chill, covered, for several hours to overnight. Combine fruit in serving bowl. Add dressing; mix lightly. **Yield:** 8 servings.

Approx Per Serving: Cal 120; Prot 1 g; Carbo 31 g; Fiber 3 g; T Fat <1 g; 3% Calories from Fat; Chol 0 mg; Sod 5 mg.

Raspberry and Spinach Salad*

"This is a beautiful and different party salad."

2 tablespoons raspberry vinegar
2 tablespoons raspberry jam
1/3 cup oil
8 cups torn spinach
3/4 cup coarsely chopped macadamia nuts
1 cup fresh raspberries
3 kiwifruit, peeled, sliced

Blend vinegar and raspberry jam in blender or small bowl. Add oil gradually, blending until smooth. Combine spinach with half the macadamia nuts, half the raspberries and half the kiwifruit in bowl. Add salad dressing; toss lightly. Top with remaining nuts, raspberries and kiwifruit. Serve immediately. **Yield:** 8 servings.

Approx Per Serving: Cal 209; Prot 3 g; Carbo 13 g; Fiber 4 g; T Fat 18 g; 71% Calories from Fat; Chol 0 mg; Sod 47 mg.

Red-White-Green Salad*

2 heads red leaf lettuce
3 heads Bibb lettuce
4 Granny Smith apples, sliced
8 ounces montrachet cheese
Garlic and Herb Vinaigrette (page 101)

Arrange lettuces on serving platter. Arrange apple slices over lettuce. Crumble cheese over top. Drizzle with dressing. **Yield:** 12 servings.

Approx Per Serving: Cal 263; Prot 5 g; Carbo 12 g; Fiber 2 g; T Fat 23 g; 75% Calories from Fat; Chol 15 mg; Sod 145 mg.

Spring Salad with Raspberry Vinaigrette*

"The name of this salad says it all."

1 head Boston lettuce, torn
1 bunch watercress
4 pears, sliced
2 ounces bleu cheese, crumbled
1/4 cup raspberry vinegar
2/3 cup olive oil
Salt and freshly ground pepper to taste

Toss lettuce with watercress, pears and cheese in large salad bowl. Blend vinegar and olive oil in small bowl. Drizzle over salad. Sprinkle with salt and pepper. **Yield:** 4 servings.

Approx Per Serving: Cal 479; Prot 5 g; Carbo 29 g; Fiber 6 g; T Fat 41 g; 73% Calories from Fat; Chol 11 mg; Sod 218 mg.

Strawberry and Grapefruit Salad*

3 heads Bibb or red leaf lettuce
Sections of 2 pink grapefruit
24 strawberries, cut into halves
Strawberry Vinaigrette (page 102)

Separate leaves of 1 head lettuce. Arrange on 8 serving plates. Tear remaining lettuce into bite-sized pieces. Place on lettuce leaves. Arrange grapefruit over lettuce; top with strawberry halves. Drizzle with salad dressing. **Yield:** 8 servings.

Approx Per Serving: Cal 354; Prot 2 g; Carbo 28 g; Fiber 4 g; T Fat 28 g; 67% Calories from Fat; Chol 0 mg; Sod 10 mg.

Strawberry and Spinach Salad*

1/3 cup oil
1/4 cup cider vinegar
1/2 cup sugar
1 small onion, finely chopped
1/4 teaspoon Worcestershire sauce
1/4 teaspoon paprika
1/4 teaspoon salt
2 tablespoons sesame seed
1 tablespoon poppy seed
1 12-ounce package fresh spinach, torn
2 cups fresh strawberries

Combine oil, vinegar, sugar, onion, Worcestershire sauce, paprika and salt in blender container; process until smooth. Stir in sesame seed and poppy seed. Toss spinach with strawberries in salad bowl. Add dressing; toss lightly. **Yield:** 8 servings.

Approx Per Serving: Cal 174; Prot 2 g; Carbo 19 g; Fiber 3 g; T Fat 11 g; 54% Calories from Fat; Chol 0 mg; Sod 104 mg.

Sunshine Salad*

1/4 cup white vinegar
1/4 cup sugar
1/2 cup corn oil
1/2 teaspoon dry mustard
1/2 teaspoon salt
1/8 teaspoon pepper
2 large heads Bibb or Boston lettuce, torn
5 green onions, chopped
1/3 cup coarsely chopped walnuts
1 11-ounce can mandarin oranges, drained

Combine vinegar, sugar, oil, dry mustard, salt and pepper in bowl; mix well. Combine lettuce, green onions, walnuts and oranges in salad bowl. Add dressing; toss lightly. **Yield:** 8 servings.

Approx Per Serving: Cal 204; Prot 2 g; Carbo 14 g; Fiber 1 g; T Fat 17 g; 71% Calories from Fat; Chol 0 mg; Sod 141 mg.

Gaucho Steak Salad

2 pounds boneless sirloin steak
Salt and pepper to taste
2 tablespoons red wine vinegar
1/2 cup corn oil
1 egg
1 tablespoon Dijon mustard
1 tablespoon minced chives
1/2 teaspoon cumin
1 bunch green onions, chopped
1 16-ounce can hearts of palm, drained, sliced
1 4-ounce can chopped green chilies, drained
8 ounces mushrooms, sliced
8 ounces snow peas
2 tomatoes, chopped
1/2 teaspoon salt
1/2 teaspoon pepper

Season sirloin with salt and pepper to taste; place in roasting pan. Roast at 350 degrees to 130 to 140 degrees on meat thermometer, medium-rare. Slice very thinly cross grain; set aside. Combine vinegar, oil, egg, mustard, chives and cumin in blender container; process until smooth. Combine steak, green onions, hearts of palm, green chilies, mushrooms, snow peas, tomatoes, 1/2 teaspoon salt and 1/2 teaspoon pepper in salad bowl; mix well. Add dressing; toss to mix well. Chill for 1 hour to overnight. Garnish with chopped cilantro. **Yield:** 8 servings.

Approx Per Serving: Cal 309; Prot 24 g; Carbo 4 g; Fiber 1 g; T Fat 22 g; 64% Calories from Fat; Chol 90 mg; Sod 503 mg.

Summer Steak Salad

1/4 cup soy sauce
1/4 cup olive oil
1/2 cup red wine vinegar
1 2-pound London broil
4 potatoes, peeled, chopped
Salt to taste
1 green bell pepper, chopped
1 red bell pepper, chopped
1 purple onion, chopped
1 egg yolk
1/3 cup red wine vinegar
1 tablespoon chopped garlic
1 tablespoon sugar
Salt and pepper to taste
1 cup olive oil
1/2 cup chopped Italian parsley

Combine soy sauce, 1/4 cup olive oil and 1/2 cup vinegar in bowl; mix well. Add beef. Marinate for 3 hours. Drain beef and pat dry. Pan-fry in skillet over high heat for 8 minutes on each side. Cut into julienne strips. Cook potatoes in salted water to cover in saucepan until tender; drain. Combine steak, potatoes, bell peppers and onion in salad bowl. Combine egg yolk, remaining 1/3 cup vinegar, garlic, sugar, salt and pepper in blender container; process until smooth. Add 1 cup olive oil gradually, processing constantly until smooth. Add to salad; toss to mix well. Add parsley. Serve on lettuce-lined serving plates. **Yield:** 4 servings.

Approx Per Serving: Cal 1112; Prot 48 g; Carbo 48 g; Fiber 4 g; T Fat 82 g; 66% Calories from Fat; Chol 181 mg; Sod 1114 mg. Nutritional information includes entire amount of marinade.

Taco Salad

"Olé!"

1 pound lean ground beef
4 teaspoons chili powder
1 clove of garlic, minced
1/2 head lettuce, chopped
1 cup chopped black olives
8 ounces sharp Cheddar cheese, shredded
5 scallions, chopped
1 16-ounce can kidney beans, drained
2 tomatoes, chopped
1 avocado, chopped
1 teaspoon salt
1/2 cup tomato juice
2 small green chili peppers, chopped
1 tablespoon olive oil
Juice of 1/2 lemon
Salt and pepper to taste
2 cups crushed corn chips

Brown ground beef in skillet, stirring until crumbly; drain. Add chili powder and garlic. Cook for several minutes. Cool slightly. Combine lettuce, olives, cheese, scallions, beans, tomatoes, avocado and salt in bowl. Add ground beef mixture; mix gently. Combine tomato juice, green chilies, olive oil, lemon juice, salt and pepper in bowl; mix well. Add to salad with corn chips; toss lightly. Serve immediately. May substitute 1 tablespoon Tabasco sauce for chili peppers if preferred. **Yield:** 8 servings.

Approx Per Serving: Cal 465; Prot 23 g; Carbo 24 g; Fiber 10 g; T Fat 33 g; 61% Calories from Fat; Chol 67 mg; Sod 1024 mg.

Chicken Salad with Thyme and Red Onion

"This is a different chicken salad. You may serve it warm or at room temperature."

4 large boneless chicken breast halves
1 tablespoon minced fresh thyme
Salt and pepper to taste
1/3 cup oil
3 tablespoons balsamic or red wine vinegar
1 small red onion, very thinly sliced
1/2 head romaine lettuce, chilled
1/2 head red leaf lettuce, chilled

Rinse chicken and pat dry. Cut into 1-inch pieces; sprinkle with thyme, salt and pepper. Heat half the oil in large skillet over medium-high heat until hot but not smoking. Add chicken. Sauté for 5 minutes or just until cooked through. Add vinegar, stirring with wooden spoon to deglaze skillet; remove from heat. Stir in onion and remaining oil. Season with salt and pepper. Spoon onto serving plates lined with romaine and red leaf lettuce. **Yield:** 4 servings.

Approx Per Serving: Cal 320; Prot 28 g; Carbo 5 g; Fiber 1 g; T Fat 21 g; 60% Calories from Fat; Chol 72 mg; Sod 69 mg.

Curried Chicken Salad

"The raisins add a special touch to the salad."

3 pounds boneless chicken breasts
2 Granny Smith apples, chopped
3 stalks celery, coarsely chopped
3/4 cup golden raisins
1 cup dry white wine
2 tablespoons fresh lime juice
2 tablespoons ginger
2 1/2 to 3 tablespoons curry powder
1 1/2 cups mayonnaise
Salt to taste

Rinse chicken. Place in water to cover in saucepan. Bring to a boil. Cook until tender. Remove chicken to plate. Let stand until cool. Cut into 3/4 to 1-inch pieces. Combine with apples and celery in bowl; mix lightly. Bring raisins and wine to a simmer in small saucepan. Simmer for 3 to 4 minutes. Add to chicken mixture; toss to mix. Add lime juice, ginger, curry powder, mayonnaise and salt; toss lightly. Chill for 1 hour or longer. Garnish with Granny Smith apple slices. **Yield:** 8 servings.

Approx Per Serving: Cal 605; Prot 41 g; Carbo 22 g; Fiber 3 g; T Fat 38 g; 58% Calories from Fat; Chol 133 mg; Sod 347 mg.

Chinese Chicken Salad

"The cilantro and sesame oil lend an unusual flavor to this delightfully different salad."

1/4 cup sesame oil
1/4 cup vegetable oil
1 tablespoon sugar
2 teaspoons soy sauce
1 or 2 teaspoons hot mustard
1 package chicken-flavored ramen noodles
1/2 head cabbage, shredded
1 bunch cilantro, chopped
1/2 cup sliced almonds, toasted
2 or 3 scallions, chopped
1 chicken breast half, cooked, chopped

Combine sesame oil, vegetable oil, sugar, soy sauce, mustard and seasoning packet from noodles in bowl; mix well. Add cabbage, cilantro, almonds, scallions and chicken; mix well. Crush noodles. Add to salad; toss lightly. **Yield:** 4 servings.

Approx Per Serving: Cal 538; Prot 15 g; Carbo 34 g; Fiber 6 g; T Fat 41 g; 65% Calories from Fat; Chol 18 mg; Sod 869 mg.

Gourmet Chicken Salad

1 tablespoon Dijon mustard
1 tablespoon fresh lemon juice
1 tablespoon red wine vinegar
Salt and pepper to taste
1/4 cup olive oil
1 tablespoon grated orange rind
2 Belgian endive, torn
1 head Bibb lettuce or radicchio, torn
Sections of 2 oranges
4 boneless chicken breast halves
1 tablespoon vegetable oil
2 tablespoons minced shallots

Combine mustard, lemon juice, vinegar, salt and pepper in bowl; beat until smooth. Add olive oil gradually, whisking until thickened to desired consistency. Stir in orange rind. Combine endive, lettuce and oranges in salad bowl. Place on 4 serving plates. Drizzle with half the dressing. Rinse chicken and pat dry; cut into 1/2-inch strips. Sprinkle with salt and pepper. Heat vegetable oil in nonstick skillet over high heat. Add chicken. Cook for 5 minutes, tossing to brown evenly. Add shallots. Cook for 1 minute. Stir in remaining salad dressing. Spoon over salads. Garnish with parsley. **Yield:** 4 servings.

Approx Per Serving: Cal 373; Prot 31 g; Carbo 15 g; Fiber 3 g; T Fat 22 g; 53% Calories from Fat; Chol 0 mg; Sod 123 mg.

Smoked Turkey and Artichoke Heart Salad

"This salad is different and tasty."

3 pounds smoked turkey
1 large red onion, chopped
2 14-ounce cans water-pack artichoke hearts, drained, cut into quarters
6 stalks celery, minced
6 tablespoons fresh lime juice
7 tablespoons olive oil
1 teaspoon freshly ground pepper
2 1/2 to 3 cups mayonnaise
2 tablespoons lemon juice
1 teaspoon tarragon
1/2 teaspoon dry mustard

Cut turkey into 1/2-inch pieces. Combine with onion, artichoke hearts and celery in large bowl. Drizzle with lime juice and olive oil; sprinkle with pepper. Let stand at room temperature for 30 to 40 minutes. Combine mayonnaise, lemon juice, tarragon and dry mustard in bowl; mix well. Add to salad; toss gently. Chill for several hours. **Yield:** 12 servings.

Approx Per Serving: Cal 691; Prot 35 g; Carbo 8 g; Fiber 1 g; T Fat 58 g; 75% Calories from Fat; Chol 119 mg; Sod 576 mg.

Crab Tostadas Salad

"This salad makes a great luncheon dish."

1 7-ounce can crab meat
1 tomato, chopped
1/2 avocado, chopped
3 green onions, sliced
1 tablespoon lemon juice
1/4 teaspoon hot pepper sauce
1/4 teaspoon salt
4 corn tortillas
1 tablespoon oil
1 cup shredded lettuce
1 cup shredded sharp Cheddar cheese

Drain and shred crab meat, reserving 4 larger pieces for garnish. Combine remaining crab meat with tomato, avocado, green onions, lemon juice, pepper sauce and salt in bowl; mix well. Chill in refrigerator. Soften tortillas 1 at a time in hot oil in skillet. Press into four 4 1/2-inch tartlet pans or custard cups. Bake at 350 degrees for 5 to 8 minutes or until crisp. Place on serving plates. Layer lettuce, cheese and crab salad in tortilla shells. Top with reserved crab meat. **Yield:** 4 servings.

Approx Per Serving: Cal 309; Prot 20 g; Carbo 18 g; Fiber 6 g; T Fat 18 g; 52% Calories from Fat; Chol 74 mg; Sod 482 mg.

Lobster and Wild Rice Salad

"Puttin' on the Ritz."

3 1/2 to 4 cups cooked wild rice
2 cups chopped cooked lobster meat
2 medium avocados, chopped
1 tablespoon lemon juice
1/2 cup coarsely chopped red onion
1 tablespoon Dijon mustard
2 1/2 tablespoons red wine vinegar
1/2 cup oil
1/2 teaspoon finely minced garlic
2 tablespoons finely chopped parsley
Salt and pepper to taste

Combine rice with lobster in bowl; mix lightly. Sprinkle avocado with lemon juice. Add avocado and onion to lobster mixture. Whisk mustard with vinegar in small bowl. Whisk in oil gradually. Add garlic, parsley, salt and pepper. Add to salad; toss gently. Serve at room temperature. **Yield:** 6 servings.

Approx Per Serving: Cal 447; Prot 16 g; Carbo 33 g; Fiber 10 g; T Fat 29 g; 57% Calories from Fat; Chol 35 mg; Sod 227 mg.

Noggin's Dilled Seafood Salad*

2 cups cooked bay scallops
2 cups peeled cooked shrimp
2 cups broccoli flowerets
1 cup sliced black olives
1 cup crumbled feta cheese
1 cup quartered artichoke hearts
1/4 cup chopped fresh parsley
1/4 cup chopped dill
1 tablespoon chopped fresh oregano
1 teaspoon each salt and pepper
Juice of 1 lemon
3/4 cup olive oil
1 cup toasted pine nuts

Combine first 11 ingredients in bowl; mix well. Add lemon juice, olive oil and pine nuts; toss gently. Chill until serving time. Serve on plates lined with Boston lettuce. **Yield:** 8 servings.

Approx Per Serving: Cal 437; Prot 26 g; Carbo 9 g; Fiber 4 g; T Fat 37 g; 70% Calories from Fat; Chol 114 mg; Sod 786 mg.

Asparagus and Shrimp Salad*

1 hard-boiled egg
2 green onions, minced
1 tablespoon chopped parsley
1/4 cup white wine vinegar
1/2 teaspoon salt
1/8 teaspoon pepper
1/2 cup olive oil
24 pencil-thin stalks asparagus, cooked, chilled
4 ounces small shrimp, cooked

Mash egg in bowl. Mix in next 5 ingredients. Whisk in olive oil gradually. Chill overnight. Arrange asparagus on lettuce-lined serving plates. Add shrimp to salad dressing. Spoon over asparagus. **Yield:** 6 servings.

Approx Per Serving: Cal 203; Prot 6 g; Carbo 3 g; Fiber 1 g; T Fat 19 g; 83% Calories from Fat; Chol 65 mg; Sod 224 mg.

Shrimp Rémoulade*

1/4 cup horseradish mustard
1/2 cup tarragon vinegar
2 tablespoons catsup
1 clove of garlic, chopped
1 cup oil
1 tablespoon paprika
1/2 cup finely chopped green onions with tops
1/2 cup finely chopped celery
1 teaspoon salt
1/2 teaspoon cayenne pepper
2 pounds cooked peeled shrimp

Combine all ingredients except shrimp in blender container; process until smooth. Combine with shrimp in bowl; mix well. Chill overnight. Serve on red leaf lettuce. **Yield:** 8 servings.

Approx Per Serving: Cal 372; Prot 25 g; Carbo 3 g; Fiber <1 g; T Fat 29 g; 70% Calories from Fat; Chol 221 mg; Sod 715 mg.

Seashells and Snow Peas with Shrimp

2 pounds small seashell pasta
$1^1/_2$ pounds snow peas
$2^1/_2$ pounds large (16 to 24-count) shrimp, peeled, cooked
1 bunch scallions, sliced
1 red bell pepper, seeded, cut into julienne strips
Shrimpy Salad Dressing (page 102)

Cook pasta *al dente* using package directions. Rinse in cold water and drain well. Blanche snow peas in boiling water in saucepan for 30 seconds. Rinse in cold water and drain. Combine pasta and snow peas with shrimp in large bowl; mix well. Stir in scallions and bell pepper. Drizzle with salad dressing; toss gently. Serve immediately or chill, covered, for several hours. **Yield:** 16 servings.

Approx Per Serving: Cal 615; Prot 25 g; Carbo 48 g; Fiber 4 g; T Fat 36 g; 52% Calories from Fat; Chol 216 mg; Sod 414 mg.

Paradise Valley Tuna Salad*

1 13-ounce can white water-pack tuna, drained
1 bunch green onions, minced
1 4-ounce can chopped green chilies, drained
$^1/_4$ cup thick and chunky medium-hot salsa
$^1/_3$ cup mayonnaise
1 teaspoon cumin

Flake tuna into bowl. Add green chilies, green onions and salsa. Add mixture of mayonnaise and cumin; mix well. Serve on bed of shredded iceberg lettuce; garnish with chopped cilantro. Serve with sliced tomato, avocado and taco chips. **Yield:** 6 servings.

Approx Per Serving: Cal 226; Prot 19 g; Carbo 4 g; Fiber <1 g; T Fat 15 g; 60% Calories from Fat; Chol 46 mg; Sod 495 mg.

Pesto Salad*

$^1/_2$ cup olive oil
3 tablespoons red wine vinegar
$^1/_2$ cup minced fresh basil
2 cloves of garlic, crushed
$^1/_2$ teaspoon salt
$^1/_4$ teaspoon sugar
1 12-ounce package bow tie egg noodles, cooked, rinsed, drained
$^1/_2$ cup grated Parmesan cheese

Mix olive oil and vinegar in bowl. Stir in basil, garlic, salt and sugar. Pour over warm noodles; mix lightly. Top with cheese. **Yield:** 6 servings.

Approx Per Serving: Cal 410; Prot 11 g; Carbo 40 g; Fiber 0 g; T Fat 23 g; 50% Calories from Fat; Chol 5 mg; Sod 312 mg.

Pasta Niçoise

"This is a good luncheon dish or light dinner entrée."

2/3 cup olive oil
1/3 cup red wine vinegar
2 cloves of garlic, minced
2 tablespoons drained capers
1 1/2 teaspoons basil
1 teaspoon salt
1/2 teaspoon pepper
1 16-ounce package rotelle or medium seashell pasta
2 7-ounce cans tuna, drained
1/3 cup Greek olives
3 medium tomatoes, chopped
2 cups sliced celery
1 cup thinly sliced red onion
1/2 cup chopped parsley

Combine olive oil, vinegar, garlic, capers, basil, salt and pepper in large salad bowl; mix well with fork. Cook pasta using package directions; drain. Add to dressing; toss to coat well. Add tuna, olives, tomatoes, celery, celery, onion and parsley; toss gently. Serve warm or chilled. **Yield:** 6 servings.

Approx Per Serving: Cal 611; Prot 30 g; Carbo 64 g; Fiber 6 g; T Fat 26 g; 38% Calories from Fat; Chol 37 mg; Sod 749 mg.

Easy Summer Pasta Salad

1/4 cup red wine vinegar
1 tablespoon mustard
1 teaspoon sugar
1/3 cup olive oil
1 teaspoon salt
1/2 teaspoon pepper
1 16-ounce package rotelle
1 large onion, coarsely chopped
1 tablespoon olive oil
8 ounces snow peas, trimmed
2 tablespoons olive oil
4 medium carrots, sliced
1 bunch broccoli, chopped
1/4 cup water
3 small tomatoes, cut into wedges
1 bunch basil, chopped
3/4 cup grated Parmesan cheese

Mix vinegar, mustard, sugar, 1/3 cup olive oil, salt and pepper with fork in small bowl; set aside. Cook pasta using package directions; drain. Sauté onion in 1 tablespoon olive oil in heavy skillet for 2 minutes. Add snow peas. Sauté for 2 to 3 minutes or until tender-crisp; remove to large bowl. Add 2 tablespoons olive oil, carrots and broccoli to skillet. Sauté just until coated with oil. Stir in water; reduce heat to medium. Cook, covered, for 3 minutes. Cook, uncovered, for 5 minutes or until vegetables are tender-crisp. Add to snow peas in bowl. Add pasta, tomatoes, basil, cheese and salad dressing; mix well. Serve warm or chilled. **Yield:** 10 servings.

Approx Per Serving: Cal 341; Prot 11 g; Carbo 45 g; Fiber 5 g; T Fat 14 g; 36% Calories from Fat; Chol 5 mg; Sod 371 mg.

Pasta Salad Génoise

"This is a hearty main dish salad."

1 tablespoon Dijon mustard
2 tablespoons fresh lemon juice
Salt and freshly ground pepper to taste
5 tablespoons olive oil
1 clove of garlic, crushed
1 16-ounce package fresh or dried fettucini
4 ounces prosciutto, cut into thin strips
4 ounces Genoa salami, cut into strips
1 tomato, finely chopped
4 ounces black olives, cut into halves
1 bunch scallions, finely chopped
1 medium zucchini, finely chopped
1 cup provolone cheese chunks

Mix mustard, lemon juice, salt and pepper in bowl. Whisk in olive oil and garlic. Cook pasta *al dente* using package directions; drain. Add to dressing; toss gently. Let stand for 30 minutes or longer. Add remaining ingredients; mix gently. Serve at room temperature. May add chicken or turkey if desired. **Yield:** 8 servings.

Approx Per Serving: Cal 427; Prot 17 g; Carbo 46 g; Fiber 4 g; T Fat 20 g; 41% Calories from Fat; Chol 27 mg; Sod 598 mg.

Chinese Noodle Salad

1 tablespoon vegetable oil
1 tablespoon sesame oil
1 tablespoon soy sauce
8 ounces uncooked linguine
1½ cups snow peas
1 cucumber
½ small red bell pepper
5 tablespoons soy sauce
¼ cup vegetable oil
2 tablespoons red wine vinegar
½ teaspoon sesame oil
¾ teaspoon dry mustard
3 tablespoons chopped parsley
⅛ teaspoon salt
⅛ teaspoon ground red pepper
¼ cup sliced scallions

Combine 1 tablespoon vegetable oil, 1 tablespoon sesame oil and 1 tablespoon soy sauce in large bowl; mix well. Cook linguine *al dente* using package directions. Rinse with cool water and drain. Add to oil mixture; toss to coat well. Chill for 1 hour. Trim snow peas and cut diagonally into 1-inch pieces. Peel and seed cucumber; cut into ¼x½-inch strips. Cut bell pepper into strips. Combine 5 tablespoons soy sauce, ¼ cup vegetable oil, vinegar, ½ teaspoon sesame oil, dry mustard, parsley, salt and red pepper in small bowl. Add to pasta. Add snow peas, cucumber, bell pepper and scallions; toss gently. **Yield:** 6 servings.

Approx Per Serving: Cal 297; Prot 7 g; Carbo 35 g; Fiber 3 g; T Fat 15 g; 44% Calories from Fat; Chol 0 mg; Sod 1078 mg.

Pasta Salad with Sun-Dried Tomatoes*

2 tablespoons minced garlic
2 tablespoons olive oil
12 basil leaves, cut into strips
3 ounces sun-dried tomatoes in oil, chopped
1 cup whole pitted black olives
8 ounces goat cheese, crumbled
Salt and freshly ground pepper to taste
16 ounces fettucini, cooked

Sauté garlic in olive oil in skillet for 2 or 3 minutes. Add basil and tomatoes. Sauté for several minutes. Add olives. Sauté just until heated through. Stir in cheese, salt and pepper. Add pasta. Toss just until cheese is partially melted. **Yield:** 4 servings.

Approx Per Serving: Cal 674; Prot 24 g; Carbo 91 g; Fiber 6 g; T Fat 25 g; 33% Calories from Fat; Chol 50 mg; Sod 795 mg.

Saffron Orzo Salad

1/4 teaspoon ground saffron
1/2 cup olive oil
2 cloves of garlic, minced
3 tablespoons fresh lemon juice
1/4 teaspoon cumin
2 teaspoons turmeric
1 teaspoon sugar
Salt and pepper to taste
16 ounces orzo, cooked
1/2 cup dried currants, plumped
2/3 cup pine nuts, toasted
1/4 cup chopped fresh mint
1/4 cup chopped parsley
3 tablespoons chopped coriander

Blend saffron into olive oil in bowl. Let stand for 15 minutes. Mix in next 7 ingredients. Add orzo; toss to coat well. Cool to room temperature. Add remaining ingredients; mix gently. **Yield:** 10 servings.

Approx Per Serving: Cal 328; Prot 8 g; Carbo 42 g; Fiber 3 g; T Fat 15 g; 41% Calories from Fat; Chol 0 mg; Sod 3 mg.

Tortellini and Greens*

8 ounces uncooked cheese tortellini
Flowerets of 1 bunch broccoli
1 head romaine lettuce, torn
1 green bell pepper, chopped
1 red bell pepper, chopped
Lemon-Garlic Salad Dressing (page 101)
1/2 cup slivered almonds
1/3 cup grated Parmesan cheese

Cook pasta using package directions. Add broccoli during last 3 minutes. Drain and cool. Combine with lettuce and bell peppers in bowl. Add salad dressing; toss gently. Sprinkle with almonds and cheese. **Yield:** 6 servings.

Approx Per Serving: Cal 476; Prot 13 g; Carbo 26 g; Fiber 4 g; T Fat 38 g; 68% Calories from Fat; Chol 22 mg; Sod 560 mg.

Tortellini and Artichoke Salad

"Serve this salad at room temperature for the best flavor."

7 or 8 cloves of garlic, crushed
1 16-ounce can artichoke hearts
1 cup sour cream
2 tablespoons mayonnaise
4 ounces ranch salad dressing
1 tablespoon onion powder
2 16-ounce packages fresh or dried spinach tortellini
1/4 cup olive oil
1 2-ounce jar sliced pimento, drained
8 ounces feta cheese, crumbled
1 cup sliced black olives

Combine garlic with undrained artichoke hearts in bowl; mix well. Marinate overnight. Combine sour cream, mayonnaise, ranch salad dressing and onion powder in bowl; mix well. Cook pasta using package directions; drain. Combine warm pasta with olive oil in large bowl; mix gently. Drain artichokes. Add to pasta. Add sour cream mixture, pimento, cheese and olives; toss gently. **Yield:** 12 servings.

Approx Per Serving: Cal 458; Prot 17 g; Carbo 41 g; Fiber 1 g; T Fat 27 g; 51% Calories from Fat; Chol 66 mg; Sod 756 mg.

Curried Rice Salad*

4 cups brown rice, cooked
1 11-ounce can mandarin oranges, drained
1 8-ounce can pineapple chunks, drained
1 cup finely chopped carrots
1 medium apple, chopped
1/2 cup raisins
1 cup seedless red grapes
1/2 cup chopped walnuts
1 tablespoon chutney
1 tablespoon lemon juice
1 tablespoon curry powder
1 teaspoon (or less) sugar
1/2 cup mayonnaise
1/2 cup whipping cream, whipped

Combine rice with oranges, pineapple, carrots, apple, raisins, grapes, walnuts, chutney, lemon juice, curry powder, sugar and mayonnaise in large bowl; mix well. Fold in whipped cream. **Yield:** 12 servings.

Approx Per Serving: Cal 423; Prot 6 g; Carbo 67 g; Fiber 4 g; T Fat 16 g; 32% Calories from Fat; Chol 19 mg; Sod 74 mg.

Combine 1 teaspoon dried basil with 1 1/2 tablespoons chopped fresh parsley to approximate fresh basil.

Elegant Wild Rice Salad

"This dish is great served with wild game."

1 1/3 cups oil
1/2 cup white vinegar
1/4 cup grated Parmesan cheese
1 clove of garlic, minced
1 tablespoon sugar
1/2 teaspoon dry mustard
1/4 teaspoon paprika
1 teaspoon celery salt
2 teaspoons salt
1/2 teaspoon white pepper
3 cups uncooked wild rice
9 cups water
2 6-ounce jars marinated artichoke hearts
1 10-ounce package frozen peas
1 green bell pepper, chopped
1 bunch green onions, chopped
1 pint cherry tomatoes, cut into halves
1/2 cup toasted slivered almonds

Combine oil, vinegar, cheese, garlic, sugar, dry mustard, paprika, celery salt, salt and white pepper in jar; cover tightly. Shake to mix well. Store in refrigerator. Cook rice, covered, in water in saucepan over low heat for 45 minutes or until tender; drain. Drain artichoke hearts, reserving marinade; cut artichoke hearts into halves. Add artichoke hearts, peas, green pepper, green onions, tomatoes and reserved marinade to rice in large bowl. Add half the dressing to rice mixture; toss to mix well. Chill, covered, in refrigerator until serving time. Toss again. Sprinkle with almonds. Add remaining salad dressing at serving time if desired. **Yield:** 10 servings.

Approx Per Serving: Cal 410; Prot 11 g; Carbo 47 g; Fiber 5 g; T Fat 22 g; 45% Calories from Fat; Chol 1 mg; Sod 554 mg. Nutritional information includes entire amount of dressing.

Asparagus in Raspberry Vinaigrette*

1 1/2 pounds fresh asparagus, trimmed
1/4 cup fresh or thawed frozen unsweetened raspberries
1/3 cup olive oil
1/2 cup raspberry vinegar
3/4 teaspoon salt
3/4 teaspoon freshly ground pepper

Cook asparagus in water in large saucepan until tender-crisp. Rinse in cold water and drain. Combine raspberries, olive oil, vinegar, salt and pepper in jar with lid; shake to mix well. Pour over asparagus in shallow dish. Chill, covered, for 1 hour or longer. Serve on plate lined with Boston lettuce. **Yield:** 6 servings.

Approx Per Serving: Cal 135; Prot 4 g; Carbo 6 g; Fiber 2 g; T Fat 12 g; 74% Calories from Fat; Chol 0 mg; Sod 269 mg. Nutritional information includes entire amount of vinaigrette.

Artichoke Heart Salad*

6 marinated artichoke hearts, drained, thinly sliced
1/2 small fennel bulb, chopped
1 stalk celery, chopped
1 tablespoon olive oil
1 bunch arugula, torn
1 small head radicchio, torn
4 ounces provolone cheese, thinly shaved
1/4 cup olive oil
2 tablespoons balsamic vinegar
Salt and freshly ground pepper to taste

Mix first 4 ingredients in bowl. Spoon into 4 salad bowls. Top with arugula, radicchio and cheese. Drizzle with remaining 1/4 cup olive oil and balsamic vinegar. Season to taste. **Yield:** 4 servings.

Approx Per Serving: Cal 306; Prot 9 g; Carbo 7 g; Fiber 4 g; T Fat 28 g; 79% Calories from Fat; Chol 20 mg; Sod 488 mg.

Broccoli Salad

Flowerets of 1 bunch broccoli
2 medium red bell peppers, cut into 1 1/2-inch pieces
1 red onion, thinly sliced
1/2 cup olive oil
1/4 cup balsamic vinegar
1 clove of garlic, crushed
1/4 teaspoon oregano
1 teaspoon basil
Salt and pepper to taste

Combine vegetables in salad bowl. Mix remaining ingredients in small bowl. Add to salad; mix well. Chill in refrigerator. Let stand at room temperature for 1 hour before serving. **Yield:** 6 servings.

Approx Per Serving: Cal 192; Prot 2 g; Carbo 7 g; Fiber 3 g; T Fat 18 g; 81% Calories from Fat; Chol 0 mg; Sod 17 mg.

Lettuce Salad with Sesame Seed

1 cup sour cream
1/2 cup mayonnaise
1 tablespoon tarragon vinegar
1 tablespoon sugar
2 tablespoons chopped onion
1 clove of garlic, minced
1 teaspoon each salt and pepper
1/2 cup sesame seed
1 tablespoon butter
1/4 cup grated Parmesan cheese
2 heads iceberg lettuce, torn
1/2 cup chopped cucumber

Mix first 8 ingredients in small bowl. Sauté sesame seed in butter in skillet. Cool to room temperature. Combine with cheese in salad bowl. Add lettuce and cucumber. Toss with dressing. **Yield:** 12 servings.

Approx Per Serving: Cal 171; Prot 4 g; Carbo 4 g; Fiber 1 g; T Fat 16 g; 83% Calories from Fat; Chol 18 mg; Sod 286 mg.

Semi-Caesar Salad

1 head romaine lettuce
2 heads Bibb lettuce
1 egg
3 tablespoons sour cream
3 tablespoons oil
1 teaspoon wine vinegar
1 teaspoon garlic salt
1/2 teaspoon freshly ground pepper
1/2 cup croutons
1/2 cup grated Parmesan cheese

Tear lettuces; place in large salad bowl. Mix egg, sour cream, oil, vinegar, garlic salt and pepper in small bowl. Add to greens with croutons and cheese; toss gently. Serve immediately. **Yield:** 6 servings.

Approx Per Serving: Cal 149; Prot 6 g; Carbo 6 g; Fiber 2 g; T Fat 12 g; 68% Calories from Fat; Chol 44 mg; Sod 526 mg.

Golden Mushroom Salad

8 ounces mushrooms, sliced
1 Golden Delicious apple, chopped
1/4 cup oil
3 tablespoons lemon juice
1 teaspoon Dijon mustard
1 clove of garlic, crushed
1/2 teaspoon sugar
1/2 teaspoon oregano
1/4 teaspoon salt
1/8 teaspoon freshly ground pepper
4 cups torn romaine lettuce
2 ounces bleu cheese, crumbled

Marinate mushrooms and apple in mixture of next 8 ingredients for 30 minutes in bowl. Discard garlic. Combine with lettuce in salad bowl. Add cheese; toss lightly. May garnish with bacon bits. **Yield:** 8 servings.

Approx Per Serving: Cal 110; Prot 3 g; Carbo 6 g; Fiber 1 g; T Fat 9 g; 71% Calories from Fat; Chol 5 mg; Sod 177 mg.

Oriental Spinach Salad

2 tablespoons sesame seed
1/3 cup oil
1/4 cup lemon juice
2 tablespoons soy sauce
1/8 teaspoon hot pepper sauce
1 teaspoon salt
8 ounces mushrooms, sliced
1 7-ounce can sliced water chestnuts, drained
10 ounces fresh spinach, torn

Toast sesame seed in skillet over medium heat. Add to mixture of next 5 ingredients in bowl. Mix in mushrooms and water chestnuts. Chill, covered, in refrigerator. Add spinach; toss to coat well. **Yield:** 8 servings.

Approx Per Serving: Cal 125; Prot 3 g; Carbo 7 g; Fiber 2 g; T Fat 11 g; 71% Calories from Fat; Chol 0 mg; Sod 556 mg.

Bacon and Potato Salad

4 pounds new potatoes
3 cups sliced celery
1/2 cup chopped scallions
1/4 cup minced parsley
8 ounces bacon
1 egg
5 tablespoons lemon juice
1 tablespoon Dijon mustard
1/2 teaspoon salt
1/4 teaspoon pepper
1/2 cup oil
1 1/2 tablespoons warm water

Cook potatoes in water to cover in saucepan until tender; drain. Peel if desired. Chop into 1/2-inch pieces. Combine with celery, scallions and parsley in bowl. Fry bacon in skillet until crisp. Remove and crumble bacon, reserving 1/4 cup drippings. Combine egg, lemon juice, mustard, salt and pepper in blender container; process until smooth. Add oil and reserved drippings gradually, processing constantly. Add warm water; process until smooth. Add to potato mixture; mix well. Toss with bacon. **Yield:** 10 servings.

Approx Per Serving: Cal 352; Prot 7 g; Carbo 48 g; Fiber 5 g; T Fat 15 g; 38% Calories from Fat; Chol 27 mg; Sod 289 mg.

Vegetable Salad

"This salad is just looking for a picnic to happen!"

1 16-ounce can Shoe Peg corn
1 16-ounce can French-style green beans
1 16-ounce can kidney beans
1 16-ounce can tiny peas
1/2 green bell pepper, finely chopped
1 medium onion, finely chopped
1/2 cup finely chopped celery
1 2-ounce jar chopped pimento
2 or 3 whole cloves of garlic
1/2 cup oil
3/4 cup vinegar
1 cup sugar
1 tablespoon water
1 teaspoon salt
1 teaspoon pepper

Drain corn, beans and peas. Combine in large bowl. Add green pepper, onion, celery, pimento and garlic. Add oil, vinegar, sugar, water, salt and pepper; mix well. Store in refrigerator. Remove garlic before serving. **Yield:** 6 servings.

Approx Per Serving: Cal 499; Prot 11 g; Carbo 77 g; Fiber 12 g; T Fat 20 g; 34% Calories from Fat; Chol 0 mg; Sod 1159 mg.

Garlic and Herb Vinaigrette*

1/4 cup Dijon mustard
1/4 cup red wine vinegar
2 cloves of garlic, minced
1 teaspoon tarragon
1 teaspoon thyme
1 teaspoon basil
1 cup oil
Salt and pepper to taste

Combine mustard, vinegar, garlic, tarragon, thyme and basil in bowl; mix well. Add oil gradually, whisking until smooth. Season with salt and pepper. **Yield:** 12 servings.

Approx Per Serving: Cal 166; Prot <1 g; Carbo 1 g; Fiber <1 g; T Fat 18 g; 97% Calories from Fat; Chol 0 mg; Sod 65 mg.

Lemon-Garlic Salad Dressing

Juice of 1 lemon
3 cloves of garlic, crushed
Salt and pepper to taste
3/4 cup oil

Combine lemon juice, garlic, salt and pepper in bowl; mix well. Add oil gradually, beating constantly with fork. Let stand for 3 hours. **Yield:** 6 servings.

Approx Per Serving: Cal 245; Prot <1 g; Carbo 1 g; Fiber <1 g; T Fat 27 g; 98% Calories from Fat; Chol 0 mg; Sod <1 mg.

Orange and Poppy Seed Dressing*

2 tablespoons honey
2 tablespoons cider vinegar
1 teaspoon dry mustard
1 tablespoon orange juice
Salt to taste
1 teaspoon poppy seed
3/4 cup oil

Whisk honey with vinegar, dry mustard, orange juice, salt and poppy seed in small bowl. Add oil gradually, whisking until slightly thickened. Chill until serving time. **Yield:** 8 servings.

Approx Per Serving: Cal 198; Prot <1 g; Carbo 5 g; Fiber <1 g; T Fat 20 g; 91% Calories from Fat; Chol 0 mg; Sod <1 mg.

Orange Vinaigrette*

2 cups olive oil
2 shallots, chopped
3 cups orange juice
1½ cups champagne vinegar
2 tablespoons chopped parsley
1 tablespoon tarragon
Salt and pepper to taste

Combine olive oil, shallots, orange juice, vinegar, parsley, tarragon, salt and pepper in blender; process until smooth. Store in refrigerator. **Yield:** 24 servings.

Approx Per Serving: Cal 180; Prot <1 g; Carbo 5 g; Fiber <1 g; T Fat 18 g; 88% Calories from Fat; Chol 0 mg; Sod 1 mg.

Shrimpy Salad Dressing*

8 ounces cooked shrimp
3 tablespoons tomato paste
½ cup dry vermouth
4 hard-boiled eggs
3 tablespoons fresh lemon juice
3 tablespoons chopped fresh tarragon
3 cups mayonnaise
Salt and freshly ground pepper to taste

Combine shrimp, tomato paste, wine, eggs, lemon juice and tarragon in food processor; process until smooth. Add mayonnaise; process until smooth. Season with salt and pepper. May add 2 tablespoons Pernod if desired. **Yield:** 12 servings.

Approx Per Serving: Cal 456; Prot 7 g; Carbo 3 g; Fiber <1 g; T Fat 46 g; 91% Calories from Fat; Chol 140 mg; Sod 381 mg.

Strawberry Vinaigrette*

8 strawberries
1 cup oil
½ cup white vinegar
¼ cup pink grapefruit juice
⅓ cup honey
1 teaspoon dry mustard
1 teaspoon celery seed
1 teaspoon paprika

Combine strawberries, oil, vinegar, grapefruit juice, honey, dry mustard, celery seed and paprika in blender container. Process until smooth. Chill until serving time. **Yield:** 8 servings.

Approx Per Serving: Cal 294; Prot <1 g; Carbo 14 g; Fiber 1 g; T Fat 27 g; 81% Calories from Fat; Chol 0 mg; Sod 1 mg.

Breads & Brunch

Baptist Church in the Valley

New Member Brunch

Tuxedo Fruit Bowl
page 83

Fresh Salmon Hash in Cheese Puff Ring
pages 131 & 120

Irish Eggs
page 127

Ham and Artichoke Casserole
page 126

A Sunday Morning Coffee Cake
page 105

Strawberry Brunch Loaf
page 115

Blintz Casserole
page 133

BREADS

A Sunday Morning Coffee Cake

"Unbelievably good!"

1 8-ounce can crushed pineapple
3 ounces cream cheese, softened
2 tablespoons sugar
1/4 teaspoon almond extract
1/4 cup butter, softened
1/2 cup sugar
1 egg
1 teaspoon vanilla extract
1 1/4 cups flour
1 1/2 teaspoons baking powder
1/4 teaspoon salt
1/4 cup packed brown sugar
2 tablespoons flour
2 tablespoons butter, softened
1/4 cup flaked coconut
1/4 teaspoon cinnamon
1/4 cup sliced almonds

Drain pineapple, reserving juice. Add enough water to reserved juice to measure 1/2 cup. Combine cream cheese, 2 tablespoons sugar, almond extract and 2 tablespoons drained pineapple in small bowl; mix well and set aside. Cream butter and 1/2 cup sugar in mixer bowl. Add egg and vanilla; beat until light and fluffy. Add mixture of 1 1/4 cups flour, baking powder and salt alternately with reserved pineapple juice, mixing well after each addition. Layer half the batter, remaining crushed pineapple and remaining batter in greased 8-inch square baking pan. Spoon cream cheese mixture 1/2 teaspoonful at a time over batter. Combine brown sugar, 2 tablespoons flour, 2 tablespoons butter, coconut, cinnamon and almonds in small bowl; mix well. Sprinkle over top. Bake at 350 degrees for 35 to 40 minutes or until coffee cake tests done. **Yield:** 8 servings.

Approx Per Serving: Cal 345; Prot 5 g; Carbo 48 g; Fiber 1 g; T Fat 16 g; 40% Calories from Fat; Chol 62 mg; Sod 247 mg.

Fresh Apple Coffee Cake

"Always light, moist and a dark golden color—a winner!"

3/4 pound Golden Delicious apples
1 egg, beaten
1 cup sugar
1/2 cup chopped walnuts
1/4 cup vegetable oil
1 teaspoon cinnamon
1/4 teaspoon nutmeg
1 cup flour
1 teaspoon baking soda
1/2 teaspoon salt

Peel and chop apples. Combine with egg in bowl; toss until mixed. Add sugar, walnuts, oil, cinnamon and nutmeg; mix well. Add mixture of flour, baking soda and salt; mix until moistened. Pour into greased 8-inch square baking pan. Bake at 350 degrees for 40 to 45 minutes or until coffee cake tests done. Cool in pan on wire rack for 10 minutes. Cut into squares. **Yield:** 8 servings.

Approx Per Serving: Cal 295; Prot 4 g; Carbo 45 g; Fiber 2 g; T Fat 12 g; 37% Calories from Fat; Chol 27 mg; Sod 246 mg.

Blueberry Coffee Cake

"This is great made with fresh peaches too!"

3 cups fresh blueberries
3 cups flour
1 tablespoon baking powder
2 cups sugar
1 cup vegetable oil
1/2 cup orange juice
4 eggs
1 tablespoon vanilla extract
1 teaspoon cinnamon
1/2 cup sugar
1 teaspoon cinnamon
Nutmeg to taste

Rinse blueberries; drain well. Combine flour, baking powder, 2 cups sugar, oil, orange juice, eggs, vanilla and 1 teaspoon cinnamon in mixer bowl. Beat at high speed for 3 minutes. Mix 1/2 cup sugar, 1 teaspoon cinnamon and nutmeg in small bowl. Pour half the batter into greased tube pan. Sprinkle with half the blueberries and half the spice-sugar. Add remaining batter; top with remaining blueberries and spice-sugar. Bake at 350 degrees for 1 3/4 to 2 hours or until coffee cake tests done. **Yield:** 20 servings.

Approx Per Serving: Cal 292; Prot 3 g; Carbo 43 g; Fiber 1 g; T Fat 12 g; 37% Calories from Fat; Chol 43 mg; Sod 66 mg.

Blue Ribbon Coffee Cake

"This won first prize in the New Jersey Blueberry Cooking Contest."

1/2 cup sugar
1/2 cup chopped pecans
1 tablespoon melted butter
1 teaspoon cinnamon
1 1/2 cups packed brown sugar
1/2 cup butter, softened
1 egg
2 cups flour
1 teaspoon baking soda
1/2 teaspoon salt
1 cup sour cream
1 1/2 cups 1/2-inch pieces rhubarb
1 cup blueberries

Combine sugar, pecans, melted butter and cinnamon in small bowl; mix well and set aside. Cream brown sugar, softened butter and egg in mixer bowl until light and fluffy. Sift in flour, baking soda and salt; mix well. Stir in sour cream. Fold in rhubarb and blueberries gently. Pour into greased and floured 9x13-inch baking pan. Sprinkle with pecan mixture. Bake at 350 degrees for 45 to 50 minutes or until coffee cake tests done. **Yield:** 20 servings.

Approx Per Serving: Cal 242; Prot 2 g; Carbo 37 g; Fiber 1 g; T Fat 10 g; 37% Calories from Fat; Chol 30 mg; Sod 158 mg.

Hearty Carrot-Apple Coffee Cake

"This makes a nice breakfast cake."

1 pound carrots
1 pound Granny Smith apples
2 cups whole wheat flour
1 cup oat bran
2 to 3 teaspoons cinnamon
1/2 teaspoon nutmeg
1 teaspoon baking soda
4 eggs, beaten
1 cup packed dark brown sugar
3/4 cup corn oil

Peel carrots; shred in food processor. Core unpeeled apples; grate apples in food processor. Measure 3 cups carrots and 2 cups apples. Combine whole wheat flour, oat bran, cinnamon, nutmeg and baking soda in large bowl; set aside. Beat eggs with brown sugar and oil in large bowl until creamy. Stir in carrots and apples. Add to flour mixture; mix well. Pour into greased 9x13-inch baking pan. Bake at 350 degrees for 50 to 55 minutes or until wooden pick inserted in center comes out clean. Cool in pan on wire rack. **Yield:** 20 servings.

Approx Per Serving: Cal 213; Prot 4 g; Carbo 31 g; Fiber 4 g; T Fat 10 g; 39% Calories from Fat; Chol 43 mg; Sod 70 mg.

Cocoa Swirl Coffee Cake

¾ cup chopped pecans
½ cup sugar
4½ teaspoons baking cocoa
2 tablespoons cinnamon
1 cup unsalted butter, softened
8 ounces cream cheese, softened
1½ cups sugar
1½ teaspoons vanilla extract
4 eggs
2¼ cups flour
1½ teaspoons baking powder
¾ cup raisins

Sprinkle pecans over bottom of generously greased tube pan; set aside. Mix ½ cup sugar, baking cocoa and cinnamon in small bowl; set aside.Cream butter in mixer bowl. Add cream cheese, 1½ cups sugar and vanilla; beat until light and fluffy. Add eggs 1 at a time, beating well after each addition. Add flour, baking powder and raisins; mix well. Layer batter and cinnamon mixture ½ at a time in prepared tube pan. Bake at 325 degrees for 65 to 75 minutes or until coffee cake tests done. Cool in pan on wire rack for 15 minutes. Invert onto wire rack to cool completely.
Yield: 16 servings.

Approx Per Serving: Cal 393; Prot 5 g; Carbo 46 g; Fiber 1 g; T Fat 22 g; 49% Calories from Fat; Chol 100 mg; Sod 94 mg.

Sweet Dutch Coffee Cake*

"This recipe is at least 100 years old and requires no eggs."

2 cups flour
2 teaspoons baking powder
1 cup sugar
½ cup melted butter
1 cup milk
2 tablespoons sugar
1 teaspoon cinnamon

Mix flour and baking powder together; set aside. Cream 1 cup sugar and butter in mixer bowl until light and fluffy. Add flour mixture and milk alternately, mixing well after each addition. Pour into greased and floured 8-inch round baking pan. Sprinkle with mixture of 2 tablespoons sugar and cinnamon. Bake at 350 degrees for 25 minutes.
Yield: 10 servings.

Approx Per Serving: Cal 275; Prot 4 g; Carbo 43 g; Fiber 1 g; T Fat 10 g; 33% Calories from Fat; Chol 28 mg; Sod 154 mg.

Sift dry ingredients onto a paper plate and bend plate for easy transfer of flour to batter.

Plum Kuchen

"Good served warm"

2 cups flour
1 tablespoon baking powder
1/2 teaspoon salt
1/4 cup sugar
6 tablespoons butter
1 egg
3/4 cup milk
2 pounds prune plums
2 tablespoons melted butter
3/4 cup sugar
1 teaspoon cinnamon
1 teaspoon nutmeg

Sift flour, baking powder, salt and 1/4 cup sugar into bowl. Cut in 6 tablespoons butter until crumbly. Beat egg with milk in bowl. Add to flour mixture; mix well. Pour into greased 9x13-inch baking pan. Pit plums; arrange skin side up in rows over batter. Drizzle with 2 tablespoons melted butter. Sprinkle with mixture of 3/4 cup sugar, cinnamon and nutmeg. Bake at 400 degrees for 40 minutes. **Yield:** 12 servings.

Approx Per Serving: Cal 266; Prot 4 g; Carbo 43 g; Fiber 2 g; T Fat 9 g; 31% Calories from Fat; Chol 41 mg; Sod 249 mg.

Streusel Loaves

1/2 cup packed brown sugar
1/2 cup oats
2 teaspoons cinnamon
1/4 cup butter, chilled
3 cups flour
1 1/2 teaspoons baking powder
1 1/2 teaspoons baking soda
1/2 teaspoon nutmeg
3/4 cup unsalted butter, softened
1 1/3 cups sugar
3 eggs
1 teaspoon vanilla extract
1 1/2 cups plain yogurt
1 medium apple, peeled, chopped

Combine brown sugar, oats and cinnamon in small bowl. Cut in chilled butter until crumbly; set aside. Sift flour, baking powder, baking soda and nutmeg together. Cream softened butter and sugar in large mixer bowl until light and fluffy. Add eggs 1 at a time, beating well after each addition. Beat in vanilla. Fold in dry ingredients alternately with yogurt. Pour about 1 1/2 cups batter into each of 2 greased 5x9-inch loaf pans. Sprinkle each with 1/3 cup streusel mixture and 1/4 of the apple. Divide remaining batter, streusel mixture and apple between loaf pans. Cut through batter with small sharp knife to create swirl. Bake at 350 degrees for 55 minutes or until golden brown and loaves test done. Cool on wire rack. Serve warm or at room temperature. **Yield:** 20 servings.

Approx Per Serving: Cal 260; Prot 4 g; Carbo 37 g; Fiber 1 g; T Fat 11 g; 37% Calories from Fat; Chol 59 mg; Sod 128 mg.

Fiesta Corn Bread*

"Delicious with taco salad"

1 cup yellow cornmeal
1 cup flour
1/4 cup sugar
1 tablespoon baking powder
1/2 teaspoon salt
1/8 teaspoon cayenne pepper
1/3 cup vegetable oil
1 egg
1 cup milk
1 8-ounce can corn, drained
1/2 cup sliced green onions
1/2 cup shredded Cheddar cheese
1 4-ounce can chopped green chilies, drained

Combine cornmeal, flour, sugar, baking powder, salt and cayenne pepper in large bowl. Combine oil, egg and milk in medium bowl; whisk until blended. Add corn, green onions, cheese and green chilies; mix well. Add to cornmeal mixture; mix well. Pour into greased 8-inch square baking pan. Bake at 400 degrees for 25 minutes. **Yield:** 8 servings.

Approx Per Serving: Cal 310; Prot 8 g; Carbo 40 g; Fiber 2 g; T Fat 14 g; 39% Calories from Fat; Chol 38 mg; Sod 489 mg.

Mother's Corn Bread

"This simple recipe comes from a long line of Kentucky cooks."

1 to 2 teaspoons bacon drippings
1 to 2 teaspoons white cornmeal
3 tablespoons flour
1 1/2 cups white cornmeal
1 teaspoon salt
1 teaspoon baking soda
2 cups buttermilk
1 egg, beaten
2 tablespoons melted bacon drippings

Melt 1 to 2 teaspoons bacon drippings in cast-iron skillet in 450-degree oven. Sprinkle with 1 to 2 teaspoons cornmeal. Place skillet in preheated oven while preparing batter. Combine flour, 1 1/2 cups cornmeal, salt and baking soda in bowl. Add buttermilk, egg and 2 tablespoons bacon drippings; mix well. Pour into hot prepared skillet. Bake at 450 degrees for 20 to 25 minutes or until golden brown. Invert onto serving plate. This is good with soup, ham, fried chicken dinners or just crumbled hot into a glass of milk and eaten with a spoon. **Yield:** 8 servings.

Approx Per Serving: Cal 184; Prot 5 g; Carbo 26 g; Fiber 2 g; T Fat 6 g; 31% Calories from Fat; Chol 57 mg; Sod 489 mg.

Crunchy Bran Bread*

"A nutritious start for the day"

1 cup (heaping) All-Bran
1/3 cup butter, softened
1/2 cup packed dark brown sugar
1 egg
1 1/2 cups sifted unbleached flour
1 teaspoon (scant) salt
1 1/2 teaspoons baking soda
1/2 teaspoon baking powder
2 tablespoons wheat germ
1/2 cup black coffee
1 cup plus 2 tablespoons water
1/4 cup dark molasses
1 cup raisins
1/2 cup coarsely chopped walnuts

Soak cereal in water to cover for 15 minutes. Cream butter and brown sugar in food processor until light and fluffy. Blend in egg. Sift flour, salt, baking soda and baking powder together. Mix in wheat germ. Stir coffee, water and molasses into cereal. Add flour mixture and cereal mixture alternately to creamed mixture, processing well after each addition. Add raisins and walnuts; pulse 2 or 3 times to mix. Pour into greased 5x9-inch loaf pan. Bake at 350 degrees for 45 minutes. Serve hot for breakfast or tea. May substitute scant 1/2 cup honey for dark brown sugar. **Yield:** 12 servings.

Approx Per Serving: Cal 248; Prot 4 g; Carbo 42 g; Fiber 3 g; T Fat 9 g; 31% Calories from Fat; Chol 31 mg; Sod 437 mg.

Great Date Bread

"A favorite from the needlework show"

1 pound chopped dates
2 cups orange juice
1/2 cup butter, softened
1 1/2 cups packed brown sugar
2 eggs
2 tablespoons orange rind
1 teaspoon vanilla extract
4 cups flour
2 teaspoons baking soda
1/2 teaspoon baking powder
1/2 teaspoon salt
1 cup chopped walnuts

Combine dates and orange juice in saucepan. Bring to a boil, stirring occasionally. Let stand until cool, stirring occasionally. Combine date mixture with butter and brown sugar in large bowl. Add eggs 1 at a time, mixing well after each addition. Mix in orange rind and vanilla. Sift in dry ingredients; mix well. Stir in walnuts. Pour into 2 greased and floured 4x8-inch loaf pans. Bake at 325 degrees for 1 hour. Cool on wire rack. **Yield:** 20 servings.

Approx Per Serving: Cal 327; Prot 5 g; Carbo 60 g; Fiber 3 g; T Fat 9 g; 25% Calories from Fat; Chol 33 mg; Sod 201 mg.

Dilly Bread*

"This is a tasty bread to serve with soup."

1 envelope dry yeast
1/4 cup lukewarm water
1 cup cream-style cottage cheese
2 tablespoons sugar
1 tablespoon butter
1 tablespoon instant minced onion
2 teaspoons dillseed
1 teaspoon salt
1/4 teaspoon baking soda
1 egg
2 1/2 cups unbleached flour

Dissolve yeast in lukewarm water. Combine cottage cheese with sugar and butter in saucepan. Heat to lukewarm. Combine with onion, dillseed, salt, baking soda, egg and yeast in large bowl. Add flour; mix well. Let rise, covered, until doubled in bulk. Stir dough down. Place in greased casserole. Let rise until doubled in bulk. Bake at 350 degrees for 40 to 50 minutes or until golden brown. **Yield:** 12 servings.

Approx Per Serving: Cal 125; Prot 5 g; Carbo 20 g; Fiber <1 g; T Fat 3 g; 19% Calories from Fat; Chol 23 mg; Sod 280 mg.

Oatmeal Bread with Honey-Orange Butter

"Honey may be substituted for the molasses to produce a lighter, sweeter bread."

2 envelopes dry yeast
1/2 cup lukewarm water
1 cup quick-cooking oats
1/2 cup molasses
1/3 cup shortening
1 tablespoon salt
1 1/2 cups boiling water
2 cups sifted flour
2 eggs, beaten
3 1/2 to 4 cups sifted flour
1 cup butter, softened
1/2 cup honey
6 tablespoons orange juice
1 tablespoon grated orange zest

Dissolve yeast in lukewarm water. Combine oats, molasses, shortening, salt and boiling water in large bowl. Cool to lukewarm. Add 2 cups flour and eggs; mix well. Beat in yeast and remaining flour; dough will be sticky. Grease top of dough lightly. Let rise, covered, for 1 1/2 to 2 hours. Punch dough down. Shape into 2 loaves; place in greased loaf pans. Let rise for 1 hour or until almost doubled in bulk. Bake at 375 degrees for 40 to 50 minutes or until brown. Combine butter, honey and orange juice in mixer bowl; beat until light and fluffy. Stir in orange zest. Spoon into decorative jar. Store in refrigerator. Serve with oatmeal bread.
Yield: 24 servings.

Approx Per Serving: Cal 238; Prot 4 g; Carbo 33 g; Fiber 1 g; T Fat 10 g; 38% Calories from Fat; Chol 34 mg; Sod 326 mg.

Orange Cinnamon Bread

1 envelope dry yeast
1/4 cup lukewarm water
1 cup warm milk
1/2 cup sugar
1/4 cup margarine
1 1/2 teaspoons salt
3/4 cup orange juice
1 tablespoon grated orange rind
2 cups flour
1 egg, slightly beaten
4 1/2 to 5 cups flour
1/2 cup sugar
1 tablespoon cinnamon
2 tablespoons water
1 cup sifted confectioners' sugar
1 teaspoon grated orange rind
4 teaspoons orange juice

Dissolve yeast in 1/4 cup lukewarm water. Combine warm milk, 1/2 cup sugar, margarine, salt, 3/4 cup orange juice and 1 tablespoon orange rind in large bowl. Let stand until cooled to lukewarm. Add 2 cups flour; beat until smooth. Beat in yeast and egg. Add enough remaining flour to make soft dough. Knead on floured surface for 8 to 10 minutes or until smooth and elastic. Place in greased bowl, turning to coat surface. Let rise, covered, for 1 hour or until doubled in bulk. Divide into 2 portions. Let rest, covered, for 10 minutes. Combine 1/2 cup sugar, cinnamon and 2 tablespoons water in small bowl; mix well. Roll dough 1 portion at a time into 7x15-inch rectangle. Sprinkle with half the cinnamon mixture; roll as for jelly roll from 7-inch side. Place seam side down in greased 5x9-inch loaf pans. Let rise, covered, for 50 to 60 minutes or until doubled in bulk. Bake at 350 degrees for 30 to 40 minutes or until golden brown. Remove from pans to cool on wire rack. Blend confectioners' sugar, 1 teaspoon orange rind and 4 teaspoons orange juice in small bowl. Spread over loaves. **Yield:** 24 servings.

Approx Per Serving: Cal 212; Prot 5 g; Carbo 42 g; Fiber 1 g; T Fat 3 g; 12% Calories from Fat; Chol 10 mg; Sod 164 mg.

Cool Peach Bread*

1/2 cup butter, softened
1/2 cup sugar
1/2 cup packed brown sugar
2 1/2 cups drained, chopped canned peaches
2 eggs
1/2 cup sour cream
1/2 teaspoon vanilla extract
2 1/2 cups flour
1 teaspoon baking soda
1/2 teaspoon salt
1/2 teaspoon cinnamon
1/2 cup finely chopped almonds

Cream butter and sugars in mixer bowl until light and fluffy. Mix in peaches, eggs, sour cream and vanilla. Add dry ingredients; mix well. Stir in almonds. Pour into greased 5x9-inch loaf pan. Bake at 350 degrees for 60 to 70 minutes or until loaf tests done. **Yield:** 12 servings.

Approx Per Serving: Cal 331; Prot 5 g; Carbo 48 g; Fiber 2 g; T Fat 14 g; 36% Calories from Fat; Chol 61 mg; Sod 247 mg.

Almond-Glazed Poppy Seed Bread

"Very Good!"

3 cups sifted flour
$2^1/_4$ cups sugar
$1^1/_2$ teaspoons salt
$1^1/_2$ teaspoons baking powder
3 eggs, beaten
$1^1/_2$ cups milk
$1^1/_3$ cups oil
$1^1/_2$ teaspoons vanilla extract
$1^1/_2$ teaspoons almond extract
2 tablespoons poppy seed
$^3/_4$ cup sugar
Juice of 1 lemon
$^1/_2$ teaspoon vanilla extract
$^1/_2$ teaspoon almond extract

Combine flour, $2^1/_4$ cups sugar, salt and baking powder in bowl; mix well. Add eggs, milk, oil, $1^1/_2$ teaspoons each vanilla and almond extracts and poppy seed; beat until well mixed. Pour into greased 5x9-inch loaf pan. Bake at 325 degrees for 1 hour or until loaf tests done. Cool on wire rack. Heat $^3/_4$ cup sugar and lemon juice in saucepan until sugar dissolves, stirring constantly; remove from heat. Blend in $^1/_2$ teaspoon each vanilla and almond extracts. Spoon over warm loaf. **Yield:** 12 servings.

Approx Per Serving: Cal 559; Prot 6 g; Carbo 74 g; Fiber 1 g; T Fat 28 g; 44% Calories from Fat; Chol 57 mg; Sod 340 mg.

Spinach and Sausage Pizza Bread*

"You can serve this as an appetizer, too."

1 10-ounce package frozen chopped spinach
1 pound hot or sweet Italian sausage
1 egg
$^1/_8$ teaspoon salt
$^1/_8$ teaspoon pepper
$^1/_8$ teaspoon garlic powder
8 ounces mozzarella cheese, shredded
1 pound pizza dough
1 egg yolk, beaten

Cook spinach using package directions; drain and squeeze dry. Remove sausage casing; crumble into skillet. Cook until brown and crumbly; drain. Add egg, seasonings, cheese and spinach. Cook until cheese melts, stirring constantly. Roll pizza dough into rectangle. Spread sausage mixture from center of rectangle evenly to all sides. Fold sides of dough to center to resemble envelope; seal seams. Place seam side down on greased baking sheet. Brush with egg yolk. Bake at 350 degrees for 40 minutes. May bake for 20 minutes, wrap tightly and freeze. Thaw at room temperature for 2 hours. Bake at 350 degrees for 20 minutes. **Yield:** 12 servings.

Approx Per Serving: Cal 231; Prot 11 g; Carbo 22 g; Fiber 1 g; T Fat 12 g; 44% Calories from Fat; Chol 65 mg; Sod 577 mg.

Strawberry Brunch Loaf*

2 cups flour
1 tablespoon baking powder
1 teaspoon salt
2 teaspoons grated lemon rind
1/2 teaspoon nutmeg
2 eggs, beaten
1/2 cup honey
1/2 cup oil
1 1/2 cups coarsely chopped strawberries
1/2 cup slivered almonds

Mix flour, baking powder, salt, lemon rind and nutmeg in large bowl. Beat eggs with honey and oil in bowl. Stir in strawberries and almonds. Add to flour mixture; mix just until moistened. Pour into greased 5x9-inch loaf pan. Bake at 350 degrees for 50 to 55 minutes. Cool in pan for 15 minutes. Remove to wire rack to cool completely. **Yield:** 12 servings.

Approx Per Serving: Cal 258; Prot 5 g; Carbo 32 g; Fiber 2 g; T Fat 13 g; 45% Calories from Fat; Chol 36 mg; Sod 274 mg.

Cheese-Stuffed French Loaf*

1 16-ounce loaf French bread
3/4 cup unsalted butter, softened
1 teaspoon dried thyme
1/2 teaspoon Tabasco sauce
1/2 cup chopped red onions
2 cups shredded sharp Cheddar cheese

Cut bread into halves horizontally. Mix butter with thyme, Tabasco sauce and onions in bowl. Spread over cut sides of bread. Sprinkle bottom half with cheese; replace top. Wrap in foil. Bake at 350 degrees for 20 minutes or until crust is hard. Slice crosswise. **Yield:** 8 servings.

Approx Per Serving: Cal 432; Prot 13 g; Carbo 30 g; Fiber 1 g; T Fat 29 g; 60% Calories from Fat; Chol 76 mg; Sod 508 mg.

Heavenly Herbed Bread*

1 16-ounce loaf French bread
1 small bunch parsley, chopped
8 to 10 scallions, chopped
1 small bunch chives, chopped
1 sprig of fresh dill, chopped
1/2 cup butter, softened
1/2 teaspoon salt

Cut bread into halves horizontally. Combine parsley, scallions, chives, dill, butter and salt in bowl; mix well. Spread over cut sides of bread; place cut sides together. Place on baking sheet. Bake at 350 degrees for 20 minutes. Cut into 1-inch slices. **Yield:** 8 servings.

Approx Per Serving: Cal 268; Prot 6 g; Carbo 30 g; Fiber 2 g; T Fat 14 g; 47% Calories from Fat; Chol 31 mg; Sod 559 mg.

Honey-Apple Muffins*

2 cups raisin bran
1/4 cup each water, orange juice, oil and Grand Marnier
1 egg, beaten
2 tablespoons honey
1 apple, peeled, grated
1 cup flour
2 1/2 teaspoons baking powder
1/2 teaspoon salt
2 teaspoons cinnamon
1/2 cup sugar
1 tablespoon grated orange rind

Mix first 7 ingredients in bowl. Stir in apple. Add remaining ingredients; mix just until moistened. Spoon into paper-lined muffin cups. Bake at 400 degrees for 25 minutes or until muffins test done. **Yield:** 12 servings.

Approx Per Serving: Cal 175; Prot 2 g; Carbo 30 g; Fiber 2 g; T Fat 5 g; 27% Calories from Fat; Chol 18 mg; Sod 213 mg.

Fresh Blueberry Muffins*

1 egg, beaten
1/2 cup milk
1 1/2 cups sifted flour
1/2 cup sugar
1/2 teaspoon salt
1 tablespoon baking powder
1/4 cup vegetable oil
1 cup fresh blueberries

Beat egg with milk in bowl. Add mixture of dry ingredients; mix while adding oil. Fold in blueberries. Fill greased muffin cups 2/3 full. Bake at 400 degrees for 20 to 25 minutes or until golden brown. **Yield:** 12 servings.

Approx Per Serving: Cal 146; Prot 2 g; Carbo 22 g; Fiber 1 g; T Fat 6 g; 34% Calories from Fat; Chol 19 mg; Sod 182 mg.

Branana Muffins

3/4 cup butter, softened
2/3 cup sugar
2 1/2 to 3 cups mashed bananas
3 eggs, beaten
2 cups cake flour
1 1/2 cups bran
3/4 teaspoon salt
1 1/2 teaspoons baking soda
1 cup chopped walnuts
1 tablespoon grated orange zest
3/4 cup granola (optional)

Cream butter and sugar in bowl until light and fluffy. Beat in bananas and eggs until light and smooth. Sift in next 4 ingredients; mix well. Stir in walnuts, orange zest and granola. Fill greased muffin cups 2/3 full. Bake at 375 degrees for 15 to 20 minutes. **Yield:** 24 servings.

Approx Per Serving: Cal 193; Prot 3 g; Carbo 24 g; Fiber 2 g; T Fat 11 g; 46% Calories from Fat; Chol 42 mg; Sod 184 mg.

Golden Carrot Muffins

"Serve these at your next meeting."

3 eggs
1 1/2 cups sugar
3/4 cup vegetable oil
2 1/4 cups sifted flour
1 3/4 teaspoons baking powder
1 teaspoon baking soda
2 teaspoons cinnamon
1 1/2 cups finely shredded carrots
1/2 cup golden raisins
3 tablespoons wheat germ
1/2 cup shredded coconut

Beat eggs, sugar and oil in large bowl until blended. Add mixture of flour, baking powder, baking soda and cinnamon; mix well. Stir in carrots, raisins, wheat germ and coconut. Fill greased muffin cups 2/3 full. Bake at 350 degrees for 20 to 25 minutes or until muffins test done. Cool in pans for 20 minutes before removing. **Yield:** 24 servings.

Approx Per Serving: Cal 183; Prot 2 g; Carbo 25 g; Fiber 1 g; T Fat 8 g; 41% Calories from Fat; Chol 27 mg; Sod 75 mg.

Eventful Muffins

"Straight from Radnor Hunt!"

1 1/4 cups sugar
2 1/4 cups flour
1 tablespoon cinnamon
2 teaspoons baking soda
1/2 teaspoon salt
1/2 cup shredded coconut
1/2 cup raisins
2 cups shredded carrots
1 apple, shredded
1 8-ounce can crushed pineapple, drained
1/2 cup chopped pecans
3 eggs
1 cup vegetable oil
1 teaspoon vanilla extract

Sift sugar, flour, cinnamon, baking soda and salt into large bowl. Stir in coconut, raisins, carrots, apple, pineapple and pecans. Combine eggs, oil and vanilla in medium bowl; whisk until blended. Add to flour mixture; mix well. Fill paper-lined muffin cups to the brim. Bake at 350 degrees for 35 minutes or until toothpick inserted in center comes out clean. Cool in pan for 10 minutes. Remove to wire rack to cool completely. Flavor improves if made 24 hours before serving. These freeze beautifully. **Yield:** 24 servings.

Approx Per Serving: Cal 221; Prot 2 g; Carbo 27 g; Fiber 1 g; T Fat 12 g; 49% Calories from Fat; Chol 27 mg; Sod 131 mg.

Good Morning Muffins

"Get the coffee ready!"

1/2 cup oats
1/2 cup orange juice
1 1/2 cups flour
2/3 cup sugar
1 1/2 teaspoons baking powder
1/4 teaspoon baking soda
1/4 teaspoon salt
1/2 cup corn oil
2 eggs, beaten
1 cup blueberries
1/8 teaspoon cinnamon
1/8 teaspoon nutmeg
2 tablespoons sugar
1/4 teaspoon cinnamon

Combine oats and orange juice in bowl; mix well. Add flour, 2/3 cup sugar, baking powder, baking soda and salt; mix well. Beat oil and eggs together in bowl. Add to oats mixture. Stir in blueberries, 1/8 teaspoon cinnamon and nutmeg. Spoon into greased giant muffin cups. Sprinkle with mixture of 2 tablespoons sugar and 1/4 teaspoon cinnamon. Bake at 400 degrees for 18 to 22 minutes or until golden brown and muffins test done. May substitute chopped strawberries or peaches for blueberries. **Yield:** 6 servings.

Approx Per Serving: Cal 451; Prot 7 g; Carbo 60 g; Fiber 2 g; T Fat 21 g; 41% Calories from Fat; Chol 71 mg; Sod 231 mg.

Mandarin Muffins

1/2 cup butter, softened
1 cup packed brown sugar
3 eggs
1 1/2 cups flour
1 1/2 cups whole wheat flour
2 teaspoons baking powder
1/8 teaspoon baking soda
1/8 teaspoon salt
1/2 teaspoon vanilla extract
1 cup orange juice
1 11-ounce can mandarin oranges, drained
1 cup chopped walnuts

Cream butter and brown sugar in mixer bowl until light and fluffy. Beat in eggs. Mix flours, baking powder, baking soda and salt together. Add to creamed mixture alternately with mixture of vanilla and orange juice, mixing well after each addition. Cut orange segments into thirds. Fold oranges and walnuts into batter. Spoon into greased muffin cups. Bake at 350 degrees for 18 to 20 minutes or until golden brown. Serve warm. **Yield:** 18 servings.

Approx Per Serving: Cal 246; Prot 5 g; Carbo 35 g; Fiber 2 g; T Fat 11 g; 37% Calories from Fat; Chol 49 mg; Sod 121 mg.

Ragamuffins*

"Wonderful texture"

1 egg, beaten
3/4 cup milk
1 cup raisins
1 apple, chopped
1/2 cup vegetable oil
1 cup flour
1 cup quick-cooking oats
1/3 cup sugar
1 tablespoon baking powder
1 teaspoon salt
1 teaspoon nutmeg
2 teaspoons cinnamon

Combine egg, milk, raisins, apple, oil, flour, oats, sugar, baking powder, salt, nutmeg and cinnamon in bowl; mix just until moistened. Fill greased muffin cups 3/4 full. Bake at 400 degrees for 15 to 20 minutes or until muffins test done. Serve cool or piping hot with butter.
Yield: 12 servings.

Approx Per Serving: Cal 230; Prot 4 g; Carbo 31 g; Fiber 2 g; T Fat 11 g; 41% Calories from Fat; Chol 20 mg; Sod 274 mg.

Raspberry Streusel Muffins

"Company fare"

1 1/2 cups flour
1/4 cup sugar
1/4 cup packed dark brown sugar
2 teaspoons baking powder
1/4 teaspoon salt
1 teaspoon cinnamon
1 egg, beaten
1/2 cup melted butter
1/2 cup milk
1 1/2 cups raspberries
1 teaspoon grated lemon zest
1/2 cup chopped pecans
1/2 cup packed brown sugar
1/4 cup flour
1 teaspoon cinnamon
1 teaspoon grated lemon zest
2 tablespoons melted butter
1/2 cup confectioners' sugar
1 tablespoon lemon juice

Combine 1 1/2 cups flour, sugar, 1/4 cup dark brown sugar, baking powder, salt and 1 teaspoon cinnamon in bowl. Add egg, 1/2 cup butter and milk; mix until moistened. Fold in raspberries and 1 teaspoon lemon zest. Fill paper-lined muffin cups 3/4 full. Combine pecans, 1/2 cup brown sugar, 1/4 cup flour, 1 teaspoon cinnamon, 1 teaspoon lemon zest and 2 tablespoons melted butter in small bowl; mix well. Sprinkle over filled muffin cups. Bake at 350 degrees for 20 to 25 minutes or until golden brown and muffins test done. Blend confectioners' sugar with lemon juice in bowl. Spoon over warm muffins. **Yield:** 12 servings.

Approx Per Serving: Cal 305; Prot 3 g; Carbo 43 g; Fiber 2 g; T Fat 14 g; 40% Calories from Fat; Chol 45 mg; Sod 198 mg.

Zucchini Muffins

"These are absolutely the best!"

3 eggs, beaten
1 cup vegetable oil
1 cup sugar
1/3 cup molasses
2 cups grated zucchini
2 teaspoons vanilla extract
1 teaspoon lemon extract
2 cups sifted flour
2 teaspoons baking soda
1/4 teaspoon baking powder
3 1/2 teaspoons cinnamon
1/2 teaspoon nutmeg
1 cup raisins
1 cup chopped walnuts
1/2 cup coconut

Combine first 7 ingredients in bowl; mix well. Add mixture of flour, baking soda, baking powder, cinnamon and nutmeg; mix well. Stir in raisins, walnuts and coconut. Fill greased muffin cups 2/3 full. Bake at 350 degrees for 20 minutes or until brown. **Yield:** 24 servings.

Approx Per Serving: Cal 232; Prot 3 g; Carbo 26 g; Fiber 1 g; T Fat 14 g; 52% Calories from Fat; Chol 27 mg; Sod 88 mg.

Cheese Puff Ring

"This popover-type bread is good served at brunch or lunch."

1 cup milk
1/4 cup butter
1/2 teaspoon salt
Pepper to taste
1 cup flour
4 eggs
1 cup shredded Swiss cheese

Combine milk, butter, salt and pepper in large saucepan. Bring to a full boil. Add flour all at once. Cook over medium heat for 2 minutes or until mixture forms ball, stirring constantly; remove from heat. Add eggs 1 at a time, beating well after each addition. Beat in half the cheese. Spoon 3/4 of the dough into 8 equal mounds shaping ring with mounds just touching. Top each large mound with small mound of remaining dough. Sprinkle with remaining cheese. Bake at 375 degrees for 55 minutes or until lightly browned and crisp. Serve hot. May be wrapped, frozen and reheated in foil. **Yield:** 8 servings.

Approx Per Serving: Cal 219; Prot 10 g; Carbo 14 g; Fiber <1 g; T Fat 14 g; 56% Calories from Fat; Chol 139 mg; Sod 266 mg.

Keep flour in a muffineer or sugar shaker to dust pastry boards or baking pans easily.

Gullifty's Golden Cheese Popovers*

2/3 cup flour
1/4 teaspoon salt
1/3 cup each milk and water
2 eggs
1/4 cup shredded Cheddar cheese
1 1/2 tablespoons melted shortening

Mix flour and salt in bowl. Stir in milk and water gradually. Add eggs; beat until smooth. Fold in cheese. Pour shortening into four 6-ounce custard cups. Preheat on baking sheet in 375-degree oven. Fill 2/3 full. Bake at 375 degrees for 45 to 50 minutes or until puffed and golden. Remove from cups; serve immediately. **Yield:** 4 servings.

Approx Per Serving: Cal 198; Prot 8 g; Carbo 17 g; Fiber 1 g; T Fat 11 g; 50% Calories from Fat; Chol 117 mg; Sod 220 mg.

Lemon Popovers*

1 cup flour
1/2 teaspoon salt
1 tablespoon sugar
1 teaspoon grated lemon zest
1 cup milk
2 eggs

Combine all ingredients in mixer bowl; beat until smooth. Fill greased 4-ounce popover or muffin cups 3/4 full. Bake at 425 degrees for 40 to 45 minutes or until golden brown. Serve immediately. **Yield:** 6 servings.

Approx Per Serving: Cal 135; Prot 6 g; Carbo 20 g; Fiber 1 g; T Fat 3 g; 23% Calories from Fat; Chol 77 mg; Sod 218 mg.

Crescent Rolls

1 envelope dry yeast
1/4 cup warm water
1/2 cup butter
1 cup milk
1/3 cup sugar
3 eggs, beaten
4 cups flour

Dissolve yeast in water in large bowl. Melt butter with milk in saucepan. Cool to lukewarm. Add milk mixture, sugar and eggs to yeast. Add flour gradually, mixing well. Place in greased bowl, turning to coat surface. Let rise, covered, until doubled in bulk. Punch dough down. Let rise until doubled in bulk. Divide into 4 portions on floured surface. Roll into 9-inch circles; cut each into 8 wedges. Roll up from wide end; place on greased baking sheet. Let rise until almost doubled in bulk. Bake at 375 degrees for 12 to 15 minutes or until golden. **Yield:** 32 servings.

Approx Per Serving: Cal 103; Prot 3 g; Carbo 14 g; Fiber <1 g; T Fat 4 g; 34% Calories from Fat; Chol 29 mg; Sod 34 mg.

BRUNCH

Adobe Eggs

"The Southwest flavor combination surprises guests."

1 pound bulk sausage
1/4 teaspoon Tabasco sauce
8 ounces mushrooms, sliced
6 eggs
1 cup sour cream
3 tablespoons chopped green onions
1 tablespoon chopped parsley
1/2 teaspoon cumin
1/2 teaspoon salt
Pepper to taste
8 ounces Monterey Jack cheese, shredded
1 4-ounce can chopped green chilies, drained
1/2 cup thick and chunky salsa
1 cup shredded sharp Cheddar cheese

Brown sausage in skillet, stirring until crumbly. Add Tabasco sauce and mushrooms. Cook until mushrooms are tender, stirring frequently; drain. Combine eggs and sour cream in mixer bowl; beat well. Add green onions, parsley, cumin, salt and pepper; mix well. Pour into greased 9x13-inch baking dish. Bake at 350 degrees for 10 to 15 minutes or until softly set, stirring several times from outside edge to center. Reduce heat to 325 degrees. Sprinkle eggs with Monterey Jack cheese; top with chilies. Spoon sausage mixture over chilies. Sprinkle with salsa and Cheddar cheese. Bake for 30 minutes. Let stand for 5 to 10 minutes at room temperature. Cut into servings. **Yield:** 8 servings.

Approx Per Serving: Cal 399; Prot 22 g; Carbo 5 g; Fiber 1 g; T Fat 32 g; 73% Calories from Fat; Chol 235 mg; Sod 900 mg.

Artichoke and Sausage Frittata

"Very flavorful and tasty brunch entrée"

1 large yellow onion, chopped
1 small red bell pepper, finely chopped
1 large clove of garlic, minced
3 tablespoons margarine
3/4 to 1 pound Italian sausage
1 14-ounce can artichoke hearts, drained
8 large eggs
1/2 cup half and half
1/2 teaspoon salt
1/2 teaspoon pepper
1/2 teaspoon basil
1/2 teaspoon oregano
1 cup shredded aged provolone cheese
1/2 cup grated Parmesan cheese

Cook onion, red pepper and garlic in margarine in skillet until vegetables are tender. Spread in bottom of greased 2-quart shallow baking dish. Remove casing from sausage. Brown sausage in skillet, stirring until crumbly; drain. Cut artichoke hearts into halves. Layer sausage and artichokes over vegetables. Combine eggs and half and half in mixer bowl; beat well. Add salt, pepper, basil and oregano; mix well. Stir in provolone cheese and Parmesan cheese. Pour over artichokes. Bake at 375 degrees for 40 to 50 minutes or until set. Let stand at room temperature for 5 minutes. Cut into servings. **Yield:** 8 servings.

Approx Per Serving: Cal 335; Prot 19 g; Carbo 7 g; Fiber <1 g; T Fat 26 g; 69% Calories from Fat; Chol 254 mg; Sod 946 mg.

Eggs in-a-Basket*

18 frozen patty shells
18 eggs
18 slices Canadian bacon, fried
6 cups Hollandaise sauce

Bake pastry shells using package directions, underbaking slightly. Let stand until cool. Scoop middle dough out carefully. Arrange shells on large baking sheet. Break 1 egg into each. Bake at 300 degrees for 30 minutes or until eggs are set. Place each shell on slice of Canadian bacon on serving plate. Top with Hollandaise sauce. **Yield:** 18 servings.

Approx Per Serving: Cal 661; Prot 19 g; Carbo 17 g; Fiber 1 g; T Fat 53 g; 77% Calories from Fat; Chol 576 mg; Sod 1286 mg.

Christmas Breakfast

"Definitely makes your holiday breakfast special"

8 slices raisin bread, crusts trimmed
8 ounces Cheddar cheese, shredded
6 eggs
3 cups milk or part mixture of milk and eggnog
1/2 teaspoon salt
1/4 teaspoon pepper
1 teaspoon dry mustard
8 ounces bacon, partially cooked

Crumble bread into bowl. Add cheese; mix well. Spread in greased 9x13-inch baking dish. Beat eggs and milk in mixer bowl. Add salt, pepper and mustard. Pour over bread mixture; arrange partially cooked bacon slices over top. Chill, covered, in refrigerator overnight. Bake, uncovered, at 350 degrees for 50 minutes or until set. Serve immediately. **Yield:** 10 servings.

Approx Per Serving: Cal 272; Prot 15 g; Carbo 14 g; Fiber <1 g; T Fat 18 g; 58% Calories from Fat; Chol 167 mg; Sod 492 mg.

Crab Strata

"A variation of the classic egg and cheese strata"

2 teaspoons butter, softened
2 tablespoons bread crumbs
8 slices white bread, crusts trimmed
8 ounces mushrooms, sliced
1/4 cup sliced green onions
1/4 cup Madeira
8 ounces crab meat
2 1/2 cups milk
4 eggs
2 cups shredded Swiss or Cheddar cheese
1/2 teaspoon salt
1/2 teaspoon dry mustard
Freshly ground pepper to taste

Butter 2-quart soufflé dish; coat with bread crumbs. Cut bread into cubes. Sauté mushrooms and green onions in Madeira in skillet over medium heat. Stir in crab meat. Remove from heat. Alternate layers of bread cubes and crab meat mixture in baking dish, ending with bread cubes. Process milk, eggs, cheese, salt, mustard and pepper in blender until well blended. Pour gradually over layers. Chill, covered, overnight. Bake, uncovered, at 325 degrees for 1 to 1 1/2 hours or until knife inserted near center comes out clean. **Yield:** 6 servings.

Approx Per Serving: Cal 429; Prot 30 g; Carbo 27 g; Fiber 2 g; T Fat 21 g; 45% Calories from Fat; Chol 232 mg; Sod 667 mg.

Four-Way Egg Bake

"Cook's choice"

1 pound sausage or 1 pound chopped ham
1 10-ounce package frozen chopped spinach or broccoli
12 eggs
1/4 cup melted margarine
1 cup sour cream
16 ounces Cheddar cheese, cubed
1 1/2 cups drained, chopped tomatoes
1 small green pepper, finely chopped

Brown sausage in skillet, stirring until crumbly; drain. Cook spinach using package directions; drain. Beat eggs in mixer bowl. Add melted margarine and sour cream; beat well. Fold in cheese, tomatoes, green pepper, sausage and spinach. Pour into greased 9x13-inch baking dish. Bake at 350 degrees for 1 hour. **Yield:** 12 servings.

Approx Per Serving: Cal 384; Prot 21 g; Carbo 5 g; Fiber <1 g; T Fat 31 g; 74% Calories from Fat; Chol 276 mg; Sod 596 mg. Nutritional information is for sausage option.

Eleven O'Clock Casserole*

"This is good anytime."

3 10-ounce packages frozen spinach
4 10-ounce packages Stouffer's frozen Welsh rarebit
2 pounds bacon, crisp-fried, crumbled
2 8-ounce cans sliced water chestnuts, drained
1 3-ounce can French-fried onions

Cook spinach partially using package directions; drain. Thaw rarebit in double boiler over boiling water. Layer 1/3 of the rarebit and all the spinach, bacon and water chestnuts in greased 9x13-inch baking dish. Top with remaining rarebit and French-fried onions. Bake at 325 degrees for 20 minutes. Serve over toasted English muffins. **Yield:** 8 servings.

Approx Per Serving: Cal 572; Prot 27 g; Carbo 26 g; Fiber 4 g; T Fat 41 g; 64% Calories from Fat; Chol 29 mg; Sod 1179 mg.

Goldrush Brunch

"The potatoes give this a hearty breakfast taste."

1 pound frozen hashed brown potatoes
1 tablespoon oil
1/4 cup butter
1/4 cup flour
1/2 teaspoon salt
1/8 teaspoon pepper
2 cups milk
1 cup sour cream
2 tablespoons chopped parsley
8 1/4-inch slices Canadian bacon
8 eggs

Brown potatoes in oil in skillet. Melt butter in 3-quart saucepan. Stir in flour, salt and pepper until well blended. Add milk. Cook until thickened, stirring constantly. Remove from heat. Stir in sour cream, parsley and hashed brown potatoes. Pour into greased 9x13-inch baking dish. Layer Canadian bacon down center of casserole, overlapping slightly. Bake, uncovered, at 350 degrees for 20 minutes. Remove from oven. Make 4 depressions on each side of Canadian bacon. Slip 1 egg carefully into each depression. Bake for 10 to 12 minutes longer or until eggs are set. **Yield:** 8 servings.

Approx Per Serving: Cal 426; Prot 17 g; Carbo 24 g; Fiber 1 g; T Fat 30 g; 63% Calories from Fat; Chol 263 mg; Sod 671 mg.

Ham and Artichoke Casserole

"This is a nice luncheon dish too."

1/4 cup butter
1/4 cup flour
2 cups warm milk
Seasoned salt and cayenne pepper to taste
1/4 teaspoon nutmeg
Paprika and white pepper to taste
2/3 cup mixed shredded Swiss cheese and Parmesan cheese
1/4 cup dry sherry
2 16-ounce cans artichoke hearts, drained
12 thin slices boiled or baked ham

Melt butter in saucepan over medium heat. Blend in flour. Remove from heat. Stir in warm milk. Cook over medium heat until thickened, stirring constantly. Add seasoned salt, cayenne pepper, nutmeg, paprika, white pepper and cheeses. Cook over low heat until cheeses are melted, stirring constantly. Remove from heat. Stir in sherry. Wrap artichoke hearts in ham slices; place seam side down with sides touching in buttered casserole. Pour sauce over rolls. Bake at 350 degrees for 25 to 30 minutes or until brown and bubbly. **Yield:** 6 servings.

Approx Per Serving: Cal 339; Prot 24 g; Carbo 16 g; Fiber <1 g; T Fat 18 g; 50% Calories from Fat; Chol 73 mg; Sod 1346 mg.

Irish Eggs

"Great do-ahead dish"

24 medium eggs
½ cup milk
1 cup butter
Salt, pepper and paprika to taste
2 10-ounce cans cream of mushroom soup
½ cup cream sherry
1 cup sliced canned mushrooms
2 cups shredded Cheddar cheese

Beat eggs with milk in mixer bowl. Scramble egg mixture in butter in skillet. Add salt, pepper and paprika. Combine soup, sherry and mushrooms in bowl; mix well. Layer scrambled eggs and soup mixture in greased 9x13-inch baking dish. Top with cheese; sprinkle with paprika. Chill, covered, in refrigerator overnight. Bake at 250 degrees for 50 minutes. **Yield:** 12 servings.

Approx Per Serving: Cal 467; Prot 18 g; Carbo 10 g; Fiber <1 g; T Fat 37 g; 74% Calories from Fat; Chol 489 mg; Sod 772 mg.

Italian Scramble

"Tastes great. Serve with Italian bread for brunch or midnight snack."

1 medium potato, cut into cubes
1 tablespoon olive oil
8 ounces Italian sausage
1 small onion, chopped
1 small green bell pepper, chopped
1 small red bell pepper, chopped
8 jumbo eggs
2 tablespoons milk
⅛ teaspoon oregano
1 tomato, chopped
¼ cup shredded mozzarella cheese
¼ cup shredded Cheddar cheese
Chopped fresh parsley

Cook potato cubes in hot olive oil in skillet, stirring occasionally. Remove casing from sausage; crumble sausage into potato cubes. Cook until sausage is brown, stirring occasionally. Add onion, green pepper and red pepper. Cook until onion is tender, stirring frequently. Beat eggs with milk and oregano in mixer bowl. Stir in tomato and mozzarella cheese. Add to potato mixture all at once. Cook over low heat until eggs are soft and fluffy, stirring lightly. Spoon into serving dish; top with Cheddar cheese and parsley. **Yield:** 8 servings.

Approx Per Serving: Cal 208; Prot 11 g; Carbo 10 g; Fiber 1 g; T Fat 14 g; 59% Calories from Fat; Chol 231 mg; Sod 281 mg.

Kentucky Splits

"Great Saturday lunch"

1/2 cup butter
1/2 cup flour
3 cups milk
1/2 teaspoon salt
2 egg yolks, beaten
1 cup shredded sharp Cheddar cheese
3 English muffins, split, toasted
6 slices cooked chicken or turkey breast
6 tomato slices
6 slices crisp-fried bacon
2 tablespoons brown sugar

Melt butter in saucepan. Add flour. Cook for 2 minutes, stirring constantly. Add milk gradually. Cook over medium heat until thickened, stirring constantly. Add salt; mix well. Stir a small amount of sauce into egg yolks; stir egg yolks into hot mixture. Add cheese, stirring until melted. Layer toasted muffin halves, chicken, tomato slices and bacon in broiler pan. Top with sauce; sprinkle with brown sugar. Broil for 5 minutes or until brown. May bake at 350 degrees for 15 minutes or until brown. Egg yolks may be omitted from sauce. **Yield:** 6 servings.

Approx Per Serving: Cal 519; Prot 24 g; Carbo 32 g; Fiber 1 g; T Fat 32 g; 56% Calories from Fat; Chol 178 mg; Sod 792 mg.

Oeufs en Cocotte

"Nice for company breakfast"

8 ounces fresh mushrooms, sliced
2 tablespoons butter
1 tablespoon lemon juice
6 slices ham or Canadian bacon
6 large eggs
Salt and pepper to taste
6 tablespoons cream
1 cup shredded Cheddar cheese

Sauté mushrooms in butter and lemon juice in skillet for 8 to 10 minutes or until light brown. Layer 1 slice ham, 1 heaping tablespoonful sautéed mushrooms, 1 whole egg, salt, pepper and 1 tablespoon cream in each of 6 greased ramekins. Sprinkle each with cheese. Bake at 425 degrees for 6 to 8 minutes or until eggs are set. **Yield:** 6 servings.

Approx Per Serving: Cal 294; Prot 19 g; Carbo 3 g; Fiber 1 g; T Fat 23 g; 70% Calories from Fat; Chol 279 mg; Sod 601 mg.

Dot egg yolk with butter or margarine before turning fried eggs to keep egg yolk from sticking or breaking.

Healthy Garden Quiche

1/4 cup chopped onion
1 clove of garlic, minced
1 teaspoon diet margarine
8 slices light Cheddar cheese, chopped
2 tablespoons flour
8 ounces egg substitute
1 cup skim milk
1/4 teaspoon Italian seasoning
1/2 cup shredded carrots
1 cup drained, thawed frozen broccoli

Sauté onion with garlic in margarine in skillet until tender. Toss cheese with flour in bowl. Add onion mixture and remaining ingredients; mix well. Pour into lightly oiled 9-inch pie plate. Bake at 350 degrees for 45 minutes or until set. **Yield:** 6 servings.

Approx Per Serving: Cal 182; Prot 18 g; Carbo 9 g; Fiber 1 g; T Fat 8 g; 41% Calories from Fat; Chol 21 mg; Sod 309 mg.

Farmer's Market Quiche

"Wonderful large quiche recipe for buffets—up to 15 servings if baked in 9x13-inch dish."

3/4 cup finely chopped onions
3 tablespoons butter
2 cups sliced, canned artichoke hearts
3 cloves of garlic, minced
Salt and pepper to taste
10 to 20 sun-dried tomato halves
1 tablespoon oil
1/4 cup chopped fresh parsley
1 tablespoon chopped fresh basil
4 eggs
1 cup ricotta cheese
2 cups half and half or cream
1/2 teaspoon salt
1/4 teaspoon pepper
1 1/2 cups grated Fontina cheese
1/3 cup grated Parmesan cheese
4 slices crisp-fried bacon, crumbled
2 baked 9 or 10-inch pie shells

Sauté onions in butter in skillet until tender. Add artichoke hearts. Sauté over medium heat until golden brown. Stir in garlic, salt and pepper to taste. Plump sun-dried tomato halves in a small amount of hot water. Sauté lightly in oil in skillet. Cut into strips. Add half the tomatoes to artichoke mixture. Combine parsley and basil in bowl; mix well. Beat eggs in mixer bowl. Add ricotta cheese gradually. Add half and half, 1/2 teaspoon salt and 1/4 teaspoon pepper; mix well. Layer half the Fontina cheese, half the Parmesan cheese, artichoke mixture, crumbled bacon, parsley mixture, egg mixture and remaining cheeses in baked pie shells. Swirl lightly with fork to mix layers. Garnish with remaining tomato strips. Bake at 375 degrees for 15 minutes. Reduce oven temperature to 325 degrees. Bake for 35 to 45 minutes longer or until centers are set. Let stand for 15 minutes before serving. **Yield:** 16 servings.

Approx Per Serving: Cal 312; Prot 10 g; Carbo 18 g; Fiber 2 g; T Fat 23 g; 65% Calories from Fat; Chol 93 mg; Sod 399 mg.

Spinach and Sausage Brunch Casserole

"This cuts beautifully."

1 pound bulk Italian sausage
1 cup chopped onions
1 7-ounce jar mild roasted red peppers, drained
1 10-ounce package frozen chopped spinach, thawed, drained
1 cup flour
1/4 cup grated Parmesan cheese
1/2 teaspoon salt
1 tablespoon chopped fresh basil
8 eggs
2 cups milk
4 ounces provolone cheese, shredded

Brown sausage with onions in skillet, stirring frequently; drain. Layer sausage mixture, half the red peppers and spinach in greased 9x13-inch baking dish. Mix flour, Parmesan cheese, salt and basil together. Beat eggs and milk in mixer bowl. Add flour mixture gradually, beating well after each addition. Pour over spinach. Bake at 425 degrees for 20 to 25 minutes or until knife inserted in center comes out clean. Top with remaining red peppers and provolone cheese. Bake at 425 degrees for 1 to 2 minutes or until cheese is melted. Let stand at room temperature for 5 minutes. Cut into squares. May refrigerate casserole for up to 2 hours before baking. **Yield:** 8 servings.

Approx Per Serving: Cal 356; Prot 21 g; Carbo 21 g; Fiber 2 g; T Fat 21 g; 53% Calories from Fat; Chol 255 mg; Sod 775 mg.

Sausage Stroganoff

"Serve this over toast points or rice."

1 clove of garlic
2 pounds hot bulk sausage
3 tablespoons flour
2 cups milk
2 large onions, chopped
1 8-ounce jar sliced mushrooms, drained
1/4 cup butter
2 teaspoons soy sauce
2 tablespoons Worcestershire sauce
Salt and pepper to taste
2 cups sour cream

Rub large skillet with garlic. Brown sausage in skillet, stirring until crumbly; drain. Sprinkle flour over sausage. Add milk. Cook until thickened, stirring constantly. Sauté onions and mushrooms in butter in skillet. Add to sausage mixture. Add soy sauce, Worcestershire sauce, salt and pepper. Cook until mixture bubbles, stirring constantly. Remove from heat. Stir in sour cream. May be frozen before adding sour cream; thaw. Reheat before adding sour cream. **Yield:** 6 servings.

Approx Per Serving: Cal 588; Prot 21 g; Carbo 17 g; Fiber 2 g; T Fat 49 g; 74% Calories from Fat; Chol 124 mg; Sod 1335 mg.

Soufflé Supreme*

2 pounds small curd cottage cheese
6 eggs, beaten
6 tablespoons flour
1 6-ounce can solid white water-pack tuna, drained
1/2 cup butter, chopped
1 12-ounce package frozen spinach soufflé, thawed
1 cup shredded sharp Cheddar cheese

Combine cottage cheese, eggs, flour, tuna, butter and spinach soufflé in bowl; mix gently. Pour into buttered 9x13-inch casserole. Top with Cheddar cheese. Bake at 350 degrees for 1 to 1 1/4 hours or until set.
Yield: 8 servings.

Approx Per Serving: Cal 451; Prot 33 g; Carbo 9 g; Fiber 1 g; T Fat 31 g; 63% Calories from Fat; Chol 292 mg; Sod 1010 mg.

Fresh Salmon Hash

"Serve this with Cheese Puff Ring (page 120)."

1 medium potato, peeled, sliced
1 tablespoon unsalted butter
1 tablespoon safflower oil
1 tablespoon unsalted butter
1 large clove of garlic, minced
1/2 cup finely chopped onion
1/3 cup finely chopped celery
2 tablespoons finely chopped green bell pepper
2 tablespoons chopped pimento
6 tablespoons whipping cream
1/2 teaspoon salt
1/4 teaspoon white pepper
1/4 cup minced fresh parsley
10 ounces cooked, flaked salmon
1 tablespoon unsalted butter
1 tablespoon safflower oil

Cook potato in a small amount of water in saucepan for 5 to 6 minutes or until tender-crisp; drain. Rinse under cold water; pat dry. Chop potato slices finely. Melt 1 tablespoon butter with 1 tablespoon oil in heavy 8-inch skillet. Add potatoes. Cook for 2 to 3 minutes or until crisp and golden brown, stirring frequently. Remove to bowl. Melt 1 tablespoon butter in skillet. Add garlic, onion, celery, green pepper and pimento. Sauté for 6 minutes or until vegetables are tender, stirring occasionally. Remove to bowl with potatoes; mix well. Add cream, salt and white pepper; mix well. Cool to room temperature. Add parsley and salmon; mix well. Chill, covered, in refrigerator for up to 24 hours. Sauté salmon hash in remaining 1 tablespoon butter and 1 tablespoon oil in skillet for 4 minutes or until crisp and golden brown. Serve immediately.
Yield: 6 servings.

Approx Per Serving: Cal 276; Prot 14 g; Carbo 8 g; Fiber 1 g; T Fat 21 g; 68% Calories from Fat; Chol 77 mg; Sod 223 mg.

Sunrise Soufflé

"Wonderful company breakfast. Sausage can be substituted for ham."

3/4 to 1 pound sugar cured ham, chopped
6 green onions, chopped
8 ounces fresh mushrooms, sliced
1/4 cup margarine
1/2 cup flour
1/4 teaspoon pepper
1/4 teaspoon thyme
4 cups milk
1 cup shredded Swiss cheese
12 jumbo eggs, beaten
1/4 teaspoon salt
3/4 cup milk
1/4 cup margarine

Sauté ham, green onions and mushrooms in 1/4 cup margarine in large skillet. Sprinkle with flour, pepper and thyme. Add 4 cups milk gradually, mixing well. Cook until thickened, stirring constantly. Remove from heat. Add cheese. Cover and set aside. Combine eggs, salt and 3/4 cup milk in bowl; beat well. Scramble egg mixture in 1/4 cup margarine in skillet. Do not overcook. Layer half the sauce, scrambled eggs and remaining sauce in buttered 3-quart casserole. Bake at 350 degrees for 20 to 25 minutes or until set. **Yield:** 8 servings.

Approx Per Serving: Cal 490; Prot 34 g; Carbo 16 g; Fiber 1 g; T Fat 32 g; 59% Calories from Fat; Chol 383 mg; Sod 1155 mg.

Brunch Tostada

"Make to order for your family with different toppings."

6 flour tortillas
12 eggs, scrambled
1 cup shredded Cheddar cheese
6 to 10 slices crisp-fried bacon, crumbled
1 medium onion, finely chopped
1 4-ounce can chopped green chilies, drained
1 cup guacamole dip or mashed avocado
1/4 cup sliced pitted black olives
6 tablespoons sour cream
1 8-ounce jar salsa

Wrap tortillas in foil. Heat in 350-degree oven for 15 minutes. Arrange warm tortillas on lightly greased baking sheet. Layer scrambled eggs, cheese, bacon, onion, green chilies, guacamole dip and olives on each tortilla. Bake at 350 degrees for 5 to 10 minutes or until heated through. Top each with 1 tablespoon sour cream. Serve with salsa. Tortillas can be wrapped in plastic wrap and microwaved on High for 1 to 2 minutes. **Yield:** 6 servings.

Approx Per Serving: Cal 539; Prot 26 g; Carbo 30 g; Fiber 2 g; T Fat 36 g; 60% Calories from Fat; Chol 460 mg; Sod 1071 mg.

Blintz Casserole

"Serve this with fresh fruit."

1 cup melted margarine
1/2 cup (scant) sugar
2 eggs
1 cup sifted flour
1 tablespoon baking powder
1/8 teaspoon salt
1/4 cup milk
1 teaspoon vanilla extract
16 ounces ricotta cheese
8 ounces cream cheese, softened
2 eggs
1/2 to 3/4 cup sugar
1/8 teaspoon salt
1/4 cup lemon juice

Combine margarine, scant 1/2 cup sugar and 2 eggs in mixer bowl; beat well. Mix flour, baking powder and salt together. Add to batter; beat well. Add milk and vanilla; mix well. Combine ricotta cheese and cream cheese in bowl; mix well. Add 2 eggs, 1/2 cup sugar, salt and lemon juice; mix well. Layer half the batter, all the cheese mixture and remaining batter in buttered 9x13-inch baking dish. Bake at 300 degrees for 1 1/2 hours. **Yield:** 6 servings.

Approx Per Serving: Cal 837; Prot 18 g; Carbo 63 g; Fiber 1 g; T Fat 58 g; 61% Calories from Fat; Chol 223 mg; Sod 837 mg.

Grand Marnier French Toast

"This makes friends and family feel special."

1 1-pound loaf unsliced white or French bread
4 eggs
1 cup milk
2 tablespoons Grand Marnier
1 tablespoon sugar
1/2 teaspoon vanilla extract
1/4 teaspoon salt
1/4 teaspoon freshly grated orange rind
Oil for frying
3 tablespoons melted butter
1 cup sifted confectioners' sugar
1 orange, thinly sliced

Cut bread into eight 3/4-inch slices. Beat eggs with milk in mixer bowl. Add liqueur, sugar, vanilla, salt and orange rind; beat well. Dip each slice of bread into egg mixture until coated. Place in buttered shallow dish. Pour remaining egg mixture over bread. Chill, covered, overnight. Cook bread in hot oil in skillet, turning to brown on both sides. Brush with melted butter; sprinkle with confectioners' sugar. Garnish with orange slice. Serve immediately with maple syrup. **Yield:** 4 servings.

Approx Per Serving: Cal 646; Prot 18 g; Carbo 94 g; Fiber 3 g; T Fat 21 g; 29% Calories from Fat; Chol 245 mg; Sod 877 mg. Nutritional information does not include oil for frying.

Banana Fritters

"These are a wonderful addition to a breakfast buffet."

4 medium firm bananas
Juice of 1/2 lemon
2 tablespoons confectioners' sugar
1/2 cup baking mix (Bisquick)
1 tablespoon sugar
1 egg
1/4 cup milk
Oil for deep frying

Cut each banana into thirds; sprinkle with lemon juice and confectioners' sugar. Let stand at room temperature for 20 minutes. Combine baking mix, sugar, egg and milk in mixer bowl; beat well. Dip banana chunks into batter. Deep-fry several at a time in 375-degree oil until brown; drain. Serve with fruit sauce or maple syrup. **Yield:** 6 servings.

Approx Per Serving: Cal 153; Prot 3 g; Carbo 30 g; Fiber 2 g; T Fat 3 g; 18% Calories from Fat; Chol 37 mg; Sod 149 mg. Nutritional information does not include oil for deep frying.

Apple Oven Pancake

"Top with syrup or sour cream."

4 cooking apples, peeled, cored
3 tablespoons butter
3 tablespoons sugar
1 teaspoon cinnamon
3 tablespoons flour
1/4 teaspoon baking powder
Salt to taste
3 tablespoons milk
2 egg yolks, beaten
2 egg whites
3 tablespoons sugar

Cut apples into 1/4-inch slices. Melt butter in heavy ovenproof skillet. Add mixture of 3 tablespoons sugar and cinnamon; mix well. Arrange apples evenly in skillet. Cook over medium heat for 5 minutes. Combine flour, baking powder, salt, milk and egg yolks in mixer bowl; beat well. Beat egg whites in mixer bowl until soft peaks form. Add 3 tablespoons sugar gradually, beating until stiff peaks form. Fold into batter. Pour over apples. Bake in skillet in 400-degree oven for 10 minutes. Invert onto warm serving plate. **Yield:** 4 servings.

Approx Per Serving: Cal 289; Prot 4 g; Carbo 43 g; Fiber 3 g; T Fat 12 g; 37% Calories from Fat; Chol 131 mg; Sod 127 mg.

Blueberry Yogurt Pancakes

1 cup flour
1 tablespoon sugar
1 teaspoon baking powder
1/2 teaspoon baking soda
1/4 teaspoon salt
1/8 teaspoon nutmeg
1 egg
1/2 cup plain yogurt
1/2 cup milk
2 tablespoons oil
3/4 cup fresh or unsweetened frozen blueberries

Mix flour, sugar, baking powder, baking soda, salt and nutmeg in bowl. Combine egg, yogurt and milk in mixer bowl; beat well. Add oil; beat well. Add flour mixture, stirring just until combined. Batter may be a little lumpy. Pour 1/4 cup at a time on hot greased griddle. Sprinkle each pancake with several blueberries. Bake until bubbles appear on surface and underside is golden brown. Turn pancake over. Bake until golden brown. Serve hot with butter and maple syrup. **Yield:** 2 servings.

Approx Per Serving: Cal 517; Prot 14 g; Carbo 68 g; Fiber 3 g; T Fat 21 g; 37% Calories from Fat; Chol 122 mg; Sod 727 mg.

Double Corn and Chili Pancakes

"Try salsa or syrup with these different pancakes."

1 1/2 cups yellow cornmeal
1/2 cup flour
2 tablespoons baking powder
1/2 teaspoon salt
1/4 teaspoon freshly ground pepper
6 large eggs
2 cups milk
1/2 cup melted unsalted butter
4 cups frozen whole kernel corn
1 4-ounce can chopped green chilies, drained
1/2 cup coarsely chopped roasted red peppers

Mix cornmeal, flour, baking powder, salt and pepper in bowl. Whisk eggs in large bowl. Add milk and melted butter; whisk to blend. Add cornmeal mixture, stirring just until mixed. Fold in corn, green chilies and red peppers. Pour 1/4 cup at a time on hot oiled griddle. Bake until brown on both sides, turning once. May keep warm in 200-degree oven for up to 30 minutes. **Yield:** 4 servings.

Approx Per Serving: Cal 793; Prot 24 g; Carbo 97 g; Fiber 11 g; T Fat 36 g; 40% Calories from Fat; Chol 398 mg; Sod 1128 mg.

Spread hot pancakes with cream cheese instead of butter, and add your favorite syrup.

Maple Bacon Oven Pancake

"It goes far and is very tasty."

$1^1/_2$ cups baking mix
2 eggs
$^1/_4$ cup maple syrup
1 teaspoon sugar
$^3/_4$ cup milk
$1^1/_2$ cups shredded Cheddar cheese
12 slices crisp-fried bacon, crumbled

Combine baking mix, eggs, maple syrup, sugar and milk in mixer bowl; beat well. Stir in half the cheese. Pour into greased 9x13-inch baking dish. Bake at 350 degrees for 10 to 15 minutes or until wooden pick inserted near center comes out clean. Sprinkle with remaining cheese and crumbled bacon. Bake for 3 to 5 minutes longer or until cheese is melted. Serve with maple syrup. **Yield:** 12 servings.

Approx Per Serving: Cal 202; Prot 8 g; Carbo 16 g; Fiber 0 g; T Fat 12 g; 52% Calories from Fat; Chol 58 mg; Sod 406 mg.

Sourdough Hotcakes

2 cups flour
2 cups warm water
1 envelope dry yeast
2 eggs
1 teaspoon baking soda
1 teaspoon salt
1 tablespoon sugar
2 tablespoons oil

Combine flour, warm water and yeast in glass bowl; mix well. Let stand, covered, in warm place overnight. Add eggs, baking soda, salt, sugar and oil; mix well with fork. Do not beat. Drop by tablespoonfuls onto hot griddle. Bake until brown on both sides, turning once. **Yield:** 6 servings.

Approx Per Serving: Cal 229; Prot 7 g; Carbo 34 g; Fiber 1 g; T Fat 7 g; 27% Calories from Fat; Chol 71 mg; Sod 517 mg.

Crisp Waffles

2 cups baking mix
1 egg
$^1/_2$ cup vegetable oil
$1^1/_3$ cups club soda

Combine baking mix, egg, oil and club soda in bowl; mix well with wire whisk. Bake batter in hot waffle iron using manufacturer's instructions. Serve with favorite topping. **Yield:** 4 servings.

Approx Per Serving: Cal 533; Prot 6 g; Carbo 42 g; Fiber 0 g; T Fat 38 g; 64% Calories from Fat; Chol 53 mg; Sod 828 mg.

Meats & Poultry

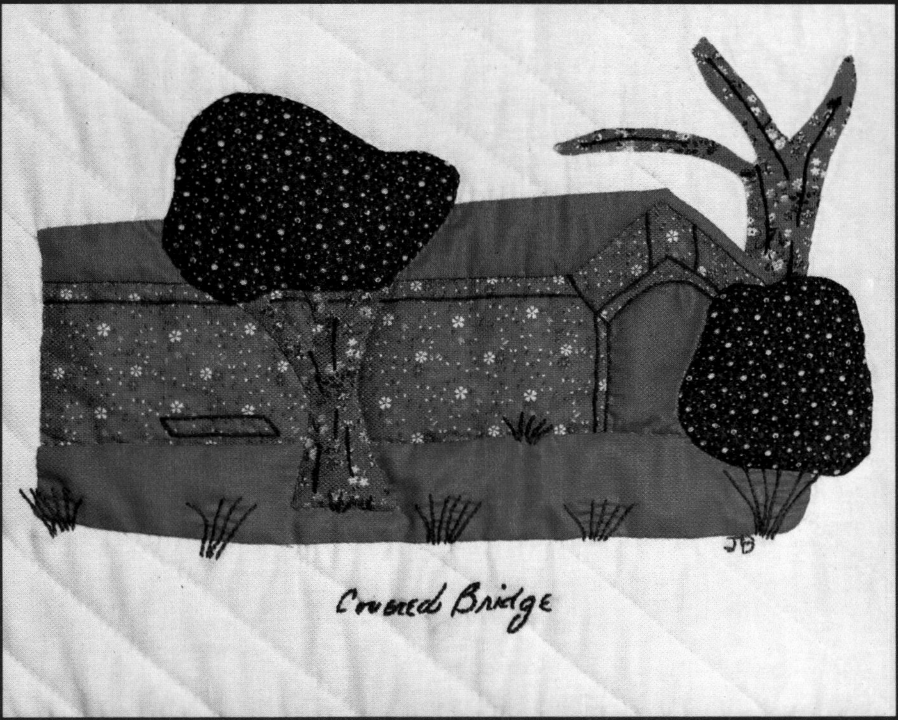

Covered Bridge

Charity Ball
Elegant Dinner

MEATS

Mushroom-Stuffed Beef Tenderloin

3/4 cup Marsala
1/4 cup minced onion
1/4 cup olive oil
2 tablespoons red wine vinegar
1/2 teaspoon salt
1/2 teaspoon pepper
1 5 to 6-pound trimmed beef tenderloin
1 pound fresh mushrooms, sliced
1/3 cup sliced scallions
2 cloves of garlic, minced
3 tablespoons butter or margarine
1/2 cup Marsala
1 1/2 cups soft whole wheat bread crumbs
Garlic salt and pepper to taste
8 slices bacon

Combine 3/4 cup wine, onion, olive oil, vinegar, salt and 1/2 teaspoon pepper in bowl; mix well. Place tenderloin in shallow dish; pour in marinade. Marinate, covered, in refrigerator for 8 hours, turning occasionally. Sauté mushrooms, scallions and garlic in butter in skillet until mushrooms are tender. Add 1/2 cup wine. Simmer until liquid evaporates. Remove from heat. Add bread crumbs; mix well. Remove tenderloin from marinade. Make a cut lengthwise down center of beef to within 1/2 inch of bottom side. Open beef to form rectangle. Spoon stuffing onto 1 side of beef; fold up other side to enclose stuffing. Tie with string at 2-inch intervals. Sprinkle with garlic salt and pepper to taste. Place seam side down on rack in roasting pan. Bake, uncovered, at 425 degrees for 30 minutes. Remove string. Arrange bacon in crisscross pattern over beef. Secure ends of beef with wooden picks. Bake for 20 minutes longer or to 140 degrees on meat thermometer for rare, 150 degrees for medium. Remove wooden picks. **Yield:** 10 servings.

Approx Per Serving: Cal 543; Prot 54 g; Carbo 10 g; Fiber 1 g; T Fat 27 g; 45% Calories from Fat; Chol 167 mg; Sod 339 mg.

Filet of Beef Stuffed with Spinach

"A wonderful combination"

1 5-pound beef tenderloin
1 cup butter, softened
2 cloves of garlic, minced
3 eggs, beaten
1 pound fresh spinach, cooked, drained
1 cup fresh bread crumbs
1/2 to 1 pound bacon

Trim fat from tenderloin. Make a lengthwise cut down center of beef, cutting within 1/2 inch of bottom side. Open beef; pound with meat mallet to flatten into rectangle. Combine butter and garlic in bowl; mix well. Spread over beef. Combine eggs, spinach and bread crumbs in bowl; mix well. Spoon onto beef. Roll from long side to enclose spinach stuffing; tie with string. Place seam side down on rack in shallow roasting pan. Cut bacon slices into halves. Lay over beef, tucking ends underneath. Bake at 400 degrees for 50 minutes for rare meat. Serve hot or cool to room temperature. **Yield:** 10 servings.

Approx Per Serving: Cal 612; Prot 51 g; Carbo 9 g; Fiber 2 g; T Fat 40 g; 60% Calories from Fat; Chol 253 mg; Sod 571 mg.

Tenderloin Deluxe*

"A dinner to impress!"

2 tablespoons butter, softened
1 2-pound beef tenderloin
1/4 cup chopped green onions
2 tablespoons butter
2 tablespoons soy sauce
1 teaspoon Dijon mustard
Pepper to taste
3/4 cup dry sherry

Spread 2 tablespoons butter over tenderloin. Place on rack in shallow roasting pan. Bake, uncovered, at 400 degrees for 20 minutes. Sauté green onions in 2 tablespoons butter in skillet until soft. Add soy sauce, mustard, pepper and sherry. Heat just to the boiling point, stirring frequently. Pour over tenderloin. Bake for 20 to 25 minutes longer for rare to medium-rare beef, basting frequently with sauce. Slice tenderloin. Serve with sauce on side. **Yield:** 4 servings.

Approx Per Serving: Cal 460; Prot 43 g; Carbo 2 g; Fiber <1 g; T Fat 25 g; 48% Calories from Fat; Chol 159 mg; Sod 701 mg.

Party Filet*

1/2 to 3/4 cup Dijon mustard
1 4 to 5-pound filet of beef

Spread mustard on trimmed filet. Place on broiler pan. Broil for 15 minutes on each side. Chill, covered, for 6 hours. Bake at 325 degrees for 1 hour. Serve immediately with sauce of your choice. **Yield:** 8 servings.

Approx Per Serving: Cal 390; Prot 54 g; Carbo 2 g; Fiber <1 g; T Fat 17 g; 41% Calories from Fat; Chol 159 mg; Sod 380 mg.

Texas Brisket

"Try this at your next roundup."

4 pounds beef brisket
1/2 5-ounce bottle of liquid smoke
1 10-ounce bottle of Worcestershire sauce
1/2 teaspoon each onion salt, garlic salt, celery salt and seasoned salt
1 18-ounce bottle of hickory-smoke barbecue sauce

Place beef brisket in Dutch oven. Mix next 6 ingredients in bowl. Pour over brisket. Marinate, covered, in refrigerator overnight. Bake in marinade at 275 degrees for 5 to 6 hours or until tender. Remove brisket to platter. Skim fat from pan drippings. Add barbecue sauce; mix well. Bring to a boil over medium heat, stirring frequently. Slice beef cross grain. Serve with sauce on buns. **Yield:** 8 servings.

Approx Per Serving: Cal 368; Prot 44 g; Carbo 13 g; Fiber <1 g; T Fat 15 g; 36% Calories from Fat; Chol 128 mg; Sod 1402 mg.

Bourbon Beef Broil*

"Old grand-dad would love this."

5 ounces soy sauce
2 tablespoons Worcestershire sauce
Juice of 1 lemon
3 tablespoons brown sugar
1/2 cup bourbon
1 or 2 cloves of garlic, minced
1/2 cup water
1 2-pound London broil steak
Pepper to taste

Mix first 7 ingredients in bowl. Place steak in shallow dish. Pour in marinade. Marinate, covered, in refrigerator overnight, turning once. Broil steak on grill or under broiler to desired doneness. Season with pepper to taste. Cut cross grain into thin slices. **Yield:** 6 servings.

Approx Per Serving: Cal 285; Prot 30 g; Carbo 11 g; Fiber <1 g; T Fat 9 g; 27% Calories from Fat; Chol 85 mg; Sod 1449 mg.

Pan-Fried Pepper Strip Steaks*

"An easy elegant entrée"

2 1/2-inch thick 6-ounce sirloin strip steaks
Salt to taste
1/4 teaspoon pepper
1 tablespoon butter
1 tablespoon vegetable oil
2 shallots, peeled, minced
1/3 cup half and half or milk
2 tablespoons prepared horseradish
2 tablespoons Dijon mustard
1/2 teaspoon pepper

Sprinkle steaks with salt and 1/4 teaspoon pepper. Fry in butter and oil in skillet for 3 minutes on each side for rare or to desired degree of doneness. Remove to warm platter; cover. Add shallots to pan drippings in skillet. Sauté for 2 minutes, stirring frequently. Add half and half, horseradish, mustard, 1/2 teaspoon pepper and any drippings from steak platter. Simmer for 2 minutes or until thickened, stirring constantly. Slice steak cross grain. Arrange on serving plate; spoon sauce over steak. Garnish with chives and peppercorns. Serve hot. **Yield:** 2 servings.

Approx Per Serving: Cal 518; Prot 38 g; Carbo 32 g; Fiber 2 g; T Fat 28 g; 47% Calories from Fat; Chol 126 mg; Sod 342 mg.

Herb-Stuffed Flank Steak

1/2 large onion, chopped
1 clove of garlic, minced
2 tablespoons butter
1/2 cup chopped mushrooms
1/4 cup chopped pistachios
1/4 cup chopped parsley
1 1/2 cups soft bread crumbs
3/4 teaspoon poultry seasoning
1/2 teaspoon salt
Pepper to taste
1 egg, slightly beaten
1 2-pound flank steak
1 tablespoon oil
1/2 cup white wine

Sauté onion and garlic in butter in skillet until soft. Add mushrooms. Sauté for 3 minutes. Remove from heat. Add pistachios, parsley, bread crumbs, poultry seasoning, salt, pepper and egg; mix well. Pound steak on both sides with meat mallet. Spread mixture on steak. Roll from short side to enclose stuffing. Tie with string at 2-inch intervals. Brown in oil in Dutch oven. Add wine. Bake, covered, at 350 degrees for 2 hours. Cut into 1-inch slices. Serve with pan drippings. **Yield:** 4 servings.

Approx Per Serving: Cal 518; Prot 48 g; Carbo 13 g; Fiber 2 g; T Fat 28 g; 51% Calories from Fat; Chol 196 mg; Sod 492 mg.

Steak alla Pizzaiolo*

2 cloves of garlic, minced
1 onion, finely chopped
1/4 cup olive oil
2 pounds boneless round steak, cut into cubes
1 teaspoon oregano
1 teaspoon basil
Salt and pepper to taste
1 16-ounce can Italian tomatoes

Sauté garlic and onion in olive oil in large skillet. Add steak. Brown on both sides. Add seasonings; toss gently. Add undrained tomatoes. Simmer for 30 minutes or until steak is tender. **Yield:** 6 servings.

Approx Per Serving: Cal 303; Prot 29 g; Carbo 6 g; Fiber 1 g; T Fat 18 g; 54% Calories from Fat; Chol 85 mg; Sod 170 mg.

Fajitas

1/2 cup fresh lime juice
1/2 cup vegetable oil
1/2 cup Tequila
3 cloves of garlic, minced
1 teaspoon cumin
1/2 teaspoon crushed red pepper
1 teaspoon oregano
2 pounds boneless sirloin steak
12 to 18 flour tortillas, warmed
1 cup tomato salsa
1 cup guacamole
1 cup sour cream

Mix first 7 ingredients in bowl in shallow dish. Add steak. Marinate, covered, in refrigerator for 4 to 6 hours. Cook steak on hot grill for 5 to 10 minutes on each side. Cut cross grain into 1/4-inch slices. Serve in warm tortillas with salsa, guacamole and sour cream. **Yield:** 6 servings.

Approx Per Serving: Cal 929; Prot 39 g; Carbo 77 g; Fiber 4 g; T Fat 49 g; 49% Calories from Fat; Chol 102 mg; Sod 796 mg.

Jim's Texas Chili

2 1/2 pounds steak, cut into small cubes
1/3 cup oil
4 cloves of garlic, minced
1 teaspoon salt
1 to 2 teaspoons pepper
5 to 6 tablespoons chili powder
1/2 cup yellow cornmeal
5 cups boiling water or beef stock
2 tablespoons vinegar
2 beef bouillon cubes

Brown steak in oil in skillet. Stir in seasonings; remove from heat. Stir in cornmeal. Add water, vinegar and bouillon; mix well. Simmer for 1 1/2 hours, stirring frequently. Adjust seasonings. **Yield:** 6 servings.

Approx Per Serving: Cal 401; Prot 37 g; Carbo 10 g; Fiber 1 g; T Fat 23 g; 53% Calories from Fat; Chol 106 mg; Sod 702 mg.

Beef Frederick

"Add a cup of wine for the cook."

2 pounds round steak, cut into cubes
1 cup chopped onion
1 clove of garlic, minced
2 tablespoons flour
1 teaspoon salt
1/2 teaspoon pepper
1 1/2 teaspoons paprika
1/4 teaspoon thyme
1 bay leaf
1 28-ounce can tomatoes
8 ounces fresh mushrooms, sliced
1 cup Burgundy
1 cup sour cream

Combine steak, onion, garlic and flour in slow cooker; mix well until steak is coated with flour. Add salt, pepper, paprika, thyme, bay leaf, tomatoes, mushrooms and wine; mix well. Cook, covered, on Low for 7 to 8 hours, stirring occasionally. Remove bay leaf. Add sour cream. Cook for 30 minutes longer. Serve over hot noodles or rice. **Yield:** 6 servings.

Approx Per Serving: Cal 363; Prot 32 g; Carbo 14 g; Fiber 3 g; T Fat 17 g; 46% Calories from Fat; Chol 102 mg; Sod 641 mg.

Beef with Broccoli and Oyster Sauce

2 teaspoons cornstarch
1/4 teaspoon black pepper
2 tablespoons red wine or dry sherry
1 1/3 pounds beef filet, thinly sliced
Flowerets of 1 bunch broccoli
1/3 cup oil
1 or 2 cloves of garlic, minced
2 or 3 tablespoons oyster sauce
2 tablespoons soy sauce
1 tablespoon lemon juice
1 tablespoon honey
1/2 teaspoon ginger
5 green onions, chopped
5 dried or fresh red chili peppers, chopped

Combine cornstarch, black pepper and red wine in shallow dish; mix well. Cut beef into 1-inch pieces; add to wine mixture, stirring to coat. Marinate, covered, in refrigerator for 15 minutes. Stir-fry broccoli in half the oil in wok or electric skillet at 350 degrees for 2 to 3 minutes or until tender-crisp. Remove to warm bowl. Add remaining oil and garlic to wok. Stir-fry for 30 seconds. Add oyster sauce, soy sauce, lemon juice, honey and ginger; mix well. Add beef. Stir-fry for 3 to 4 minutes. Add onions and chili peppers. Stir-fry for 30 seconds. Add broccoli. Stir-fry for 1 minute or until heated through. **Yield:** 6 servings.

Approx Per Serving: Cal 302; Prot 22 g; Carbo 12 g; Fiber 3 g; T Fat 19 g; 55% Calories from Fat; Chol 57 mg; Sod 433 mg.

"Main Line Poverty" Casserole

1 medium onion, finely chopped
2 cloves of garlic, minced
3 tablespoons olive oil
1 pound lean ground beef
8 whole sun-dried tomatoes packed in oil
1 28-ounce can crushed tomatoes in purée
2 tablespoons oregano
2 teaspoons marjoram
1 14-ounce package ziti
2 eggs
2/3 cup whipping cream
2 cups shredded mozzarella cheese
3 tablespoons Parmesan cheese

Sauté onion and garlic in hot olive oil in skillet for 5 minutes. Add ground beef. Cook until ground beef is brown, stirring until crumbly; drain. Drain sun-dried tomatoes; finely chop. Add sun-dried tomatoes, crushed tomatoes, oregano and marjoram to ground beef. Simmer, uncovered, for 15 minutes, stirring occasionally. Cook ziti using package directions; drain. Whisk eggs and cream together in 3-quart casserole. Add zita; toss to coat. Stir in ground beef mixture and 1 1/2 cups mozzarella cheese. Sprinkle with Parmesan cheese; top with remaining 1/2 cup mozzarella cheese. Bake, uncovered, at 350 degrees for 30 to 40 minutes or until hot and bubbly. **Yield:** 6 servings.

Approx Per Serving: Cal 765; Prot 37 g; Carbo 68 g; Fiber 7 g; T Fat 39 g; 46% Calories from Fat; Chol 187 mg; Sod 495 mg.

Unstuffed Cabbage*

1 pound ground beef
1 onion, chopped
1/2 cup uncooked rice
1 small head cabbage, shredded
Salt and pepper to taste
1 10-ounce can tomato soup
1/2 soup can water

Brown ground beef with onion in skillet, stirring frequently; drain. Layer rice, cabbage, salt and pepper over ground beef. Pour soup and water over all. Simmer, covered, until cabbage is tender.
Yield: 6 servings.

Approx Per Serving: Cal 258; Prot 17 g; Carbo 23 g; Fiber 2 g; T Fat 12 g; 40% Calories from Fat; Chol 49 mg; Sod 379 mg.

Mark cup capacity on bottom of casserole with permanent china marker to take the guesswork out of matching recipes and dishes.

Super Bowl Casserole*

"You too can enjoy the game."

2 pounds ground beef
2 green bell peppers, chopped
2 large onions, chopped
2 cups chopped celery and leaves
2 tablespoons oil
2 4-ounce jars sliced mushrooms
1 10-ounce can tomato soup
1 7-ounce jar green olives, sliced
1 soup can water
1 6-ounce can tomato paste
1 8-ounce can tomato sauce
8 ounces uncooked narrow egg noodles
4 ounces sharp Cheddar cheese, shredded

Brown ground beef in skillet, stirring until crumbly; drain. Sauté green peppers, onions and celery in oil in skillet until soft. Mix with soup, mushrooms, olives, water, tomato paste, tomato sauce, ground beef and uncooked noodles in bowl. Spoon into 2½ to 3-quart casserole. Top with cheese. Bake at 325 degrees for 1 hour. **Yield:** 10 servings.

Approx Per Serving: Cal 421; Prot 25 g; Carbo 29 g; Fiber 3 g; T Fat 25 g; 51% Calories from Fat; Chol 71 mg; Sod 1082 mg.

Nevada Chili

"For hotter chili add more jalapeño peppers. But be careful!"

1½ medium onions, chopped
1 medium green bell pepper, chopped
1 large stalk celery, chopped
2 small cloves of garlic, minced
2 jalapeño peppers, chopped
3 tablespoons vegetable oil
4 pounds lean ground beef
8 tablespoons chili powder
1 tablespoon cumin
2 teaspoons garlic salt
½ teaspoon Tabasco sauce
1 cup beer
1¼ cups water
Salt and pepper to taste
1 14-ounce can stewed tomatoes
1 8-ounce can tomato sauce
1 4-ounce can chopped green chilies
1 bay leaf
1 16-ounce can kidney beans

Sauté first 5 ingredients in oil in skillet. Add ground beef. Cook until ground beef is brown, stirring until crumbly; drain. Add chili powder, cumin, garlic salt, Tabasco sauce, beer, water, salt and pepper; mix well. Let stand for 2 minutes. Add stewed tomatoes, tomato sauce, green chilies and bay leaf. Simmer, covered, for 2¾ hours, skimming off fat and stirring frequently. Stir in kidney beans. Cook for 15 minutes longer. Remove bay leaf. Serve with corn bread. **Yield:** 10 servings.

Approx Per Serving: Cal 505; Prot 38 g; Carbo 19 g; Fiber 6 g; T Fat 31 g; 55% Calories from Fat; Chol 118 mg; Sod 1083 mg.

Meat-Stuffed Eggplant

2 medium eggplant
Salt and pepper to taste
$1^1/_2$ pounds ground beef
2 small cloves of garlic, minced
$^1/_2$ cup grated Parmesan cheese
2 eggs
$^1/_4$ cup chopped parsley
1 cup dry bread crumbs
1 16-ounce can tomatoes, chopped

Cut eggplant into halves lengthwise. Scoop out pulp, leaving 1-inch shell. Chop pulp. Combine with salt to taste and a small amount of water in saucepan. Simmer until very tender, stirring occasionally; drain. Mash in bowl. Cool to room temperature. Blanch eggplant shells in boiling water; drain. Cool to room temperature. Add pepper, ground beef, garlic, Parmesan cheese, eggs, parsley and bread crumbs to mashed eggplant; mix well. Spoon into shells. Place in baking dish. Spoon tomatoes over stuffed eggplant. Bake, wrapped in foil, at 350 degrees for 30 minutes. Remove foil. Bake for 1 hour longer. **Yield:** 6 servings.

Approx Per Serving: Cal 397; Prot 30 g; Carbo 23 g; Fiber 5 g; T Fat 21 g; 47% Calories from Fat; Chol 151 mg; Sod 465 mg.

Spinach Enchilada Casserole

"A winning combination of tastes and textures"

$1^1/_2$ pounds lean ground beef
1 clove of garlic, minced
$^1/_2$ cup chopped onion
Salt and pepper to taste
2 tomatoes, chopped
1 8-ounce can tomato sauce
2 4-ounce cans chopped green chilies
Juice of $^1/_2$ lime
1 tablespoon sugar
1 10-ounce package frozen chopped spinach, thawed, drained
10 6-inch corn tortillas
$^1/_2$ cup melted butter
3 cups shredded Monterey Jack cheese
1 cup sour cream

Brown ground beef with garlic, onion, salt and pepper in skillet, stirring frequently; drain. Add next 6 ingredients; mix well. Simmer, covered, for 10 minutes, stirring occasionally. Cut tortillas into quarters; dip in melted butter. Layer half the tortilla quarters slightly overlapping in greased 9x13-inch baking dish. Layer half the ground beef mixture and cheese over tortillas. Layer remaining tortillas, sour cream, ground beef mixture and cheese on top. Bake at 350 degrees for 30 minutes.
Yield: 8 servings.

Approx Per Serving: Cal 618; Prot 32 g; Carbo 27 g; Fiber 5 g; T Fat 44 g; 63% Calories from Fat; Chol 138 mg; Sod 796 mg.

Sue's "Pasta Fazool"

1/2 pound sweet Italian sausage
1/2 pound hot Italian sausage
1 pound ground beef
4 cloves of garlic, minced
1/2 teaspoon thyme
1 large onion, chopped
1 teaspoon oregano
1 28-ounce can Italian plum tomatoes, drained
2 tablespoons tomato paste
1/4 teaspoon cayenne pepper
1 15-ounce can kidney beans, rinsed, drained
Salt and pepper to taste
1 pound mostaccioli pasta
1/2 cup grated Parmesan cheese
1/4 cup chopped fresh Italian parsley
12 ounces Fontina or provolone cheese, shredded

Remove casings from Italian sausage. Brown sausage and ground beef with garlic, thyme, onion and oregano in skillet, stirring frequently; drain. Chop plum tomatoes. Add tomatoes, tomato paste and cayenne pepper to sausage mixture. Simmer for 5 minutes, stirring occasionally. Add kidney beans, salt and pepper. Cook pasta using package directions; drain. Add pasta, Parmesan cheese and parsley to sauce; mix well. Spoon into greased 9x13-inch baking dish. Sprinkle with Fontina cheese. Bake at 350 degrees for 30 minutes or until hot and bubbly. **Yield:** 8 servings.

Approx Per Serving: Cal 685; Prot 40 g; Carbo 58 g; Fiber 8 g; T Fat 32 g; 42% Calories from Fat; Chol 112 mg; Sod 821 mg.

Sicilian Meat Roll

"Family recipe with a little extra oomph"

2 eggs, beaten
3/4 cup soft bread crumbs
1/2 cup tomato juice
2 tablespoons chopped parsley
1/2 teaspoon oregano
Salt to taste
1/4 teaspoon pepper
1 small clove of garlic, minced
2 pounds ground beef
8 thin slices boiled ham
6 ounces mozzarella cheese, shredded
3 slices mozzarella cheese, cut diagonally

Combine first 8 ingredients in bowl; mix well. Add ground beef; mix well. Pat mixture into 10x12-inch rectangle on waxed paper. Arrange ham slices on top, leaving a small border around edge; sprinkle with shredded cheese. Roll mixture to enclose filling, using waxed paper to lift; press edges and ends to seal. Place meat roll seam-side down in 9x13-inch baking dish. Bake at 350 degrees for 1 1/4 hours or until cooked through. Arrange triangles of cheese on top. Bake until cheese is melted. **Yield:** 8 servings.

Approx Per Serving: Cal 398; Prot 36 g; Carbo 4 g; Fiber <1 g; T Fat 26 g; 59% Calories from Fat; Chol 168 mg; Sod 654 mg.

Beef and Broccoli Scramble*

1 10-ounce package frozen broccoli
1 pound ground beef
1 large onion, chopped
1 4-ounce jar sliced mushrooms, drained
1 tablespoon corn oil
Salt and pepper to taste
1 10-ounce can cream of broccoli soup
6 ounces sharp Cheddar cheese, shredded

Cook broccoli using package directions; drain. Brown ground beef with onion and mushrooms in oil in skillet, stirring frequently; drain. Add salt and pepper. Layer broccoli, ground beef mixture and soup in greased 8-inch baking dish. Sprinkle with cheese. Bake at 350 degrees for 20 minutes. May be microwaved for 5 to 7 minutes. **Yield:** 6 servings.

Approx Per Serving: Cal 448; Prot 25 g; Carbo 19 g; Fiber 2 g; T Fat 31 g; 61% Calories from Fat; Chol 79 mg; Sod 1627 mg.

Mexican Torta

2 cloves of garlic, minced
1 medium onion, chopped
3 tablespoons olive oil
3 small fresh jalapeño peppers, seeded, minced
1 green bell pepper, finely chopped
1 red bell pepper, finely chopped
1½ pounds lean ground beef
2 tablespoons cumin
1 tablespoon chili powder
½ cup fresh lime juice
½ cup dry red wine
½ cup raisins
½ cup slivered almonds, toasted
1 16-ounce can refried beans
2 tablespoons chopped fresh coriander
Salt and pepper to taste
1½ pounds Monterey Jack cheese, thinly sliced

Sauté garlic and onion in oil in skillet for 2 minutes. Add jalapeño, green and red peppers. Sauté for 5 minutes. Add ground beef. Cook until ground beef is brown, stirring until crumbly; drain. Add cumin and chili powder. Cook for 1 minute. Stir in lime juice, wine and raisins. Simmer, uncovered, for 20 minutes. Add almonds, beans, coriander, salt and pepper. Remove from heat. Alternate layers of cheese slices and ground beef mixture in 3-quart soufflé dish, ending with cheese. Cover dish with buttered foil. Place dish in larger baking pan. Pour in hot water to half the depth of dish. Bake at 350 degrees for 50 minutes. Remove dish from water bath. Let stand for 15 minutes. Unmold onto serving dish. Cut into wedges. Serve at once. **Yield:** 8 servings.

Approx Per Serving: Cal 705; Prot 43 g; Carbo 26 g; Fiber 7 g; T Fat 48 g; 61% Calories from Fat; Chol 133 mg; Sod 748 mg.

Deviled Lamb Chops*

1/4 cup olive oil
1 tablespoon lime juice
1 clove of garlic, minced
1/4 teaspoon liquid smoke
1/4 teaspoon hot pepper sauce
8 1-inch thick loin lamb chops
1/4 cup jalapeño jelly
2 red bell peppers, roasted

Mix first 5 ingredients in bowl. Place chops in skillet. Brush both sides with oil mixture. Cook, covered, for 8 minutes on each side or until tender. Place on ovenproof serving dish. Brush with 2 tablespoons jelly. Cut red peppers into 16 strips. Place 2 strips on each chop. Spoon remaining jelly onto chops. Broil until glazed. **Yield:** 4 servings.

Approx Per Serving: Cal 490; Prot 43 g; Carbo 15 g; Fiber 1 g; T Fat 27 g; 51% Calories from Fat; Chol 133 mg; Sod 125 mg.

Grilled Chops with Mustard-Herb Butter*

2 tablespoons Dijon mustard
1 teaspoon dry mustard
Salt and pepper to taste
2 tablespoons butter, softened
4 lamb chops
2 tablespoons chopped parsley
1 tablespoon chopped chives
1 teaspoon lemon juice
2 tablespoons butter, softened

Mix first 5 ingredients in bowl. Spread mixture on both sides of chops. Grill over hot coals for 4 to 6 minutes. Wrap each chop in foil. Grill for 10 to 15 minutes longer or until tender. Combine remaining ingredients in bowl. Brush onto chops just before serving. **Yield:** 4 servings.

Approx Per Serving: Cal 263; Prot 22 g; Carbo 1 g; Fiber <1 g; T Fat 19 g; 65% Calories from Fat; Chol 98 mg; Sod 254 mg.

Ginger Lamb Kabobs*

1/2 cup olive oil
1/2 cup fresh lemon juice
1 clove of garlic, minced
1 small onion, finely chopped
1 teaspoon grated fresh gingerroot
1 1/2 teaspoons salt
2 teaspoons coriander seed
2 teaspoons curry powder
1 teaspoon turmeric
1 crushed cardamom seed
5 to 6 pounds boned leg of lamb

Mix first 10 ingredients in shallow dish. Cut lamb into 1 1/2-inch cubes. Add to marinade. Marinate, covered, in refrigerator overnight. Place on skewers. Grill over hot coals for 8 minutes or until tender. **Yield:** 10 servings.

Approx Per Serving: Cal 416; Prot 45 g; Carbo 2 g; Fiber <1 g; T Fat 24 g; 54% Calories from Fat; Chol 146 mg; Sod 432 mg.

Butterflied Leg of Lamb

1 cup dry red wine
1 tablespoon marjoram
1 tablespoon rosemary
2 bay leaves, crumbled
1 teaspoon seasoned salt
1/4 teaspoon ginger
2 cloves of garlic, minced
3 tablespoons orange marmalade
2 tablespoons red wine vinegar
3/4 to 1 cup beef broth
1 tablespoon minced onion
1 6 to 7-pound leg of lamb, butterflied

Combine red wine, marjoram, rosemary, bay leaves, seasoned salt, ginger, garlic, orange marmalade, vinegar, beef broth and onion in saucepan; mix well. Simmer, uncovered, for 20 minutes, stirring occasionally. Place lamb in shallow roasting pan, fat side down. Pour hot mixture over lamb. Marinate, covered, in refrigerator for 6 to 7 hours, turning frequently. Remove lamb; reserve marinade. Place lamb over hot coals fat side up. Grill for 35 to 45 minutes, turning several times and brushing with marinade. Cut cross grain into very thin slices.
Yield: 8 servings.

Approx Per Serving: Cal 502; Prot 66 g; Carbo 6 g; Fiber <1 g; T Fat 20 g; 35% Calories from Fat; Chol 213 mg; Sod 426 mg.

Grilled Leg of Lamb

1 onion, cut into quarters
3 cloves of garlic, minced
1 1-inch cube fresh ginger, peeled
1/2 jalapeño pepper, seeded
1/4 cup soy sauce
1/4 cup honey
2 tablespoons peanut oil
1 3 1/2 to 3 3/4-pound trimmed, boned leg of lamb, butterflied

Process onion, garlic, ginger and pepper in blender until puréed. Add soy sauce, honey and oil; process until well mixed. Place leg of lamb in plastic bag. Pour in marinade, turning to coat both sides; seal bag. Marinate in refrigerator overnight, turning several times. Remove lamb; reserve marinade. Place lamb boned side up on grill 2 to 3 inches from hot coals. Cook for 5 to 6 minutes on each side or until seared and lightly charred, basting with marinade frequently. Remove to shallow roasting pan. Bake at 175 degrees for 30 to 60 minutes or to 130 degrees on meat thermometer for medium rare. **Yield:** 6 servings.

Approx Per Serving: Cal 427; Prot 48 g; Carbo 15 g; Fiber <1 g; T Fat 19 g; 40% Calories from Fat; Chol 152 mg; Sod 804 mg.

Leg of Lamb à la George

1/4 cup oil
3 tablespoons lemon juice
2 cloves of garlic, minced
2 teaspoons dry oregano
2 teaspoons salt
1/2 teaspoon pepper
1 large onion, thinly sliced
1/3 cup olive oil
2 pounds spinach, cooked, drained
1/4 cup parsley
1 tablespoon salt
1/4 cup bread crumbs
1 egg, beaten
1/4 teaspoon dillweed
1/4 teaspoon oregano
1/8 teaspoon pepper
1 7-pound boned leg of lamb
4 ounces Feta cheese, cut into cubes
1/2 cup hot water

Process oil, lemon juice, garlic, 2 teaspoons oregano, 2 teaspoons salt and 1/2 teaspoon pepper in food processor. Sauté onion in hot olive oil in skillet until soft. Add spinach and parsley. Sauté for 2 minutes. Cool for 5 minutes. Stir in 1 tablespoon salt, bread crumbs, egg, dillweed, 1/4 teaspoon oregano and 1/8 teaspoon pepper. Place lamb skin side down. Flatten with meat mallet. Rub half the oil mixture over lamb. Spread spinach mixture over lamb; sprinkle with cheese cubes. Fold half the lamb over from narrow shank end to enclose filling. Fold opposite end over, to resemble envelope. Tie with string. Rub with remaining oil mixture; place in roasting pan. Add hot water. Bake at 400 degrees for 30 minutes. Reduce oven temperature to 350 degrees. Bake for 2 hours longer or until done to taste. **Yield:** 10 servings.

Approx Per Serving: Cal 551; Prot 58 g; Carbo 7 g; Fiber 3 g; T Fat 32 g; 52% Calories from Fat; Chol 202 mg; Sod 1419 mg.

Rack of Lamb with Herbed Mustard Coating*

3 tablespoons Dijon mustard
1 tablespoon chopped fresh sage
1 tablespoon chopped fresh mint
1 1/2 tablespoons chopped fresh rosemary
1 1/2 tablespoons chopped fresh thyme
1 1 1/2 to 2-pound rack of lamb, boned, trimmed
Salt to taste
2 tablespoons olive oil
1 cup fresh bread crumbs

Combine mustard and herbs in bowl; mix well. Season lamb with salt. Brown lamb on all sides in hot olive oil in skillet. Remove to platter. Brush with herbed mustard. Roll in bread crumbs, pressing to coat. Broil lamb 8 inches from heat source for about 6 minutes or until crumbs are golden brown and lamb is 135 degrees on meat thermometer for medium rare, turning every 2 to 3 minutes. Cut into slices. **Yield:** 2 servings.

Approx Per Serving: Cal 953; Prot 79 g; Carbo 38 g; Fiber 2 g; T Fat 51 g; 49% Calories from Fat; Chol 241 mg; Sod 881 mg.

Lamb in Red Wine

1½ cups dry red wine
1 small onion, finely chopped
2 cloves of garlic, minced
1 tablespoon Worcestershire sauce
1 bay leaf
1 teaspoon salt
¼ teaspoon freshly ground pepper
2 pounds lamb, cut into 2-inch cubes
1 cup chili sauce
½ cup catsup
1 to 2 tablespoons prepared horseradish
1 tablespoon chutney
1 teaspoon honey

Combine red wine, onion, garlic, Worcestershire sauce, bay leaf, salt and pepper in bowl; mix well. Place lamb cubes in bowl. Add marinade, stirring to coat. Marinate, covered, in refrigerator for 10 hours to overnight, stirring several times. Remove lamb to 10-inch round glass bowl, placing smaller pieces near center. Microwave, covered loosely with waxed paper, on Medium for 6 to 7 minutes, stirring several times; drain. Lamb will be rare. Combine chili sauce, catsup, horseradish, chutney and honey in glass bowl; mix well. Microwave, loosely covered with waxed paper, on High for 4 minutes or until mixture bubbles, stirring 1 or 2 times. Pour sauce over lamb, stirring to coat lamb. Microwave, uncovered, on Medium for 2 to 3 minutes or until heated through, stirring 1 or 2 times. Serve over rice. **Yield:** 6 servings.

Approx Per Serving: Cal 331; Prot 29 g; Carbo 22 g; Fiber 1 g; T Fat 9 g; 24% Calories from Fat; Chol 85 mg; Sod 1325 mg.

Irish Lamb Stew

2 pounds lean lamb, cut into cubes
2 cups condensed beef broth
2 cups water
2 onions, chopped
2 potatoes, finely chopped
2 leeks with green tops, chopped
2 stalks celery, chopped
2 cloves of garlic, minced
2 bay leaves
1 tablespoon summer savory
1 teaspoon each salt and pepper
1 3-ounce jar onions, drained
3 medium potatoes, cut into quarters
3 carrots, sliced
1 tablespoon chopped parsley

Place lamb in large saucepan. Add broth, water, chopped onions, potatoes, leeks, celery, garlic, bay leaves, savory, salt and pepper. Simmer, covered, over low heat for 1 hour, stirring occasionally. Remove lamb to bowl. Remove bay leaves. Purée broth and vegetables 2 cups at a time in blender. Combine with lamb, drained onions, remaining potatoes and carrots in saucepan. Simmer for 30 to 45 minutes or until tender. Add parsley just before serving. **Yield:** 6 servings.

Approx Per Serving: Cal 386; Prot 32 g; Carbo 42 g; Fiber 5 g; T Fat 9 g; 22% Calories from Fat; Chol 85 mg; Sod 784 mg.

Alcohol Is Good for Your Liver

1½ pounds calf's liver, sliced
1 large sweet onion, thinly sliced
3 tablespoons oil
2 tablespoons cognac
1 clove of garlic, minced
1 8-ounce can tomato sauce
1 cup Cabernet Sauvignon
2 tablespoons Dijon mustard
½ teaspoon pepper
8 ounces fresh mushrooms, coarsely sliced

Rinse liver; pat dry. Stack slices on plastic wrap; fold to seal. Freeze for about 30 minutes or until very firm. Remove wrap. Cut into ½-inch strips. Sauté onion in oil in skillet. Add liver. Cook over high heat until liver begins to brown, stirring constantly. Add cognac; ignite. Combine garlic, tomato sauce, Cabernet Sauvignon, mustard and pepper in bowl; mix well. Add with mushrooms to liver. Reduce heat. Simmer, covered, for 3 to 5 minutes or until tender. **Yield:** 4 servings.

Approx Per Serving: Cal 363; Prot 28 g; Carbo 17 g; Fiber 3 g; T Fat 16 g; 40% Calories from Fat; Chol 397 mg; Sod 518 mg.

Calf's Liver with Onions and Apples*

"Do not overcook. Should be light pink inside."

1 pound calf's liver, sliced, sinew removed
2 tablespoons safflower oil
Salt and pepper to taste
2 onions, thinly sliced
2 apples, peeled, thinly sliced
½ cup condensed beef broth
1 tablespoon cider vinegar
1 teaspoon honey
1 teaspoon Bovril meat extract
1 teaspoon cornstarch
¼ cup water
1 tablespoon finely chopped fresh parsley

Fry liver in hot oil in skillet for 1 minute on each side. Remove to warm plate. Season with salt and pepper. Brown onions and apples in pan drippings in skillet, adding more oil if needed. Add beef broth, cider vinegar, honey, meat extract and mixture of cornstarch and water. Simmer for 1 minute, stirring constantly. Add liver. Cook for 1 to 2 minutes or until thickened. Add parsley just before serving.
Yield: 4 servings.

Approx Per Serving: Cal 243; Prot 18 g; Carbo 20 g; Fiber 3 g; T Fat 11 g; 39% Calories from Fat; Chol 265 mg; Sod 147 mg.

Baked Ham

"This makes ham taste like the expensive circular cut one."

1/2 10-pound ham, semi-boneless
1/2 cup whole cloves
1 cup packed light brown sugar
2 tablespoons prepared mustard
2 tablespoons dry sherry

Score ham; push cloves in where lines cross. Combine brown sugar, mustard and sherry in bowl; mix glaze well. Place ham on 5 sheets of foil, each sheet large enough to wrap ham. Pour glaze over ham. Wrap ham 1 sheet at a time, until wrapped 5 times. Place in baking pan. Bake at 275 degrees for 5 hours, turning once. Foil will contain hot liquid so use care in unwrapping. Serve hot or cold. **Yield:** 12 servings.

Approx Per Serving: Cal 386; Prot 48 g; Carbo 22 g; Fiber <1 g; T Fat 11 g; 25% Calories from Fat; Chol 104 mg; Sod 2551 mg.

Tennessee Barbecued Pork

"Excellent served with coleslaw, corn bread and baked beans"

1/4 teaspoon red pepper
3 tablespoons brown sugar
1/4 teaspoon black pepper
3 tablespoons prepared mustard
1 teaspoon salt
1 cup vinegar
1 1/2 cups water
1/2 cup catsup
1/2 cup Worcestershire sauce
1 onion, chopped
1 5 to 6-pound pork shoulder
Tabasco sauce to taste

Combine red pepper, brown sugar, black pepper, mustard, salt, vinegar, water, catsup and Worcestershire sauce in large Dutch oven; mix well. Add onion; mix well. Remove and discard rind and most of fat from pork shoulder. Add pork to sauce. Bake, covered, at 325 degrees for 5 to 6 hours, turning occasionally. Remove pork to platter. Cool until it can be handled. Shred pork, removing fat and bone. Chill sauce until fat solidifies; remove fat. Add water and Tabasco sauce to sauce. Reheat to serving temperature. Add shredded pork or serve pork with sauce on side. **Yield:** 18 servings.

Approx Per Serving: Cal 245; Prot 30 g; Carbo 7 g; Fiber <1 g; T Fat 10 g; 38% Calories from Fat; Chol 92 mg; Sod 370 mg.

Add several teaspoons instant mashed potatoes to gravy to reduce saltiness. Thin with additional liquid if necessary.

Chop Suey

"Translation: Miscellaneous fragments"

1 pound boneless lean pork
2 tablespoons cornstarch
3 tablespoons soy sauce
1 tablespoon dry sherry
1½ teaspoons salt
¼ teaspoon ginger
¼ teaspoon MSG
½ cup water
2 tablespoons oil
2 cups thinly shredded Chinese cabbage
1 cup thinly sliced celery
1 bunch of green onions, cut into 1-inch pieces
1 16-ounce can bean sprouts, drained
1 8-ounce can sliced water chestnuts, drained
1 6-ounce can bamboo shoots, drained
3 cups hot cooked rice

Cut meat into thin, bite-sized pieces. Combine cornstarch, soy sauce, sherry, salt, ginger, MSG and water in bowl; mix well. Brown pork in hot oil in skillet over medium high heat, stirring frequently. Add cornstarch mixture; mix well. Add Chinese cabbage, celery, green onions, bean sprouts, water chestnuts and bamboo shoots. Cook for 5 minutes or until vegetables are tender-crisp, stirring frequently. Serve over hot rice. **Yield:** 4 servings.

Approx Per Serving: Cal 486; Prot 30 g; Carbo 57 g; Fiber 7 g; T Fat 15 g; 28% Calories from Fat; Chol 69 mg; Sod 1948 mg.

Piquant Pork with Peppers

"A southwestern mouthful"

12 ounces boneless lean pork
1 to 2 tablespoons safflower oil
1½ cups sliced red onions
4 cups sliced red bell peppers
2 teaspoons cumin
2 tablespoons red wine vinegar
Pepper to taste
2 cups hot cooked noodles
3 large scallions, sliced
3 tablespoons (heaping) chopped fresh cilantro

Wash pork; pat dry. Trim off fat; cut pork into cubes or strips. Rub skillet with trimmed fat. Sauté pork in hot skillet until brown on all sides. Remove to warm bowl. Add oil to skillet. Sauté onions and red peppers with cumin for 10 minutes or until onions are tender. Turn off heat. Add vinegar and pepper to skillet; mix well. Add pork; mix well. Serve over hot noodles. Sprinkle with scallions and cilantro. **Yield:** 2 servings.

Approx Per Serving: Cal 437; Prot 36 g; Carbo 17 g; Fiber 5 g; T Fat 26 g; 52% Calories from Fat; Chol 104 mg; Sod 91 mg.

Pork Chops with Apples and Raisins

4 1 1/2 to 2-inch thick center-cut pork chops
Salt and pepper to taste
1 tablespoon oil
1/4 cup butter
1 large yellow onion, sliced
1 large sweet apple, cut into wedges
1/4 cup raisins
1/2 cup Port

Season pork chops with salt and pepper. Brown in oil and butter in skillet. Place 1 slice onion on each chop. Cook, covered, on low heat for 15 minutes. Turn chops so onions will be on bottom. Arrange apple wedges and raisins around chops. Add wine. Simmer, covered, for 15 minutes, turning apple wedges once. Simmer, uncovered, for 5 minutes or until sauce is thickened, stirring gently. **Yield:** 4 servings.

Approx Per Serving: Cal 481; Prot 33 g; Carbo 23 g; Fiber 3 g; T Fat 26 g; 51% Calories from Fat; Chol 129 mg; Sod 179 mg.

Cantonese Spareribs

1/2 cup molasses
1/2 cup orange juice
1/4 cup soy sauce
3 tablespoons sherry
1 teaspoon ginger
1 teaspoon dry mustard
1/4 teaspoon garlic powder
4 pounds lean spareribs

Mix first 7 ingredients in shallow dish. Add ribs. Marinate, covered, in refrigerator overnight, turning occasionally. Drain, reserving marinade. Place ribs in shallow baking dish. Bake, covered with foil, at 350 degrees for 1 hour. Remove fat from ribs. Add reserved marinade. Bake for 30 to 45 minutes longer, basting several times. **Yield:** 4 servings.

Approx Per Serving: Cal 807; Prot 51 g; Carbo 27 g; Fiber <1 g; T Fat 52 g; 60% Calories from Fat; Chol 208 mg; Sod 1197 mg.

Roast Pork with Tasty Sauerkraut*

2 pounds drained sauerkraut
2 cups applesauce
1 tablespoon brown sugar
1 cup dry white wine
1/2 teaspoon dry mustard
1/4 teaspoon pepper
1 teaspoon caraway seed
4 pounds boneless loin pork roast

Combine first 7 ingredients in casserole; mix well. Place roast in well in center. Bake, covered, at 350 degrees for 40 minutes per pound or until tender. **Yield:** 10 servings.

Approx Per Serving: Cal 337; Prot 37 g; Carbo 16 g; Fiber 2 g; T Fat 12 g; 34% Calories from Fat; Chol 111 mg; Sod 691 mg.

Pork Crown Roast with Wild Rice Stuffing

"Stuffing has a wonderful nutty flavor."

2 6-ounce packages wild rice mix
1/2 cup chopped onion
1/3 cup chopped celery
1 clove of garlic, minced
1/4 cup butter
1/2 cup chopped walnuts
4 to 5 tablespoons finely chopped preserved ginger
1/2 teaspoon allspice
1 Granny Smith apple, peeled, chopped
1 8 to 10-pound crown roast of pork

Cook rice using package directions. Sauté onion, celery and garlic in butter in skillet until tender. Combine rice, sautéed vegetables, walnuts, ginger, allspice and apple in bowl; mix well. Place pork roast on rack in large shallow roasting pan. Spoon stuffing lightly into center. Spoon any remaining stuffing into buttered shallow baking dish. Cover ends of bones and top of stuffing with foil. Roast pork at 400 degrees for 10 minutes. Reduce oven temperature to 325 degrees. Roast for 3 1/2 hours longer. Place remaining stuffing in oven with roast. Bake for 30 minutes or until roast is 185 degrees on meat thermometer. **Yield:** 10 servings.

Approx Per Serving: Cal 905; Prot 94 g; Carbo 35 g; Fiber 1 g; T Fat 41 g; 42% Calories from Fat; Chol 290 mg; Sod 986 mg.

Gingered Pork Tenderloin

"Melts in your mouth"

1 3-pound boneless pork tenderloin
1 1/2 cups vinegar
1/2 cup soy sauce
1/2 cup sherry
1/2 cup lemon juice
2 teaspoons fresh minced garlic
2 tablespoons grated fresh ginger

Place pork and vinegar in large saucepan with water to cover. Boil for 20 to 30 minutes, stirring occasionally; drain. Combine soy sauce, sherry, lemon juice, garlic and ginger in bowl; mix well. Pour over pork in shallow dish. Marinate, covered, in refrigerator for 4 to 5 hours, turning occasionally. Drain pork. Place on hot grill. Grill for 45 minutes or until cooked through. **Yield:** 6 servings.

Approx Per Serving: Cal 374; Prot 46 g; Carbo 8 g; Fiber <1 g; T Fat 15 g; 38% Calories from Fat; Chol 139 mg; Sod 1484 mg.

Great Grilled Pork

"The name says it all. There is a hint of the Southwest in flavor."

1/3 cup packed fresh oregano
1/3 cup packed cilantro
1/4 medium onion
1/2 teaspoon grated orange rind
1/3 cup orange juice
Juice of 1 lime
Pepper to taste
1 teaspoon olive oil
1 12 to 14-ounce pork tenderloin, trimmed
1/2 bunch of watercress or arugula, washed, dried
Sections of 2 small oranges

Process oregano and cilantro in food processor until finely chopped. Add onion, orange rind, orange juice, lime juice, pepper and olive oil 1 at a time, processing until well blended. Place pork in shallow dish. Pour in marinade. Marinate, covered, in refrigerator until cooking time. Grease grill or cover broiler pan with foil to prevent marinade sticking. Drain pork, reserving marinade. Place pork on grill. Grill until brown on 1 side, basting with reserved marinade occasionally; turn. Grill for 10 minutes longer or until brown and slightly pink inside. Arrange on bed of watercress. Garnish with orange sections. **Yield:** 4 servings.

Approx Per Serving: Cal 202; Prot 21 g; Carbo 12 g; Fiber 3 g; T Fat 8 g; 34% Calories from Fat; Chol 61 mg; Sod 57 mg.

Pork Tenderloin with Apricot Jam*

1 1/2 tablespoons sweet hot mustard
1/8 teaspoon garlic powder
1/4 teaspoon coarsely ground pepper
1/4 teaspoon rosemary
1 1-pound pork tenderloin
1/8 cup sugarless apricot preserves

Combine mustard, garlic powder, pepper and rosemary in bowl; mix well. Slice tenderloin lengthwise, cutting to but not through outer edge. Spread mustard mixture in pocket. Press gently to close; tie securely with heavy string at 2-inch intervals. Place in roasting pan. Spread apricot preserves over surface. Bake at 325 degrees for 40 to 45 minutes or until cooked through. **Yield:** 4 servings.

Approx Per Serving: Cal 169; Prot 23 g; Carbo 1 g; Fiber <1 g; T Fat 8 g; 42% Calories from Fat; Chol 69 mg; Sod 131 mg.

Kielbasa in Beer

2 large onions, sliced
2 tablespoons butter
1 cup beer
2 chicken bouillon cubes
1½ cups water
½ teaspoon pepper
1 tablespoon vinegar
4 large carrots
5 medium potatoes
1½ pounds kielbasa
1 medium tomato, chopped
3 tablespoons chopped parsley

Sauté onions in butter in skillet until translucent. Add beer, bouillon cubes, water, pepper and vinegar; mix well. Cut each carrot into 2 pieces; cut each potato into thirds. Cut kielbasa into ½ to ¾-inch slices. Add carrots, potatoes, kielbasa and tomato to skillet. Simmer, covered, for 35 minutes, stirring occasionally. Add parsley just before serving. May substitute turkey kielbasa for kielbasa and beef bouillon cubes for chicken bouillon cubes. **Yield:** 6 servings.

Approx Per Serving: Cal 446; Prot 16 g; Carbo 56 g; Fiber 7 g; T Fat 17 g; 35% Calories from Fat; Chol 44 mg; Sod 1120 mg.

Lentils with Italian Sausage

8 ounces mild or hot Italian sausage
1 cup chopped onion
1 cup chopped green bell pepper
1 clove of garlic, minced
1 teaspoon basil
2 cups lentils, rinsed, drained
¾ teaspoon salt
5 cups water
1 28-ounce can plum tomatoes

Remove casing from sausage. Brown sausage with onion, pepper and garlic in skillet, stirring frequently; drain. Stir in basil, lentils and salt. Add water. Simmer, uncovered, for 30 minutes or until lentils are tender and liquid has evaporated, stirring occasionally. Add undrained tomatoes, stirring to break up tomatoes. Simmer, uncovered, for 20 minutes or until almost all liquid has evaporated, stirring occasionally. **Yield:** 6 servings.

Approx Per Serving: Cal 322; Prot 23 g; Carbo 46 g; Fiber 10 g; T Fat 7 g; 18% Calories from Fat; Chol 15 mg; Sod 721 mg.

Add fresh parsley to floral centerpieces for an attractive—and appetizing—accent.

Osso Buco

3/4 cup flour
Salt and pepper to taste
3 pounds veal shank
3 tablespoons olive oil
2 tablespoons unsalted butter
3 leeks, rinsed, dried, minced
6 carrots, peeled, minced
5 oil-packed sun-dried tomatoes
3 plum tomatoes, seeded, chopped
6 cloves of garlic, minced
2 cups beef stock
1 cup dry white wine
Finely grated rind of 1 lemon
1/2 cup minced fresh parsley
3 cloves of garlic, minced

Season flour with salt and pepper. Cut veal into eight 1 1/2 to 2-inch thick pieces. Dredge in flour until coated. Brown veal on all sides in olive oil and butter in Dutch oven. Remove veal to plate. Sauté leeks and carrots in pan drippings for 7 minutes. Chop sun-dried tomatoes finely. Add with plum tomatoes and 6 cloves of garlic to carrots. Cook for 5 minutes. Add beef stock and wine. Adjust seasonings. Add veal. Bring to a boil, stirring occasionally. Place in oven. Bake, covered, at 300 degrees for 1 1/2 hours or until veal is tender. Combine lemon rind, parsley and 3 cloves of garlic in bowl; mix well. Serve osso buco in wide shallow bowls; sprinkle with parsley mixture. **Yield:** 6 servings.

Approx Per Serving: Cal 611; Prot 51 g; Carbo 36 g; Fiber 7 g; T Fat 27 g; 41% Calories from Fat; Chol 197 mg; Sod 430 mg.

Company Roast Veal

1 3-pound boneless veal rump or loin roast, tied
3 tablespoons vegetable oil
3 medium carrots, thinly sliced
2 medium onions, thinly sliced
1 tablespoon vegetable oil
2 tablespoons butter
1 teaspoon salt
1/2 teaspoon freshly ground pepper
1/2 teaspoon thyme
1 bunch of parsley
2 bay leaves
1 10-ounce can chicken stock

Brown veal on all sides in 3 tablespoons hot oil in Dutch oven; drain. Remove veal to warm platter. Sauté carrots and onions in 1 tablespoon oil and butter in Dutch oven for 10 minutes or until soft. Add veal. Sprinkle with salt, pepper and thyme. Tie parsley and bay leaves together. Add with chicken stock to veal. Roast, covered, at 350 degrees for 1 1/2 hours, basting every 15 minutes with stock. Remove veal to warm platter. Discard parsley and bay leaves. Remove vegetables to bowl. Strain stock; skim off fat. Press vegetables through sieve into stock. Simmer until thickened, stirring frequently. Adjust seasonings. Cut veal into 3/4-inch slices. Serve with vegetable gravy. **Yield:** 6 servings.

Approx Per Serving: Cal 404; Prot 47 g; Carbo 8 g; Fiber 3 g; T Fat 20 g; 44% Calories from Fat; Chol 197 mg; Sod 670 mg.

A Veal Caper

- 2 pounds stew veal
- 2 stalks celery, cut into 2-inch lengths
- 1 small whole onion
- 1 1/2 cups chicken stock
- 6 peppercorns
- 2 tablespoons melted butter
- 2 tablespoons flour
- 2 tablespoons lemon juice
- 2 teaspoons capers
- Salt and white pepper to taste

Combine veal, celery, onion, stock and peppercorns in 2-quart casserole. Bake, covered, at 350 degrees for 1 1/2 hours or until veal is very tender. Discard celery, onion and peppercorns, reserving stock. Melt butter in skillet. Stir in flour until well mixed. Add reserved stock; mix well. Simmer until thickened, stirring constantly. Add lemon juice, capers, salt and white pepper; mix well. Add veal. Cook until heated through. Serve over hot rice or noodles. **Yield:** 4 servings.

Approx Per Serving: Cal 341; Prot 48 g; Carbo 7 g; Fiber 1 g; T Fat 13 g; 34% Calories from Fat; Chol 202 mg; Sod 473 mg.

Veal Capri

- 1 1/2 pounds veal scallops
- 3 tablespoons flour
- Salt and pepper to taste
- 3 tablespoons olive oil
- 1 tablespoon butter
- 2 tablespoons brandy, warmed
- 2 tablespoons chopped onion
- 4 ounces fresh mushrooms, sliced
- 2 tablespoons Amaretto
- 2 tablespoons brown stock
- 1 1/2 tablespoons whipping cream
- 1 tablespoon minced fresh parsley

Dredge veal in mixture of flour, salt and pepper. Brown on both sides in olive oil and butter in skillet. Ignite brandy; pour over veal. Remove veal to warm platter when flame dies; keep warm. Sauté onion in pan drippings. Stir in mushrooms and Amaretto. Simmer until liquid is reduced by half. Stir in brown stock and cream. Pour over veal; sprinkle with parsley. **Yield:** 4 servings.

Approx Per Serving: Cal 398; Prot 35 g; Carbo 13 g; Fiber 1 g; T Fat 20 g; 48% Calories from Fat; Chol 155 mg; Sod 151 mg.

Add a very thin lemon slice to each glass of water at the dinner table for a touch of color and a refreshing drink.

Veal Divan

3 slices bacon
3 tablespoons (about) butter
1½ cups herb-seasoned stuffing mix
6 thin veal steaks
Salt to taste
1 tablespoon butter
2 10-ounce packages frozen broccoli spears, thawed
1 chicken bouillon cube
½ cup hot water
1 10-ounce can condensed shrimp soup
⅓ cup milk

Fry bacon in skillet until crisp; drain, reserving drippings. Add enough melted butter to bacon drippings to measure ¼ cup. Prepare stuffing mix using package directions with mixture of bacon drippings and butter. Crumble bacon into stuffing; mix well. Pound veal steaks until ⅛ inch thick. Sprinkle with salt. Place ⅓ cup stuffing on each steak. Roll to enclose filling; tie with string. Brown veal rolls in 1 tablespoon butter in skillet. Arrange veal rolls and broccoli in 7x12-inch baking dish. Combine bouillon cube and hot water in bowl; stir until bouillon is dissolved. Pour over veal rolls. Bake, covered with foil, at 350 degrees for 1 hour. Heat soup and milk in saucepan. Remove ties from veal rolls. Pour hot soup over veal. **Yield:** 6 servings.

Approx Per Serving: Cal 338; Prot 25 g; Carbo 22 g; Fiber 3 g; T Fat 18 g; 46% Calories from Fat; Chol 124 mg; Sod 1010 mg.

Veal à la Madelon*

"A piquant dish with gourmet aspirations"

1 clove of garlic
2 tablespoons butter
2 pounds boneless veal
2 tablespoons flour
1 teaspoon salt
¼ teaspoon pepper
2 1-inch wide pieces of lemon rind
1 cup boiling water
1 cup whipping cream

Sauté garlic in hot butter in heavy skillet. Remove garlic. Cut veal into bite-sized pieces. Brown veal in pan drippings. Sprinkle with flour, salt and pepper. Brown again. Add lemon rind and water. Simmer, covered, for 1 hour or until tender. Remove lemon rind. Stir in cream. Heat to serving temperature. Serve over hot rice. **Yield:** 6 servings.

Approx Per Serving: Cal 345; Prot 31 g; Carbo 3 g; Fiber <1 g; T Fat 23 g; 60% Calories from Fat; Chol 189 mg; Sod 480 mg.

Veal Marengo

"A welcome variation on the now familiar boeuf Bourguignon"

1/2 cup flour
Salt and pepper to taste
3 pounds boneless lean veal
1/4 cup olive oil
1 large onion, chopped
1 cup dry white wine
1 cup chicken stock
4 ripe tomatoes, seeded
3 cloves of garlic, minced
1 tablespoon chopped fresh tarragon
1 teaspoon thyme
2 tablespoons fine strips orange rind
12 ounces fresh small button mushrooms
1/2 cup chopped fresh parsley

Season flour with salt and pepper. Cut veal into 2-inch cubes. Coat veal lightly with flour. Brown veal on all sides in hot olive oil in skillet. Remove to warm plate. Add onion to pan drippings. Sauté for 5 to 7 minutes or until translucent. Add wine and chicken stock, stirring well. Cut tomatoes into 1/2-inch pieces. Add veal, tomatoes, garlic, tarragon, thyme and orange rind to onion. Simmer, uncovered, for 1 1/4 hours or until veal is very tender, stirring occasionally. Stir in mushrooms. Simmer for 10 to 15 minutes longer, stirring occasionally. Remove veal and vegetables to warm bowl if sauce is too thin. Reduce sauce over high heat until thickened, stirring constantly. Add veal and vegetables. Heat to serving temperature. Serve over hot buttered noodles. Sprinkle with parsley. **Yield:** 8 servings.

Approx Per Serving: Cal 331; Prot 37 g; Carbo 13 g; Fiber 3 g; T Fat 12 g; 35% Calories from Fat; Chol 140 mg; Sod 194 mg.

Veal Scallopini*

1 1/2 pounds thinly sliced veal
1/4 teaspoon oregano
1 clove of garlic, minced
Salt and pepper to taste
1/2 cup flour
1/2 cup olive oil
2 tablespoons butter
1 cup white wine or Madeira
6 slices mozzarella cheese
1/2 cup Parmesan cheese

Cut veal into 6 portions. Season with oregano, garlic, salt and pepper. Dredge in flour. Sauté veal in hot olive oil and butter in skillet until golden brown on both sides. Remove to shallow baking dish. Add wine to pan drippings. Simmer for several minutes, stirring constantly. Pour over veal. Place 1 slice of mozzarella cheese on each serving of veal; sprinkle with Parmesan cheese. Bake at 400 degrees until cheese is melted. **Yield:** 6 servings.

Approx Per Serving: Cal 492; Prot 32 g; Carbo 9 g; Fiber <1 g; T Fat 33 g; 64% Calories from Fat; Chol 131 mg; Sod 324 mg.

POULTRY

Roast Chicken on Waffles

"Try this for a special mid-week treat."

1 2½ to 3-pound chicken
Rosemary, salt and pepper to taste
1 tablespoon shortening
2 tablespoons chopped onion
3 tablespoons melted butter
1 tablespoon finely chopped shallots
1 clove of garlic, crushed
1 cup sliced mushrooms
3 tablespoons flour
½ cup white wine
1 cup chicken stock
Nutmeg, cayenne pepper, salt and white pepper to taste
6 frozen whole grain waffles

Rinse chicken inside and out; pat dry. Sprinkle cavity with rosemary, salt and pepper. Truss chicken; rub with shortening. Place on rack in shallow roasting pan. Sprinkle with additional rosemary, salt and pepper. Place in oven preheated to 450 degrees; reduce oven temperature to 350 degrees. Roast for 1 hour or until tender. Cool until easy to handle. Chop into bite-sized pieces, discarding skin and bones. Sauté onion in butter in saucepan until tender. Stir in shallots, garlic and mushrooms. Cook over low heat for 5 minutes. Stir in flour. Add wine and chicken stock. Cook until thickened and bubbly, stirring constantly; reduce heat. Simmer for 10 minutes longer. Stir in chicken, nutmeg, cayenne pepper, salt and white pepper. Cook until heated through. Keep warm in chafing dish over hot water. Toast waffles using package directions. Spoon chicken mixture over waffles. Garnish with chopped parsley and pimento. Serve with gingered fruits. **Yield:** 6 servings.

Approx Per Serving: Cal 423; Prot 37 g; Carbo 19 g; Fiber 1 g; T Fat 20 g; 45% Calories from Fat; Chol 137 mg; Sod 519 mg.

Amaretto Chicken Bake

"A neat dish for a dinner party"

3 tablespoons flour
1½ teaspoons paprika
1½ teaspoons garlic salt
1½ teaspoons salt
1½ teaspoons white pepper
1 3-pound chicken, cut up
3 tablespoons butter
1 tablespoon oil
1 6-ounce can frozen orange juice concentrate, thawed
1 tablespoon Dijon mustard
½ cup water
1 cup Amaretto

Combine flour, paprika, garlic salt, salt and white pepper in bowl; mix well. Rinse chicken and pat dry. Coat with flour mixture. Brown on both sides in mixture of butter and oil in skillet; drain. Arrange in baking dish. Add orange juice concentrate, mustard, water and Amaretto to skillet, stirring to deglaze. Bring to a boil, stirring until smooth. Pour over chicken. Bake at 325 degrees for 45 minutes, basting occasionally with sauce. **Yield:** 4 servings.

Approx Per Serving: Cal 755; Prot 51 g; Carbo 54 g; Fiber 1 g; T Fat 25 g; 30% Calories from Fat; Chol 175 mg; Sod 1842 mg.

Chicken in Cilantro Sauce

"This is good made with chicken breasts and served over rice."

2 tablespoons red wine vinegar
1 teaspoon oregano
1 tablespoon garlic salt
1 teaspoon pepper
1 2½ to 3-pound chicken, cut up, skinned
Leaves of 1 bunch cilantro
1 onion, cut into quarters
2 medium tomatoes, cut into quarters
1 green bell pepper, chopped
1 yellow chili pepper, seeded
1 medium onion, chopped
Paprika to taste
2 tablespoons oil

Combine vinegar, oregano, garlic salt and pepper in bowl. Rinse chicken and pat dry. Add to vinegar mixture, coating well. Marinate in refrigerator. Combine cilantro, quarters of 1 onion, tomatoes, green pepper and yellow chili in blender container; process until smooth. Sauté chopped onion with paprika in oil in skillet until onion is golden brown. Stir in cilantro sauce. Cook for 2 minutes. Add chicken and water to cover. Cook for 45 to 55 minutes or until chicken is tender.
Yield: 4 servings.

Approx Per Serving: Cal 435; Prot 51 g; Carbo 12 g; Fiber 3 g; T Fat 20 g; 42% Calories from Fat; Chol 152 mg; Sod 1691 mg.

Kahlua Stir-Fry Chicken

3 tablespoons beaten egg
3 tablespoons oil
3 tablespoons cornstarch
2 pounds chicken, boned, skinned
1/4 cup oil
1/2 cup sliced water chestnuts
1 green bell pepper, chopped
1 cup asparagus tips
1 4-ounce can sliced mushrooms, drained
4 ounces snow peas
3 tablespoons Kahlua
1 teaspoon cornstarch
1 cup whole cashews
3 green onions, finely chopped

Mix egg, 3 tablespoons oil and 3 tablespoons cornstarch in bowl. Rinse chicken and pat dry. Cut into 1/2-inch pieces. Add to egg mixture; mix well. Stir-fry chicken in 1/4 cup oil in skillet or wok until golden brown. Remove to warm bowl. Drain most of drippings from skillet. Add next 5 ingredients to skillet. Stir-fry for 3 minutes or until vegetables are tender-crisp. Combine Kahlua with 1 teaspoon cornstarch in bowl. Stir into skillet. Bring to a simmer, stirring constantly. Add chicken and cashews. Cook until heated through. Top with green onions. **Yield:** 4 servings.

Approx Per Serving: Cal 741; Prot 42 g; Carbo 30 g; Fiber 5 g; T Fat 50 g; 61% Calories from Fat; Chol 151 mg; Sod 245 mg.

Lemon Chicken

2 whole chicken breasts
1 tablespoon soy sauce
2 teaspoons salt
1 cup chicken broth
3 tablespoons sugar
1 tablespoon cornstarch
1/2 cup flour
2 tablespoons cornstarch
1/4 teaspoon sugar
1/4 teaspoon baking powder
1/8 teaspoon baking soda
1/2 cup water
2 cups peanut oil
1 scallion, split, cut into 2-inch pieces
2 large lemons, thinly sliced

Rinse chicken and pat dry. Split into halves. Sprinkle with soy sauce and 1 teaspoon salt. Let stand for 15 minutes. Mix remaining 1 teaspoon salt, broth, 3 tablespoons sugar and 1 tablespoon cornstarch in bowl; set aside. Combine flour, 2 tablespoons cornstarch, 1/4 teaspoon sugar, baking powder, baking soda and water in bowl; mix well. Heat oil in wok. Add 1 tablespoon heated oil to flour batter; mix well. Coat chicken with batter. Deep-fry in hot oil in wok for 7 to 8 minutes or until golden brown. Remove to warm platter; keep warm. Drain all but 2 tablespoons oil from wok. Add scallion. Stir-fry until tender. Add lemon slices. Stir-fry for 30 seconds. Add chicken broth mixture. Cook until thickened, stirring constantly. Spoon sauce over chicken. **Yield:** 4 servings.

Approx Per Serving: Cal 348; Prot 30 g; Carbo 21 g; Fiber <1 g; T Fat 10 g; 26% Calories from Fat; Chol 72 mg; Sod 1607 mg. Nutritional information does not include peanut oil for deep frying.

Beijing Chicken

4 7-ounce boneless chicken breast halves
1 cup chicken broth
4 scallions, minced
3 tablespoons soy sauce
2 tablespoons sherry
2 tablespoons Dijon mustard
1 tablespoon hoisen sauce
2 teaspoons toasted sesame oil
1 teaspoon honey
2 teaspoons minced ginger

Rinse chicken and pat dry. Pound thin. Place in shallow dish. Add mixture of remaining ingredients. Marinate at room temperature for 30 minutes. Drain, reserving marinade. Grill or broil chicken until tender. Serve with heated marinade. Garnish with cilantro. **Yield:** 4 servings.

Approx Per Serving: Cal 309; Prot 49 g; Carbo 5 g; Fiber <1 g; T Fat 8 g; 26% Calories from Fat; Chol 127 mg; Sod 1433 mg.

Belgian Chicken with Almonds

4 4-ounce boneless chicken breast halves
1/4 cup butter
2 tablespoons flour
1/2 teaspoon salt
Cinnamon, nutmeg and ginger to taste
1 1/2 cups fresh orange juice
1/4 cup seedless raisins
1/4 cup blanched almonds

Rinse chicken and pat dry. Brown lightly in butter in heavy skillet. Remove to warm platter. Stir flour, salt and spices into drippings. Add orange juice gradually. Cook until thickened, stirring constantly. Add chicken. Sprinkle with raisins and almonds. Simmer, covered, for 45 minutes or until chicken is tender. Garnish with orange slice twists. **Yield:** 4 servings.

Approx Per Serving: Cal 397; Prot 30 g; Carbo 26 g; Fiber 3 g; T Fat 20 g; 44% Calories from Fat; Chol 103 mg; Sod 429 mg.

Broiled Chicken Tarragon*

4 4-ounce boneless chicken breast halves
3 tablespoons low-calorie mayonnaise
4 teaspoons Dijon mustard
1 teaspoon tarragon
Salt and pepper to taste

Rinse chicken and pat dry. Pound thin. Brush with mixture of remaining ingredients. Place on rack in broiler pan. Broil for 3 to 4 minutes. Turn chicken; brush with remaining mixture. Broil until tender. **Yield:** 4 servings.

Approx Per Serving: Cal 171; Prot 27 g; Carbo 2 g; Fiber <1 g; T Fat 5 g; 30% Calories from Fat; Chol 75 mg; Sod 185 mg.

Chicken Breasts with Fennel Sauce

"Fennel gives chicken an unusually pleasant flavor."

4 5-ounce boneless chicken breast halves
Salt and pepper to taste
2 tablespoons olive oil
1/4 cup finely chopped shallots
1 1/2 cups chopped fennel bulb
1/4 cup dry white wine
1/4 cup chicken broth
1 bay leaf
2 fresh thyme sprigs
Tabasco sauce to taste
2 tablespoons butter
4 fennel leaves, finely chopped

Rinse chicken and pat dry; sprinkle with salt and pepper. Sauté in olive oil in nonstick skillet over medium-high heat for 3 minutes on each side. Add shallots and fennel; shake skillet to distribute evenly. Cook for 3 minutes. Add wine, broth, bay leaf, thyme and Tabasco sauce. Cook for 10 minutes longer, turning chicken occasionally. Remove chicken to warm platter; cover with foil. Remove and discard bay leaf and thyme. Remove 1/2 cup fennel with slotted spoon and reserve. Combine remaining fennel mixture with butter in food processor container; process until smooth. Return to saucepan; season with salt and pepper. Add juices from chicken platter, reserved fennel and chopped fennel leaves. Bring to a simmer. Spoon over chicken. Serve immediately. **Yield:** 4 servings.

Approx Per Serving: Cal 305; Prot 34 g; Carbo 2 g; Fiber <1 g; T Fat 16 g; 51% Calories from Fat; Chol 106 mg; Sod 178 mg.

Chicken Breasts with Shrimp

"A different and delightful combination"

1 pound peeled shrimp
2 small onions, chopped
1/4 cup margarine
2 eggs, beaten
1/4 cup water
1/2 cup grated Parmesan cheese
1 cup bread crumbs
Seasoned salt, red pepper and black pepper to taste
8 4-ounce boneless chicken breast halves
1/4 cup melted margarine
1/2 cup sherry

Sauté shrimp and onions in 1/4 cup margarine in skillet; set aside. Beat eggs with water in bowl. Mix cheese, bread crumbs, seasoned salt, red pepper and black pepper in bowl. Rinse chicken and pat dry. Dip in egg mixture; coat with bread crumb mixture. Spoon shrimp mixture onto chicken; roll to enclose filling. Place in 1/4 cup melted margarine in baking dish. Add sherry. Bake at 350 degrees for 1 1/2 hours, basting occasionally. **Yield:** 8 servings.

Approx Per Serving: Cal 406; Prot 42 g; Carbo 12 g; Fiber 1 g; T Fat 19 g; 44% Calories from Fat; Chol 234 mg; Sod 486 mg.

Chicken with Artichokes*

"A quick and easy dinner for unexpected company, this dish can also be made with medallions of veal."

8 4-ounce boneless chicken breast halves, cooked
2 9-ounce packages frozen artichoke hearts, cooked, drained
8 ounces fresh mushrooms, sliced
1/4 cup butter
1/4 cup flour
2 cups chicken stock
3 cups shredded Cheddar cheese
1/2 teaspoon freshly grated nutmeg
1/2 cup fine dry bread crumbs
1 teaspoon savory
1 teaspoon thyme
2 tablespoons butter

Combine chicken and artichoke hearts in 3-quart baking dish. Sauté mushrooms in 1/4 cup butter in saucepan. Stir in flour. Add chicken stock. Cook until thickened, stirring constantly. Stir in cheese and nutmeg. Pour over chicken. Mix bread crumbs with savory and thyme in bowl. Sprinkle over casserole. Dot with 2 tablespoons butter. Bake at 350 degrees for 30 minutes. Broil just until topping is brown. May substitute 1/4 cup sherry for part of the chicken stock. **Yield:** 8 servings.

Approx Per Serving: Cal 471; Prot 42 g; Carbo 16 g; Fiber 6 g; T Fat 27 g; 51% Calories from Fat; Chol 141 mg; Sod 674 mg.

Chicken with Cashews and Broccoli*

6 4-ounce boneless chicken breast halves
1 tablespoon cornstarch
1 cup chicken broth
3 tablespoons dry sherry
2 tablespoons soy sauce
1/4 to 1/2 teaspoon Tabasco sauce
2 slices fresh ginger
1/4 cup peanut oil
3 cups broccoli flowerets
1 medium red bell pepper, cut into 1-inch pieces
8 ounces mushrooms, sliced
1 bunch scallions, slivered
1 clove of garlic, minced
1/3 cup dry-roasted cashews

Rinse chicken and pat dry; cut into 1-inch pieces. Combine cornstarch, chicken broth, sherry, soy sauce and Tabasco sauce in small bowl; mix well. Stir-fry chicken and ginger in hot oil in wok or skillet until cooked through. Remove and discard ginger; push chicken up sides of wok or remove to warm plate. Add broccoli, bell pepper, mushrooms, scallions and garlic. Stir-fry for 3 minutes. Stir in chicken and cornstarch mixture. Cook until thickened to desired consistency, stirring constantly. Sprinkle with cashews. Serve with hot rice. **Yield:** 6 servings.

Approx Per Serving: Cal 317; Prot 31 g; Carbo 10 g; Fiber 3 g; T Fat 16 g; 47% Calories from Fat; Chol 72 mg; Sod 554 mg.

Chicken Crêpes

4 eggs
1½ cups flour
½ teaspoon salt
¾ cup milk
¾ cup chicken broth
2 tablespoons melted butter
2 cups chopped cooked chicken
1 tablespoon chopped parsley
1 teaspoon grated onion
½ cup light cream
6 tablespoons flour
6 tablespoons melted butter
3 cups chicken broth, strained
1 egg yolk
Sage to taste
3 slices bacon, crisp-fried, crumbled
½ cup shredded Swiss cheese
½ cup grated Parmesan cheese
2 tablespoons light cream

Beat 4 eggs at medium speed in mixer bowl for 1 minute. Mix 1½ cups flour and salt in small bowl. Add to eggs ½ at a time, mixing well. Mix in milk gradually. Add ¾ cup chicken broth; beat until smooth. Add 2 tablespoons butter; mix well. Let stand, covered, for 1 to 2 hours. Spoon thin layer into greased heated crêpe pan, swirling to coat evenly. Bake until light brown on both sides. Repeat using remaining batter. Combine chicken, parsley, onion and ½ cup cream in saucepan. Simmer for 10 minutes. Blend 6 tablespoons flour into 6 tablespoons butter in saucepan. Stir in 3 cups chicken broth. Cook until thickened, stirring constantly. Mix egg yolk with half the cream sauce. Stir in sage. Add to chicken mixture; mix well. Cook until thickened to desired consistency. Stir in bacon and half the cheeses. Spoon onto crêpes; roll to enclose filling. Arrange seam side down in greased rectangular baking dish. Stir remaining 2 tablespoons cream into remaining sauce. Spoon over crêpes; sprinkle with mixture of remaining cheeses. Bake at 350 degrees for 20 to 30 minutes or until heated through. **Yield:** 8 servings.

Approx Per Serving: Cal 473; Prot 25 g; Carbo 25 g; Fiber 1 g; T Fat 30 g; 57% Calories from Fat; Chol 232 mg; Sod 827 mg.

Easy Chicken Cutlets*

"These are wonderful for lunch the next day."

4 4-ounce boneless chicken breast halves
1 cup melted margarine
1 cup grated Parmesan cheese
1 cup cornflake crumbs

Rinse chicken and pat dry. Dip in margarine; coat with mixture of cheese and crumbs. Place on lightly oiled baking sheet. Bake at 375 degrees for 30 minutes, turning once. May substitute Italian bread crumbs for cornflake crumbs and mayonnaise or Dijon mustard for margarine. **Yield:** 4 servings.

Approx Per Serving: Cal 706; Prot 37 g; Carbo 16 g; Fiber <1 g; T Fat 55 g; 70% Calories from Fat; Chol 88 mg; Sod 1186 mg.

Chicken Dijonaise*

4 8-ounce chicken breast halves, boned, skinned
3 tablespoons butter
1/4 cup chopped onion
1/2 cup white wine
2 tablespoons Dijon mustard
1 1/2 cups cream
Rosemary, thyme, tarragon, salt and pepper to taste

Rinse chicken and pat dry. Sauté in 2 tablespoons butter in skillet until cooked through. Remove to warm platter. Add 1 tablespoon butter and onion to skillet. Sauté for several minutes. Stir in wine and mustard. Cook until reduced by 1/2. Stir in cream. Cook until mixture coats spoon, stirring frequently. Stir in rosemary, thyme, tarragon, salt and pepper. Spoon over chicken. May substitute yogurt for cream. **Yield:** 4 servings.

Approx Per Serving: Cal 554; Prot 29 g; Carbo 4 g; Fiber <1 g; T Fat 45 g; 76% Calories from Fat; Chol 218 mg; Sod 268 mg.

Chicken Fajitas

"You can marinate whole chicken breast filets, grill and slice to serve."

8 4-ounce boneless skinned chicken breasts
1 cup fresh lime juice
3/4 teaspoon garlic salt
1 teaspoon pepper
3 or 4 onions, sliced
2 green bell peppers, sliced into thin strips
3 tablespoons oil
12 warm flour tortillas

Rinse chicken and pat dry. Slice into long 1/2-inch strips. Combine with lime juice, garlic salt and pepper in bowl. Marinate in refrigerator for 2 hours or longer. Sauté onions and green peppers in 2 tablespoons oil in large skillet for 4 to 5 minutes. Remove with slotted spoon. Add 1 tablespoon oil. Increase heat to 375 to 400 degrees. Drain chicken; add to skillet. Sauté for 4 to 5 minutes or until cooked through; remove pan from heat. Spoon chicken with onions and pepper onto tortillas; roll or fold as desired. Serve with salsa, guacamole, shredded Cheddar cheese and sour cream. **Yield:** 6 servings.

Approx Per Serving: Cal 511; Prot 42 g; Carbo 52 g; Fiber 4 g; T Fat 17 g; 30% Calories from Fat; Chol 96 mg; Sod 612 mg.

Use empty Parmesan or Romano cheese jars as shakers for crumbs or breading mixes.

Chicken Marsala

"The ham flavor in this dish makes it outstanding."

2 pounds boneless chicken breast halves
1/2 cup grated Locatelli cheese
1/4 cup margarine
1 onion, chopped
12 ounces mushrooms, sliced
1 clove of garlic, crushed
2 tablespoons flour
1/4 cup hot water
1 10-ounce can consommé
5 to 6 slices ham, chopped
1/2 to 3/4 cup Marsala

Rinse chicken and pat dry. Cut into 2-inch pieces. Coat lightly with cheese. Sauté in margarine in skillet over medium-high heat until light brown. Remove chicken to warm platter. Add onion, mushrooms and garlic to drippings in skillet. Sauté until onion is tender. Remove to bowl; sprinkle with flour. Add water and consommé to skillet, stirring to deglaze. Return chicken and onion mixture to skillet. Cook until thickened, stirring constantly. Sauté ham in nonstick skillet until light brown. Add wine and ham to chicken mixture; reduce heat. Simmer for 15 minutes. Serve over pasta. **Yield:** 6 servings.

Approx Per Serving: Cal 513; Prot 66 g; Carbo 11 g; Fiber 2 g; T Fat 17 g; 31% Calories from Fat; Chol 168 mg; Sod 937 mg.

Chicken Provençal

"Serve this dish on rice pilaf cooked in chicken broth."

4 pounds chicken breasts, boned, skinned, fat removed
Juice of 1 lemon
2 teaspoons thyme
Salt and pepper to taste
3 medium onions, chopped
2 small cloves of garlic, minced
3 tablespoons olive oil
1 tablespoon butter
1 16-ounce can Italian tomatoes
1/2 cup dry white wine
8 ounces mushrooms
Chopped parsley to taste
2 bay leaves
Sesame seed to taste

Rinse chicken and pat dry. Sprinkle with mixture of lemon juice, thyme, salt and pepper. Sauté onions and garlic in mixture of olive oil and butter in large skillet for several minutes. Add chicken. Sauté until light brown. Add tomatoes, wine, mushrooms, parsley, bay leaves and sesame seed; mix well. Simmer until chicken is tender. Remove bay leaves.
Yield: 8 servings.

Approx Per Serving: Cal 389; Prot 55 g; Carbo 9 g; Fiber 2 g; T Fat 13 g; 31% Calories from Fat; Chol 148 mg; Sod 234 mg.

Chicken in Sour Cream

"Excellent served cold at picnics"

2 cups sour cream
1/4 cup fresh lemon juice
4 teaspoons Worcestershire sauce
1 clove of garlic, crushed
2 teaspoons paprika
2 teaspoons celery salt
2 teaspoons pepper
6 8-ounce chicken breast halves, skinned
3/4 cup bread crumbs
1/2 cup melted butter

Combine sour cream, lemon juice, Worcestershire sauce, garlic, paprika, celery salt and pepper in large deep bowl; mix well. Rinse chicken and pat dry. Add to sour cream mixture, coating well. Marinate, covered, in refrigerator overnight; drain. Coat chicken with bread crumbs. Spread in baking dish; drizzle with butter. Bake at 350 degrees for 45 minutes or until tender. **Yield:** 6 servings.

Approx Per Serving: Cal 543; Prot 40 g; Carbo 14 g; Fiber 1 g; T Fat 36 g; 60% Calories from Fat; Chol 172 mg; Sod 1063 mg. Nutritional information includes entire amount of marinade.

Chicken and Tortilla Casserole

2 8-ounce whole boneless chicken breasts
1 cup water
1 medium onion, chopped
1/4 cup margarine
1 clove of garlic, chopped
1 teaspoon chili powder
1 4-ounce can chopped green chilies
1 10-ounce can cream of chicken soup
1 cup chicken stock
1 16-ounce can mild enchilada sauce
1/2 cup shredded sharp Cheddar cheese
10 corn tortillas
1 16-ounce can kidney beans, drained
1 1/2 cups shredded sharp Cheddar cheese

Rinse chicken well. Combine with water in 9x13-inch glass dish. Microwave, covered, on High for 10 minutes. Sauté onion lightly in margarine in 2-quart saucepan. Add garlic, chili powder, green chilies, soup, chicken stock and enchilada sauce. Drain and chop chicken, reserving liquid. Add reserved liquid to saucepan; mix well. Cook until heated through. Stir in 1/2 cup cheese. Arrange half the tortillas in 9x13-inch glass dish. Top with chicken, beans, half the sauce, remaining tortillas, remaining sauce and 1 1/2 cups cheese. Bake at 350 degrees for 30 minutes. Serve with rice. May substitute refried beans for kidney beans. **Yield:** 6 servings.

Approx Per Serving: Cal 642; Prot 39 g; Carbo 56 g; Fiber 11 g; T Fat 31 g; 42% Calories from Fat; Chol 92 mg; Sod 2210 mg.

Cranberry-Glazed Chicken*

8 4-ounce boneless chicken breast halves
1 8-ounce bottle of French salad dressing
1 16-ounce can whole cranberry sauce
1 envelope onion soup mix

Rinse chicken and pat dry. Arrange in 9x13-inch baking dish. Combine remaining ingredients in bowl; mix well. Pour over chicken. Bake at 350 degrees for 1 hour. Serve over rice. **Yield:** 8 servings.

Approx Per Serving: Cal 378; Prot 27 g; Carbo 24 g; Fiber 1 g; T Fat 19 g; 46% Calories from Fat; Chol 72 mg; Sod 491 mg.

Dynamite Chicken

8 4-ounce chicken breast halves
3 10-ounce packages frozen spinach, thawed, drained
2 10-ounce cans cream of chicken soup
1 cup mayonnaise
1 tablespoon fresh lemon juice
1 teaspoon curry powder
1/2 cup shredded sharp Cheddar cheese

Rinse chicken well. Poach in water in saucepan until tender; drain. Discard skin and bones. Layer spinach and chicken in 9x13-inch baking dish. Combine soup, mayonnaise, lemon juice and curry powder in bowl; mix well. Spread over chicken; top with cheese. Bake at 350 degrees for 30 to 40 minutes or until bubbly. **Yield:** 8 servings.

Approx Per Serving: Cal 462; Prot 34 g; Carbo 12 g; Fiber 3 g; T Fat 32 g; 61% Calories from Fat; Chol 102 mg; Sod 912 mg.

Inside-Out Chicken*

"Do not crush the stuffing mix in this recipe."

8 4-ounce boneless chicken breast halves
1 10-ounce can cream of mushroom soup
2 cups herb-flavored stuffing mix

Rinse chicken and pat dry. Dip in soup; coat with stuffing mix. Arrange in lightly greased 9x13-inch baking dish. Bake, covered, at 350 degrees for 1 hour or until tender. Bake, uncovered, for 10 to 15 minutes or until brown. **Yield:** 8 servings.

Approx Per Serving: Cal 242; Prot 29 g; Carbo 15 g; Fiber <1 g; T Fat 6 g; 24% Calories from Fat; Chol 73 mg; Sod 583 mg.

Italian Chicken Bake

"Microwave the potatoes or even the whole dish for a quick meal."

6 4-ounce boneless chicken breast halves
3 to 4 onions, sliced
6 to 8 potatoes, peeled, sliced 1/4 to 1/2-inch thick
Salt and pepper to taste
1 large clove of garlic, minced
1/2 cup olive oil
Oregano to taste
1/2 10-ounce can consommé
1/2 10-ounce can water

Rinse chicken and pat dry. Arrange in large baking pan. Spread onions and potatoes around chicken; sprinkle with salt, pepper and garlic. Drizzle with oil; sprinkle with oregano. Bake, covered with foil, at 325 degrees for 1 hour. Pour mixture of consommé and water over chicken. Bake, uncovered, for 35 to 45 minutes longer or until chicken and potatoes are tender. Serve with tossed salad. **Yield:** 6 servings.

Approx Per Serving: Cal 535; Prot 33 g; Carbo 53 g; Fiber 5 g; T Fat 22 g; 36% Calories from Fat; Chol 72 mg; Sod 199 mg.

Lime Chicken Kabobs*

"This easy dish is great for a summer barbecue."

1/2 cup oil
1/2 cup Rose's lime juice
2 tablespoons chopped onion
2 tablespoons tarragon
1/2 teaspoon Tabasco sauce
6 4-ounce boneless chicken breast halves, skinned

Combine oil, lime juice, onion, tarragon and Tabasco sauce in bowl. Rinse chicken and pat dry; cut into cubes. Add to marinade; mix well. Marinate in refrigerator for 3 hours; drain. Thread onto skewers. Grill until cooked through. Serve over wild rice. **Yield:** 6 servings.

Approx Per Serving: Cal 308; Prot 27 g; Carbo 2 g; Fiber <1 g; T Fat 21 g; 62% Calories from Fat; Chol 72 mg; Sod 65 mg. Nutritional information includes entire amount of marinade.

For a different garnish, mince leftover corned beef and sauté in butter until crisp. Drain and use in place of crumbled bacon for topping casseroles.

Touch of Lemon Chicken

1½ pounds boneless chicken breasts
⅓ cup flour
1 teaspoon salt
¼ teaspoon pepper
4 tablespoons corn oil
2 tablespoons butter
1 medium onion, chopped
1 pound mushrooms, sliced
2 to 3 tablespoons flour
½ cup water
1 10-ounce can consommé
1 cup dry white wine
Juice of 2 or 3 medium lemons

Rinse chicken and pat dry. Cut into 2-inch pieces. Coat with mixture of ⅓ cup flour, salt and pepper. Heat 2 tablespoons oil and butter in 12-inch skillet over medium heat or electric skillet set at medium heat. Add chicken. Sauté until brown on all sides. Remove chicken to warm dish. Add 2 tablespoons oil, onion and mushrooms. Sauté until tender; reduce heat. Sprinkle with 2 to 3 tablespoons flour. Stir in water, consommé and wine. Cook until thickened, stirring constantly. Return chicken to skillet. Stir in lemon juice. Simmer for 10 to 15 minutes or until chicken is tender. Serve over rice or linguine. **Yield:** 5 servings.

Approx Per Serving: Cal 438; Prot 38 g; Carbo 20 g; Fiber 3 g; T Fat 20 g; 43% Calories from Fat; Chol 99 mg; Sod 842 mg.

Monte Carlo Chicken

6 6-ounce boneless chicken breast halves
1 pound fresh spinach
6 ounces ricotta cheese
2 ounces pine nuts
½ teaspoon basil
Salt and pepper to taste
½ cup chicken broth
1 small onion, chopped
1 tablespoon olive oil
1 clove of garlic, crushed
1 pound tomatoes, skinned, chopped
1 tablespoon tomato paste
1 teaspoon sugar
Salt and pepper to taste
2 tablespoons chopped fresh basil

Rinse chicken and pat dry. Pound with meat mallet to flatten. Rinse and drain spinach. Cook in large skillet until wilted, stirring constantly. Drain and chop. Combine with ricotta cheese, pine nuts, ½ teaspoon basil, salt and pepper in bowl; mix well. Spoon onto chicken, leaving ½ inch edge on long side. Roll from opposite side to enclose filling; tie loosely with thread. Wrap individually with foil. Arrange in baking dish; add chicken broth. Bake at 400 degrees for 30 minutes to poach or until chicken is tender. Sauté onion in olive oil in saucepan. Stir in next 6 ingredients. Simmer for 30 minutes. Stir in 2 tablespoons basil. Spoon sauce onto serving plates. Cut chicken into slices, discarding foil; arrange slices in circle over sauce. **Yield:** 6 servings.

Approx Per Serving: Cal 376; Prot 49 g; Carbo 11 g; Fiber 4 g; T Fat 16 g; 37% Calories from Fat; Chol 123 mg; Sod 252 mg.

New Orleans Chicken

"This can be reheated in a slow oven."

8 boneless chicken breast halves
Salt and pepper to taste
1/2 cup butter
2 teaspoons olive oil
1 cup bottled small cooked onions with liquid
8 ounces mushrooms, sliced
1/4 cup Burgundy
2 shallots, chopped
3/4 cup Burgundy
1/2 cup whipping cream

Rinse chicken and pat dry; cut into halves. Sprinkle with salt and pepper. Sauté in butter and olive oil in electric skillet until brown. Remove chicken to warm platter. Add onions, mushrooms and 1/4 cup wine to skillet. Cook for 5 minutes. Return chicken to skillet; set skillet temperature to 350 degrees. Cook, covered, for 20 minutes. Sauté shallots in small nonstick skillet until tender. Add remaining 3/4 cup wine. Cook until reduced by 1/2. Stir in cream. Heat just for 2 minutes; do not boil. Place chicken mixture on serving plate; spoon sauce over top. **Yield:** 8 servings.

Approx Per Serving: Cal 365; Prot 29 g; Carbo 10 g; Fiber 1 g; T Fat 21 g; 55% Calories from Fat; Chol 124 mg; Sod 276 mg.

Chinese Chicken

"A health-conscious recipe"

3 tablespoons soy sauce
1 tablespoon sherry
1 teaspoon sugar
1 teaspoon salt
2 tablespoons cornstarch
5 4-ounce boneless chicken breast halves
1 egg white, beaten
1/2 cup cornstarch
1 clove of garlic, minced
2 slices ginger
2 chili peppers, chopped
3 scallions
2 tablespoons peanut oil
1/2 cup water
1/2 cup unsalted peanuts
2 green bell peppers, chopped

Mix first 5 ingredients in bowl. Rinse chicken and pat dry. Cut into bite-sized pieces. Dip into egg white; coat with 1/2 cup cornstarch. Stir-fry garlic, ginger, chili peppers and scallions in 1 tablespoon peanut oil in skillet. Remove with slotted spoon. Add remaining tablespoon peanut oil and chicken. Stir-fry for 5 minutes or until cooked through. Return vegetables to skillet. Add soy sauce mixture and water; mix well. Simmer for 5 minutes or until chicken is tender. Add peanuts and green peppers. Cook for 1 minute. Serve over rice. **Yield:** 4 servings.

Approx Per Serving: Cal 453; Prot 40 g; Carbo 28 g; Fiber 3 g; T Fat 20 g; 40% Calories from Fat; Chol 90 mg; Sod 1403 mg.

Raspberry Chicken*

"For an elegant company dish, spoon sauce onto individual plates and place chicken in sauce."

4 4-ounce boneless chicken breast halves
2 tablespoons butter
1 medium onion, chopped
3 tablespoons raspberry jam
3 tablespoons raspberry vinegar
1/2 cup half and half

Rinse chicken and pat dry. Sauté in butter in 10-inch skillet over medium heat for 5 minutes. Turn chicken and add onion. Sauté until chicken is tender and golden brown. Remove to warm platter. Add jam and vinegar to skillet, stirring to deglaze. Cook until slightly reduced, stirring constantly; remove from heat. Stir in half and half. Bring just to a simmer; do not boil. Spoon over chicken. **Yield:** 4 servings.

Approx Per Serving: Cal 286; Prot 28 g; Carbo 15 g; Fiber 1 g; T Fat 12 g; 39% Calories from Fat; Chol 99 mg; Sod 126 mg.

Santa Fe Chicken

6 6-ounce boneless whole chicken breasts, skinned
6 1/2x1x3-inch sharp Cheddar cheese sticks
6 canned whole green chilies
1/2 cup flour
2 tablespoons olive oil
1 bunch scallions, chopped
1 4-ounce can chopped green chilies
2 tablespoons margarine
1/4 cup flour
1 14-ounce can (or less) chicken broth
1 tablespoon lemon juice
1/4 cup chopped cilantro
2 tablespoons tomato paste
1/2 cup shredded sharp Cheddar cheese
Salt and pepper to taste

Rinse chicken and pat dry. Cut each chicken breast in half. Slice thick part of each breast nearly through; open and spread flat. Place 1 cheese stick in each whole green chili. Place chilies on 6 pieces chicken. Top with remaining chicken pieces; secure with wooden picks. Coat with 1/2 cup flour. Brown on both sides in olive oil in skillet. Place in shallow baking dish. Bake at 350 degrees for 30 minutes. Sauté scallions in drippings in skillet. Add chopped green chilies and 2 tablespoons margarine. Sauté for several minutes. Sprinkle with 1/4 cup flour. Cook over low heat, adding chicken broth gradually and stirring until thickened to desired consistency. Stir in lemon juice and cilantro. Mix 1/2 cup sauce with tomato paste in small bowl. Stir into hot sauce. Stir in shredded cheese, salt and pepper. Spoon sauce over chicken to serve. **Yield:** 6 servings.

Approx Per Serving: Cal 530; Prot 53 g; Carbo 19 g; Fiber 1 g; T Fat 26 g; 45% Calories from Fat; Chol 148 mg; Sod 1043 mg.

Well Dressed Chicken

"You may substitute four or five ounces of Boursin cheese for the cream cheese mixture for an even easier preparation."

4 ounces cream cheese, softened
¾ cup packed watercress
1 clove of garlic
⅛ teaspoon salt
Freshly ground pepper to taste
1 17-ounce package frozen puff pastry, thawed
4 8-ounce boneless chicken breast halves
1 egg, beaten

Process first 5 ingredients in food processor or blender container until smooth. Roll pastry sheets to 10x14-inch rectangles on lightly floured surface. Cut each into halves. Spread cream cheese mixture in oval about the size of chicken on each piece of pastry. Rinse chicken and pat dry. Place skinned side down on cream cheese. Pull up long sides of pastry to cover chicken and fold to close. Press ends and folds to seal well. Place seam side down 2 inches apart on greased baking sheet. Brush with egg. Bake at 425 degrees for 20 minutes or until pastry is puffed and golden brown and chicken is tender. **Yield:** 4 servings.

Approx Per Serving: Cal 912; Prot 65 g; Carbo 45 g; Fiber <1 g; T Fat 51 g; 51% Calories from Fat; Chol 229 mg; Sod 867 mg.

Chicken Enchiladas

1 cup chopped onion
½ cup chopped green pepper
2 tablespoons butter
2 cups chopped cooked chicken
1 4-ounce can chopped green chilies, drained
¼ cup flour
1 teaspoon coriander
Salt to taste
3 tablespoons melted butter
2½ cups chicken broth
1 cup sour cream
2 cups shredded Monterey Jack cheese
12 corn tortillas

Sauté onion and green pepper in 2 tablespoons butter in skillet. Stir in chicken and green chilies; set aside. Blend flour, coriander and salt into 3 tablespoons melted butter in saucepan. Cook for several minutes. Stir in chicken broth. Cook over medium heat until thickened, stirring constantly; remove from heat. Stir in sour cream and ½ cup cheese. Stir ½ cup sauce into chicken mixture. Dip tortillas 1 at a time into remaining sauce for 5 seconds to soften. Spoon chicken mixture onto tortillas; roll to enclose filling. Place seam side down in 9x13-inch baking dish. Pour remaining sauce over top. Sprinkle with remaining cheese. Bake at 350 degrees for 25 minutes. Serve with salsa, guacamole and additional sour cream. **Yield:** 6 servings.

Approx Per Serving: Cal 581; Prot 31 g; Carbo 36 g; Fiber 6 g; T Fat 36 g; 56% Calories from Fat; Chol 121 mg; Sod 818 mg.

Chicken Florentine

2 10-ounce packages frozen spinach
1 small onion, chopped
3 tablespoons margarine
1/2 teaspoon thyme
1/4 teaspoon salt
1/4 teaspoon pepper
3 tablespoons (or more) margarine
1 small onion, chopped
4 ounces fresh mushrooms, sliced
3 tablespoons flour
1 10-ounce can consommé
Worcestershire sauce to taste
1/2 teaspoon basil
1 egg yolk
1 teaspoon lemon juice
2 cups chopped cooked chicken

Microwave spinach on High in glass bowl for 10 minutes; drain well. Sauté 1 onion in 3 tablespoons margarine in skillet until tender. Add spinach, thyme, salt and pepper; mix well. Spoon into 2-quart baking dish. Melt remaining 3 tablespoons margarine in same skillet. Add remaining onion and mushrooms. Sauté until tender. Stir in flour, consommé, Worcestershire sauce and basil. Cook until thickened, stirring constantly; reduce heat. Stir a small amount of hot sauce into mixture of egg yolk and lemon juice; stir egg yolk mixture into hot sauce. Cook over low heat for 1 minute, stirring constantly; do not boil. Stir in chicken. Pour over spinach mixture. Bake at 350 degrees for 15 to 20 minutes or until heated through. May omit egg yolk and mushrooms if preferred. **Yield:** 4 servings.

Approx Per Serving: Cal 407; Prot 31 g; Carbo 19 g; Fiber 5 g; T Fat 24 g; 53% Calories from Fat; Chol 139 mg; Sod 861 mg.

Chicken Pizzazz*

"Hot chicken salad with pizzazz"

2 cups chopped cooked chicken
3/4 cup toasted slivered almonds
1 8-ounce can sliced water chestnuts, drained
1 2-ounce jar chopped pimento, drained
1 tablespoon fresh lemon juice
1/2 cup mayonnaise
1/2 cup low-fat yogurt
3 tablespoons dry vermouth
1 teaspoon curry powder
1/4 teaspoon salt
1/4 teaspoon white pepper
1 cup shredded Cheddar cheese
3/4 cup canned French-fried onions, crushed

Combine chicken, almonds, water chestnuts, pimento, lemon juice, mayonnaise, yogurt, wine, curry powder, salt and white pepper in bowl; mix well. Spread in 9x13-inch baking dish. Top with cheese and onions. Bake at 350 degrees for 25 to 30 minutes or until bubbly. May substitute mayonnaise for yogurt. **Yield:** 6 servings.

Approx Per Serving: Cal 459; Prot 19 g; Carbo 17 g; Fiber 2 g; T Fat 35 g; 69% Calories from Fat; Chol 55 mg; Sod 416 mg.

Yankee Chicken Hash

"For healthier hash, substitute chicken or turkey sausage for the sausage in this dish."

3 cups chopped cooked chicken
1½ cups crumbled cooked sausage
¾ cup chopped green bell pepper
¾ cup chopped onion
½ teaspoon thyme
2 tablespoons chopped parsley
½ cup coarse bread crumbs
½ teaspoon grated lemon rind
1 tablespoon flour
1 tablespoon melted butter
½ cup milk
Salt and pepper to taste
¼ cup butter

Combine chicken, sausage, green pepper, onion, thyme and parsley in large bowl; mix well. Stir in bread crumbs and lemon rind. Blend flour into 1 tablespoon melted butter in small saucepan. Cook until smooth. Add milk gradually. Cook until thickened, stirring constantly. Simmer for 5 minutes. Season with salt and pepper. Stir sauce into chicken mixture. Melt ¼ cup butter in heavy skillet. Spread hash in skillet. Cook over low heat until bottom is brown and crusty. Fold in half and slide onto serving platter. **Yield:** 6 servings.

Approx Per Serving: Cal 370; Prot 28 g; Carbo 11 g; Fiber 1 g; T Fat 24 g; 58% Calories from Fat; Chol 112 mg; Sod 535 mg.

Oriental Chicken over Cheese Soufflé

8 slices white bread
¼ cup butter, softened
1 pound medium sharp Cheddar cheese, shredded
6 eggs
3 cups milk
1 cup sliced mushrooms
½ cup flour
2 teaspoons salt
½ cup melted butter
½ to 1 cup cream
3 cups milk
2 cups chicken stock
3½ cups chopped cooked chicken
2 7-ounce cans sliced water chestnuts
½ cup sliced pimento
¼ cup dry white wine

Trim crusts from bread and spread softened butter on both sides; cut into cubes. Layer bread and cheese in 9x13-inch baking dish. Beat eggs in bowl. Beat in 3 cups milk. Pour over layers. Chill overnight. Bake at 350 degrees for 1 hour or until set. Sauté mushrooms in nonstick skillet for several minutes; set aside. Blend flour and salt into ½ cup melted butter in saucepan. Stir in cream, 3 cups milk and chicken stock. Cook for 20 minutes or until thickened and smooth, stirring frequently. Add chicken, water chestnuts, mushrooms, pimento and wine. Cook until heated through. Serve over soufflé. **Yield:** 10 servings.

Approx Per Serving: Cal 736; Prot 39 g; Carbo 30 g; Fiber 2 g; T Fat 51 g; 62% Calories from Fat; Chol 309 mg; Sod 1252 mg.

Hot Chicken Salad*

5 cups chopped cooked chicken
1½ cups chopped celery
1½ to 2 cups cooked rice
1 teaspoon chopped onion
2 5-ounce cans water chestnuts, drained, chopped
1 teaspoon lemon juice
¾ cup mayonnaise
1 10-ounce can cream of chicken soup
1½ cups crushed cornflakes
¼ cup melted butter

Mix first 8 ingredients in bowl. Spoon into 9x13-inch baking dish. Top with mixture of cornflakes and melted butter. Bake at 350 degrees for 30 minutes or until bubbly. Serve with fresh asparagus. **Yield:** 8 servings.

Approx Per Serving: Cal 525; Prot 29 g; Carbo 32 g; Fiber 2 g; T Fat 31 g; 53% Calories from Fat; Chol 109 mg; Sod 700 mg.

Lancaster Chicken Spaghetti*

1 green bell pepper, chopped
1 large onion, chopped
1 clove of garlic, chopped
½ cup margarine
3 cups chopped cooked chicken
1 4-ounce can sliced mushrooms
½ 8-ounce can tomato sauce
1 10-ounce can tomatoes with green chilies
Salt and pepper to taste
12 ounces spaghetti, cooked
1 cup shredded Cheddar cheese

Sauté green pepper, onion and garlic in margarine in saucepan. Add chicken, mushrooms, tomato sauce, tomatoes, salt and pepper. Add spaghetti; mix well. Spoon into buttered baking dish; top with cheese. Bake at 350 degrees for 45 minutes. **Yield:** 6 servings.

Approx Per Serving: Cal 584; Prot 34 g; Carbo 50 g; Fiber 4 g; T Fat 28 g; 43% Calories from Fat; Chol 82 mg; Sod 741 mg.

Roasted Cornish Hens Supreme*

2 Cornish game hens
2 tablespoons Dijon mustard
2 teaspoons soy sauce
1 medium onion, thinly sliced
2 tablespoons mayonnaise
¼ cup shredded Cheddar cheese

Rinse hens and pat dry. Cut into halves and remove backbone. Arrange skin side up in shallow baking dish. Brush with mixture of mustard and soy sauce. Top with onion slices. Spread with mixture of mayonnaise and cheese. Bake, covered with foil, at 375 degrees for 20 minutes. Bake, uncovered, for 20 to 25 minutes or until golden brown. **Yield:** 4 servings.

Approx Per Serving: Cal 314; Prot 36 g; Carbo 4 g; Fiber 1 g; T Fat 17 g; 49% Calories from Fat; Chol 113 mg; Sod 450 mg.

Duck Breasts with Raspberry Sauce

"You may also use domestic duck or turkey tenderloin in this recipe."

1/2 cup dry red wine
1/4 cup soy sauce
1/4 cup oil
1/4 teaspoon pepper
4 wild duck breasts, skinned, boned
1/4 cup seedless raspberry jam
1/4 cup water
1 1/2 tablespoons Dijon mustard
1 teaspoon lime juice
1 teaspoon soy sauce
1/2 teaspoon steak sauce
1/2 teaspoon salt
1/2 teaspoon pepper

Combine wine, 1/4 cup soy sauce, oil and 1/4 teaspoon pepper in bowl; mix well. Rinse duck and pat dry. Add to marinade. Marinate in refrigerator for 2 to 3 hours, turning occasionally; drain. Place duck on rack in broiler pan. Broil 5 inches from heat source for 15 minutes or until cooked through, turning once. Combine jam, water, mustard, lime juice, 1 teaspoon soy sauce, steak sauce, 1/2 teaspoon salt and 1/2 teaspoon pepper in saucepan. Simmer until thickened to desired consistency. Serve with duck. **Yield:** 4 servings.

Approx Per Serving: Cal 315; Prot 18 g; Carbo 17 g; Fiber <1 g; T Fat 18 g; 53% Calories from Fat; Chol 62 mg; Sod 1506 mg. Nutritional information includes entire amount of marinade.

Kingdom Come Goose

"This is a good substitute for the Christmas turkey. It can also be prepared with two to four Muscovy ducks in season."

1 8 to 10-pound goose
2 green cooking apples
2 stalks celery, coarsely chopped
2 10-ounce cans consommé
1 10-ounce can water
3/4 cup butter
1/3 cup sherry
1/4 cup bourbon
2 1/2 ounces currant jelly
2 tablespoons Worcestershire sauce

Rinse goose inside and out and pat dry. Stuff with apples and celery. Place breast side down in large roasting pan. Add consommé and water. Roast, tightly covered, at 350 degrees for 3 hours or until very tender. Combine butter, sherry, bourbon, jelly and Worcestershire sauce in saucepan. Cook until heated through, stirring to mix well. Slice breast from goose, discarding skin. Place in baking dish. Spoon sauce over top. Bake at 350 degrees just until heated through. **Yield:** 6 servings.

Approx Per Serving: Cal 396; Prot 18 g; Carbo 18 g; Fiber 1 g; T Fat 25 g; 61% Calories from Fat; Chol 143 mg; Sod 750 mg.

Pheasant in Casserole

4 slices bacon, chopped
2 pheasant
1/2 cup flour
2 large onions, sliced
1 pound fresh mushrooms, sliced
3/4 cup dry red wine
1/2 clove of garlic, crushed
2 tablespoons tarragon

Fry bacon in large skillet until brown; remove with slotted spoon. Rinse pheasant and pat dry. Cut into serving pieces, discarding backbones and ribs. Coat with flour. Cook in drippings in skillet until brown on all sides. Remove to baking dish. Add onions and mushrooms to drippings in skillet. Sauté until light brown. Remove to baking dish with slotted spoon; drain skillet. Add wine and garlic to skillet. Cook for several minutes, stirring to deglaze skillet. Pour over pheasant. Sprinkle with tarragon and bacon. Roast, covered, at 325 degrees for 2 hours. **Yield:** 8 servings.

Approx Per Serving: Cal 283; Prot 28 g; Carbo 12 g; Fiber 2 g; T Fat 12 g; 40% Calories from Fat; Chol 82 mg; Sod 98 mg.

Turkey Meat Loaf

1 1/2 pounds ground uncooked turkey
4 slices bread, torn
1 egg
1 cup milk
1/4 cup chopped onion
1 tablespoon Worcestershire sauce
1 small green bell pepper, chopped
1 medium carrot, coarsely shredded
1 4-ounce can chopped mushrooms, drained
3 tablespoons catsup
1/8 teaspoon garlic powder
1/4 teaspoon sage
1/2 teaspoon dry mustard
Salt to taste
1/4 teaspoon pepper
1 tomato, thinly sliced
3 slices American cheese, cut into halves diagonally

Combine turkey, bread crumbs, egg, milk, onion, Worcestershire sauce, green pepper, carrot, mushrooms, catsup, garlic powder, sage, dry mustard, salt and pepper in bowl; mix well. Shape into loaf in greased 5x9-inch loaf pan. Bake at 350 degrees for 1 to 1 1/4 hours. Arrange tomato slices and cheese over top. Bake for 3 to 5 minutes or until cheese melts. May brush with mixture of 1/2 cup catsup, 2 tablespoons brown sugar, 1 tablespoon lemon juice, 1 teaspoon dry mustard and nutmeg to taste. Microwave, covered, on Medium-high for 30 minutes, turning dish after 15 minutes. Drain and let stand for 5 minutes. **Yield:** 6 servings.

Approx Per Serving: Cal 362; Prot 30 g; Carbo 18 g; Fiber 2 g; T Fat 19 g; 47% Calories from Fat; Chol 126 mg; Sod 618 mg.

Turkey and Pumpkin Stew

"The faces of your guests and family will light up when you present dinner in a pumpkin!"

1 10-inch pumpkin
2 tablespoons flour
1/8 teaspoon ginger
1 teaspoon salt
2 pounds uncooked turkey, cubed
2 tablespoons oil
1 medium onion, chopped
2 to 3 carrots, cut into quarters
1 cup chopped yellow squash
8 to 12 ounces green beans, cut
1 cup beef bouillon

Slice off and reserve top of pumpkin. Discard seed. Scoop out and reserve pumpkin pulp, leaving 3/4-inch shell. Combine flour, ginger and salt in bowl. Rinse turkey and pat dry. Add to flour mixture; toss to coat well. Brown in oil in saucepan. Add pumpkin pulp, onion, carrots, squash, green beans and bouillon. Bring to a boil; reduce heat. Simmer for 10 minutes. Place pumpkin shell in baking pan. Spoon stew into pumpkin; replace top of pumpkin. Pour 1-inch hot water into baking pan. Bake, uncovered, at 350 degrees for 1 hour. Bake, covered with foil, for 1 3/4 hours or until tender. **Yield:** 6 servings.

Approx Per Serving: Cal 271; Prot 28 g; Carbo 21 g; Fiber 6 g; T Fat 9 g; 30% Calories from Fat; Chol 63 mg; Sod 562 mg.

Turkey Tolstoy*

"A low-cholesterol recipe"

1 1/2 to 2 pounds uncooked boneless turkey breast
1 clove of garlic, crushed
1 large onion, chopped
12 ounces mushrooms, sliced
1/4 cup (or more) corn oil
3 tablespoons flour
Salt to taste
1/4 teaspoon pepper
1 10-ounce can consommé
1/2 to 3/4 10-ounce can water
1/4 cup dry white wine
1 cup plain low-fat yogurt
2 teaspoons Dijon mustard

Rinse turkey and pat dry; cut into bite-sized pieces. Sauté garlic, onion and mushrooms in oil in heavy skillet. Remove with slotted spoon. Brown turkey quickly in drippings in skillet, adding additional oil if needed. Return vegetables to skillet. Stir in flour, salt and pepper. Stir in consommé and water. Cook until thickened, stirring constantly; reduce heat. Simmer for 5 minutes or until turkey is tender. Add wine, yogurt and mustard. Cook until heated through. Serve over rice or egg noodles. **Yield:** 5 servings.

Approx Per Serving: Cal 360; Prot 36 g; Carbo 14 g; Fiber 2 g; T Fat 17 g; 44% Calories from Fat; Chol 78 mg; Sod 426 mg.

Seafood & Pasta

Warren Tavern

Golf Tournament Cocktail Buffet

Bacon 'n Cheese on Rye
page 42

Bleu Cheese Pâté
page 67

Filet of Beef Stuffed with Spinach
page 140

Fusilli with Tomato and Cheese Sauce
page 208

Tortellini in Cheese Sauce
page 210

Chocolate Buttersweets
page 271

Fruit Pizzas
page 249

SEAFOOD

Flounder Véronique

"This tasty dish can also be prepared with sole."

8 ounces mushrooms, sliced
3 tablespoons butter
Salt and pepper to taste
2 pounds flounder filets
1 cup milk
8 ounces seedless green grapes
1/4 cup butter
1 1/2 tablespoons flour
2 tablespoons grated Parmesan cheese
1/2 cup light cream
1/4 cup grated Parmesan cheese

Sauté mushrooms in 3 tablespoons butter in skillet. Season with salt and pepper; set aside. Poach fish in milk in saucepan for 5 to 10 minutes or until fish flakes easily. Remove fish gently and season with salt and pepper; reserve poaching liquid. Alternate layers of fish, mushrooms and grapes in buttered baking dish. Melt 1/4 cup butter in saucepan; remove from heat. Blend in flour. Add reserved poaching liquid gradually. Add 2 tablespoons cheese and cream. Cook until thickened, stirring constantly. Spoon over layers in baking dish. Sprinkle with 1/4 cup cheese. Bake at 400 degrees for 15 minutes. May chill until baking time and let stand until room temperature. **Yield:** 4 servings.

Approx Per Serving: Cal 614; Prot 52 g; Carbo 19 g; Fiber 2 g; T Fat 37 g; 54% Calories from Fat; Chol 225 mg; Sod 540 mg.

Fishing for Compliments*

4 flounder filets
1 sweet onion, thinly sliced
1/2 cup mayonnaise
3 tablespoons grated Parmesan cheese
1 teaspoon Dijon mustard

Arrange fish in broiler pan lined with greased foil. Place onion rings over fish. Combine mayonnaise, cheese and mustard in bowl; mix well. Spread over onions. Cover with foil. Broil for 15 to 20 minutes; remove foil. Broil until topping is bubbly and brown. May substitute sole filets for flounder. **Yield:** 4 servings.

Approx Per Serving: Cal 335; Prot 24 g; Carbo 4 g; Fiber 1 g; T Fat 25 g; 66% Calories from Fat; Chol 81 mg; Sod 339 mg.

Flounder Incognito*

"Even children like this dish."

1 1/2 pounds flounder filets
1 16-ounce can stewed Italian-style tomatoes
2 cups shredded mozzarella cheese

Arrange fish in greased 9x13-inch baking dish. Pour tomatoes over fish; sprinkle with cheese. Bake at 350 degrees for 25 minutes. **Yield:** 4 servings.

Approx Per Serving: Cal 354; Prot 45 g; Carbo 10 g; Fiber 0 g; T Fat 14 g; 36% Calories from Fat; Chol 137 mg; Sod 719 mg.

Golden Puff Flounder

1/2 cup mayonnaise
2 egg yolks, beaten
2 tablespoons chopped parsley
1/4 teaspoon cayenne pepper
2 egg whites, stiffly beaten
2 pounds flounder filets
1/3 cup oil
1 teaspoon salt
Pepper to taste

Combine mayonnaise, egg yolks, parsley and cayenne pepper in bowl; mix well. Fold in egg whites. Place fish in greased broiler pan. Brush with mixture of oil, salt and pepper. Broil 3 to 4 inches from heat source for 3 to 4 minutes. Turn fish and brush with remaining oil. Broil for 3 to 4 minutes. Spread with mayonnaise mixture. Broil 5 inches from heat source for 2 to 3 minutes or until golden brown. **Yield:** 4 servings.

Approx Per Serving: Cal 608; Prot 47 g; Carbo 1 g; Fiber <1 g; T Fat 45 g; 68% Calories from Fat; Chol 247 mg; Sod 909 mg.

Finnegan's Flounder

"Add a green vegetable for a St. Patrick's day dinner."

2 pounds flounder filets
1 small onion, chopped
1 teaspoon salt
Freshly ground pepper to taste
3/4 cup apple juice
1/4 cup Irish Mist
1/4 cup lemon juice
2 tablespoons flour
2 tablespoons melted butter
1/4 cup whipping cream
1/4 cup grated Parmesan cheese

Arrange fish in buttered baking dish; sprinkle with onion, salt and pepper. Combine apple juice, liqueur and lemon juice in small bowl; mix well. Pour over fish. Bake, covered, at 350 degrees for 15 minutes. Strain and reserve cooking liquid; keep fish warm. Blend flour into butter in small saucepan. Cook for 2 minutes. Stir in reserved cooking liquid and cream. Cook until thickened, stirring constantly. Pour over fish. Sprinkle with cheese. Broil just until brown. Garnish with parsley. Serve with boiled new potatoes. **Yield:** 4 servings.

Approx Per Serving: Cal 418; Prot 47 g; Carbo 13 g; Fiber 1 g; T Fat 16 g; 34% Calories from Fat; Chol 164 mg; Sod 873 mg.

Double Orange Roughy

"This is a moist and tender fish dish!"

4 orange roughy filets
2 1/2 cups (or more) orange juice
2 tablespoons cornstarch
1 tablespoon Dijon mustard
Basil and thyme to taste
15 to 20 coriander seeds, crushed
1 ounce Tequila

Poach fish in orange juice in large skillet over low heat for 5 to 6 minutes on each side or until fish flakes easily. Remove fish to shallow baking dish, reserving poaching liquid. Blend cornstarch and mustard in saucepan. Strain in reserved poaching liquid and additional orange juice if desired. Cook over medium heat until thickened, stirring constantly. Stir in basil, thyme, coriander and Tequila. Strain over fish. Bake at 325 degrees for 10 to 12 minutes or until heated through. May omit Tequila if preferred. **Yield:** 4 servings.

Approx Per Serving: Cal 220; Prot 23 g; Carbo 23 g; Fiber 1 g; T Fat 2 g; 8% Calories from Fat; Chol 62 mg; Sod 146 mg.

Cook frozen fish while still icy in center. Fish will stay moist and juicy.

Red Snapper Vera Cruz

"A touch of Acapulco"

3 pounds red snapper filets
1/4 cup fresh lemon juice
Salt and freshly ground pepper to taste
1 cup chopped onion
1 clove of garlic, minced
2 tablespoons oil
1 cup finely chopped fresh cilantro leaves
3 or 4 jalapeño peppers, chopped
1 cup canned tomatoes, puréed
1 tablespoon olive oil

Arrange fish in single layer in 9x13-inch baking dish; sprinkle with lemon juice, salt and pepper. Sauté onion and garlic in 2 tablespoons oil in small skillet over medium heat until tender. Drain lemon juice from fish. Sprinkle with onion, garlic, cilantro and peppers. Pour tomatoes over fish; drizzle with olive oil. Bake at 350 degrees for 20 minutes or until fish flakes easily. Serve with rice. **Yield:** 6 servings.

Approx Per Serving: Cal 317; Prot 49 g; Carbo 6 g; Fiber 1 g; T Fat 10 g; 29% Calories from Fat; Chol 85 mg; Sod 169 mg.

Salmon in Pastry with Champagne Sauce

1 cup chicken stock
1/2 cup champagne
1/4 cup minced shallots
1/4 cup sliced fresh mushrooms
3/4 cup whipping cream
1 1 1/4-pound thick salmon filet, skinned
1/2 cup unsalted butter, softened
2 teaspoons fresh lemon juice
1 teaspoon tarragon
Salt and pepper to taste
8 ounces frozen puff pastry, thawed
1 egg, slightly beaten
1 teaspoon mixed parsley, tarragon, dill and chives

Combine chicken stock, champagne, shallots and mushrooms in saucepan. Cook until liquid is reduced by 1/2. Stir in cream. Cook over low heat until thickened enough to coat spoon, stirring constantly. Strain sauce and keep warm. Cut salmon into 4 serving pieces. Cut deep pocket into side of each piece. Combine butter, lemon juice, tarragon, salt and pepper in small bowl; mix well. Stuff into pockets in fish. Roll puff pastry 1/8 inch thick on lightly floured surface. Cut into 4 squares. Brush lightly with cold water. Place 1 piece fish on each square pastry. Roll to enclose fish, pressing edges to seal. Arrange on ungreased baking sheet; brush with egg. Chill for 30 minutes or longer. Bake at 400 degrees for 12 to 15 minutes or until pastry is light brown. Stir mixed herbs into sauce. Serve with fish. **Yield:** 4 servings.

Approx Per Serving: Cal 903; Prot 39 g; Carbo 25 g; Fiber <1 g; T Fat 69 g; 71% Calories from Fat; Chol 275 mg; Sod 577 mg.

Salmon Steaks Poached in Wine*

"Absolutely wonderful—with so little time."

1/2 cup chopped green onions
1/4 cup margarine
1/4 cup white wine
3 tablespoons chopped fresh parsley or 1 tablespoon parsley flakes
1 teaspoon salt
1 tablespoon chopped fresh dill or 1 teaspoon dry dill
1/4 teaspoon pepper
4 fresh salmon steaks, 1/2 inch thick
2 teaspoons capers

Cook green onions, covered, in margarine in skillet until tender. Add wine, parsley, salt, dill and pepper; reduce heat to medium-low. Add salmon. Poach, covered, for 5 to 8 minutes or just until fish flakes easily. Remove salmon to warm serving dish. Sprinkle with capers. Spoon sauce over salmon. Garnish with lemon wedges and fresh parsley or dill. **Yield:** 4 servings.

Approx Per Serving: Cal 365; Prot 37 g; Carbo 1 g; Fiber 1 g; T Fat 21 g; 77% Calories from Fat; Chol 0 mg; Sod 669 mg.

Baked Stuffed Sole with Lobster Sauce

2 slices bread, crusts trimmed, finely cubed
1 tablespoon cracker crumbs
1/4 cup melted butter
1 ounce sherry
1 teaspoon grated Parmesan cheese
Salt to taste
8 ounces lobster meat, finely chopped
4 large sole filets
1 tablespoon butter
1/4 cup milk
2 tablespoons flour
1/4 cup melted butter
3/4 cup milk, scalded
3/4 cup cream, scalded
Paprika to taste
1 tablespoon butter
1 ounce sherry

Combine bread cubes, cracker crumbs, 1/4 cup butter, 1 ounce wine, cheese, salt and 1/4 of the lobster meat in bowl; mix well. spoon onto fish filets. Roll to enclose stuffing. Melt 1 tablespoon butter in baking dish. Arrange fish rolls in prepared dish. Add 1/4 cup milk; sprinkle with salt. Bake at 400 degrees for 20 minutes or until fish flakes. Blend flour into 1/4 cup melted butter in saucepan. Cook for several minutes. Add 3/4 cup warm milk and cream. Cook until thickened, stirring constantly. Season with salt and paprika. Sauté remaining lobster in remaining 1 tablespoon butter in skillet. Stir in remaining 1 ounce wine. Add to sauce; mix gently. Cook just until heated through. Serve over fish. **Yield:** 4 servings.

Approx Per Serving: Cal 669; Prot 36 g; Carbo 16 g; Fiber <1 g; T Fat 50 g; 68% Calories from Fat; Chol 242 mg; Sod 649 mg.

Marinated Fish Filets*

"Delicious—with so little effort"

1/4 cup orange juice
1/4 cup soy sauce
1 small tomato, chopped
2 tablespoons oil
1 1/2 teaspoons lemon juice
1 clove of garlic, chopped
1/4 teaspoon oregano
2 teaspoons chopped parsley
1/4 teaspoon pepper
4 sole filets

Combine first 9 ingredients in shallow dish; mix well. Add fish. Marinate for 1 hour. Drain, reserving marinade. Arrange on foil-covered rack in broiler pan. Broil 4 inches from heat source for 8 to 10 minutes or until fish flakes easily, basting occasionally with reserved marinade. May bake at 350 degrees for 30 minutes if preferred. **Yield:** 4 servings.

Approx Per Serving: Cal 188; Prot 23 g; Carbo 5 g; Fiber <1 g; T Fat 8 g; 40% Calories from Fat; Chol 62 mg; Sod 1126 mg. Nutritional information includes entire amount of marinade.

Wellington Sole

2 shallots, minced
1 red bell pepper, minced
1 tablespoon olive oil
8 ounces crab meat, flaked
1 teaspoon sherry or balsamic wine vinegar
1/2 teaspoon dry mustard
1/4 cup dry white wine
2 tablespoons bread crumbs
Salt and pepper to taste
4 4-ounce sole filets
1/4 cup dry white wine
1 cup water
8 sheets frozen phyllo dough, thawed
1/4 cup melted butter
2 tablespoons bread crumbs

Sauté shallots and bell pepper in olive oil in 10-inch skillet for 2 minutes. Add crab meat, vinegar, dry mustard and 1/4 cup wine. Cook for 3 minutes, stirring frequently; remove to bowl. Add 2 tablespoons bread crumbs, salt and pepper to crab meat mixture; mix gently. Spoon onto fish filets; roll to enclose filling. Add remaining 1/4 cup wine to skillet, stirring to deglaze. Stir in water. Bring to a simmer. Place fish rolls seam side down in skillet. Simmer, covered, for 5 minutes. Remove fish; drain on paper towel. Place on plate. Chill in refrigerator. Place 1 sheet phyllo dough on work surface. Brush with melted butter; sprinkle with 1/2 tablespoon bread crumbs. Top with second sheet of dough; brush with butter. Place 1 fish roll on dough. Gather up corners of dough to enclose fish, twisting to seal packet. Repeat process with remaining ingredients. Place on greased baking sheet. Bake at 400 degrees for 10 to 12 minutes or until light brown. **Yield:** 4 servings.

Approx Per Serving: Cal 535; Prot 41 g; Carbo 47 g; Fiber 3 g; T Fat 18 g; 31% Calories from Fat; Chol 150 mg; Sod 559 mg.

Florentine Fish Pronto*

2 fish filets
1/2 cup white wine
1 10-ounce package frozen spinach soufflé, thawed

Place fish in baking dish. Pour wine into dish. Top with spinach. Bake at 350 degrees for 20 minutes or until spinach is set and fish flakes easily. **Yield:** 2 servings.

Approx Per Serving: Cal 372; Prot 33 g; Carbo 3 g; Fiber 4 g; T Fat 21 g; 50% Calories from Fat; Chol 254 mg; Sod 893 mg.

Swordfish with Lemon-Soy Marinade*

1/3 cup soy sauce
1/4 cup fresh lemon juice
1/2 cup oil
2 teaspoons Dijon mustard
1 clove of garlic, minced
1 teaspoon grated lemon rind
6 swordfish filets

Combine soy sauce, lemon juice, oil, mustard, garlic and lemon rind in bowl; mix well. Pierce fish with fork. Place in marinade. Marinate in refrigerator for 1 to 3 hours; drain. Grill over hot coals for 5 to 6 minutes on each side or until fish flakes easily. **Yield:** 6 servings.

Approx Per Serving: Cal 314; Prot 24 g; Carbo 3 g; Fiber <1 g; T Fat 23 g; 66% Calories from Fat; Chol 45 mg; Sod 1032 mg. Nutritional information includes entire amount of marinade.

Broiled Swordfish with Pesto Sauce*

"The pesto sauce is also good with salmon, sea bass or halibut."

1/2 cup fresh spinach
1/2 cup fresh Italian parsley
1 cup light cream
2 tablespoons grated Parmesan cheese
1 cup chopped fresh basil
1 tablespoon flour
1 clove of garlic
1/2 teaspoon salt
1/8 teaspoon freshly ground pepper
6 swordfish steaks

Chop spinach and parsley in blender or food processor. Add cream, cheese, basil, flour, garlic, salt and pepper; process until smooth. Pour into small saucepan. Grill or broil swordfish for 10 minutes for each inch of thickness or until fish flakes easily, turning once. Simmer sauce until heated through, stirring frequently. Serve with fish. **Yield:** 6 servings.

Approx Per Serving: Cal 273; Prot 25 g; Carbo 3 g; Fiber <1 g; T Fat 18 g; 59% Calories from Fat; Chol 91 mg; Sod 333 mg.

Nutty Frangelica Swordfish

"A wonderful dinner party entrée"

8 6-ounce swordfish steaks
Juice of 1 lemon
1 clove of garlic, crushed
2 tablespoons oil
9 egg yolks
Juice of 1 lemon
Salt and pepper to taste
$1\frac{1}{2}$ cups melted margarine
$\frac{1}{2}$ cup chopped hazelnuts
$\frac{1}{4}$ to $\frac{1}{2}$ cup Frangelica
1 pound lump crab meat

Combine swordfish steaks with juice of 1 lemon, garlic and oil in shallow dish. Marinate in refrigerator for 6 hours or longer. Combine egg yolks, juice of 1 lemon, salt and pepper in blender container; process at high speed for 3 seconds. Add margarine gradually, processing constantly. Stir in hazelnuts and Frangelica. Pour into double boiler. Cook over hot water until heated through; keep warm. Place crab meat in baking dish. Heat in 350-degree oven until heated through. Grill steaks for 7 minutes on each side or until they flake easily. Place steaks on serving plates; top with crab meat. Spoon sauce over steaks. May refrigerate sauce and reheat by whisking 2 tablespoons in double boiler, whisking in remaining sauce and heating to serving temperature. **Yield:** 8 servings.

Approx Per Serving: Cal 782; Prot 51 g; Carbo 11 g; Fiber 1 g; T Fat 56 g; 67% Calories from Fat; Chol 364 mg; Sod 726 mg.

Swordfish Portuguese

3 pounds swordfish steaks
Salt and freshly ground pepper to taste
$\frac{1}{4}$ cup fresh lemon juice
1 large yellow onion, chopped
4 cloves of garlic, minced
3 tablespoons olive oil
3 large tomatoes, finely chopped, seeded
$\frac{1}{2}$ cup tomato paste
1 tablespoon brown sugar
$\frac{1}{2}$ cup dry sherry
$\frac{3}{4}$ cup dry white wine
$\frac{1}{2}$ cup chopped parsley or coriander
1 lemon, thinly sliced

Arrange swordfish in single layer in lightly oiled shallow baking dish. Sprinkle with salt and pepper; rub with lemon juice. Sauté onion and garlic in olive oil in medium saucepan over medium-high heat for 10 minutes, stirring frequently. Stir in tomatoes, tomato paste, brown sugar, sherry and white wine. Simmer for 15 minutes. Stir in parsley, salt and pepper. Spoon over fish; top with lemon slices. Bake, tightly covered with foil, at 375 degrees for 25 to 30 minutes or until fish flakes easily. **Yield:** 6 servings.

Approx Per Serving: Cal 442; Prot 48 g; Carbo 14 g; Fiber 3 g; T Fat 17 g; 34% Calories from Fat; Chol 91 mg; Sod 235 mg.

Grilled Tuna with Lime and Cilantro*

1 small onion, chopped
1 cup butter
Juice of 1 lime
5 ounces dry white wine
1/2 cup light cream
6 8-ounce tuna steaks
1/4 cup (scant) olive oil
Salt and pepper to taste
1 tablespoon chopped fresh cilantro

Sauté onion in 1 tablespoon butter in saucepan. Stir in lime juice and wine. Bring to a boil. Stir in cream. Heat just to the boiling point. Whisk in remaining butter. Keep sauce warm. Brush fish with olive oil; season with salt and pepper. Grill or broil for 5 to 8 minutes on each side or until fish flakes easily. Stir cilantro into sauce. Spoon onto serving plates. Place fish on sauce. Garnish with sprig of fresh cilantro. **Yield:** 6 servings.

Approx Per Serving: Cal 823; Prot 51 g; Carbo 3 g; Fiber <1 g; T Fat 66 g; 74% Calories from Fat; Chol 263 mg; Sod 386 mg.

Piquant Tuna*

4 6-ounce tuna steaks
1 tablespoon olive oil
2 tablespoons balsamic vinegar
2 tablespoons fresh parsley
3 tablespoons Dijon mustard
1 clove of garlic, crushed
2 tablespoons chopped onion
3 tablespoons capers

Place tuna steaks on rack in broiler pan. Process remaining ingredients in blender container until smooth. Spread half the mixture on steaks. Broil for 3 to 4 minutes. Turn steaks; spread with remaining mustard mixture. Broil for 5 to 6 minutes or until fish flakes easily. **Yield:** 4 servings.

Approx Per Serving: Cal 336; Prot 38 g; Carbo 2 g; Fiber <1 g; T Fat 19 g; 52% Calories from Fat; Chol 118 mg; Sod 237 mg.

Skillet-Blackened Tuna*

1 tablespoon paprika
1 teaspoon onion powder
1 teaspoon garlic powder
2 teaspoons salt
1 teaspoon cayenne pepper
3/4 teaspoon each oregano, thyme, black pepper and white pepper
4 tuna steaks
2 or 3 tablespoons oil

Rub mixture of seasonings onto fish, coating well. Heat oil in skillet until very hot. Add fish. Sear for 1 minute on each side; reduce heat. Cook for 10 minutes or until fish flakes easily. **Yield:** 4 servings.

Approx Per Serving: Cal 236; Prot 23 g; Carbo 1 g; Fiber <1 g; T Fat 15 g; 58% Calories from Fat; Chol 45 mg; Sod 1171 mg.

Radnor Deviled Clams

1 10-ounce can minced clams
1/2 cup (about) milk
1 teaspoon minced celery
1 teaspoon minced onion
1 teaspoon minced green bell pepper
2 tablespoons margarine
6 tablespoons flour
1/8 teaspoon thyme
Salt and pepper to taste
1/2 cup bread crumbs
1 tablespoon melted margarine

Drain clams, reserving liquid. Add enough milk to reserved liquid to measure 1 cup. Sauté celery, onion and green pepper in 2 tablespoons margarine in saucepan until tender but not brown. Stir in flour. Add milk mixture. Cook until thickened, stirring constantly. Add clams, thyme, salt and pepper. Spoon into baking dish or 4 medium scallop shells. Top with mixture of bread crumbs and 1 tablespoon melted margarine. Bake at 370 degrees for 20 minutes. May double recipe, but do not double thyme. **Yield:** 4 servings.

Approx Per Serving: Cal 224; Prot 10 g; Carbo 22 g; Fiber 1 g; T Fat 15 g; 52% Calories from Fat; Chol 49 mg; Sod 236 mg.

Crab Meat Cobbler

1/2 cup butter
1/2 cup chopped onion
1/2 cup chopped green bell pepper
1/2 cup flour
1 teaspoon prepared mustard
1 cup milk
1 cup shredded Cheddar cheese
1 pound crab meat, cleaned
1 1/2 cups drained canned tomatoes
2 teaspoons Worcestershire sauce
1/2 teaspoon salt
2 cups herb-seasoned stuffing mix
1/4 cup melted butter
1/2 cup boiling water

Melt 1/2 cup butter in double boiler. Add onion and green pepper. Cook for 10 minutes or until vegetables are tender. Stir in flour, mustard, milk and cheese. Cook until sauce is thickened and cheese is melted, stirring constantly. Stir in crab meat, tomatoes, Worcestershire sauce and salt. Spoon into buttered 2-quart baking dish. Combine stuffing mix, 1/4 cup melted butter and water in bowl; mix well. Spread over casserole. Bake at 350 degrees for 25 to 30 minutes or until bubbly and brown.
Yield: 4 servings.

Approx Per Serving: Cal 789; Prot 40 g; Carbo 47 g; Fiber 2 g; T Fat 50 g; 56% Calories from Fat; Chol 245 mg; Sod 1728 mg.

Nothing But Crab Cakes*

"Three cheers for these."

1 pound crab meat
1 egg yolk
1 tablespoon chopped parsley
1 tablespoon mayonnaise
2 teaspoons Worcestershire sauce
1 tablespoon melted butter
1 teaspoon paprika
1 teaspoon dry mustard
1/2 teaspoon salt
1/2 teaspoon pepper
1/2 cup dry bread crumbs
2 tablespoons oil

Combine crab meat, egg yolk, parsley, mayonnaise, Worcestershire sauce, butter, paprika, dry mustard, salt and pepper in bowl; mix well. Shape into patties. Coat with bread crumbs. Chill in refrigerator. Fry in medium-hot oil in skillet until brown on both sides. **Yield:** 4 servings.

Approx Per Serving: Cal 293; Prot 25 g; Carbo 10 g; Fiber 1 g; T Fat 17 g; 51% Calories from Fat; Chol 177 mg; Sod 745 mg.

Creamy Crab Soufflé

"This has a delicate flavor and consistency."

1 cup chopped scallions
1/2 teaspoon tarragon
1 tablespoon butter
5 tablespoons flour
1 cup milk
1 cup shredded Cheddar cheese
2 tablespoons tomato paste
1 teaspoon salt
1/2 teaspoon pepper
6 egg yolks
1 pound fresh crab meat
6 egg whites
1/8 teaspoon cream of tartar

Sauté scallions and tarragon in butter in small skillet. Blend flour with milk in saucepan. Cook until thickened and smooth, stirring constantly. Cook for 1 minute longer; remove from heat. Add cheese, tomato paste, salt and pepper, stirring until cheese melts. Beat in egg yolks 1 at a time. Stir in crab meat and scallion mixture. Beat egg whites with cream of tartar in mixer bowl until stiff peaks form. Stir 1/4 of the egg whites into crab mixture; fold crab mixture into egg whites. Spoon into greased 1 1/2-quart soufflé dish. Bake at 375 degrees for 25 minutes for creamy center. Bake for 35 minutes for firm center. **Yield:** 4 servings.

Approx Per Serving: Cal 460; Prot 43 g; Carbo 14 g; Fiber 1 g; T Fat 25 g; 49% Calories from Fat; Chol 479 mg; Sod 1167 mg.

Lobster Frittata

1 medium onion, thinly sliced
2 cloves of garlic, minced
3 zucchini, sliced 1/4-inch thick
1 green bell pepper, cut into 1/4-inch strips
2 red bell peppers, cut into 1/4-inch strips
3 tablespoons olive oil
6 eggs
1/4 cup heavy cream
3 tablespoons chopped fresh basil
Salt and freshly ground pepper to taste
2 5-ounce packages Boursin cheese, crumbled
1 pound chopped cooked lobster meat
2 cup shredded Swiss cheese

Sauté onion, garlic, zucchini and bell peppers in olive oil in large saucepan over medium-high heat for 10 to 15 minutes or until tender-crisp. Whisk eggs with cream in large bowl. Whisk in basil, salt and pepper. Add Boursin cheese, lobster meat and sautéed vegetables. Stir in Swiss cheese. Spoon into buttered 10-inch springform pan. Place on baking sheet. Bake at 350 degrees for 45 to 60 minutes or just until firm. Let stand for 10 minutes. Place on serving plate; remove side of pan. Cut into wedges to serve. **Yield:** 8 servings.

Approx Per Serving: Cal 432; Prot 33 g; Carbo 7 g; Fiber 1 g; T Fat 30 g; 63% Calories from Fat; Chol 271 mg; Sod 568 mg.

Lobster and Capon Madeira

"Serve this from chafing dish over saffron rice."

1/2 cup butter
1 tablespoon chopped onion
1 tablespoon chopped celery
1 clove of garlic, minced
1/2 cup flour
1 tablespoon tomato paste
1/8 teaspoon thyme
1/8 teaspoon rosemary
1 small bay leaf
3 cups hot consommé
1 tablespoon sugar
1 tablespoon orange juice
1/4 to 1/2 cup Madeira
2 cups chopped cooked lobster
2 cups chopped cooked capon or chicken

Heat butter in skillet until foamy. Add onion, celery and garlic. Sauté for 5 minutes. Stir in flour. Cook until golden brown, stirring constantly. Stir in tomato paste, thyme, rosemary and bay leaf. Cook over low heat for 5 minutes, stirring constantly. Add consommé. Simmer, covered, for 1 hour; strain. Blend sugar and orange juice in saucepan. Cook until light caramel color. Add wine. Simmer for several minutes. Stir into strained sauce in saucepan. Cook for 5 minutes. Add lobster and capon. Simmer for 10 minutes longer. Discard bay leaf. **Yield:** 8 servings.

Approx Per Serving: Cal 273; Prot 23 g; Carbo 10 g; Fiber <1 g; T Fat 14 g; 50% Calories from Fat; Chol 88 mg; Sod 747 mg.

The Captain's Lobster Thermidor

8 6-ounce lobster tails
1 lemon, sliced
Salt
3 tablespoons sherry
2 tablespoons brandy
1/4 cup flour
1/8 teaspoon mace
Paprika to taste
1 teaspoon salt
1/2 cup melted butter
1 1/2 cups light cream
1 egg yolk, slightly beaten
1/2 cup shredded sharp Cheddar cheese

Bring enough water to cover lobster tails to a boil in large saucepan, adding lemon slices and 1 teaspoon salt for each quart water. Add lobster tails. Cook for 6 minutes; drain and cool. Remove meat from shells, reserving shells; chop lobster meat. Toss lobster meat with sherry and brandy in bowl. Cover and set aside. Blend flour, mace, paprika and salt into melted butter in large saucepan. Stir in cream. Bring to a boil, stirring constantly; reduce heat. Simmer for several minutes. Stir a small amount of hot mixture into egg yolk; stir egg yolk into hot mixture. Add lobster meat mixture. Cook until thickened and heated through, stirring frequently. Rinse reserved lobster shells; pat dry. Arrange on baking sheet. Fill with lobster mixture, mounding in shells. Sprinkle with cheese. Bake at 450 degrees for 8 to 10 minutes or until cheese is golden brown. **Yield:** 8 servings.

Approx Per Serving: Cal 433; Prot 32 g; Carbo 8 g; Fiber <1 g; T Fat 29 g; 62% Calories from Fat; Chol 212 mg; Sod 941 mg. Nutritional information does not include salt used in cooking lobster.

Scalloped Oysters and Corn*

"A nice buffet dish"

3 1/2 cups coarse cracker crumbs
1 cup melted margarine
2 16-ounce cans cream-style corn
1/2 cup light cream
3/4 teaspoon Tabasco sauce
1 teaspoon salt
1/2 teaspoon pepper
1 quart oysters, drained, coarsely chopped
1/2 cup coarse cracker crumbs

Mix 3 1/2 cups cracker crumbs with melted margarine in bowl. Combine corn, light cream, Tabasco sauce, salt and pepper in bowl; mix well. Layer crumb mixture, corn mixture and oysters 1/2 at a time in 2-quart baking dish. Top with remaining 1/2 cup cracker crumbs. Bake at 375 degrees for 40 minutes. **Yield:** 10 servings.

Approx Per Serving: Cal 496; Prot 16 g; Carbo 47 g; Fiber 3 g; T Fat 27 g; 49% Calories from Fat; Chol 57 mg; Sod 1268 mg.

Oysters and Spinach

"If you double this recipe, do not double the sauce."

2 10-ounce packages frozen chopped spinach
1 pint oysters
1/2 cup thinly sliced scallions
1/4 cup butter
1/2 cup flour
Paprika, salt and pepper to taste
1/2 cup white wine
1 1/2 cups light cream
1 cup shredded Cheddar cheese

Cook spinach using package directions; drain well. Spread in baking dish. Drain oysters and pat dry. Spread over spinach. Sauté scallions in butter in saucepan. Stir in flour, paprika, salt and pepper. Cook for several minutes, stirring constantly. Add wine and cream. Cook until thickened and smooth, stirring constantly. Pour over layers. Top with cheese. Bake at 350 degrees for 30 minutes. Garnish with parsley or chives. **Yield:** 6 servings.

Approx Per Serving: Cal 476; Prot 18 g; Carbo 17 g; Fiber 7 g; T Fat 95 g; 86% Calories from Fat; Chol 407 mg; Sod 411 mg.

Scallops Florentine*

1 10-ounce package frozen chopped spinach, thawed
1 egg, slightly beaten
2 tomatoes, peeled, cut into wedges
2 cloves of garlic, minced
4 scallions with stems, finely chopped
3 tablespoons butter
1 pound scallops
1/4 cup white wine
1/4 cup bread crumbs
1/4 cup grated Parmesan cheese
3 tablespoons melted butter

Mix spinach and egg in bowl. Spread in greased 9-inch pie plate. Arrange tomato wedges around edge of pie plate. Sauté garlic and scallions in 3 tablespoons butter in skillet for 1 minute. Add scallops. Cook for 1 minute. Stir in wine. Simmer for 1 minute. Spread over spinach. Sprinkle with bread crumbs and cheese; drizzle with 3 tablespoons melted butter, Bake, covered, at 325 degrees for 15 minutes. Bake, uncovered, for 5 minutes longer. **Yield:** 4 servings.

Approx Per Serving: Cal 369; Prot 28 g; Carbo 15 g; Fiber 3 g; T Fat 22 g; 53% Calories from Fat; Chol 144 mg; Sod 549 mg.

Clarify oil used for deep frying by pouring through a funnel lined with paper coffee filter.

Bahama Mama Shrimp

"These are also good with plum sauce or a mixture of 1 cup duck sauce, 2 teaspoons horseradish and 2 tablespoons bourbon."

1/3 cup dry mustard
1 tablespoon honey
2 teaspoons vinegar
1/4 cup cold water
1 pound (24-count) shrimp
1/4 cup flour
1/2 teaspoon dry mustard
1/2 teaspoon salt
1 egg
2 tablespoons cream
1 1/4 cups coconut
3/4 cup bread crumbs
Oil for frying

Combine 1/3 cup dry mustard, honey, vinegar and cold water in bowl; mix well. Chill until serving time. Shell and devein shrimp, leaving tails. Mix flour, 1/2 teaspoon dry mustard and salt in small bowl. Beat egg and cream in small bowl. Mix coconut and bread crumbs on plate. Roll shrimp in flour mixture, dip in egg mixture and coat with crumbs; press coating onto shrimp. Chill in refrigerator. Fry in 2 inches oil in skillet for 2 minutes or until golden brown. Serve with mustard sauce.
Yield: 3 servings.

Approx Per Serving: Cal 561; Prot 37 g; Carbo 52 g; Fiber 5 g; T Fat 24 g; 37% Calories from Fat; Chol 322 mg; Sod 844 mg. Nutritional information does not include oil for frying.

Shrimp Stuffed with Crab

24 jumbo shrimp
1 small onion, minced
1/4 cup chopped celery
1/2 cup chopped green bell pepper
2 tablespoons butter
1 tablespoon chopped parsley
1 pound crab meat
1/2 cup seasoned bread crumbs
1 egg, beaten
1/2 to 1 cup light cream
1 teaspoon Worcestershire sauce
1/4 teaspoon thyme
Tabasco sauce to taste
1 teaspoon salt
2 cloves of garlic, crushed
1/2 cup butter
Paprika to taste

Shell, devein and butterfly shrimp. Arrange, open, in buttered shallow baking dish. Sauté onion, celery and green pepper in 2 tablespoons butter in saucepan just until onion is translucent; remove from heat. Add parsley and crab meat; toss to mix well. Stir in bread crumbs, egg, cream, Worcestershire sauce, thyme, Tabasco sauce and salt. Mound onto shrimp. Sauté garlic in 1/2 cup butter in skillet; discard garlic. Drizzle butter over shrimp; sprinkle with paprika. Bake at 400 degrees for 10 to 15 minutes or until shrimp are cooked through. **Yield:** 4 servings.

Approx Per Serving: Cal 763; Prot 56 g; Carbo 15 g; Fiber 1 g; T Fat 53 g; 63% Calories from Fat; Chol 571 mg; Sod 1540 mg.

Spicy Shrimp and Bacon Kabobs

1 pound jumbo shrimp
3 tablespoons oil
2 tablespoons duck sauce
1 tablespoon honey
1 tablespoon maple syrup
1 clove of garlic, minced
1/4 teaspoon basil
1/4 teaspoon oregano
1/4 teaspoon rosemary
1 teaspoon red pepper
1 teaspoon black pepper
8 slices bacon, cut into halves

Peel and devein shrimp. Combine oil, duck sauce, honey, maple syrup and seasonings in bowl; mix well. Add shrimp. Marinate in refrigerator for 2 hours. Fry bacon just until partially cooked; drain. Drain shrimp, reserving marinade. Wrap each shrimp with bacon piece; thread onto skewers. Brush with reserved marinade; place on rack in broiler pan. Broil for 3 minutes on each side. Serve over steamed shredded zucchini or wild rice. **Yield:** 4 servings.

Approx Per Serving: Cal 292; Prot 23 g; Carbo 10 g; Fiber <1 g; T Fat 17 g; 54% Calories from Fat; Chol 188 mg; Sod 431 mg. Nutritional information includes entire amount of marinade.

Hot and Sour Shrimp and Walnuts

1 pound large shrimp, peeled, deveined
2 tablespoons sherry
1 tablespoon grated fresh ginger
1/2 cup chicken stock
2 tablespoons dry sherry
2 tablespoons soy sauce
2 tablespoons catsup
1 tablespoon cornstarch
1 tablespoon rice vinegar
1 tablespoon sugar
1 teaspoon sesame oil
1/4 teaspoon cayenne pepper
2 tablespoons chopped walnuts
6 teaspoons peanut oil
2 medium red bell pepper, cut into strips
2 cloves of garlic, chopped
4 ounces mushrooms
4 ounces pea pods
8 green onions, sliced diagonally into 1-inch pieces

Combine shrimp with 2 tablespoons sherry and ginger in bowl; mix well. Chill, covered, for 30 minutes. Combine chicken stock, 2 tablespoons sherry, soy sauce, catsup, cornstarch, vinegar, sugar, sesame oil and cayenne pepper in small bowl; mix well. Stir-fry walnuts in 2 teaspoons peanut oil in wok or heavy skillet over high heat for 1 minute. Remove with slotted spoon. Add 2 teaspoons peanut oil, bell peppers and garlic to wok. Stir-fry for 1 minute. Add mushrooms and pea pods. Stir-fry for 1 minute. Add remaining 2 teaspoons peanut oil, shrimp mixture and green onions. Stir-fry for 1 minute. Stir in chicken stock mixture. Cook for 2 minutes or until thickened and clear, stirring frequently. Sprinkle with walnuts. Serve over rice. **Yield:** 4 servings.

Approx Per Serving: Cal 272; Prot 23 g; Carbo 15 g; Fiber 3 g; T Fat 12 g; 41% Calories from Fat; Chol 177 mg; Sod 910 mg.

Shrimp Chinoiserie-Bourbon Duck Sauce

"Out of this world!"

1/2 cup chopped green onions
1/2 cup chopped red bell pepper
2 teaspoons chopped garlic
2 teaspoons minced ginger
2 teaspoons oil
2 tablespoons bourbon
1 cup duck sauce
24 shrimp
1 tablespoon minced garlic
1 tablespoon minced ginger
1 tablespoon oil
1/2 cup chopped green onions
2 tablespoons shredded carrot
2 tablespoons minced celery
4 ounces prosciutto, minced
2 teaspoons soy sauce
1 1/2 teaspoons balsamic vinegar
2 tablespoons chopped cilantro
8 9-inch egg roll wrappers
Oil for frying

Sauté 1/2 cup green onions, bell pepper, 2 teaspoons chopped garlic and 2 teaspoons minced ginger in 2 teaspoons oil in saucepan. Add bourbon and duck sauce; mix well. Cook until heated through; keep warm. Peel shrimp, leaving tails. Chop 8 shrimp, discarding tails; set aside. Butterfly remaining shrimp; pound to flatten slightly. Sauté 1 tablespoon garlic and 1 tablespoon ginger in 1 tablespoon oil in large skillet for 30 seconds. Add 1/2 cup green onions, carrot and celery. Sauté for 2 minutes. Stir in chopped shrimp. Sauté until shrimp are pink. Stir in prosciutto, soy sauce and vinegar. Cool slightly. Add cilantro. Trim edges from egg roll wrappers with scissors to form circles; cut circles into halves. Place 1 butterflied shrimp 1/2 inch from end of each wrapper; top with vegetable mixture. Brush edges of wrappers with water. Roll wrappers around shrimp, leaving tails out; press wrappers around shrimp to seal. Heat 2 inches oil in saucepan. Add shrimp. Fry for 3 minutes or until golden brown. Serve with Bourbon Duck Sauce. **Yield:** 6 servings.

Approx Per Serving: Cal 229; Prot 24 g; Carbo 16 g; Fiber 1 g; T Fat 6 g; 25% Calories from Fat; Chol 184 mg; Sod 699 mg. Nutritional information does not include oil for frying.

Easy Stuffed Shrimp*

2 cups seasoned stuffing mix
1/2 cup melted butter
16 jumbo shrimp, butterflied

Combine stuffing mix, half the butter and enough hot water to moisten in bowl; mix well. Spoon into shrimp. Place in baking pan. Bake at 400 degrees for 20 minutes. Drizzle with remaining butter. Serve immediately. **Yield:** 4 servings.

Approx Per Serving: Cal 421; Prot 23 g; Carbo 25 g; Fiber 0 g; T Fat 25 g; 54% Calories from Fat; Chol 235 mg; Sod 859 mg.

PASTA

Linguine with Artichoke Sauce

"Gourmet delight!"

1/4 cup butter
1/4 cup olive oil
1 tablespoon flour
1 cup chicken broth
1 clove of garlic, minced
1 tablespoon minced fresh parsley
2 to 3 teaspoons fresh lemon juice
Salt and white pepper to taste
1 14-ounce can artichoke hearts packed in water, drained
2 tablespoons freshly grated Parmesan cheese
2 teaspoons capers, rinsed, drained
1 tablespoon butter
2 tablespoons olive oil
1 tablespoon freshly grated Parmesan cheese
1/4 teaspoon salt
1 pound linguine, cooked, drained
2 ounces minced prosciutto or cooked ham

Melt 1/4 cup butter with 1/4 cup olive oil in saucepan over medium heat. Stir in flour until well mixed. Blend in broth. Simmer for 1 minute or until thickened, stirring constantly. Reduce heat to low. Add garlic, parsley, lemon juice, salt to taste and white pepper. Cook for 5 minutes, stirring constantly. Cut artichokes into slices. Add with 2 tablespoons cheese and capers to sauce. Simmer, covered, for 8 minutes, stirring frequently. Melt 1 tablespoon butter with 2 tablespoons olive oil in large skillet over medium heat. Stir in remaining cheese and 1/4 teaspoon salt. Add linguine, tossing lightly. Arrange linquine on platter. Cover with artichoke sauce; top with prosciutto. **Yield:** 6 servings.

Approx Per Serving: Cal 531; Prot 13 g; Carbo 62 g; Fiber 3 g; T Fat 26 g; 43% Calories from Fat; Chol 28 mg; Sod 513 mg.

Pasta with Broccoli Sauce*

"Eat this with friends."

Flowerets of 1 large bunch broccoli
2 tablespoons salt
3 quarts water
8 cloves of garlic, minced
1/2 teaspoon pepper
3 tablespoons unsalted butter
3 tablespoons olive oil
1/4 cup dry white wine
1 pound fresh white linguine, cooked
4 ounces Parmesan cheese, grated

Cook broccoli with salt in water in saucepan for 3 minutes or until tender-crisp; drain. Rinse under cold running water. Sauté garlic with pepper in butter and olive oil in skillet until mixture is light brown. Add wine. Bring to a boil. Simmer for 3 minutes, stirring frequently. Add broccoli. Heat to serving temperature. Add cooked linguine; mix well. Spoon into bowl; top with cheese. **Yield:** 6 servings.

Approx Per Serving: Cal 492; Prot 18 g; Carbo 62 g; Fiber 5 g; T Fat 19 g; 34% Calories from Fat; Chol 28 mg; Sod 2454 mg. Nutritional information includes entire amount of salt for cooking broccoli.

Baked Ziti with Broccoli

"Looks good and tastes good"

1 pound uncooked ziti
2 cloves of garlic, crushed
2 tablespoons olive oil
2 10-ounce packages frozen chopped broccoli, thawed
1 cup grated Parmesan cheese
4 cups whipping cream
2 cups shredded mozzarella cheese

Cook ziti using package directions for 10 minutes; drain. Sauté garlic in olive oil in skillet for 1 minute. Drain thawed broccoli. Combine zita, garlic, broccoli, Parmesan cheese and cream in bowl; mix lightly. Pour into 9x12-inch baking dish. Top with mozzarella cheese. Bake, covered, at 350 degrees for 30 minutes or until hot and bubbly. **Yield:** 10 servings.

Approx Per Serving: Cal 637; Prot 17 g; Carbo 41 g; Fiber 4 g; T Fat 46 g; 64% Calories from Fat; Chol 154 mg; Sod 286 mg.

Add a touch of color to the kitchen by recycling interesting color-printed French ratatouille or Italian olive oil cans. Wash and use to hold kitchen utensils.

Pasta with Caviar

"Serve with pride and a green salad."

2 cloves of garlic, minced
1 small onion, minced
2 tablespoons unsalted butter
3 tablespoons olive oil
Rind of 1 lemon, cut into fine strips
1 1/4 cups bottled clam juice
1/4 cup vodka
1 1/2 cups half and half
3/4 cup freshly grated Parmesan cheese
Salt and pepper to taste
1 pound uncooked linguine or fettuccine
4 ounces (about) golden caviar

Sauté garlic and onion in butter and olive oil in skillet for 5 minutes. Add lemon rind, clam juice and vodka. Simmer for 15 minutes or until reduced by about half, stirring frequently. Add cream. Simmer for 15 minutes or until thickened, stirring frequently. Stir in cheese until melted. Add salt and pepper. Cook linguine using package directions just until tender; drain well. Combine hot pasta and sauce in bowl; toss well. Spoon onto serving plates; top with 1 heaping tablespoonful caviar. **Yield:** 4 servings.

Approx Per Serving: Cal 864; Prot 31 g; Carbo 94 g; Fiber 5 g; T Fat 37 g; 40% Calories from Fat; Chol 225 mg; Sod 910 mg.

Fusilli with Tomato and Cheese Sauce*

"Committee's favorite"

1 pound ripe plum tomatoes
8 ounces mozzarella cheese, shredded
1/2 cup chopped fresh basil
6 tablespoons olive oil
2 tablespoons balsamic vinegar or red wine vinegar
2 cloves of garlic, minced
1/4 teaspoon dried red pepper flakes
Salt and black pepper to taste
12 ounces uncooked fusilli or rotelle
1/4 cup pine nuts, toasted

Cut tomatoes into halves; remove seeds. Cut into 1/2-inch pieces. Combine tomatoes and cheese in bowl; toss to mix. Add basil, olive oil, vinegar, garlic, red pepper flakes, salt and black pepper; mix well. Let stand at room temperature for 30 minutes. Cook pasta using package directions for about 9 minutes or until just tender; drain. Add sauce to pasta. Cook over low heat until cheese starts to melt, tossing gently. Remove to serving platter. Sprinkle with pine nuts. Garnish with fresh basil leaves. **Yield:** 4 servings.

Approx Per Serving: Cal 716; Prot 25 g; Carbo 72 g; Fiber 5 g; T Fat 37 g; 46% Calories from Fat; Chol 44 mg; Sod 223 mg.

Linguine with Brie and Fresh Tomato Sauce

"Put your fresh tomatoes to good use."

4 tomatoes
1 pound Brie
1 cup basil leaves
3 cloves of garlic, minced
1 cup plus 1 tablespoon olive oil
1½ teaspoons salt
½ teaspoon pepper
1½ pounds uncooked linguine
½ cup grated Parmesan cheese

Cut tomatoes into ½-inch cubes. Remove rind from cheese; cut cheese into cubes. Cut basil leaves into strips. Combine tomatoes, cheese, basil, garlic, olive oil, salt and pepper in bowl; mix well. Let stand, covered, for 2 hours or longer. Cook linguine using package directions for 8 to 10 minutes or until just tender; drain. Toss with sauce. Serve immediately with Parmesan cheese. **Yield:** 6 servings.

Approx Per Serving: Cal 1059; Prot 34 g; Carbo 90 g; Fiber 6 g; T Fat 63 g; 53% Calories from Fat; Chol 80 mg; Sod 1142 mg.

Montrachet Linguine*

"Tempting blend of flavors"

1 bunch green onions, sliced
4 plum tomatoes, chopped
1 red bell pepper, chopped
6 oil-pack sun-dried tomatoes
2 cloves of garlic, minced
¼ teaspoon oregano
3 tablespoons olive oil
1 tablespoon chopped parsley
1 tablespoon chopped fresh basil
8 ounces uncooked spinach linguine
4 ounces montrachet (soft goat cheese), sliced

Sauté green onions, tomatoes, bell pepper, sun-dried tomatoes and garlic with oregano in olive oil in skillet. Stir in parsley and basil. Cook linguine using package directions; drain. Add to sauce; mix well. Top each serving with cheese. **Yield:** 2 servings.

Approx Per Serving: Cal 1137; Prot 35 g; Carbo 111 g; Fiber 11 g; T Fat 64 g; 50% Calories from Fat; Chol 41 mg; Sod 378 mg.

Make instant garlic butter by puréeing 1 cup softened butter with 1 or 2 cloves of garlic. Store in freezer and use for sautéing or garlic bread.

Tortellini in Cheese Sauce*

"Great!"

12 ounces fresh cheese tortellini
2 cups half and half
1 cup finely grated Romano cheese
Pinch of white pepper
1 teaspoon basil

Cook tortellini using package directions; drain. Heat half and half in saucepan over medium heat. Add Romano cheese, white pepper and basil. Cook slowly until cheese is melted, stirring frequently. Fold in tortellini gently. Serve immediately. **Yield:** 6 servings.

Approx Per Serving: Cal 341; Prot 16 g; Carbo 30 g; Fiber 0 g; T Fat 18 g; 46% Calories from Fat; Chol 72 mg; Sod 430 mg.

Fettucini Abruzzi

"Just spicy enough!"

1 pound boneless chicken breast halves
3 cloves of garlic, minced
1 small onion, chopped
3 tablespoons olive oil
1/4 teaspoon basil
1/4 teaspoon thyme
1/4 teaspoon marjoram
2 35-ounce cans whole plum tomatoes, drained
1 3-ounce can small pitted olives
2 tablespoons capers
1/2 cup sun-dried tomatoes, slivered
2 teaspoons salt
Pepper to taste
1 pound uncooked fettucini

Rinse chicken; pat dry. Cut into bite-sized pieces. Sauté garlic and onion in olive oil in skillet until onion is translucent. Add chicken, basil, thyme and marjoram. Cook over medium-high heat for 10 minutes or until chicken is golden brown, stirring occasionally. Chop plum tomatoes coarsely. Add with olives, capers and sun-dried tomatoes to chicken mixture; mix well. Add salt and pepper. Bring to a boil, stirring occasionally. Reduce heat. Simmer, covered, for 20 minutes or until chicken is tender, stirring occasionally. Cook fettucini using package directions; drain. Serve chicken sauce over fettucini. Garnish with grated Parmesan cheese. **Yield:** 4 servings.

Approx Per Serving: Cal 794; Prot 46 g; Carbo 110 g; Fiber 11 g; T Fat 21 g; 23% Calories from Fat; Chol 72 mg; Sod 2099 mg.

Linguine with Chicken, Walnuts and Rosemary

"This is a special recipe from a special friend."

1 pound boneless chicken breast
3 tablespoons flour
1 1/2 tablespoons chopped fresh rosemary
Salt and pepper to taste
3 cloves of garlic, minced
1/4 cup butter
2/3 cup dry white wine
12 ounces strong chicken broth
2/3 cup whipping cream
1/4 cup chopped walnuts
1 pound linguine, cooked
1/4 cup chopped walnuts

Rinse chicken; pat dry. Cut into bite-sized pieces. Mix flour, rosemary, salt and pepper together. Toss chicken in flour mixture until coated. Sauté chicken with garlic in hot butter in skillet until light brown. Remove chicken to warm platter. Add wine to skillet. Bring to a boil, stirring to deglaze skillet. Add chicken broth. Cook until mixture is reduced to 1 cup, stirring frequently. Add cream. Cook until slightly thickened, stirring constantly. Add 1/4 cup walnuts, linguine and chicken; toss to coat linguine well. Spoon onto serving plates. Sprinkle with remaining 1/4 cup walnuts. **Yield:** 4 servings.

Approx Per Serving: Cal 957; Prot 46 g; Carbo 95 g; Fiber 6 g; T Fat 40 g; 39% Calories from Fat; Chol 157 mg; Sod 451 mg.

Angel Hair Pasta with Basil and Crab Meat*

2 tablespoons chopped shallots
2 tablespoons minced fresh basil
2 tablespoons minced fresh parsley
1/2 cup butter
3 16-ounce cans chopped peeled tomatoes, drained
1/2 cup dry white wine
1 1/2 pounds crab meat
1 pound angel hair pasta, cooked
Pepper to taste
1/2 cup grated Parmesan cheese

Sauté shallots with basil and parsley in hot butter in skillet for 2 to 3 minutes. Add tomatoes. Bring to a boil. Simmer until mixture is reduced by half, stirring frequently. Add wine. Simmer for 5 minutes, stirring frequently. Add crab meat. Simmer for 2 to 3 minutes, stirring frequently. Place warm pasta in serving dish; top with sauce. Sprinkle with pepper and Parmesan cheese. **Yield:** 6 servings.

Approx Per Serving: Cal 630; Prot 38 g; Carbo 68 g; Fiber 2 g; T Fat 22 g; 30% Calories from Fat; Chol 153 mg; Sod 860 mg.

King Crab Fettucini*

1 clove of garlic, minced
1/2 cup butter
8 ounces crab meat
3/4 cup whipping cream
1/2 cup grated Parmesan cheese
1/2 teaspoon salt
1/8 teaspoon white pepper
12 ounces fettucini, cooked
1 tablespoon chopped fresh parsley

Sauté garlic in butter in heavy skillet over medium heat until golden brown. Stir in crab meat. Add cream, Parmesan cheese, salt and white pepper; mix well. Place warm fettucini in serving bowl. Add crab sauce; mix well. Sprinkle with fresh parsley. **Yield:** 4 servings.

Approx Per Serving: Cal 776; Prot 28 g; Carbo 66 g; Fiber 4 g; T Fat 45 g; 52% Calories from Fat; Chol 188 mg; Sod 825 mg.

Linguine with Tuna and Clams*

1 30-ounce jar thick spaghetti sauce
1 8-ounce can white clam sauce
1 13-ounce can water-pack white tuna, drained
1 pound linguine, cooked

Combine first 3 ingredients in saucepan. Cook until heated through. Serve over hot linguine. Garnish with Parmesan cheese. **Yield:** 4 servings.

Approx Per Serving: Cal 835; Prot 49 g; Carbo 121 g; Fiber 7 g; T Fat 18 g; 18% Calories from Fat; Chol 70 mg; Sod 1408 mg.

Fusilli with Eggplant Sauce

1 large onion, chopped
2 cloves of garlic, minced
1 medium eggplant, peeled, chopped
3 to 4 tablespoons olive oil
1 28-ounce can Italian plum tomatoes, coarsely chopped
1/2 teaspoon basil
1/2 teaspoon oregano
Salt and pepper to taste
1/4 cup minced Italian parsley
1 pound fusilli, cooked
3 to 4 tablespoons grated Romano cheese

Sauté onion, garlic and eggplant in hot olive oil in skillet for 7 to 8 minutes. Add tomatoes with liquid, basil, oregano, salt, pepper and parsley to sautéed mixture; mix well. Simmer for 10 to 15 minutes or until of desired consistency, stirring frequently. Pour 1 cup sauce into heated serving dish. Add pasta; sprinkle with Romano cheese. Toss to mix well. Add remaining sauce; toss gently. **Yield:** 4 servings.

Approx Per Serving: Cal 639; Prot 20 g; Carbo 103 g; Fiber 11 g; T Fat 17 g; 24% Calories from Fat; Chol 6 mg; Sod 401 mg.

Lasagna Pinwheels with Tomato Béchamel

"This is impressive and worth the work."

1 cup finely chopped yellow onion
1 cup finely chopped carrots
3 tablespoons olive oil
3 tablespoons unsalted butter
2 teaspoons minced garlic
2 35-ounce cans Italian plum tomatoes
1/2 teaspoon salt
1 teaspoon freshly ground pepper
2 teaspoons sugar
3 tablespoons minced fresh basil
2 tablespoons unsalted butter
2 tablespoons flour
1 cup milk
1/2 teaspoon salt
1 1/4 pounds whole milk ricotta cheese
1 cup grated Parmesan cheese
4 ounces lean prosciutto, finely chopped
3 tablespoons minced Italian parsley
1 teaspoon salt
1/2 teaspoon freshly ground pepper
2 egg yolks, slightly beaten
1 tablespoon salt
6 quarts boiling water
1 pound uncooked curly lasagna noodles
Sprigs of 1 small bunch curly parsley
2 cups grated Parmesan cheese

Sauté onion and carrots in olive oil and 3 tablespoons butter in skillet for 5 minutes or until tender. Add garlic. Sauté for 2 minutes. Chop tomatoes coarsely. Add tomatoes, 1/2 teaspoon salt, 1 teaspoon pepper, sugar and basil to sautéed mixture. Cook for 35 minutes or until sauce is thickened, stirring frequently. Cool, covered, to room temperature. Purée sauce 3 cups at a time in food processor fitted with steel blade. Melt 2 tablespoons butter in 2 1/2-quart saucepan. Stir in flour until well mixed. Add milk and 1/2 teaspoon salt. Simmer for 5 minutes or until thickened and creamy, stirring constantly. Add tomato mixture; mix well. Pour 1 1/2 cups sauce into 9x13-inch baking dish. Combine ricotta cheese, 1 cup Parmesan cheese, prosciutto, 3 tablespoons parsley, 1 teaspoon salt and 1/2 teaspoon pepper in bowl; mix well. Add egg yolks; mix well. Add 1 tablespoon salt to 6 quarts boiling water in saucepan. Add noodles 1 at a time. Cook for 4 minutes or until just tender. Drain; rinse with cold water. Drain again. Lay noodles on towel-lined surface. Spread 1 heaping tablespoonful ricotta cheese filling over each noodle. Roll to enclose filling; place seam side down in baking dish. Spoon 1 tablespoon sauce over each roll. Cover pasta rolls with buttered parchment paper. Cover dish with foil. Bake at 350 degrees for 45 minutes. Let stand at room temperature for 10 minutes before serving. Garnish with parsley. Heat remaining sauce. Serve sauce and remaining 2 cups Parmesan cheese with pasta pinwheels. **Yield:** 12 servings.

Approx Per Serving: Cal 475; Prot 25 g; Carbo 42 g; Fiber 2 g; T Fat 24 g; 45% Calories from Fat; Chol 96 mg; Sod 1778 mg.

Chicken Lasagna

2 whole chicken breasts, boned, cut into 1-inch cubes
3 cups sliced mushrooms
2 cloves of garlic
1 large onion, chopped
1 teaspoon each oregano, basil and thyme
2 tablespoons olive oil
1 28-ounce can Italian tomatoes with basil
1 15-ounce can tomato sauce
3 tablespoons freshly grated Romano cheese
2 cups grated carrots
1/2 teaspoon salt
1 teaspoon pepper
8 ounces lasagna noodles, cooked
1/2 cup freshly grated Romano cheese
8 slices mozzarello cheese

Sauté first 7 ingredients in olive oil in skillet until chicken is cooked through. Stir in tomatoes, tomato sauce, 3 tablespoons Romano cheese, carrots, salt and pepper. Cook for 5 minutes. Layer lasagna noodles, sauce, Romano cheese and mozzarella cheese 1/2 at a time in oiled 9x13-inch baking dish. Bake, covered, at 350 degrees for 20 minutes. Bake, uncovered, for 10 minutes longer or until cheese is bubbly.
Yield: 6 servings.

Approx Per Serving: Cal 506; Prot 37 g; Carbo 48 g; Fiber 5 g; T Fat 19 g; 33% Calories from Fat; Chol 88 mg; Sod 1150 mg.

Vegetarian Lasagna

"A delightful way to serve an old favorite"

1 10-ounce package frozen chopped spinach
1/4 cup chopped onion
2 teaspoons oil
1/2 cup grated carrots
1 cup sliced mushrooms
1 8-ounce can tomato sauce
1 6-ounce can tomato paste
1/2 cup chopped black olives
3/4 teaspoon oregano
5 lasagna noodles, cooked, cut into halves
1 cup ricotta cheese
4 ounces Monterey Jack cheese, sliced
1/4 cup grated Parmesan cheese

Cook spinach using package directions; drain. Sauté onion in hot oil in skillet until tender. Add carrots and mushrooms. Cook until tender. Stir in tomato sauce, tomato paste, olives and oregano. Remove from heat. Layer half the noodles, half the ricotta cheese, half the spinach and half the sauce in 8-inch square baking dish. Add 1/3 of the Monterey Jack cheese. Repeat layers. Add remaining Monterey Jack cheese. Top with Parmesan cheese. Bake at 375 degrees for 30 minutes. Let stand at room temperature for 10 minutes before serving. **Yield:** 4 servings.

Approx Per Serving: Cal 220; Prot 12 g; Carbo 21 g; Fiber 3 g; T Fat 12 g; 45% Calories from Fat; Chol 27 mg; Sod 401 mg.

Macaroni and Cheese*

3 cups uncooked elbow macaroni
8 ounces pepperoni, thinly sliced
Salt and pepper to taste
1 28-ounce can Italian tomatoes, chopped
12 ounces extra-sharp Cheddar cheese, cut into cubes

Cook macaroni using package directions; drain. Combine with remaining ingredients in bowl; mix well. Spoon into greased 9x13-inch baking dish. Baked, covered with foil, at 350 degrees for 1 hour. **Yield:** 6 servings.

Approx Per Serving: Cal 611; Prot 30 g; Carbo 29 g; Fiber 3 g; T Fat 42 g; 62% Calories from Fat; Chol 59 mg; Sod 1779 mg.

Spinach Pasta with Salmon-Cream Sauce*

2 cups whipping cream
2 tablespoons butter
1 teaspoon salt
Nutmeg to taste
1 tablespoon grated Parmesan cheese
1/3 cup chopped fresh dill
1 1/2 to 2 cups flaked poached salmon
1 pound uncooked spinach linguine
4 quarts water
Salt to taste
2 tablespoons butter

Combine cream, 2 tablespoons butter, 1 teaspoon salt and nutmeg in saucepan. Simmer until mixture is reduced by 1/3, stirring frequently. Add cheese, dill and salmon; mix well. Remove from heat. Cook linguine in 4 quarts boiling water with 2 tablespoons salt for 2 minutes or just until tender; drain. Add 2 tablespoons butter, tossing until butter is melted. Spoon into serving dish. Pour sauce over pasta. Garnish with additional fresh dill. **Yield:** 6 servings.

Approx Per Serving: Cal 734; Prot 32 g; Carbo 54 g; Fiber 0 g; T Fat 43 g; 53% Calories from Fat; Chol 168 mg; Sod 925 mg.

Linguine with Sausage and Leeks*

1 pound sausage
2 leeks, thinly sliced
3/4 cup half and half
6 ounces linguine, cooked
1/2 cup grated Parmesan cheese

Brown sausage with leeks in skillet, stirring until crumbly; drain. Add half and half. Heat to serving temperature. Pour linguine into serving bowl. Add sausage sauce. Sprinkle with Parmesan cheese. **Yield:** 4 servings.

Approx Per Serving: Cal 491; Prot 22 g; Carbo 42 g; Fiber 3 g; T Fat 26 g; 47% Calories from Fat; Chol 68 mg; Sod 907 mg.

Pasta with Scallops and Snow Peas

"A winning combination"

1 pound snow peas
3 quarts water
Salt to taste
1 pound uncooked fettucini
1 tablespoon minced garlic
2 tablespoons olive oil
5 ripe plum tomatoes, chopped
1 jalapeño pepper, seeded, chopped
Pepper to taste
1 pound sea scallops
1/3 cup whipping cream
1/2 cup chopped fresh basil
Juice of 1/2 lemon
1/2 cup grated Parmesan cheese

Trim ends of snow peas; remove strings. Bring 3 quarts water to a boil in saucepan. Add salt and snow peas. Cook for 3 minutes. Remove snow peas to bowl. Bring water to a boil again. Add fettucini. Cook for 6 minutes or until just tender; drain, reserving 1/2 cup water. Sauté garlic in hot olive oil in skillet. Add tomatoes, jalapeño pepper, salt, pepper, scallops, fettucini and reserved 1/2 cup water. Bring to a boil, stirring constantly. Add snow peas, cream, basil and lemon juice; mix well. Simmer for 2 minutes, stirring frequently. Serve with Parmesan cheese. **Yield:** 4 servings.

Approx Per Serving: Cal 781; Prot 44 g; Carbo 106 g; Fiber 10 g; T Fat 20 g; 23% Calories from Fat; Chol 75 mg; Sod 395 mg.

Fettucini with Scallops*

15 ounces sea scallops
1 tablespoon olive oil
1/2 cup sliced green onions
3 cloves of garlic, minced
2 medium tomatoes, peeled, chopped
1/4 cup dry white wine
1 tablespoon cornstarch
1/2 cup nonfat yogurt
1 cup thawed frozen artichoke hearts
3 tablespoons chopped fresh basil
3 cups hot cooked fettucini
3 tablespoons grated Parmesan cheese

Sauté scallops in olive oil in skillet for 2 minutes. Remove to warm bowl. Add green onions, garlic and tomatoes to pan drippings. Cook for 1 to 2 minutes. Add wine. Simmer for 2 to 3 minutes. Mix cornstarch and yogurt in bowl. Stir into wine mixture. Add artichoke hearts, basil and scallops. Simmer for 3 to 4 minutes or until thickened, stirring constantly. Spoon hot fettucini onto serving plates; top with scallop sauce. Sprinkle with Parmesan cheese. **Yield:** 6 servings.

Approx Per Serving: Cal 220; Prot 19 g; Carbo 26 g; Fiber 4 g; T Fat 4 g; 17% Calories from Fat; Chol 27 mg; Sod 193 mg.

Pasta with Scampi Primavera*

"All preparations can be done early in the day including cooking spaghetti. Reheat briefly in boiling water and other ingredients in saucepan."

1 pound uncooked thin spaghetti
3 cloves of garlic, minced
1/2 teaspoon finely chopped lemon rind
3/4 cup olive oil
1 medium zucchini, cut into thin strips
1 medium red bell pepper, cut into thin strips
2 carrots, cut into thin strips
1 1/2 pounds uncooked shrimp, peeled, deveined
2 tablespoons lemon juice
3/4 teaspoon salt
1/8 teaspoon pepper
2 teaspoons basil
2 tablespoons chopped parsley

Cook spaghetti using package directions; drain. Sauté garlic and lemon rind in hot olive oil in skillet for 30 seconds, stirring constantly. Add zucchini, red pepper, carrots and shrimp. Cook over medium heat for 3 to 4 minutes or until shrimp are pink, stirring constantly. Sprinkle with lemon juice, salt and pepper. Stir in basil and parsley. Spoon spaghetti into serving bowl. Add shrimp sauce; toss well. **Yield:** 8 servings.

Approx Per Serving: Cal 473; Prot 22 g; Carbo 47 g; Fiber 4 g; T Fat 22 g; 42% Calories from Fat; Chol 133 mg; Sod 361 mg.

Pasta and Shrimp Kiev*

"Delicious!"

2 cloves of garlic, minced
1 large green bell pepper, cut into strips
1 cup thinly sliced fresh mushrooms
1/4 cup margarine
1 pound uncooked shrimp, peeled, deveined
1/2 teaspoon salt
Pepper to taste
1/2 teaspoon oregano
1/8 teaspoon tarragon
2 plum tomatoes, chopped
1/2 cup wine
1 tablespoon lemon juice
12 ounces linguine, cooked

Sauté half the garlic, green pepper and mushrooms in 2 tablespoons margarine in skillet until green peppers are tender-crisp. Remove to warm bowl. Add remaining 2 tablespoons margarine to skillet. Heat until bubbly. Add shrimp, salt, pepper, oregano, tarragon and remaining garlic; mix well. Sauté until shrimp are slightly firm. Stir in tomatoes, wine and lemon juice. Simmer, covered, for 2 to 4 minutes or just until shrimp are opaque. Add green pepper mixture. Heat to serving temperature. Spoon over hot linguine in serving bowl. **Yield:** 4 servings.

Approx Per Serving: Cal 554; Prot 31 g; Carbo 69 g; Fiber 2 g; T Fat 14 g; 24% Calories from Fat; Chol 177 mg; Sod 611 mg.

Tuna and Linguine*

"Good low-fat dinner fare"

1 large onion, finely chopped
1/4 cup olive oil
1 large green bell pepper, sliced
1 large red bell pepper, sliced
1 medium zucchini, sliced
2 cloves of garlic, minced
8 ounces fresh mushrooms, sliced
1 10-ounce can consommé
1/2 cup grated Romano cheese
1/2 teaspoon oregano
1/2 teaspoon basil
1/2 teaspoon salt
1/2 teaspoon pepper
1 13-ounce can water-pack solid white tuna
1 pound linguine, cooked

Sauté onion in hot olive oil in skillet for 2 minutes. Add green pepper, red pepper, zucchini, garlic and mushrooms. Cook for 5 minutes, stirring constantly. Add consommé, cheese, oregano, basil, salt and pepper; mix well. Add undrained tuna. Heat to serving temperature, stirring frequently. Serve over hot linguine. Garnish with additional cheese. **Yield:** 4 servings.

Approx Per Serving: Cal 764; Prot 51 g; Carbo 96 g; Fiber 8 g; T Fat 19 g; 23% Calories from Fat; Chol 64 mg; Sod 1112 mg.

Bolognese Sauce for Pasta

"A thick, meaty pasta sauce"

1 pound pork sausage
2 pounds ground round
4 large onions, chopped
4 cloves of garlic, minced
1 cup chopped parsley
12 ounces mushrooms, thinly sliced
3 15-ounce cans tomato sauce
1 25-ounce bottle of hearty Burgundy
1 1/2 teaspoons salt
1 teaspoon sage
1 teaspoon rosemary
1/2 teaspoon marjoram
1/2 teaspoon thyme
Pepper to taste

Brown sausage and ground round in large skillet, stirring until crumbly. Add onions. Cook until onions are tender, stirring frequently; drain. Add garlic, parsley and mushrooms; mix well. Add tomato sauce, Burgundy, salt, sage, rosemary, marjoram, thyme and pepper. Simmer, covered, for 3 hours or until thickened, stirring occasionally. Skim off fat. Serve over pasta. May be frozen and reheated slowly. **Yield:** 10 servings.

Approx Per Serving: Cal 387; Prot 25 g; Carbo 18 g; Fiber 4 g; T Fat 20 g; 47% Calories from Fat; Chol 77 mg; Sod 1428 mg.

Angela's Spaghetti Sauce*

"A chef in Florence gave me this recipe—in Italian."

2 16-ounce cans Italian plum tomatoes
1 clove of garlic, minced
1/4 cup olive oil
3 or 4 tablespoons Marsala
10 to 12 fresh basil leaves, chopped
Salt to taste

Drain tomatoes, reserving juice and discarding seed. Purée tomatoes in food processor. Sauté garlic in hot olive oil in skillet. Add puréed tomatoes, reserved juice, wine, basil and salt. Simmer for 15 minutes, stirring frequently. **Yield:** 6 servings.

Approx Per Serving: Cal 125; Prot 1 g; Carbo 8 g; Fiber 2 g; T Fat 9 g; 69% Calories from Fat; Chol 0 mg; Sod 247 mg.

Pesto Sauce*

"Keeps in refrigerator for 3 to 4 days"

1/2 bunch fresh basil
1/2 bunch fresh parsley, stemmed
2 tablespoons grated Romano cheese
1/4 cup pine nuts, toasted
1 tablespoon minced garlic
1/8 teaspoon salt
1/4 teaspoon pepper
1/2 cup olive oil

Combine first 7 ingredients in blender container. Process until finely chopped. Add olive oil gradually, blending until sauce is smooth. **Yield:** 16 (1-tablespoon) servings.

Approx Per Serving: Cal 74; Prot 1 g; Carbo 1 g; Fiber <1 g; T Fat 8 g; 92% Calories from Fat; Chol 1 mg; Sod 26 mg.

Low-Fat Pesto Sauce*

2 cups fresh spinach
1/2 cup fresh basil
1/2 cup fresh parsley
4 cloves of garlic, minced
2 cups canned or fresh tomatoes
1/2 cup low-fat Parmesan cheese
Juice of 1 lemon
1/4 cup pine nuts

Process spinach, basil, parsley, garlic, tomatoes, cheese, lemon juice and pine nuts in blender container until finely chopped. Serve over pasta. **Yield:** 32 (1-tablespoon) servings.

Approx Per Serving: Cal 17; Prot 1 g; Carbo 1 g; Fiber <1 g; T Fat 1 g; 43% Calories from Fat; Chol 1 mg; Sod 68 mg.

Rose's Spaghetti Sauce with Meatballs

"This is the best."

1 pound ground sirloin
1 cup seasoned bread crumbs
1 medium onion, finely chopped
1 clove of garlic, minced
2 eggs
1/3 cup grated locatelli cheese
1/2 teaspoon salt
1/4 teaspoon pepper
1/4 cup oil
1 large onion, chopped
1 clove of garlic, chopped
1 tablespoon oil
1 12-ounce can tomato paste
1 12-ounce can water
1 28-ounce can Italian tomatoes, crushed
1 28-ounce can tomato sauce
1 teaspoon salt
1 teaspoon pepper
1 tablespoon sugar
1 teaspoon basil

Combine ground sirloin, bread crumbs, 1 chopped onion, 1 clove of garlic, eggs, cheese, 1/2 teaspoon salt and 1/4 teaspoon pepper in bowl; mix well. Shape into 2-inch balls. Brown quickly on all sides in 1/4 cup hot oil in skillet. Remove to warm plate. Sauté remaining onion and remaining garlic in 1 tablespoon oil in large saucepan until tender. Add tomato paste. Simmer for 4 to 5 minutes, stirring constantly. Add water, tomatoes, tomato sauce, 1 teaspoon salt, 1 teaspoon pepper, sugar and basil; mix well. Bring to a boil. Add meatballs. Simmer for 2 1/2 hours, stirring occasionally. May substitute ground turkey for ground sirloin. **Yield:** 6 servings.

Approx Per Serving: Cal 504; Prot 25 g; Carbo 45 g; Fiber 7 g; T Fat 27 g; 47% Calories from Fat; Chol 126 mg; Sod 1798 mg.

Pasta Puttanesca*

"Anchovy lovers delight!"

2 28-ounce cans peeled Italian plum tomatoes
1 teaspoon oregano
1/8 teaspoon dried red pepper flakes
1/2 cup black olives
1/4 cup drained capers
4 cloves of garlic, minced
8 anchovy filets, chopped
1/2 cup chopped Italian parsley

Chop tomatoes coarsely. Bring tomatoes and liquid to a boil in saucepan. Add oregano, red pepper flakes, olives, capers, garlic, anchovy filets and parsley in order listed, stirring frequently. Simmer, until sauce is thickened, stirring frequently. Serve over hot linguine. Garnish with additional parsley. **Yield:** 4 servings.

Approx Per Serving: Cal 555; Prot 21 g; Carbo 104 g; Fiber 10 g; T Fat 8 g; 12% Calories from Fat; Chol 0 mg; Sod 1105 mg.

Vegetables & Side Dishes

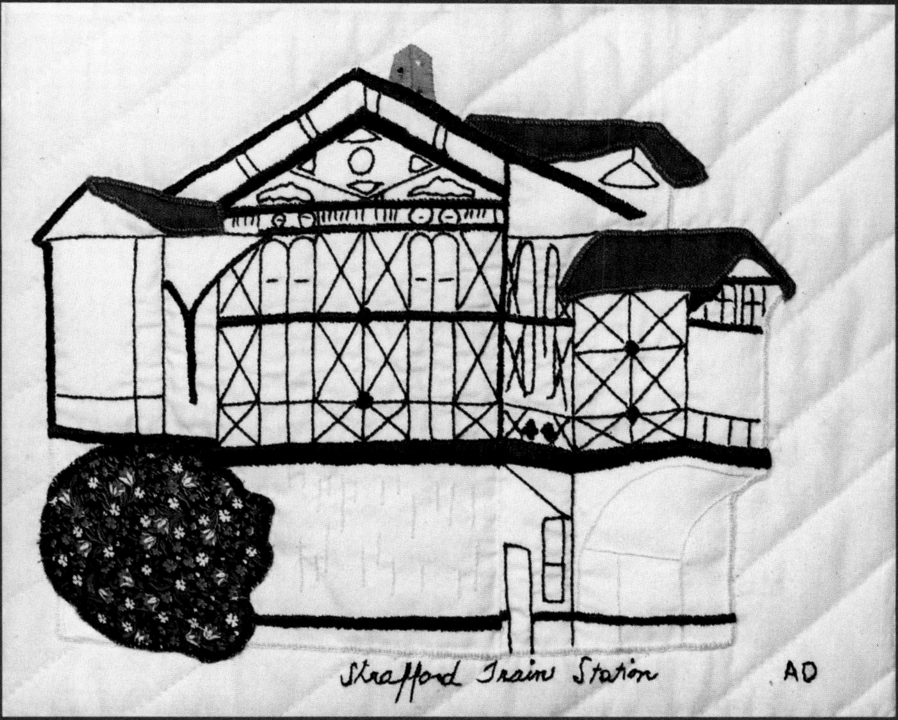

Strafford Train Station

Radnor Hunt Tailgate Picnic

Cold Filet of Beef Appetizer
page 38

Vegetable Basket with Yogurt-Dill Dressing
page 15

Glazed Ham with Cranberry-Pear Chutney
page 32

Saffron Pasta Salad
page 14

Tomatoes Stuffed with 'Chokes and Hearts
page 54

Eventful Muffins
page 117

Double Dark Decadent Brownie Cake
page 258

VEGETABLES

Asparagus in the Clouds*

1 pound asparagus, cooked
3 egg whites, at room temperature
1/4 teaspoon cream of tartar
3 tablespoons mayonnaise
1/4 teaspoon dry mustard
1 tablespoon lemon juice
1/2 teaspoon salt

Arrange asparagus in baking dish. Beat egg whites with cream of tartar in mixer bowl until stiff peaks form. Fold in mixture of remaining ingredients. Spread egg white mixture over top gently. Broil for 1 minute or just until light brown. **Yield:** 4 servings.

Approx Per Serving: Cal 112; Prot 6 g; Carbo 5 g; Fiber 2 g; T Fat 8 g; 63% Calories from Fat; Chol 6 mg; Sod 365 mg.

Sesame Asparagus*

1 1/2 pounds asparagus, cooked
1 large shallot, sliced
1/2 cup olive oil
1/4 cup rice wine vinegar
2 tablespoons orange juice
2 teaspoons Dijon mustard
1/2 teaspoon sesame oil
1/2 teaspoon salt

Arrange asparagus in serving dish. Combine remaining ingredients in glass dish. Microwave on High for 1 minute; mix well. Pour over asparagus. **Yield:** 6 servings.

Approx Per Serving: Cal 211; Prot 4 g; Carbo 10 g; Fiber 2 g; T Fat 19 g; 75% Calories from Fat; Chol 0 mg; Sod 204 mg.

Black Beans and Rice

½ cup dried black beans, soaked
3 cups water
3 cups cooked rice
½ cup thick and chunky medium salsa

Cook black beans in water in saucepan for 2½ hours or until tender. Drain beans and cool. Combine with rice and salsa in glass bowl; mix gently with wooden spoon. Microwave on High for 3 minutes or until heated through. **Yield:** 4 servings.

Approx Per Serving: Cal 255; Prot 9 g; Carbo 53 g; Fiber 6 g; T Fat 1 g; 4% Calories from Fat; Chol 0 mg; Sod 33 mg.

Green Beans with Bell Pepper Sauce

1 onion, sliced
2 cloves of garlic, crushed
3 tablespoons olive oil
2 yellow bell peppers, cut into strips
2 tomatoes, skinned, chopped
1½ pounds green beans, trimmed
Salt and pepper to taste
2 tablespoons chopped fresh oregano or 1 teaspoon dried oregano

Sauté onion and garlic in olive oil in skillet. Add bell peppers. Sauté for 5 minutes. Add tomatoes. Cook over medium-low heat for 30 minutes. Cook beans in boiling water in saucepan for 3 minutes; drain. Add tomato mixture; mix well. Season with salt and pepper. Cook for 3 to 4 minutes or until heated through. Top with oregano. **Yield:** 6 servings.

Approx Per Serving: Cal 120; Prot 3 g; Carbo 14 g; Fiber 4 g; T Fat 7 g; 49% Calories from Fat; Chol 0 mg; Sod 11 mg.

Lemon Crumb Green Beans*

2 pounds tender whole green beans, cooked
½ cup slivered almonds
⅓ cup butter
1 cup Italian-style bread crumbs
1 teaspoon grated lemon rind
Juice of 1 lemon

Place hot beans in serving dish. Sauté almonds in butter in skillet over medium heat for 1 to 2 minutes. Add bread crumbs. Sauté until bread crumbs are crisp. Stir in lemon rind. Drizzle lemon juice over beans. Spoon crumb mixture over top. **Yield:** 6 servings.

Approx Per Serving: Cal 269; Prot 7 g; Carbo 26 g; Fiber 5 g; T Fat 17 g; 54% Calories from Fat; Chol 28 mg; Sod 217 mg.

Broccoli Cantonese

"Add chopped cooked chicken to this recipe for a main dish."

3 pounds broccoli
1 cup chicken broth
1 tablespoon cornstarch
1 tablespoon soy sauce
1/2 teaspoon MSG
Dry mustard, ginger and salt to taste
2 tablespoons oil
4 to 5 green onions, chopped

Separate broccoli into flowerets. Peel broccoli stems, discarding tough ends. Slice stems 1/4 to 1/2 inch thick. Combine chicken broth, cornstarch, soy sauce, MSG, dry mustard, ginger and salt in small bowl; mix well. Stir-fry broccoli stems in hot oil in skillet or wok for 1 minute. Add flowerets and green onions. Stir-fry for 1 to 2 minutes; push vegetables to the side. Add chicken broth mixture. Cook until thickened, stirring constantly. Stir in vegetables. Cook, covered, for 2 to 3 minutes over low heat. **Yield:** 8 servings.

Approx Per Serving: Cal 88; Prot 6 g; Carbo 11 g; Fiber 6 g; T Fat 4 g; 36% Calories from Fat; Chol <1 mg; Sod 540 mg.

Broccoli Sauté*

"This is a nice company vegetable that goes well with beef."

2 pounds broccoli spears
1 tablespoon water
1/2 cup fresh whole wheat bread crumbs
3 tablespoons margarine
1/2 cup minced onion
1 clove of garlic, minced
3 tablespoons oil
3 slices bacon, chopped, crisp-fried
Salt and pepper to taste

Combine broccoli with water in glass dish. Microwave on High for 5 minutes or until tender; drain. Sauté bread crumbs in margarine in skillet until light brown. Remove and set aside. Add onion and garlic to oil in skillet. Sauté over low heat until tender. Add broccoli. Sauté until heated through. Add bread crumbs, bacon, salt and pepper; toss lightly. Serve immediately. May substitute green beans for broccoli. **Yield:** 6 servings.

Approx Per Serving: Cal 209; Prot 7 g; Carbo 15 g; Fiber 6 g; T Fat 15 g; 61% Calories from Fat; Chol 3 mg; Sod 220 mg.

Sprinkle potatoes lightly with flour before frying for easier browning.

Brussels Sprouts with Caraway Seed*

1½ pounds Brussels sprouts
2½ cups chicken broth
¼ cup melted butter
2 tablespoons lemon juice
1½ tablespoons caraway seed
½ teaspoon salt
Freshly ground pepper to taste
¼ cup bread crumbs
2 tablespoons butter

Cook Brussels sprouts in chicken broth in saucepan for 5 to 6 minutes or just until tender; drain well. Add melted butter, lemon juice, caraway seed, salt and pepper; toss to coat well. Spoon into 1-quart baking dish. Sprinkle with bread crumbs; dot with 2 tablespoons butter. Broil for 1 minute or until topping is golden brown. **Yield:** 8 servings.

Approx Per Serving: Cal 142; Prot 5 g; Carbo 11 g; Fiber 4 g; T Fat 10 g; 57% Calories from Fat; Chol 24 mg; Sod 493 mg. Nutritional information includes entire amount of chicken broth.

Hearty Skillet Cabbage

2 onions, chopped
6 tablespoons margarine
1 head cabbage, finely chopped
1 tablespoon brown sugar
Salt and pepper to taste

Sauté onion in margarine in electric skillet heated to 300 degrees. Add cabbage. Cook for 10 minutes. Stir in brown sugar, salt and pepper; reduce heat. Cook for 15 to 25 minutes or until tender. **Yield:** 6 servings.

Approx Per Serving: Cal 137; Prot 1 g; Carbo 9 g; Fiber 2 g; T Fat 11 g; 71% Calories from Fat; Chol 0 mg; Sod 105 mg.

Martini Cauliflower

Flowerets of 1 head cauliflower
1 carrot, peeled, minced
1 onion, minced
¼ cup unsalted butter
1 cup chicken broth
3 tablespoons dry vermouth
Salt and freshly ground pepper to taste

Slice cauliflowerets ½ inch thick. Sauté carrot and onion in butter in large skillet over medium-high heat for 3 minutes. Add cauliflower; toss to coat with butter. Add chicken broth and vermouth; reduce heat to medium. Cook, covered, for 7 minutes or until cauliflower is tender-crisp. Season with salt and pepper. Serve immediately. **Yield:** 6 servings.

Approx Per Serving: Cal 113; Prot 3 g; Carbo 7 g; Fiber 3 g; T Fat 8 g; 65% Calories from Fat; Chol 21 mg; Sod 146 mg.

Apricot Carrots

3 or 4 green onions
10 to 12 carrots
4 ounces dried apricots
1/4 cup butter
1 tablespoon honey
1 tablespoon sherry wine vinegar
1/2 cup water
Salt and freshly ground pepper to taste

Cut green onions, carrots and apricots into julienne strips. Sauté green onions and carrots in butter in large sauté pan over medium heat for 3 to 4 minutes or until green onions are tender. Add apricots, honey, vinegar and water. Cook, covered, for 4 to 5 minutes or until carrots are tender and mixture is heated through; remove from heat. Season with salt and pepper. Serve hot. **Yield:** 6 servings.

Approx Per Serving: Cal 188; Prot 2 g; Carbo 30 g; Fiber 6 g; T Fat 8 g; 36% Calories from Fat; Chol 21 mg; Sod 117 mg.

Nutty Carrots*

"Flame these in a chafing dish at the table for spectacular entertaining."

1 pound carrots, diagonally sliced
3/4 cup shelled natural pistachios
2 tablespoons butter
Salt and freshly ground pepper to taste
2 tablespoons brandy or ginger brandy

Steam carrots in saucepan until tender. Combine with pistachios, butter, salt and pepper in serving dish. Sprinkle with brandy. Flame if desired. Do not use dyed pistachios for this recipe. **Yield:** 6 servings.

Approx Per Serving: Cal 170; Prot 4 g; Carbo 13 g; Fiber 4 g; T Fat 12 g; 60% Calories from Fat; Chol 10 mg; Sod 60 mg.

Sun-Kissed Carrots*

1 medium bunch carrots, sliced
1/4 to 1/2 cup margarine
1/3 cup packed brown sugar
3 to 4 tablespoons fresh orange juice
1 teaspoon nutmeg

Steam carrots in saucepan until tender-crisp; drain. Sauté in margarine for several minutes. Add brown sugar, orange juice and nutmeg. Cook until carrots are glazed, stirring gently. Serve immediately. **Yield:** 6 servings.

Approx Per Serving: Cal 238; Prot 1 g; Carbo 26 g; Fiber 3 g; T Fat 15 g; 56% Calories from Fat; Chol 0 mg; Sod 218 mg.

Celery Scallop Amandine

"This is good served with grilled chicken."

6 cups 1-inch celery pieces
1 cup half and half
1 cup water
1/4 cup flour
1 1/2 teaspoons salt
Pepper to taste
3/4 teaspoon dried dillweed or 1 tablespoon chopped fresh dill
1/4 cup sliced almonds, toasted

Combine celery with 1 inch boiling water in saucepan. Cook, covered, for 2 to 3 minutes or until tender-crisp; drain. Place in 2-quart baking dish. Combine half and half, 1 cup water, flour, salt, pepper and dillweed in bowl; mix until smooth. Pour over celery. Bake at 350 degrees for 30 to 35 minutes or until sauce is thickened and celery is tender, stirring occasionally. Sprinkle with almonds. **Yield:** 6 servings.

Approx Per Serving: Cal 95; Prot 3 g; Carbo 13 g; Fiber 4 g; T Fat 6 g; 57% Calories from Fat; Chol 15 mg; Sod 657 mg.

Eggplant di Napoli

"Delicious!"

1/2 cup grated Romano cheese
1/2 cup flour
Salt and pepper to taste
2 small eggplant
1 large clove of garlic
1/2 cup (or more) olive oil
1 32-ounce jar tomato and basil pasta sauce
1 cup grated Romano cheese

Mix 1/2 cup cheese, flour, salt and pepper in shallow bowl. Slice eggplant 1/4 inch thick. Coat with cheese mixture. Sauté garlic in olive oil in heavy skillet over medium heat; discard garlic. Fry several eggplant slices at a time in olive oil in skillet, removing to paper towels to drain and adding additional olive oil as needed. Spread a small amount of pasta sauce in 7x11-inch baking dish. Alternate layers of eggplant, remaining sauce and remaining 1 cup cheese in prepared dish until all ingredients are used. Bake at 325 degrees for 20 to 25 minutes or until bubbly.
Yield: 10 servings.

Approx Per Serving: Cal 214; Prot 7 g; Carbo 15 g; Fiber 3 g; T Fat 15 g; 60% Calories from Fat; Chol 14 mg; Sod 720 mg.

Caponata

"Serve this hot or cold."

3 stalks celery, chopped
1 green bell pepper, chopped
1 medium onion, chopped
3 tablespoons olive oil
1 small eggplant, peeled, chopped
1 16-ounce can tomatoes
8 to 10 black olives, sliced
1 2½-ounce package sliced almonds
3 tablespoons vinegar
1 tablespoon sugar
½ teaspoon basil
½ teaspoon salt
Pepper to taste
1 6-ounce can tomato paste

Sauté celery, green pepper and onion in olive oil in large skillet until tender. Add eggplant, tomatoes, olives, almonds, vinegar, sugar, basil, salt and pepper; mix well. Simmer for 30 minutes. Stir in tomato paste. **Yield:** 6 servings.

Approx Per Serving: Cal 192; Prot 4 g; Carbo 14 g; Fiber 5 g; T Fat 15 g; 65% Calories from Fat; Chol 0 mg; Sod 381 mg.

Ratatouille Niçoise

2 large onions, thinly sliced
2 or 3 cloves of garlic, minced
½ cup oil
1 small eggplant, peeled, chopped
4 large tomatoes, chopped
4 zucchini, chopped
2 green bell peppers, chopped
½ teaspoon basil
½ teaspoon thyme
Salt and pepper to taste

Sauté onions and garlic lightly in oil in heavy saucepan over high heat. Add eggplant and tomatoes; crush with wooden spoon. Add zucchini, green peppers, basil, thyme, salt and pepper; mix well. Cook for 2 to 3 minutes over high heat, stirring constantly; reduce heat. Simmer, covered, for 1 hour or until thickened to desired consistency, stirring occasionally. Store in refrigerator for up to 15 days. Serve hot or cold as vegetable, salad or appetizer. May substitute one 28-ounce can tomatoes for fresh tomatoes. **Yield:** 6 servings.

Approx Per Serving: Cal 226; Prot 3 g; Carbo 14 g; Fiber 5 g; T Fat 19 g; 71% Calories from Fat; Chol 0 mg; Sod 12 mg.

Mushrooms Supreme

"This is a nice brunch or buffet dish."

1½ pounds mushrooms, sliced
1 tablespoon grated onion
2 tablespoons butter
½ teaspoon tarragon
½ teaspoon salt
¼ teaspoon pepper
2 tablespoons flour
¼ cup shredded Swiss cheese
2 egg yolks
¾ cup whipping cream
2 tablespoons fine bread crumbs
2 tablespoons melted butter

Cook mushrooms and onion, covered, in 2 tablespoons butter in saucepan over low heat for 4 minutes. Sprinkle with tarragon, salt and pepper. Stir in flour and cheese. Spoon into buttered baking dish. Beat egg yolks with cream in bowl. Pour over mushrooms. Top with bread crumbs; drizzle with remaining 2 tablespoons butter. Bake at 400 degrees for 20 minutes or until set. May prepare in advance and freeze, adding topping at baking time. May substitute Parmesan cheese for Swiss cheese. **Yield:** 4 servings.

Approx Per Serving: Cal 384; Prot 9 g; Carbo 15 g; Fiber 3 g; T Fat 34 g; 76% Calories from Fat; Chol 205 mg; Sod 432 mg.

Gourmet Onions

"Try Vidalia onions in this dish for a sweeter taste."

4 cups sliced or chopped onions
5 tablespoons butter
2 eggs
1 cup sour cream
Salt and pepper to taste
3 tablespoons grated Parmesan cheese
6 tablespoons grated sharp Cheddar cheese

Sauté onions in butter in skillet until tender. Place in 2-quart baking dish. Beat eggs in mixer bowl. Add sour cream, salt and pepper; mix well. Spoon over onions; sprinkle with cheeses. Bake at 375 degrees for 35 to 40 minutes or until set. **Yield:** 4 servings.

Approx Per Serving: Cal 402; Prot 11 g; Carbo 15 g; Fiber 3 g; T Fat 34 g; 76% Calories from Fat; Chol 188 mg; Sod 397 mg.

Use an egg slicer to slice mushrooms uniformly.

Peas with Mint and Scallions*

2 10-ounce packages frozen tiny peas
1/4 cup butter
1 bunch scallions, chopped
1/4 cup minced fresh mint
Salt and pepper to taste

Rinse peas in sieve with warm water. Microwave butter on High in 1 1/2-quart glass dish for 2 minutes. Stir in peas, scallions and mint. Microwave, tightly covered with plastic wrap, on High for 3 minutes. Stir in salt and pepper. Let stand for several minutes. **Yield:** 6 servings.

Approx Per Serving: Cal 144; Prot 5 g; Carbo 14 g; Fiber 5 g; T Fat 8 g; 49% Calories from Fat; Chol 21 mg; Sod 171 mg.

Snow Peas with Basil*

1 pound fresh snow peas, trimmed
1/2 cup chopped green onions
3 tablespoons corn oil
1/4 cup consommé
Salt and pepper to taste
2 tablespoons freshly chopped basil

Rinse snow peas; do not dry. Microwave on High in glass dish for 3 minutes. Sauté green onions in oil in saucepan until tender. Add snow peas, consommé, salt and pepper; mix gently. Cook for 2 minutes or until heated through. Sprinkle with basil. **Yield:** 4 servings.

Approx Per Serving: Cal 145; Prot 4 g; Carbo 10 g; Fiber 3 g; T Fat 11 g; 63% Calories from Fat; Chol 0 mg; Sod 85 mg.

Purée of Peas

"Sprinkle with finely grated or chopped carrot for a colorful effect."

3 10-ounce packages frozen peas
1 small carrot, cut into quarters
2 green onions, chopped
1/2 cup water
1/2 teaspoon thyme
Salt and freshly ground pepper to taste
1/4 cup butter, chopped
1/4 cup whipping cream

Combine first 7 ingredients in saucepan. Simmer, covered, until peas are tender; drain, discarding carrot. Purée in several batches in blender or food processor. Add butter and cream; process until smooth. Place in buttered baking dish; set in larger pan of warm water. Bake at 300 degrees for 20 to 30 minutes or until heated through. **Yield:** 8 servings.

Approx Per Serving: Cal 162; Prot 6 g; Carbo 16 g; Fiber 6 g; T Fat 9 g; 48% Calories from Fat; Chol 26 mg; Sod 173 mg.

New Potato Bake*

3 pounds small new potatoes
2 or 3 tablespoons olive oil
1/2 teaspoon lemon pepper
1/4 teaspoon garlic powder
1/2 teaspoon oregano
1/2 teaspoon salt

Cut unpeeled potatoes into halves or quarters, depending on size. Mix remaining ingredients in deep bowl. Add potatoes; mix with wooden spoon to coat well. Spread on baking sheet. Bake at 400 degrees for 30 to 35 minutes or until potatoes are tender. **Yield:** 5 servings.

Approx Per Serving: Cal 368; Prot 6 g; Carbo 69 g; Fiber 6 g; T Fat 8 g; 20% Calories from Fat; Chol 0 mg; Sod 235 mg.

Onion Barbecued Potatoes

"Serve these easy potatoes with pepper-butter or your favorite topping."

6 russet potatoes, peeled
1 onion, thinly sliced
6 tablespoons melted butter
1/2 envelope onion soup mix

Slice potatoes into thirds, cutting to but not through bottom. Place onion slices into cuts. Place each potato on square of foil. Brush with butter; sprinkle with soup mix. Fold foil to enclose potatoes; seal tightly. Grill over hot coals for 50 to 60 minutes or until fork tender, turning occasionally. **Yield:** 6 servings.

Approx Per Serving: Cal 257; Prot 4 g; Carbo 36 g; Fiber 3 g; T Fat 12 g; 40% Calories from Fat; Chol 31 mg; Sod 158 mg.

Party Potatoes

8 to 10 medium potatoes, peeled
8 ounces light cream cheese, softened
1 cup sour cream
1/4 cup butter
1/2 cup chopped green onions
8 slices crisp-fried bacon, crumbled
Salt and pepper to taste
2 tablespoons minced parsley
1/2 cup bread crumbs

Cook potatoes in water in saucepan until tender; drain. Mash potatoes in bowl. Add cream cheese, sour cream and butter; beat well. Stir in green onions, bacon, salt and pepper. Spoon into buttered 1 or 2-quart baking dish. Sprinkle with parsley and bread crumbs. Bake at 375 degrees for 20 to 30 minutes or until heated through. **Yield:** 8 servings.

Approx Per Serving: Cal 419; Prot 11 g; Carbo 50 g; Fiber 3 g; T Fat 20 g; 43% Calories from Fat; Chol 50 mg; Sod 383 mg.

Red Potatoes with Pepperoni and Chives*

1/4 cup chopped pepperoni
2 cloves of garlic, minced
2 pounds small red potatoes, cut into quarters, cooked
1/4 cup butter, chopped, softened
1/2 cup chicken broth
1 tablespoon vinegar
1/4 cup chopped chives
Pepper to taste

Sauté pepperoni and garlic in nonstick skillet for 4 to 5 minutes; drain on paper towels. Toss potatoes with butter, broth and vinegar in bowl. Add pepperoni mixture, chives and pepper; toss to mix. **Yield:** 6 servings.

Approx Per Serving: Cal 285; Prot 6 g; Carbo 39 g; Fiber 4 g; T Fat 12 g; 38% Calories from Fat; Chol 24 mg; Sod 334 mg.

Spinach and Artichoke Bake*

1 16-ounce can artichoke hearts, rinsed, sliced
3 10-ounce packages frozen chopped spinach, cooked
8 ounces cream cheese, softened
2 tablespoons mayonnaise
6 tablespoons milk
1 teaspoon thyme
Salt and pepper to taste
2 tablespoons Parmesan cheese

Layer artichokes and spinach in shallow greased baking dish. Combine next 6 ingredients in bowl; mix well. Spread over spinach. Sprinkle with Parmesan cheese. Bake at 325 degrees for 25 minutes. **Yield:** 8 servings.

Approx Per Serving: Cal 181; Prot 7 g; Carbo 10 g; Fiber 3 g; T Fat 14 g; 64% Calories from Fat; Chol 35 mg; Sod 341 mg.

Baked Herbed Spinach*

1 cup minced onion
2 cloves of garlic, minced
1/4 cup butter
5 10-ounce packages frozen chopped spinach, thawed, drained
1 cup whipping cream
1 cup milk
1/4 cup grated Parmesan cheese
1/2 cup bread crumbs
1 teaspoon each marjoram and salt
1/4 teaspoon pepper
2 tablespoons grated Parmesan cheese

Sauté onion and garlic in butter in skillet until tender. Mix next 8 ingredients in bowl. Stir in onion mixture. Spoon into greased 2-quart baking dish. Sprinkle with remaining 2 tablespoons cheese. Bake at 350 degrees for 25 to 30 minutes or until bubbly. **Yield:** 12 servings.

Approx Per Serving: Cal 181; Prot 7 g; Carbo 12 g; Fiber 4 g; T Fat 13 g; 61% Calories from Fat; Chol 42 mg; Sod 405 mg.

"Sun-Dried" Tomatoes

40 plum tomatoes
Salt to taste
Fresh basil leaves to taste
2 cups extra-virgin olive oil

Slice tomatoes into halves lengthwise. Arrange cut side up on rack in baking pan. Sprinkle with salt. Bake at 250 degrees for 8 hours; tomatoes should resemble prunes. Cool to room temperature. Pack with basil into sterilized jars. Add enough olive oil to cover; seal with 2-piece lids. Discard tomatoes that change color. **Yield:** 20 servings.

Approx Per Serving: Cal 239; Prot 2 g; Carbo 11 g; Fiber 4 g; T Fat 22 g; 79% Calories from Fat; Chol 0 mg; Sod 20 mg.

Zucchini-Stuffed Love Apple

4 small zucchini, grated, drained
2 tablespoons unsalted butter
5 tablespoons grated Parmesan cheese
1 tablespoon whipping cream
4 small tomatoes
1 fresh basil leaf, chopped
Seasoned salt and freshly ground pepper to taste
4 teaspoons butter

Sauté zucchini in 2 tablespoons butter in skillet until tender. Add 1 tablespoon cheese and cream; mix well. Cut off tops of tomatoes and scoop out centers. Pat dry inside and out. Sprinkle with seasonings. Fill with zucchini mixture. Arrange in baking dish. Top with 4 tablespoons cheese; dot with 4 teaspoons butter. Bake at 350 degrees for 20 minutes or until topping is brown. **Yield:** 4 servings.

Approx Per Serving: Cal 159; Prot 5 g; Carbo 7 g; Fiber 2 g; T Fat 13 g; 71% Calories from Fat; Chol 36 mg; Sod 162 mg.

Green and Gold Squash Scallop

1 medium onion, chopped
2 tablespoons oil
2 each zucchini and summer squash, grated
3 eggs, slightly beaten
2 tablespoons chopped parsley
1/2 teaspoon each oregano and salt
1/4 teaspoon pepper
1 cup cracker crumbs
1 cup shredded Cheddar cheese

Sauté onion in oil in skillet; remove from heat. Stir in squash, eggs, parsley, oregano, salt and pepper. Layer squash, cracker crumbs and cheese 1/3 at a time in baking dish. Bake at 325 degrees for 45 minutes. **Yield:** 6 servings.

Approx Per Serving: Cal 238; Prot 10 g; Carbo 16 g; Fiber 2 g; T Fat 15 g; 57% Calories from Fat; Chol 131 mg; Sod 513 mg.

Spaghetti Squash Monterey

1 spaghetti squash
1 large onion, chopped
1/4 cup butter
1 4-ounce can chopped green chilies, drained
1 teaspoon cumin
Salt and pepper to taste
1/2 cup sour cream
2 cups shredded Cheddar cheese
Chili powder to taste

Pierce squash in several places with knife. Microwave on High for 15 to 20 minutes or until soft when pressed, turning once. Cut into halves, discarding seed. Separate into strands with fork. Sauté onion in butter in skillet. Stir in green chilies, cumin, salt and pepper; remove from heat. Add sour cream and 1 cup cheese. Combine with squash in bowl; mix well. Spoon into greased 3-quart baking dish; top with remaining 1 cup cheese. Sprinkle lightly with chili powder. Bake at 325 degrees for 30 minutes. **Yield:** 8 servings.

Approx Per Serving: Cal 228; Prot 8 g; Carbo 8 g; Fiber 2 g; T Fat 18 g; 71% Calories from Fat; Chol 52 mg; Sod 346 mg.

Sweet Potato and Apple Casserole

3 tablespoons sugar
1/2 teaspoon cinnamon
White pepper to taste
2 cooking apples, sliced
4 small sweet potatoes, peeled, sliced
2 tablespoons melted reduced-calorie margarine

Combine sugar, cinnamon and white pepper in small bowl. Layer apples, sweet potatoes, sugar mixture and margarine 1/2 at a time in 8x8-inch baking dish sprayed with nonstick cooking spray. Bake, covered, at 350 degrees for 1 hour. **Yield:** 8 servings.

Approx Per Serving: Cal 110; Prot 1 g; Carbo 24 g; Fiber 3 g; T Fat 2 g; 13% Calories from Fat; Chol 0 mg; Sod 42 mg.

Maple Sweet Potatoes*

5 or 6 sweet potatoes, peeled, sliced
1/2 cup pure maple syrup
2 tablespoons margarine

Place sweet potatoes in glass dish. Drizzle with maple syrup; dot with margarine. Microwave on High for 20 to 25 minutes or until tender. **Yield:** 8 servings.

Approx Per Serving: Cal 195; Prot 2 g; Carbo 41 g; Fiber 3 g; T Fat 3 g; 15% Calories from Fat; Chol 0 mg; Sod 51 mg.

SIDE DISHES

Couscous with Mushrooms*

"This is a good substitute for rice."

3 to 4 cups chicken broth
2 cups precooked couscous
8 ounces mushrooms, sliced
6 scallions, finely chopped
1/4 cup pine nuts

Bring 3 to 4 cups chicken broth to a boil in saucepan using package directions. Stir in remaining ingredients; remove from heat. Let stand for 5 minutes or until liquid is absorbed. **Yield:** 4 servings.

Approx Per Serving: Cal 210; Prot 11 g; Carbo 29 g; Fiber 2 g; T Fat 5 g; 23% Calories from Fat; Chol 1 mg; Sod 787 mg.

Lemon-Dill Rice

1 large onion, minced
2 cups uncooked rice
3 tablespoons butter
5 cups water
1/4 cup fresh lemon juice
2 tablespoons dillweed or dillseed
2 teaspoons salt

Sauté onion and rice in butter in saucepan until lightly browned. Stir in water, lemon juice, dillweed and salt. Bring to a boil. Spoon into 2-quart baking dish. Bake, covered, at 325 degrees for 45 to 60 minutes or until rice is tender and liquid is absorbed. **Yield:** 8 servings.

Approx Per Serving: Cal 216; Prot 4 g; Carbo 40 g; Fiber 1 g; T Fat 5 g; 19% Calories from Fat; Chol 12 mg; Sod 573 mg.

Argentine Rice

1 14-ounce can asparagus spears
1 onion, chopped
1 green bell pepper, chopped
1 clove of garlic, crushed
1 tablespoon oil
2 tablespoons butter
1½ cups uncooked long grain rice
½ cup grated Parmesan cheese
Salt and pepper to taste
1 cup sour cream
8 ounces Monterey Jack cheese, shredded

Drain asparagus, reserving liquid. Add enough water to reserved liquid to measure 2½ cups. Sauté onion, green pepper and garlic in oil in saucepan. Stir in reserved liquid, butter, rice, Parmesan cheese, salt and pepper. Simmer, covered, for 25 minutes or until rice is tender. Stir in sour cream. Layer rice mixture, asparagus and Monterey Jack cheese in 2-quart baking dish. Bake at 350 degrees for 30 minutes. May substitute nonfat yogurt for sour cream. **Yield:** 8 servings.

Approx Per Serving: Cal 376; Prot 14 g; Carbo 33 g; Fiber 2 g; T Fat 21 g; 51% Calories from Fat; Chol 50 mg; Sod 460 mg.

Rice Milano

1 large onion, finely chopped
1 red bell pepper, finely chopped
5 tablespoons margarine
1 cup dry white wine
2 cups uncooked long grain rice
1 teaspoon salt
½ teaspoon white pepper
½ teaspoon saffron thread
4 to 5 cups consommé
½ cup toasted pine nuts
1 cup grated Romano cheese
3 tablespoons margarine

Sauté onion and bell pepper in margarine in 4-quart saucepan over medium heat until tender but not brown. Stir in wine. Cook until wine has evaporated. Add rice, salt and pepper. Sauté lightly, tossing to coat rice well with margarine. Add saffron and 2 cups consommé. Cook until consommé has nearly evaporated. Add 2 cups consommé. Simmer, covered, for 20 to 25 minutes or until tender, adding remaining 1 cup consommé if needed for desired consistency. Remove from heat. Stir in pine nuts, cheese and remaining 3 tablespoons margarine. May cook uncovered for a firmer textured rice. **Yield:** 6 servings.

Approx Per Serving: Cal 557; Prot 21 g; Carbo 58 g; Fiber 2 g; T Fat 25 g; 40% Calories from Fat; Chol 16 mg; Sod 1774 mg.

Mixed Grain Pilaf

"This is a nice dish for a picnic or barbecue."

1/3 cup slivered almonds
1 large onion, chopped
1 large carrot, shredded
1 clove of garlic, minced
1/3 cup chopped parsley
1/4 cup butter
1/3 cup uncooked barley
1/3 cup uncooked brown rice
1/3 cup uncooked bulgur
2 1/2 cups chicken broth
1/4 cup sherry
3/4 teaspoon basil
3/4 teaspoon oregano
Salt and pepper to taste

Spread almonds in shallow baking pan. Toast at 350 degrees for 8 minutes; cool to room temperature. Sauté onion, carrot, garlic and parsley in butter in 3-quart saucepan over medium-high heat until onion is tender. Stir in barley, rice and bulgur. Sauté until grains are lightly browned. Stir in broth, wine, basil, oregano, salt and pepper. Bring to a boil; reduce heat. Simmer, covered, for 45 to 55 minutes or until grains are tender. Let stand, covered, for 10 minutes. Top with toasted almonds. Serve warm or cold. May substitute oat groats for 1 of the grains or beef broth for chicken broth. **Yield:** 6 servings.

Approx Per Serving: Cal 264; Prot 7 g; Carbo 29 g; Fiber 6 g; T Fat 13 g; 44% Calories from Fat; Chol 21 mg; Sod 397 mg.

Noodles Florence

12 ounces uncooked wide noodles
1 clove of garlic, minced
1/2 green bell pepper, chopped
1 onion, chopped
1 tablespoon chopped parsley
2 cups cottage cheese
2 cups sour cream
1 tablespoon Worcestershire sauce
1 teaspoon horseradish
Tabasco sauce to taste
1/2 teaspoon dry mustard
Salt to taste

Cook noodles using package directions for 10 minutes; rinse in cold water and drain. Combine with garlic, green pepper, onion and parsley in bowl; mix well. Combine cottage cheese, sour cream, Worcestershire sauce, horseradish, Tabasco sauce, dry mustard and salt in small bowl. Add to noodles; mix gently. Spoon into buttered large baking dish. Bake at 325 degrees for 40 minutes. May sprinkle with Parmesan cheese or substitute plain yogurt for sour cream. Serve with baked ham, sautéed mushrooms, salad and rolls. **Yield:** 8 servings.

Approx Per Serving: Cal 351; Prot 15 g; Carbo 36 g; Fiber <1 g; T Fat 17 g; 42% Calories from Fat; Chol 33 mg; Sod 270 mg.

Desserts

Conestoga Wagon

The Chairman's Wrap-Up Luncheon

Provençal Summer Soup
page 79

Raspberry and Spinach Salad
page 84

Chicken Pizzazz
page 181

Sesame Asparagus
page 223

Lemon Popovers
page 121

Chocolate Mousse Crown
page 246

Lemon Delight
page 251

DESSERTS

Bavarian Apple Torte

1/2 cup butter, softened
1/3 cup sugar
1/4 teaspoon vanilla extract
1 cup flour
8 ounces cream cheese, softened
1/4 cup sugar
1 egg
1/2 teaspoon vanilla extract
4 cups chopped apples
1/3 cup sugar
1/2 teaspoon cinnamon
1/4 cup sliced almonds

Cream butter, 1/3 cup sugar and 1/4 teaspoon vanilla in mixer bowl until light and fluffy. Stir in flour. Spread in 9-inch springform pan. Combine cream cheese and 1/4 cup sugar in bowl; mix well. Stir in egg and remaining 1/2 teaspoon vanilla. Spread over flour mixture. Toss apples with mixture of remaining 1/3 cup sugar and cinnamon. Arrange in concentric circles over cream cheese mixture. Sprinkle with almonds. Bake at 450 degrees for 10 minutes. Reduce temperature to 400 degrees. Bake for 25 to 30 minutes longer or until wooden pick comes out clean. **Yield:** 8 servings.

Approx Per Serving: Cal 408; Prot 5 g; Carbo 46 g; Fiber 2 g; T Fat 24 g; 52% Calories from Fat; Chol 89 mg; Sod 190 mg.

Sour Cream-Apple Squares

2 cups flour
2 cups packed brown sugar
1/2 cup margarine, softened
1 cup chopped pecans
1 egg
1 teaspoon baking soda
1 cup sour cream
2 teaspoons cinnamon
1 1/2 teaspoons vanilla extract
2 cups chopped peeled apples

Mix flour and brown sugar in large bowl. Cut in margarine until crumbly. Stir in pecans. Press 2 3/4 cups of the mixture into ungreased 9x13-inch baking pan. Add remaining ingredients to remaining crumb mixture; mix well. Spoon into prepared pan. Bake at 350 degrees for 25 minutes or until set. Cool for 20 minutes. Cut into squares. **Yield:** 15 servings.

Approx Per Serving: Cal 352; Prot 3 g; Carbo 53 g; Fiber 1 g; T Fat 15 g; 38% Calories from Fat; Chol 21 mg; Sod 155 mg.

Bananas Hawaiian*

3 tablespoons butter
1/2 cup firmly packed brown sugar
1 cup dark rum
1/4 teaspoon ground cinnamon
6 bananas, peeled, sliced
2 quarts vanilla ice cream
3/4 cup flaked coconut, toasted

Melt butter in skillet. Add brown sugar, rum and cinnamon. Cook until bubbly. Add bananas. Cook until heated through. Pour over ice cream in individual serving dishes. Sprinkle with coconut. **Yield:** 8 servings.

Approx Per Serving: Cal 545; Prot 6 g; Carbo 71 g; Fiber 3 g; T Fat 21 g; 35% Calories from Fat; Chol 71 mg; Sod 162 mg.

Maine Blueberry Shaker Pudding

2 tablespoons butter
1/2 cup sugar
1 cup flour
1 teaspoon baking powder
1/2 teaspoon salt
1/2 cup milk
3/4 cup sugar
1 cup water
2 cups blueberries
1/2 teaspoon cinnamon
1 tablespoon butter

Cream 2 tablespoons butter and 1/2 cup sugar in bowl. Add flour, baking powder, salt and milk; beat well. Pour into greased 2 1/2-quart casserole. Combine remaining ingredients in saucepan. Boil for 3 minutes. Pour over batter. Bake at 350 degrees for 45 minutes. **Yield:** 4 servings.

Approx Per Serving: Cal 492; Prot 5 g; Carbo 98 g; Fiber 3 g; T Fat 10 g; 18% Calories from Fat; Chol 27 mg; Sod 441 mg.

Nantucket Blueberry Crunch

"Delicious summertime dessert"

3/4 cup chopped walnuts
2 pints fresh blueberries
1/2 cup sugar
1/2 teaspoon cinnamon
1/4 teaspoon nutmeg
Finely grated rind of 1 lemon
1 tablespoon lemon juice
3/4 cup flour, sifted
1/4 teaspoon salt
1/2 cup packed dark brown sugar
6 tablespoons cold unsalted butter
6 cups vanilla ice cream

Place walnuts on foil-lined baking pan. Bake at 350 degrees for 8 to 10 minutes or until very hot. Break into small pieces when cooled. Rinse and dry blueberries. Combine with mixture of sugar, cinnamon and nutmeg in bowl; toss to mix well. Sprinkle with lemon rind and juice; toss gently. Spoon mixture into greased 9x13-inch baking pan. Sprinkle with walnuts. Combine flour, salt and brown sugar in bowl; mix well. Cut in butter until crumbly. Sprinkle over top. Bake at 350 degrees for 30 minutes. Serve hot in tall glasses with ice cream. **Yield:** 6 servings.

Approx Per Serving: Cal 727; Prot 10 g; Carbo 98 g; Fiber 4 g; T Fat 36 g; 44% Calories from Fat; Chol 90 mg; Sod 224 mg.

Blueberry Tart

"Beautiful to serve"

1 1/2 cups flour
1/3 cup sugar
3/4 teaspoon baking powder
7 tablespoons unsalted butter
1 egg
4 cups fresh blueberries
1 tablespoon flour
1/3 cup seedless red raspberry preserves
1/2 teaspoon cinnamon

Combine 1 1/2 cups flour, sugar and baking powder in bowl; mix well. Cut in butter until crumbly. Add egg; stir with fork or spoon until smooth and well blended. Pat onto bottom and 1 1/2 inches up side of ungreased 9-inch springform pan for crust. Chill in refrigerator. Rinse and dry blueberries. Combine 1 tablespoon flour, preserves and cinnamon in bowl; mix well. Coat blueberries with flour mixture. Spread evenly over crust. Bake at 350 degrees for 55 to 60 minutes or until crust is lightly browned. Loosen edge of tart with knife; remove side of pan. Cool on wire rack for 1 hour. May substitute damson plum or strawberry preserves for raspberry preserves. **Yield:** 10 servings.

Approx Per Serving: Cal 237; Prot 3 g; Carbo 37 g; Fiber 2 g; T Fat 9 g; 34% Calories from Fat; Chol 43 mg; Sod 38 mg.

Amaretto Cheesecake

"Every now and then you need a little cheesecake."

1/4 cup butter
2 tablespoons sugar
1/2 teaspoon vanilla extract
1/2 cup flour
24 ounces cream cheese, softened
1 cup sugar
4 eggs
1/3 cup whipping cream
1/3 cup Amaretto
1 teaspoon vanilla extract
2 tablespoons flour
2 cups sour cream
2 tablespoons sugar
3 tablespoons Amaretto

Combine butter, 2 tablespoons sugar, 1/2 teaspoon vanilla and 1/2 cup flour in bowl; mix well. Press into springform pan. Combine cream cheese, 1 cup sugar, eggs, whipping cream, 1/3 cup Amaretto, remaining 1 teaspoon vanilla and 2 tablespoons flour in mixer bowl. Beat until light and well blended. Pour into springform pan. Bake at 350 degrees for 50 minutes. Let stand for 5 minutes; it will not be fully set. Combine sour cream, remaining 2 tablespoons sugar and 3 tablespoons Amaretto in bowl; mix well. Spread over cheesecake. Bake at 350 degrees for 5 minutes. Chill in pan overnight. Place on serving plate. Remove side of pan. **Yield:** 15 servings.

Approx Per Serving: Cal 405; Prot 7 g; Carbo 28 g; Fiber <1 g; T Fat 29 g; 65% Calories from Fat; Chol 135 mg; Sod 198 mg.

Low-Fat Pumpkin Cheesecakes

"A Thanksgiving blessing"

24 ounces light cream cheese, softened
1 cup sugar
1 teaspoon ground cinnamon
1 teaspoon ground ginger
1/2 teaspoon ground cloves
1 16-ounce can pumpkin
1 cup egg substitute
2 9-inch graham cracker pie shells

Combine cream cheese, sugar, cinnamon, ginger and cloves in food processor container. Process until light and fluffy. Add pumpkin; mix well. Add egg substitute 1/4 cup at a time, beating at low speed until well mixed. Spoon into pie shells. Bake at 300 degrees for 1 1/4 hours or until center is set. Cool to room temperature. Chill, covered, for 3 hours. May frost with favorite cream cheese frosting. **Yield:** 16 servings.

Approx Per Serving: Cal 517; Prot 11 g; Carbo 45 g; Fiber 1 g; T Fat 33 g; 57% Calories from Fat; Chol 71 mg; Sod 634 mg.

Black Forest Crêpes

3 eggs
1 cup flour
1 cup milk
2 tablespoons sugar
2 tablespoons melted butter
2 17-ounce cans pitted dark sweet cherries
1 cup confectioners' sugar
2½ tablespoons cornstarch
½ cup Amaretto
1 cup whipping cream, whipped
2 cups chocolate syrup

Combine eggs, flour, milk, sugar and melted butter in blender container. Process for 1 minute. Scrape sides. Process for 30 seconds longer or until smooth. Chill for 1 hour. Spoon batter a small amount at a time into small skillet or electric crêpe pan. Cook until golden brown. Drain cherries, reserving ⅓ cup juice. Combine confectioners' sugar and cornstarch in saucepan; mix well. Stir in liqueur and reserved juice. Add cherries. Cook over medium heat until slightly thickened, stirring constantly. Cool. Spoon into crêpes; fold over. Top with whipped cream and chocolate syrup. Serve immediately. **Yield:** 15 servings.

Approx Per Serving: Cal 341; Prot 5 g; Carbo 60 g; Fiber 2 g; T Fat 10 g; 25% Calories from Fat; Chol 71 mg; Sod 75 mg.

Chocolate Mint Squares

½ cup low-fat margarine, softened
1 cup sugar
1 cup sifted unbleached bread flour
4 eggs
1 16-ounce can chocolate syrup
½ cup low-fat margarine, softened
2 cups sifted confectioners' sugar
½ teaspoon mint extract
3 drops of green food coloring
6 tablespoons low-fat margarine
1 cup semisweet chocolate chips

Combine ½ cup margarine, sugar, flour, eggs and chocolate syrup in bowl; mix well. Spoon into greased 9x13-inch baking pan. Bake at 350 degrees for 30 minutes or until top springs back when lightly touched; do not overbake. Cool. Combine ½ cup margarine, confectioners' sugar, mint and food coloring in bowl; mix well. Spread on baked layer. Chill in refrigerator. Combine remaining 6 tablespoons margarine and chocolate chips in saucepan. Cook over low heat until smooth, stirring frequently. Cool slightly. Pour over dessert. Chill until serving time. Cut into squares. **Yield:** 12 servings.

Approx Per Serving: Cal 437; Prot 5 g; Carbo 71 g; Fiber 2 g; T Fat 18 g; 34% Calories from Fat; Chol 71 mg; Sod 307 mg.

Chocolate Mousse Crown

"Wonderful served with whipped cream and fresh raspberries or strawberries—rich!"

2 16-ounce packages ladyfingers
1/2 cup dry sherry
2 cups chocolate chips
16 ounces cream cheese, softened
3/4 cup packed light brown sugar
1/4 teaspoon salt
4 eggs, separated
1/2 teaspoon vanilla extract
3/4 cup packed light brown sugar
2 cups whipping cream, whipped

Split ladyfingers into halves lengthwise. Place cut side up on baking sheet. Bake at 350 degrees for 4 to 5 minutes or until lightly browned. Cool for 10 minutes. Brush cut sides with sherry. Arrange over bottom and around side of springform pan. Melt chocolate chips in double boiler. Let stand for 10 minutes. Combine cream cheese, 3/4 cup brown sugar and salt in bowl; mix well. Add egg yolks 1 at a time, beating well after each addition. Stir in cooled chocolate. Beat egg whites with vanilla in mixer bowl until stiff but not dry. Beat in remaining 3/4 cup brown sugar until stiff and satiny. Fold into chocolate mixture alternately with whipped cream. Bake at 350 degrees for 30 minutes. **Yield:** 20 servings.

Approx Per Serving: Cal 510; Prot 8 g; Carbo 60 g; Fiber 1 g; T Fat 27 g; 48% Calories from Fat; Chol 100 mg; Sod 159 mg.

Kahlua-Chocolate Mousse*

"The name says it all!"

1 cup semisweet chocolate chips
2 tablespoons Kahlua
1 tablespoon orange juice
2 eggs
2 egg yolks
1 teaspoon vanilla extract
1/4 cup extra fine sugar
1 cup whipping cream

Combine chocolate chips and Kahlua in top of double boiler. Cook until chocolate is melted, stirring frequently. Combine orange juice, eggs, egg yolks, vanilla and sugar in blender container. Add chocolate mixture. Process until blended. Add whipping cream. Process until well blended. Spoon into serving dishes. Chill for 4 to 6 hours. Garnish with additional whipped cream, shaved chocolate or candied violets.
Yield: 6 servings.

Approx Per Serving: Cal 380; Prot 5 g; Carbo 29 g; Fiber 1 g; T Fat 29 g; 66% Calories from Fat; Chol 196 mg; Sod 45 mg.

Chocolate Torte

"Chocolate wafers become cake-like; very impressive dessert when sliced."

8 ounces sweet chocolate
2 tablespoons boiling water
2 eggs, separated
4 cups whipping cream, whipped
1/2 teaspoon vanilla extract
1/2 teaspoon almond extract
1 16-ounce package thin chocolate wafers

Melt chocolate in top of double boiler. Stir in water. Cool. Beat in slightly beaten egg yolks until glossy. Beat egg whites in mixer bowl until stiff. Fold in whipped cream. Fold into chocolate mixture. Stir in flavorings. Alternate layers of wafers and filling in 9-inch springform pan until all ingredients are used, ending with filling. Chill, covered, for 24 hours. Remove side of pan. Garnish with additional whipped cream. **Yield:** 8 servings.

Approx Per Serving: Cal 838; Prot 10 g; Carbo 62 g; Fiber 1 g; T Fat 63 g; 66% Calories from Fat; Chol 222 mg; Sod 490 mg.

Crème de Menthe Torte

"Relatively easy and very impressive! It is a fun finish on St. Patrick's Day."

1 16-ounce package chocolate wafers, finely crushed
1/2 cup melted butter
1/2 gallon vanilla ice cream
1 16-ounce package chocolate-covered mint cookies, coarsely chopped
3 to 6 tablespoons crème de menthe
6 egg whites, at room temperature
1/2 teaspoon cream of tartar
1/4 teaspoon salt
3/4 cup extra fine sugar
1 teaspoon vanilla extract
2 or 3 drops of green food coloring (optional)

Combine wafer crumbs and melted butter in bowl; mix well. Press into 9-inch pie plate. Bake at 350 degrees for 7 minutes. Cool for 20 minutes. Layer ice cream, cookie crumbs and 1 or 2 tablespoons crème de menthe 1/3 at a time over crust. Shape into mound. Freeze for 1 to 2 hours or until set. Beat egg whites at low speed in mixer bowl until foamy. Add cream of tartar and salt. Beat at medium speed until soft peaks form. Add sugar, vanilla and food coloring gradually, beating constantly at high speed until stiff peaks form; do not underbeat. Spread 3/4 inch thick over frozen pie. Bake at 475 degrees for 3 to 5 minutes or until lightly browned. Freeze for 1 hour. **Yield:** 8 servings.

Approx Per Serving: Cal 1048; Prot 15 g; Carbo 139 g; Fiber 0 g; T Fat 46 g; 40% Calories from Fat; Chol 90 mg; Sod 865 mg.

Meringue Pie Dessert

3 egg whites
1 cup sugar
1/4 teaspoon baking powder
1 teaspoon vanilla extract
1/2 cup chopped pecans
12 saltine crackers, crumbled
6 scoops ice cream
1 cup chocolate sauce

Beat egg whites in mixer bowl until soft peaks form. Add sugar gradually, beating constantly until stiff peaks form. Beat in baking powder, vanilla, pecans and crackers. Spread in buttered 9-inch pie plate. Bake at 350 degrees for 25 minutes. Let stand, covered, at room temperature until cool. Cut into wedges. Top with ice cream and chocolate sauce. **Yield:** 6 servings.

Approx Per Serving: Cal 535; Prot 7 g; Carbo 81 g; Fiber 2 g; T Fat 21 g; 35% Calories from Fat; Chol 32 mg; Sod 272 mg.

White Chocolate Mousse Cake

"Absolutely elegant"

3 cups crushed chocolate wafers
1/2 cup melted unsalted butter
1 cup milk
1 envelope plus 1 teaspoon unflavored gelatin
12 ounces white chocolate, slightly softened
2 cups whipping cream
2 teaspoons vanilla extract
4 egg whites, at room temperature
1/8 teaspoon salt
2 tablespoons sugar
2 10-ounce packages frozen raspberries with syrup
1 tablespoon cornstarch
1 tablespoon water
Sugar to taste (optional)

Mix wafer crumbs and butter in bowl. Press into 10-inch springform pan. Chill for 1 hour. Sprinkle gelatin in milk in top of double boiler. Let stand for 5 minutes. Add white chocolate. Cook over very hot water until melted, stirring frequently. Let stand for 30 minutes or chill for 10 minutes. Whip cream with vanilla in mixer bowl. Beat egg whites, salt and 2 tablespoons sugar in mixer bowl until stiff. Fold 1/3 at a time into chocolate mixture. Fold in whipped cream 1/3 at a time. Spoon into prepared pan. Chill for several hours to overnight. Purée raspberries in blender; strain. Combine with remaining ingredients in saucepan. Cook until thickened, stirring constantly. Cool. Remove side of pan from dessert. Serve with sauce. **Yield:** 18 servings.

Approx Per Serving: Cal 371; Prot 5 g; Carbo 35 g; Fiber 2 g; T Fat 24 g; 58% Calories from Fat; Chol 56 mg; Sod 205 mg.

Coffee Cream*

32 ounces whole-milk ricotta cheese
3/4 cup confectioners' sugar
2 tablespoons instant coffee
1 cup whipping cream
3 tablespoons brandy

Combine cheese, confectioners' sugar and coffee granules in blender container. Process for several seconds. Add cream and brandy. Process until smooth and slightly thickened. Spoon into six 8-ounce custard cups. Cover with plastic wrap. Chill in refrigerator. **Yield:** 6 servings.

Approx Per Serving: Cal 476; Prot 18 g; Carbo 24 g; Fiber <1 g; T Fat 34 g; 65% Calories from Fat; Chol 131 mg; Sod 143 mg.

Fruit Pizzas

"Impressive summer dessert"

2 1/2 cups flour
2 1/2 teaspoons baking soda
1 cup butter, softened
1 cup confectioners' sugar
1/3 cup sugar
1 egg
2 1/2 teaspoons cream of tartar
1/2 teaspoon vanilla extract
1/4 teaspoon almond extract
1 cup confectioners' sugar
16 ounces cream cheese, softened
1 teaspoon vanilla extract
1 cup sliced peaches
1 cup sliced strawberries
1 cup sliced apples
1 cup sliced grapes
1/2 cup sugar
1 cup orange juice
1/4 cup lemon juice
4 teaspoons cornstarch
1/4 teaspoon grated orange rind
1/4 teaspoon grated lemon rind

Sift flour and baking soda together. Cream butter, 1 cup confectioners' sugar and 1/3 cup sugar in mixer bowl until light and fluffy. Beat in cream of tartar, 1/2 teaspoon vanilla and almond extract. Stir in flour mixture. Divide into 2 portions. Pat onto 2 lightly greased pizza pans. Bake at 325 degrees for 12 to 15 minutes or until brown. Cream remaining 1 cup confectioners' sugar, cream cheese and 1 teaspoon vanilla in mixer bowl until light and fluffy. Spread over cooled crust. Cover completely with fruit slices. Combine remaining 1/2 cup sugar, juices and cornstarch in saucepan. Cook over medium heat until thickened, stirring constantly. Stir in grated rinds. Let stand until cool. Brush over fruit slices. May add or substitute kiwifruit, bananas, mandarin oranges or any berries. **Yield:** 16 servings.

Approx Per Serving: Cal 418; Prot 5 g; Carbo 52 g; Fiber 2 g; T Fat 22 g; 47% Calories from Fat; Chol 75 mg; Sod 315 mg.

Crème de Cassis Ice Cream

4 cups half and half
1¼ cups seedless blackberry jam or preserves
¾ cup Crème de Cassis
½ cup sugar
2¼ teaspoons vanilla extract

Combine half and half, jam, Crème de Cassis, sugar and vanilla in large bowl. Whisk until thoroughly blended. Pour into ice cream freezer container. Freeze using manufacturer's directions. Garnish servings with additional Crème de Cassis and chopped walnuts. **Yield:** 16 servings.

Approx Per Serving: Cal 214; Prot 2 g; Carbo 32 g; Fiber <1 g; T Fat 7 g; 31% Calories from Fat; Chol 22 mg; Sod 28 mg.

Cinnamon Brandy Ice Cream

1 cup milk
1 cup whipping cream
½ teaspoon vanilla extract
1 teaspoon cinnamon
⅔ cup sugar
5 egg yolks
1 ounce brandy

Bring milk and cream to a boil over medium heat in saucepan. Stir in vanilla and cinnamon. Beat sugar and egg yolks in mixer bowl. Stir into milk mixture. Cook until mixture will coat metal spoon, stirring constantly. Cool. Stir in brandy. Pour into ice cream freezer container. Freeze using manufacturer's directions. **Yield:** 12 servings.

Approx Per Serving: Cal 155; Prot 2 g; Carbo 13 g; Fiber 0 g; T Fat 10 g; 60% Calories from Fat; Chol 119 mg; Sod 20 mg.

Roadrunner Coconut Ice Cream*

"Sweet ending for the fiesta"

1 gallon vanilla ice cream, slightly softened
2 to 3 teaspoons coconut extract
1 15-ounce can cream of coconut

Combine ice cream, flavoring and cream of coconut in large bowl; mix well. Spoon into ice cream container. Freeze until firm. Garnish servings with toasted coconut. **Yield:** 30 servings.

Approx Per Serving: Cal 173; Prot 3 g; Carbo 17 g; Fiber 0 g; T Fat 11 g; 54% Calories from Fat; Chol 32 mg; Sod 64 mg.

Coconut Coffee Ice Cream with Tia Maria*

1/8 cup coconut
1/2 cup coffee ice cream
1 ounce Tia Maria

Toast coconut under broiler. Sprinkle over ice cream. Top with Tia Maria. **Yield:** 1 serving.

Approx Per Serving: Cal 272; Prot 3 g; Carbo 33 g; Fiber 1 g; T Fat 10 g; 34% Calories from Fat; Chol 30 mg; Sod 62 mg.

Snickers Ice Cream Cake*

"I'll diet tomorrow."

30 Oreo cookies, crushed
6 tablespoons melted margarine
1 16-ounce package snack-sized Snicker bars
1/2 gallon vanilla ice cream, softened
1 cup hot fudge sauce, heated
1 cup caramel sauce, heated

Combine cookie crumbs and margarine in bowl; mix well. Press onto bottom and side of buttered 9-inch springform pan. Bake at 350 degrees for 8 to 10 minutes or until lightly browned. Cool in pan. Combine candy and ice cream in bowl; mix well. Spoon into cooled crust. Cover with plastic wrap; top with foil. Freeze until firm. Let stand in refrigerator for 10 to 15 minutes. Remove side of pan. Drizzle thin lines of heated sauces across top of dessert. **Yield:** 16 servings.

Approx Per Serving: Cal 514; Prot 8 g; Carbo 69 g; Fiber 1 g; T Fat 24 g; 42% Calories from Fat; Chol 30 mg; Sod 347 mg.

Lemon Delight*

"Very light and lemony"

1 16-ounce angel food cake
1 14-ounce can sweetened condensed milk
2/3 cup lemon juice
1 cup whipping cream, whipped
12 maraschino cherries

Tear cake into small pieces. Mix condensed milk and lemon juice in bowl. Combine cake and 3/4 of the lemon mixture in bowl; mix well. Fold in 3/4 of the whipped cream. Spread in 9-inch square serving dish. Layer remaining lemon mixture and whipped cream over dessert. Cut into squares. Top each serving with cherry. **Yield:** 12 servings.

Approx Per Serving: Cal 273; Prot 5 g; Carbo 42 g; Fiber <1 g; T Fat 10 g; 33% Calories from Fat; Chol 38 mg; Sod 241 mg.

Peaches Chablis*

"A light and easy company dessert"

8 large ripe peaches
1½ cups pink Chablis
½ cup sugar
¼ teaspoon nutmeg
1 cinnamon stick
4 whole cloves

Peel peaches; cut into slices. Combine Chablis, sugar and nutmeg in large glass bowl. Stir until sugar is dissolved. Add cinnamon stick, cloves and peaches. Chill, covered with plastic wrap, for 6 hours to overnight. Remove cloves and cinnamon stick. **Yield:** 6 servings.

Approx Per Serving: Cal 152; Prot 1 g; Carbo 30 g; Fiber 2 g; T Fat <1 g; 1% Calories from Fat; Chol 0 mg; Sod 4 mg.

Peaches Foster*

"A summertime favorite!"

2 tablespoons butter
¼ cup packed brown sugar
⅛ teaspoon cinnamon
⅛ teaspoon nutmeg
4 peaches, peeled, sliced
2 tablespoons rum
2 cups peach ice cream

Melt butter in saucepan. Add brown sugar, cinnamon and nutmeg; mix well. Cook until bubbly, stirring frequently. Add peaches. Cook over medium heat for 3 to 4 minutes or until heated through, stirring constantly. Stir in rum. Pour over ice cream. **Yield:** 4 servings.

Approx Per Serving: Cal 302; Prot 3 g; Carbo 42 g; Fiber 1 g; T Fat 13 g; 39% Calories from Fat; Chol 45 mg; Sod 114 mg.

Macaroon-Almond Baked Pears

"A favorite with everyone; it looks like you've gone to a lot of effort!"

4 fresh pears, split, cored
¼ cup orange liqueur
⅓ cup apricot preserves
1 cup crushed soft macaroons
¼ cup sliced almonds
1 cup whipping cream, whipped

Place pears cut side up in 6x10-inch glass baking dish. Combine liqueur and preserves in bowl; mix well. Spoon over pears. Sprinkle with crumbs and almonds. Bake at 350 degrees for 20 to 25 minutes or until heated through and bubbly. Top with whipped cream. **Yield:** 8 servings.

Approx Per Serving: Cal 333; Prot 3 g; Carbo 38 g; Fiber 2 g; T Fat 19 g; 51% Calories from Fat; Chol 41 mg; Sod 23 mg.

Piña Colada Bread Pudding

1 10-ounce loaf day-old French bread
1 6-ounce can piña colada mix
3 1/4 cups (about) milk
2 cups sugar
1/2 cup melted butter
3 eggs
2 tablespoons vanilla extract
1 cup grated coconut
2 cups crushed pineapple, drained
1/2 cup butter
1 1/2 cups confectioners' sugar
2 egg yolks
1/2 cup rum

Crumble bread into bowl. Add next 8 ingredients; mix well. Spoon into buttered 9x12-inch baking dish. Place in cold oven. Bake at 350 degrees for 1 1/4 hours or until top is golden brown. Cream 1/2 cup butter and confectioners' sugar in saucepan. Cook over medium heat until all butter is absorbed. Remove from heat. Stir in egg yolks. Add rum gradually, stirring constantly. Pour over dessert. Sauce will thicken as it cools. **Yield:** 20 servings.

Approx Per Serving: Cal 339; Prot 4 g; Carbo 45 g; Fiber 1 g; T Fat 14 g; 40% Calories from Fat; Chol 83 mg; Sod 194 mg.

Strawberries Cassis*

2 10-ounce packages frozen raspberries
2 tablespoons sugar
4 ounces Cassis syrup
2 pints strawberries

Purée first 3 ingredients in blender. Chill in refrigerator. Pour over strawberries in long-stemmed glasses. **Yield:** 4 servings.

Approx Per Serving: Cal 309; Prot 2 g; Carbo 67 g; Fiber 10 g; T Fat 1 g; 2% Calories from Fat; Chol 0 mg; Sod 6 mg.

Fresh Strawberry Dip*

1/2 cup butter
1 14-ounce can sweetened condensed milk
2 cups confectioners' sugar
1 cup chocolate chips
1 to 2 tablespoons Grand Marnier (optional)
1 quart fresh strawberries

Melt butter in saucepan over low heat. Stir in condensed milk. Add confectioners' sugar gradually. Stir in chocolate chips. Bring to a boil. Simmer for 3 minutes, stirring frequently. Stir in Grand Marnier. Pour into serving bowl. Serve with hulled strawberries. **Yield:** 8 servings.

Approx Per Serving: Cal 506; Prot 5 g; Carbo 74 g; Fiber 3 g; T Fat 24 g; 40% Calories from Fat; Chol 48 mg; Sod 164 mg.

Irish Cream Turtle Torte

"Incredible!"

1½ cups shortbread cookie crumbs
¼ cup packed light brown sugar
¼ teaspoon nutmeg
¼ cup melted butter
1 quart butter pecan ice cream, slightly softened
¾ cup Irish cream liqueur
1 12-ounce jar caramel ice cream topping
1 cup coarsely chopped pecans, toasted
1 quart chocolate ice cream, slightly softened
1 12-ounce jar fudge ice cream topping

Butter side of 10-inch springform pan. Line side with strips of waxed paper. Butter bottom of pan and paper-lined side. Combine crumbs, brown sugar and nutmeg in bowl; mix well. Stir in butter. Pat onto bottom of pan. Chill in refrigerator. Combine butter pecan ice cream and ½ cup Irish cream in bowl; mix lightly. Pack into chilled crust. Combine caramel topping and 2 tablespoons Irish cream in bowl; mix well. Drizzle over butter pecan layer. Sprinkle with ¾ cup pecans. Freeze for 1 hour. Spread with chocolate ice cream. Combine fudge topping and remaining 2 tablespoons Irish cream in bowl; mix well. Spoon over chocolate ice cream. Freeze, covered with foil, for 6 hours to overnight. Remove side of pan. Remove waxed paper carefully. Sprinkle with remaining ¼ cup pecans. Let stand for 10 minutes. **Yield:** 14 servings.

Approx Per Serving: Cal 514; Prot 6 g; Carbo 68 g; Fiber 1 g; T Fat 23 g; 41% Calories from Fat; Chol 51 mg; Sod 234 mg.

Wild Rice and Rum Pudding

"A gourmet rice pudding with a nutty flavor"

4 cups milk
⅔ cup white rice
½ cup wild rice
½ teaspoon salt
2 eggs
½ cup sugar
½ cup whipping cream
½ teaspoon nutmeg
½ teaspoon cinnamon
½ cup raisins (optional)
2 tablespoons dark rum

Combine milk, rices and salt in 3-quart saucepan. Bring to a boil; reduce heat. Simmer, covered, for 1 hour, stirring occasionally. Whisk eggs in bowl. Add sugar, cream, nutmeg, cinnamon and raisins; mix well. Stir into rice mixture. Cook over low heat until thickened, stirring constantly. Stir in rum. Serve warm or cold. **Yield:** 8 servings.

Approx Per Serving: Cal 293; Prot 8 g; Carbo 39 g; Fiber <1 g; T Fat 11 g; 35% Calories from Fat; Chol 90 mg; Sod 209 mg.

CAKES

Queen Elizabeth's Cake

"Melts in your mouth."

1 cup boiling water
1 cup chopped dates
1 teaspoon baking soda
1/4 cup butter, softened
1 cup sugar
1 egg, beaten
1 teaspoon vanilla extract
1 1/2 cups sifted flour
1 teaspoon baking powder
1/2 teaspoon salt
1/2 cup chopped pecans
5 tablespoons brown sugar
5 tablespoons cream
2 tablespoons butter
1/2 cup coconut
1/2 cup chopped pecans

Pour boiling water over dates and baking soda in bowl; mix well. Cream butter and sugar in mixer bowl until light and fluffy. Add egg and vanilla; mix well. Mix flour, baking powder and salt together. Add to batter; mix well. Stir in 1/2 cup pecans and date mixture. Pour into greased 9x13-inch cake pan. Bake at 350 degrees for 35 minutes or until cake tests done. Combine brown sugar, cream and 2 tablespoons butter in saucepan. Bring to a boil. Boil for 3 minutes, stirring frequently. Mixture will be thin. Pour over cake. Sprinkle with coconut and 1/2 cup pecans. **Yield:** 15 servings.

Approx Per Serving: Cal 272; Prot 3 g; Carbo 38 g; Fiber 2 g; T Fat 13 g; 42% Calories from Fat; Chol 33 mg; Sod 196 mg.

Apple-Raisin Cake

2¼ cups whole wheat flour
⅓ cup nonfat dry milk
½ teaspoon ground cinnamon
¼ teaspoon ground cloves
½ teaspoon baking soda
1 teaspoon baking powder
¼ teaspoon salt
½ cup shortening
1 cup honey
2 eggs
1 cup applesauce
1 cup raisins
1 cup chopped pecans
¼ cup confectioners' sugar, sifted
¼ teaspoon vanilla extract
2 tablespoons (about) milk

Sift flour, dry milk powder, cinnamon, cloves, baking soda, baking powder and salt together. Cream shortening and honey in mixer bowl until light and fluffy. Beat in eggs 1 at a time. Stir in applesauce. Add flour mixture to creamed mixture gradually, beating well after each addition. Fold in raisins and pecans. Spoon into greased and floured bundt pan. Bake at 325 degrees for 60 to 70 minutes or until wooden pick inserted near center comes out clean. Cool in pan for several minutes. Invert onto serving plate. Combine confectioners' sugar and vanilla in bowl; mix well. Stir in enough milk to make of glaze consistency. Drizzle over cooled cake. **Yield:** 16 servings.

Approx Per Serving: Cal 294; Prot 5 g; Carbo 45 g; Fiber 3 g; T Fat 13 g; 36% Calories from Fat; Chol 27 mg; Sod 100 mg.

Anna Banana Cake

"Yummy banana cake"

2 cups flour
1½ cups sugar
1 teaspoon baking powder
½ teaspoon salt
1 teaspoon vanilla extract
½ cup shortening
2 bananas, sliced
2 eggs
½ cup chopped walnuts
½ banana, sliced
¼ cup butter, softened
1 teaspoon lemon juice
2 cups confectioners' sugar

Grease bottoms of two 8-inch round cake pans. Combine flour, sugar, baking powder, salt, vanilla, shortening, 2 bananas and eggs in mixer bowl; mix just until moistened. Beat at medium speed for 3 minutes. Stir in walnuts. Spoon into prepared pans. Bake at 350 degrees for 30 to 35 minutes or until cake springs back when lightly touched. Cool in pans for several minutes. Remove to wire rack to cool completely. Cream ½ banana, butter and lemon juice in mixer bowl until light and fluffy. Add confectioners' sugar gradually, beating until creamy. Spread between layers and over top and side of cooled cake. **Yield:** 12 servings.

Approx Per Serving: Cal 426; Prot 4 g; Carbo 67 g; Fiber 1 g; T Fat 17 g; 34% Calories from Fat; Chol 46 mg; Sod 162 mg.

Southern Glazed Teacake

3 eggs
2 cups sugar
1 1/4 cups oil
1/4 cup orange juice
3 cups flour
1/4 teaspoon salt
1 teaspoon baking soda
1 teaspoon cinnamon
1 teaspoon vanilla extract
1 cup chopped apples
1 cup coconut
1 cup chopped pecans
1/2 cup margarine
1/2 teaspoon baking soda
1 cup sugar
1/2 cup buttermilk
1/2 teaspoon vanilla extract

Combine eggs, 2 cups sugar, oil, orange juice, flour, salt, 1 teaspoon baking soda, cinnamon and 1 teaspoon vanilla in large bowl; mix well. Stir in apples, coconut and pecans. Spoon into greased and floured tube pan. Bake at 325 degrees for 1 1/2 hours. Cool in pan. Combine margarine, remaining 1/2 teaspoon baking soda, 1 cup sugar, buttermilk and 1/2 teaspoon vanilla in saucepan. Bring to a rolling boil. Pour over cooled cake in pan. Let stand until cool. **Yield:** 16 servings.

Approx Per Serving: Cal 526; Prot 5 g; Carbo 61 g; Fiber 2 g; T Fat 31 g; 51% Calories from Fat; Chol 40 mg; Sod 201 mg.

Easy Carrot Cake*

1 1/2 cups flour
1 1/4 cups sugar
1 1/2 teaspoons baking soda
1 1/2 teaspoons cinnamon
1/4 teaspoon salt (optional)
1 1/2 6-ounce jars baby food strained carrots
2/3 cup oil
2 eggs, slightly beaten
1 teaspoon vanilla extract
1 8-ounce can crushed pineapple, drained
2/3 cup coconut
1/2 cup chopped walnuts
3 ounces cream cheese, softened
1/4 cup margarine, softened
1/2 teaspoon vanilla extract
2 cups confectioners' sugar

Combine flour, sugar, baking soda, cinnamon and salt in 9-inch square or 7x12-inch cake pan; mix well. Add carrots, oil, eggs and 1 teaspoon vanilla. Mix thoroughly with fork. Stir in pineapple, coconut and walnuts. Bake at 350 degrees for 40 to 45 minutes or until cake tests done. Cool in pan on wire rack. Combine cream cheese, margarine and remaining 1/2 teaspoon vanilla in bowl; blend well with wooden spoon. Beat in confectioners' sugar gradually. Spread over cooled cake.
Yield: 12 servings.

Approx Per Serving: Cal 459; Prot 4 g; Carbo 60 g; Fiber 2 g; T Fat 24 g; 46% Calories from Fat; Chol 43 mg; Sod 193 mg.

Jack Daniel's Chocolate Birthday Cake

"This cake is so rich it doesn't need any frosting, but it doesn't hurt to serve it with a lot of whipped cream or vanilla ice cream. It's also good warm, right out of the pan."

2 cups flour
2 teaspoons baking powder
1/8 teaspoon salt
1 1/2 cups water
1/2 cup Jack Daniel's Tennessee whiskey
1 tablespoon instant coffee
1 1/4 cups unsalted butter
1 cup baking cocoa
2 cups sugar
2 eggs
1 cup coarsely chopped pecans
2 tablespoons Jack Daniel's Tennessee whiskey

Sift flour, baking powder and salt together. Combine water, 1/2 cup whiskey, coffee, butter and cocoa in large saucepan. Cook until butter is melted, stirring occasionally. Remove from heat. Beat in sugar. Cool slightly. Whisk in eggs, blending thoroughly. Add flour mixture to cooked mixture gradually, beating well after each addition. Stir in pecans. Spoon into greased and floured 9-inch tube pan. Smooth with spatula. Bake at 325 degrees for 1 to 1 1/4 hours or until cake tests done. Sprinkle with remaining 2 tablespoons whiskey. Cool in pan on wire rack. Invert onto serving plate. **Yield:** 16 servings.

Approx Per Serving: Cal 424; Prot 4 g; Carbo 41 g; Fiber 3 g; T Fat 27 g; 57% Calories from Fat; Chol 81 mg; Sod 71 mg.

Double-Dark Decadent Brownie Cake

1/2 cup corn syrup
1/2 cup butter
5 ounces semisweet chocolate
3/4 cup sugar
3 eggs
1 teaspoon vanilla extract
1 cup flour
1 cup chopped walnuts
3 ounces semisweet chocolate
1 tablespoon butter
2 tablespoons corn syrup
1 teaspoon milk

Bring 1/2 cup corn syrup to a boil in large saucepan, stirring occasionally. Remove from heat. Add 1/2 cup butter and 5 ounces chocolate, stirring until melted. Stir in sugar. Beat in eggs 1 at a time. Stir in vanilla, flour and walnuts. Spoon into greased and floured 9-inch round cake pan. Bake at 350 degrees for 30 minutes or until cakes tests done. Cool in pan for 10 minutes. Remove to wire rack to cool completely. Combine remaining 3 ounces chocolate and 1 tablespoon butter in saucepan. Cook over low heat until melted, stirring frequently. Remove from heat. Stir in remaining 2 tablespoons corn syrup and milk. Pour over cake; spread over side. Let stand for 1 hour. **Yield:** 8 servings.

Approx Per Serving: Cal 584; Prot 7 g; Carbo 69 g; Fiber 2 g; T Fat 35 g; 51% Calories from Fat; Chol 115 mg; Sod 153 mg.

Deep Dark and Rich Chocolate Cake*

"This is served on very special occasions, and shared with us by a special friend in memory of her dad."

16 ounces semisweet chocolate
1 cup strong black coffee, cooled
2 cups sugar
2 cups unsalted butter
8 eggs, beaten

Combine chocolate, coffee, sugar and butter in saucepan. Bring to a boil, stirring constantly. Cool completely. Add eggs gradually, beating well after each addition. Spoon into buttered 9-inch springform pan. Bake at 250 degrees for 1 hour and 40 minutes; cake will not be completely set. Cool in pan. Chill, covered, overnight. Remove sides of pan. Garnish with whipped cream. **Yield:** 12 servings.

Approx Per Serving: Cal 643; Prot 6 g; Carbo 55 g; Fiber 1 g; T Fat 48 g; 64% Calories from Fat; Chol 225 mg; Sod 311 mg.

Chocolate Suicide Cake

"Chocolate on the inside, chocolate on the outside! Cut into small servings; this is very rich."

1 2-layer package devil's food cake mix
2²/₃ cups semisweet chocolate chips
1¹/₃ cups whipping cream
¹/₄ cup unsalted butter, cut into 4 pieces
1 tablespoon cinnamon (optional)
16 maraschino cherries with stems, well drained

Prepare and bake cake mix using package directions for 9x13-inch cake pan. Cool in pan. Cut cake into small pieces. Microwave chocolate chips on Medium for 5 to 7 minutes or until melted. Heat whipping cream in saucepan over medium heat. Add butter. Bring to a slow boil. Add melted chocolate; mix well. Cool for 20 minutes. Place cake pieces, 1¹/₃ cups chocolate mixture and cinnamon in food processor container. Process with plastic blade until blended to fudge-like consistency. Spoon into waxed paper-lined 9-inch springform pan. Smooth with spatula. Freeze, covered with plastic, for 1 hour or until firm enough to unmold. Remove side of pan, leaving plastic intact. Invert onto plate; remove bottom of pan and waxed paper. Invert onto serving plate; remove plastic. Dip cherries in ¹/₄ cup chocolate mixture. Spread remaining chocolate mixture over top and side of cake. Arrange cherries around border of cake. Chill for 1 hour. **Yield:** 20 servings.

Approx Per Serving: Cal 388; Prot 4 g; Carbo 47 g; Fiber 1 g; T Fat 23 g; 51% Calories from Fat; Chol 31 mg; Sod 136 mg.

Fresh Coconut Cake

"This will transport you back to Hawaii."

2¼ cups cake flour
2¼ teaspoons baking powder
½ teaspoon salt
¾ cup shortening
½ teaspoon vanilla extract
1 cup sugar
3 egg yolks, well beaten
1¼ cups freshly grated coconut
¾ cup fresh coconut milk
3 egg whites
½ cup sugar
1 recipe Fluffy Five-Minute Frosting (below)
½ cup freshly grated coconut

Line two 9-inch cake pans with waxed paper. Spray with nonstick cooking spray. Sift cake flour, baking powder and salt together. Cream shortening in mixer bowl until light and fluffy. Add vanilla. Beat in 1 cup sugar. Add egg yolks; beat well. Stir in 1¼ cups coconut. Add cake flour mixture and coconut milk alternately to creamed mixture, beating well after each addition. Beat egg whites in mixer bowl until stiff but not dry. Beat in remaining ½ cup sugar 2 tablespoons at a time. Fold into batter gently. Spoon into prepared pans. Bake at 375 degrees for 25 to 30 minutes or until cake tests done. Cool in pan for several minutes. Remove to wire rack to cool completely. Spread Fluffy Five-Minute Frosting between layers and over top and side of cake. Sprinkle with remaining ½ cup coconut. **Yield:** 12 servings.

Approx Per Serving: Cal 484; Prot 4 g; Carbo 70 g; Fiber 2 g; T Fat 22 g; 40% Calories from Fat; Chol 53 mg; Sod 203 mg.

Fluffy Five-Minute Frosting

2 egg whites
1½ cups sugar
⅛ teaspoon salt
¼ teaspoon cream of tartar
½ cup cold water
1 tablespoon light corn syrup
1 teaspoon vanilla extract

Combine egg whites, sugar, salt, cream of tartar, water and corn syrup in double boiler. Beat at low speed over boiling water until well mixed. Beat at high speed for 5 minutes or until peaks form when beaters are lifted. Beat in vanilla. **Yield:** 12 servings.

Approx Per Serving: Cal 104; Prot 1 g; Carbo 26 g; Fiber 0 g; T Fat 0 g; 0% Calories from Fat; Chol 0 mg; Sod 32 mg.

For instant cake decorating, fill zip-type plastic bag with icing or whipped cream. Seal and clip off one corner.

Coconut-Sour Cream Cake

"Fun dessert for Easter"

3 cups sifted cake flour
2 teaspoons baking powder
3/4 teaspoon baking soda
3/4 teaspoon salt
3/4 cup butter, softened
1 1/2 cups sugar
3/4 cup sour cream
1 teaspoon vanilla extract
1 1/4 cups milk
1 3-ounce can flaked coconut
4 egg whites, stiffly beaten
3/4 cup butter, softened
1/2 teaspoon vanilla extract
1/8 teaspoon salt
6 cups sifted confectioners' sugar
1 egg white
2 to 3 tablespoons milk

Sift cake flour, baking powder, baking soda and 3/4 teaspoon salt together. Cream 3/4 cup butter and sugar in mixer bowl until light and fluffy. Blend in sour cream and 1 teaspoon vanilla. Add cake flour mixture and milk alternately, beating well after each addition. Stir in 3/4 cup coconut. Fold in beaten egg whites gently. Spoon into 3 greased and floured 9-inch cake pans. Bake at 350 degrees for 30 to 35 minutes or until wooden pick inserted in center comes out clean. Cool in pans for 10 minutes. Remove to wire rack to cool completely. Cream 3/4 cup butter in mixer bowl until light and fluffy. Blend in 1/2 teaspoon vanilla and salt. Add confectioners' sugar alternately with egg white and milk, beating well after each addition. Spread between layers and over top and side of cake. Sprinkle with remaining coconut. **Yield:** 12 servings.

Approx Per Serving: Cal 667; Prot 5 g; Carbo 99 g; Fiber 2 g; T Fat 30 g; 39% Calories from Fat; Chol 73 mg; Sod 500 mg.

Coffee Royale Cake*

1 baked 9-inch yellow cake layer
1 baked 9-inch chocolate cake layer
1 1/2 cups whipping cream
2 tablespoons instant coffee
1/3 cup sugar
1 12-ounce jar raspberry jam

Split each layer into 2 layers horizontally. Combine whipping cream, coffee powder and sugar in bowl. Chill in refrigerator. Beat until stiff. Place 1 yellow layer on cake plate. Spread with half the jam and 1/3 of the whipped cream. Top with 1 chocolate layer and half the remaining whipped cream. Layer remaining yellow layer, jam, whipped cream and chocolate layer on top. Garnish with additional whipped cream and shaved chocolate. **Yield:** 12 servings.

Approx Per Serving: Cal 511; Prot 5 g; Carbo 79 g; Fiber <1 g; T Fat 21 g; 36% Calories from Fat; Chol 41 mg; Sod 223 mg.

Eggnog Refrigerator Cake*

1 12-ounce angel food cake
1 cup butter, softened
2 cups confectioners' sugar
3 egg yolks
1/4 cup brandy
1 cup slivered almonds, toasted
1 cup whipping cream
1/4 cup sugar

Slice cake into 5 layers horizontally. Cream butter and confectioners' sugar in mixer bowl until light and fluffy. Beat in egg yolks 1 at a time. Stir in brandy and almonds. Alternate layers of cake and filling on buttered cake plate, ending with cake layer. Chill for 24 hours. Beat whipping cream in mixer bowl until soft peaks form, adding sugar gradually. Spread over top of cake. **Yield:** 10 servings.

Approx Per Serving: Cal 549; Prot 6 g; Carbo 53 g; Fiber 2 g; T Fat 36 g; 58% Calories from Fat; Chol 146 mg; Sod 341 mg.

Hummingbird Cake

"Everyone will want seconds!"

3 cups cake flour
1 cup packed brown sugar
1 cup sugar
1 teaspoon salt
1 teaspoon baking soda
1 teaspoon cinnamon
3 eggs, beaten
1 1/2 cups oil
1 1/2 teaspoons vanilla extract
2 cups chopped bananas
1 8-ounce can crushed pineapple
1 cup chopped pecans
3/4 cup butter, softened
11 ounces cream cheese, softened
6 3/4 cups sifted confectioners' sugar
1 1/2 teaspoons vanilla extract
1 cup chopped pecans

Combine cake flour, brown sugar, sugar, salt, baking soda and cinnamon in bowl; mix well. Stir in eggs and oil until just mixed. Do not beat. Stir in 1 1/2 teaspoons vanilla, bananas, undrained pineapple and 1 cup pecans. Spoon into 3 well greased and floured 9-inch cake pans. Bake at 350 degrees for 25 to 30 minutes or until cake tests done. Cool in pans for 10 minutes. Remove to wire racks to cool completely. Combine butter and cream cheese in mixer bowl; beat well. Add confectioners' sugar gradually, beating until light and fluffy. Add remaining 1 1/2 teaspoons vanilla; mix well. Spread frosting between layers and on top and side of cake. Sprinkle with remaining 1 cup pecans. May also bake this cake in bundt or tube pan for about 1 1/4 hours. **Yield:** 12 servings.

Approx Per Serving: Cal 1087; Prot 7 g; Carbo 129 g; Fiber 3 g; T Fat 63 g; 51% Calories from Fat; Chol 113 mg; Sod 450 mg.

Italian Love Cake*

1 2-layer package fudge marble or chocolate cake mix
2 pounds ricotta cheese
4 large eggs
1/4 cup sugar
1 teaspoon vanilla extract
1 4-ounce package chocolate instant pudding mix
1 cup milk
8 ounces whipped topping

Prepare cake mix using package directions. Pour into greased and floured 9x13-inch cake pan. Combine ricotta cheese, eggs, sugar and vanilla in mixer bowl; beat well. Spoon over cake batter. Do not mix. Bake at 350 degrees for 1 hour or until cake tests done. Cool in pan on wire rack. Combine pudding mix and milk in bowl; beat well. Add whipped topping; beat at low speed until creamy. Spread frosting over cooled cake. Garnish with chocolate shavings. Store in refrigerator. **Yield:** 12 servings.

Approx Per Serving: Cal 593; Prot 15 g; Carbo 74 g; Fiber <1 g; T Fat 28 g; 41% Calories from Fat; Chol 112 mg; Sod 372 mg.

Mocha Cake Roll

3/4 cup sifted cake flour
1/2 teaspoon baking powder
1/2 teaspoon salt
5 eggs
3/4 cup sugar
2 ounces unsweetened chocolate
1/4 teaspoon baking soda
1/4 cup cold water
2 tablespoons sugar
1/4 cup confectioners' sugar
1 tablespoon instant coffee
1 tablespoon cold water
9 ounces whipped topping
1/4 cup chocolate sprinkles

Grease sides and bottom of 10x15-inch cake pan. Line with greased waxed paper. Sift cake flour, baking powder and salt together. Beat eggs in mixer bowl for 5 minutes or until lemon-colored. Add 3/4 cup sugar gradually, beating until light and fluffy. Beat in cake flour mixture gradually. Melt chocolate in double boiler over hot water. Stir in baking soda, 1/4 cup water and 2 tablespoons sugar. Cook for 5 minutes or until thickened and smooth, stirring constantly. Add to batter; beat well. Spread in prepared cake pan. Bake at 350 degrees for 18 to 20 minutes or until cake tests done. Sprinkle towel with confectioners' sugar. Loosen cake from pan; turn onto towel. Remove waxed paper. Roll as for jelly roll. Cool on wire rack for 1 hour. Combine instant coffee and 1 tablespoon cold water in bowl; mix well. Add whipped topping; mix well. Unroll cake carefully. Reserve 1 1/2 to 2 cups coffee mixture. Spread remaining coffee mixture over cake to within 1 inch of sides. Roll gently to enclose filling. Place seam side down on serving plate. Cover with reserved coffee mixture; top with chocolate sprinkles. Store in refrigerator. **Yield:** 10 servings.

Approx Per Serving: Cal 270; Prot 5 g; Carbo 36 g; Fiber 1 g; T Fat 13 g; 42% Calories from Fat; Chol 107 mg; Sod 188 mg.

Peanut Butter Meltaway Cake

"The whole family will love it."

1 cup margarine
$1/4$ cup baking cocoa
1 cup water
$1/2$ cup buttermilk
2 eggs, beaten
2 cups flour
2 cups sugar
1 teaspoon baking soda
1 teaspoon vanilla extract
1 cup peanut butter
1 tablespoon oil
$1/2$ cup margarine
$1/4$ cup baking cocoa
1 1-pound package confectioners' sugar
6 tablespoons buttermilk
1 teaspoon vanilla extract

Combine 1 cup margarine, $1/4$ cup cocoa, water, $1/2$ cup buttermilk and eggs in saucepan. Heat until margarine melts and mixture blends, stirring constantly. Mix flour, sugar and baking soda in mixer bowl. Add warm mixture and 1 teaspoon vanilla; beat well. Pour into greased and floured 9x13-inch cake pan. Bake at 350 degrees for 30 minutes. Cool to room temperature. Mix peanut butter and oil in bowl until creamy. Spread over cooled cake. Combine $1/2$ cup margarine and $1/4$ cup cocoa in saucepan. Heat until margarine melts and mixture is blended, stirring constantly. Add confectioners' sugar, 6 tablespoons buttermilk and 1 teaspoon vanilla; beat well. Spread over peanut butter. **Yield:** 15 servings.

Approx Per Serving: Cal 601; Prot 9 g; Carbo 81 g; Fiber 2 g; T Fat 30 g; 43% Calories from Fat; Chol 29 mg; Sod 364 mg.

Great Valley Pineapple Cake

"This cake is great with or without frosting."

2 cups flour
2 cups sugar
2 teaspoons baking soda
2 eggs
1 29-ounce can crushed pineapple
2 teaspoons vanilla extract
1 cup chopped pecans
8 ounces cream cheese, softened
$1/2$ cup margarine, softened
$1\frac{1}{3}$ cups confectioners' sugar
1 teaspoon vanilla extract
$1/2$ cup chopped pecans

Mix flour, sugar and baking soda in bowl. Add eggs, undrained pineapple, 2 teaspoons vanilla and 1 cup pecans; mix well. Pour into greased 9x13-inch cake pan. Bake at 350 degrees for 35 to 40 minutes or until cake tests done. Cool in pan for 5 minutes. Beat cream cheese, margarine, confectioners' sugar and 1 teaspoon vanilla in mixer bowl. Stir in $1/2$ cup pecans. Spread over warm cake. **Yield:** 15 servings.

Approx Per Serving: Cal 447; Prot 5 g; Carbo 64 g; Fiber 2 g; T Fat 20 g; 40% Calories from Fat; Chol 45 mg; Sod 237 mg.

Lemon Yogurt Pound Cake*

"Very moist and good served plain or topped with strawberries."

2 1/4 cups unbleached flour
2 cups sugar
1/2 teaspoon salt
1/2 teaspoon baking soda
1 teaspoon grated lemon rind
1 teaspoon vanilla extract
1 cup butter, softened
1 cup lemon yogurt
3 large eggs, at room temperature
1/4 cup sifted confectioners' sugar

Combine flour, sugar, salt, baking soda, lemon rind, vanilla, butter, yogurt and eggs in large mixer bowl; beat at low speed until well mixed. Beat at medium speed for 3 minutes. Pour into lightly greased and floured 9-inch tube pan. Bake at 325 degrees for 60 to 70 minutes or until cake tests done. Cool in pan for 15 minutes. Invert onto wire rack to cool completely. Sprinkle with confectioners' sugar. **Yield:** 16 servings.

Approx Per Serving: Cal 288; Prot 4 g; Carbo 40 g; Fiber <1 g; T Fat 13 g; 40% Calories from Fat; Chol 72 mg; Sod 212 mg.

Helen's Old-Fashioned Pound Cake

"This cake will bring back memories."

4 cups flour
2 teaspoons baking powder
12 egg yolks
2 cups butter, softened
2 cups sugar
1/2 teaspoon milk
1 teaspoon vanilla extract
1/2 teaspoon almond extract
12 egg whites, stiffly beaten

Sift flour and baking powder together 2 times. Beat egg yolks in mixer bowl until lemon-colored. Cream butter and sugar in mixer bowl until light and fluffy. Add beaten egg yolks gradually, beating well after each addition. Add flour mixture alternately with milk, vanilla and almond extract, beating well after each addition. Fold in stiffly beaten egg whites gently. Spoon into well greased tube pan. Bake at 350 degrees for 30 minutes. Reduce oven temperature to 300 degrees. Bake for 1 1/4 hours longer or until cake tests done. Cool in pan for several minutes. Invert onto wire rack to cool completely. **Yield:** 16 servings.

Approx Per Serving: Cal 475; Prot 8 g; Carbo 49 g; Fiber 1 g; T Fat 28 g; 52% Calories from Fat; Chol 222 mg; Sod 279 mg.

Amazin' Raisin Cake

"This is good just sprinkled with confectioners' sugar."

3 cups flour
2 cups sugar
1 cup mayonnaise
1/3 cup milk
2 eggs
2 teaspoons baking soda
1 1/2 teaspoons cinnamon
1/2 teaspoon nutmeg
1/2 teaspoon salt
1/2 teaspoon cloves
3 cups chopped, peeled apples
1 cup raisins
1/2 cup coarsely chopped walnuts
2 cups whipped cream

Grease and flour two 9-inch round cake pans. Combine flour, sugar, mayonnaise, milk and eggs in mixer bowl; beat well. Add baking soda, cinnamon, nutmeg, salt and cloves; beat well. Stir in apples, raisins and walnuts. Spoon into prepared cake pans. Bake at 350 degrees for 45 minutes or until layers test done. Cool in pans for 10 minutes. Remove to wire rack to cool completely. Spread whipped cream between layers and over top and side of cake. **Yield:** 12 servings.

Approx Per Serving: Cal 550; Prot 6 g; Carbo 75 g; Fiber 3 g; T Fat 27 g; 42% Calories from Fat; Chol 74 mg; Sod 355 mg.

Walnut-Buttermilk Lemon Cake

"This is the best lemon cake of all! Slice thin as it is very rich."

3 cups sifted flour
2 teaspoons baking powder
Salt to taste
1/2 cup butter, softened
2 cups sugar
1 teaspoon vanilla extract
5 large eggs
2/3 cup buttermilk
2 tablespoons grated lemon rind
1/3 cup fresh lemon juice
2 cups chopped walnuts
1/2 cup sugar
1/3 cup fresh lemon juice

Butter and flour 10-inch bundt pan. Sift flour, baking powder and salt together. Cream butter and 2 cups sugar in mixer bowl until light and fluffy. Add vanilla. Add eggs 1 at a time, beating well after each addition. Add flour mixture alternately with buttermilk. Add lemon rind and 1/3 cup lemon juice; beat well. Stir in walnuts. Spoon into prepared pan. Bake at 350 degrees for 60 to 70 minutes or until cake tests done. Cool in pan for 10 minutes. Invert onto foil-lined rack. Mix 1/2 cup sugar and 1/3 cup lemon juice in bowl. Brush onto hot cake until all glaze is absorbed. Let stand until cool. **Yield:** 16 servings.

Approx Per Serving: Cal 379; Prot 7 g; Carbo 52 g; Fiber 2 g; T Fat 17 g; 40% Calories from Fat; Chol 83 mg; Sod 124 mg.

COOKIES, ETC.

Apricot Squares

"Worth the work"

1/2 cup unsalted butter
1 cup flour
1/4 cup sugar
1/2 cup dried apricots
1 cup packed light brown sugar
2 eggs, beaten
1/3 cup flour
1/2 teaspoon baking powder
1/4 teaspoon salt
1/2 teaspoon vanilla extract
1/2 cup chopped pecans
1/2 cup confectioners' sugar

Cut butter into 1 cup flour and 1/4 cup sugar in bowl until mixture is crumbly. Press into greased 8-inch square baking dish. Bake at 350 degrees for 25 minutes. Snip apricots into small pieces. Cook apricots in a small amount of water in saucepan until softened but not tearing apart. Cool in saucepan for several minutes. Beat brown sugar and eggs in mixer bowl until light and fluffy. Add mixture of remaining 1/3 cup flour, baking powder and salt; mix well. Stir in vanilla, pecans and apricots. Spread over baked layer. Bake at 350 degrees for 30 minutes. Cool in baking dish. Cut into squares with knife dipped into iced water. Sprinkle with confectioners' sugar. **Yield:** 24 servings.

Approx Per Serving: Cal 173; Prot 3 g; Carbo 30 g; Fiber <1 g; T Fat 6 g; 32% Calories from Fat; Chol 35 mg; Sod 47 mg.

My Mother's Almond Crescents

"Everyone's favorite Christmas cookie"

2 cups butter
1/2 cup sugar
2 teaspoons vanilla extract
1 teaspoon almond extract
4 cups flour
1 1/2 cups unblanched ground almonds
1 1/2 cups confectioners' sugar

Cream butter and sugar in mixer bowl until light and fluffy. Add vanilla, almond extract and flour; mix well. Stir in almonds. Chill, covered, for 1 hour. Roll dough between sheets of waxed paper to 1/4 to 1/2-inch thickness. Cut with small cutter dipped in flour to make crescents. Place on ungreased cookie sheets. Bake at 325 degrees for 20 minutes. Cool on cookie sheet for several minutes. Roll in confectioners' sugar while still warm. Place on wire rack to cool completely. Roll in confectioners' sugar again before storing. **Yield:** 120 servings.

Approx Per Serving: Cal 61; Prot 1 g; Carbo 6 g; Fiber <1 g; T Fat 4 g; 57% Calories from Fat; Chol 8 mg; Sod 26 mg.

Almond Lace Cookies

"An elegant cookie—serve with ice cream, sherbet or sugared fruit."

2/3 cup finely ground blanched almonds
1/2 cup sugar
1/2 cup butter
1 tablespoon flour
2 tablespoons milk

Combine almonds, sugar, butter, flour and milk in 10-inch skillet. Cook over low heat until butter is melted and ingredients are well mixed, stirring constantly. Drop warm mixture 1 heaping teaspoonful at a time 2 inches apart on greased cookie sheet. Do not place more than 4 on each cookie sheet. Bake at 350 degrees for 5 minutes or until golden brown. Remove quickly with large spatula; roll around handle of wooden spoon. Reheat in oven for 1 minute if cookies get too hard to roll. Cool on wire rack. Repeat with remaining batter, greasing cookie sheet each time. Store cooled cookies in covered container. **Yield:** 30 servings.

Approx Per Serving: Cal 58; Prot 1 g; Carbo 4 g; Fiber <1 g; T Fat 5 g; 68% Calories from Fat; Chol 8 mg; Sod 27 mg.

Use an extra oven or refrigerator rack as an oversized cooling rack when baking large batches of cookies.

Cherry Butterballs

3/4 cup butter, softened
1 cup packed brown sugar
1 egg, beaten
1 teaspoon vanilla extract
1/4 teaspoon almond extract
2 cups sifted flour
1 1/2 teaspoons baking powder
1/4 teaspoon salt
1 cup sugar
36 candied cherries

Cream butter and brown sugar in mixer bowl until light and fluffy. Add egg and flavorings; mix well. Add mixture of flour, baking powder and salt; mix well. Shape into balls; coat with sugar. Place on ungreased cookie sheet; press 1 candied cherry into center of each. Bake at 375 degrees for 10 minutes or until light brown. **Yield:** 36 servings.

Approx Per Serving: Cal 130; Prot 1 g; Carbo 23 g; Fiber <1 g; T Fat 4 g; 28% Calories from Fat; Chol 16 mg; Sod 66 mg.

Cranberry-Pecan Bars

1/3 cup margarine
1 cup flour
2 tablespoons sugar
1 cup chopped pecans
1 1/4 cups sugar
2 tablespoons flour
2 eggs, beaten
2 tablespoons milk
1 tablespoon grated orange rind
1 teaspoon vanilla extract
1 cup chopped cranberries
1/2 cup coconut

Cut margarine into 1 cup flour and 2 tablespoons sugar in bowl until crumbly. Stir in half the pecans. Press into 9x13-inch baking dish. Bake at 350 degrees for 15 minutes. Beat next 4 ingredients in bowl. Stir in remaining ingredients. Spread over crust. Bake at 350 degrees for 25 minutes or until golden brown. Cool in baking dish. Cut into bars. **Yield:** 36 servings.

Approx Per Serving: Cal 93; Prot 1 g; Carbo 13 g; Fiber 1 g; T Fat 5 g; 43% Calories from Fat; Chol 12 mg; Sod 24 mg.

Date and Nut Kisses*

2 egg whites
1 cup confectioners' sugar
1 1/2 cups chopped walnuts
1 1/2 cups chopped dates

Beat egg whites until soft peaks form. Beat in confectioners' sugar gradually until stiff. Fold in walnuts and dates. Drop by teaspoonfuls onto greased cookie sheet. Bake at 250 degrees for 10 minutes or until light brown. Cool on wire rack. **Yield:** 24 servings.

Approx Per Serving: Cal 99; Prot 2 g; Carbo 15 g; Fiber 1 g; T Fat 5 g; 40% Calories from Fat; Chol 0 mg; Sod 5 mg.

Alyce's Brownies*

1 16-ounce package caramels
1/3 cup evaporated milk
1 2-layer package German chocolate cake mix
1/3 cup evaporated milk
3/4 cup butter or margarine, softened
1 cup finely chopped pecans
2 cups chocolate chips

Combine caramels and 1/3 cup evaporated milk in double boiler. Cook over boiling water until caramels are melted, stirring frequently. Remove from heat; keep covered. Combine cake mix, remaining 1/3 cup evaporated milk and butter in mixer bowl; mix well. Stir in pecans. Spoon half the batter into greased 9x13-inch baking dish. Bake at 350 degrees for 6 minutes. Sprinkle with chocolate chips. Drizzle with melted caramel mixture. Top with remaining batter. Bake at 350 degrees for 15 to 18 minutes or until brownies test done. Cool slightly in refrigerator. Cut into servings. **Yield:** 15 servings.

Approx Per Serving: Cal 530; Prot 5 g; Carbo 67 g; Fiber 2 g; T Fat 30 g; 48% Calories from Fat; Chol 29 mg; Sod 480 mg.

Raspberry Brownies

"A nice touch to an old favorite"

4 ounces unsweetened chocolate
1 cup unsalted butter
1 teaspoon salt
1 teaspoon vanilla extract
2 cups sugar
4 eggs
1 cup flour
2 cups chopped walnuts
1 cup raspberry jam

Melt chocolate and butter in large saucepan over low heat, stirring occasionally. Remove from heat. Add salt, vanilla and sugar; mix well. Cool to room temperature. Add eggs; beat well. Add flour; beat until smooth. Stir in walnuts. Pour half the batter into greased 9x13-inch baking dish. Freeze, covered, for 30 minutes. Spread raspberry jam over frozen batter; top with remaining batter. Bake at 350 degrees for 40 to 45 minutes or until brownies test done. **Yield:** 15 servings.

Approx Per Serving: Cal 462; Prot 6 g; Carbo 53 g; Fiber 3 g; T Fat 28 g; 51% Calories from Fat; Chol 90 mg; Sod 167 mg.

Soften hardened cookies by storing with an apple wedge in airtight container in refrigerator for several days.

Chocolate Buttersweets

1/2 cup margarine, softened
1/2 cup confectioners' sugar
1/4 teaspoon salt
1 teaspoon vanilla extract
1 1/4 cups flour
3 ounces cream cheese, softened
1 cup confectioners' sugar
2 tablespoons flour
1 teaspoon vanilla extract
1/2 cup chopped walnuts
1/2 cup flaked coconut
1/2 cup semisweet chocolate chips
2 tablespoons margarine
2 tablespoons water
1/2 cup confectioners' sugar

Cream 1/2 cup margarine and 1/2 cup confectioners' sugar in mixer bowl until light and fluffy. Add salt and 1 teaspoon vanilla; mix well. Add 1 1/4 cups flour gradually, beating well after each addition. Shape by teaspoonfuls into balls; place on ungreased cookie sheets. Press indentation into each cookie. Bake at 350 degrees for 12 to 15 minutes or until light brown. Remove to wire rack. Combine cream cheese and 1 cup confectioners' sugar in bowl. Add 2 tablespoons flour and 1 teaspoon vanilla; mix well. Stir in walnuts and coconut. Spoon into indentations in warm cookies. Melt chocolate chips and 2 tablespoons margarine with water in saucepan over low heat, stirring occasionally. Add 1/2 cup confectioners' sugar; beat until smooth. Cool slightly. Place a dollop on top of filling in each cookie. **Yield:** 18 servings.

Approx Per Serving: Cal 217; Prot 2 g; Carbo 25 g; Fiber 1 g; T Fat 13 g; 51% Calories from Fat; Chol 5 mg; Sod 120 mg.

Chocolate Coffee-Nut Cookies

"These are fantastic!"

1/4 cup instant coffee
1 tablespoon boiling water
2/3 cup butter or margarine
2/3 cup sugar
1/2 cup packed dark brown sugar
1 egg
1 teaspoon vanilla extract
1 1/2 cups flour
2 3-ounce bars Swiss dark chocolate
1 1/2 cups chopped walnuts

Dissolve coffee in water in bowl. Cream butter, sugar and brown sugar in mixer bowl until light and fluffy. Add egg, vanilla and coffee; beat well. Add flour; mix well. Cut chocolate into 1/2-inch pieces. Stir chocolate and walnuts into batter. Drop by heaping tablespoonfuls 2 1/2 inches apart on greased cookie sheets. Bake, 1 cookie sheet at a time, at 325 degrees for 17 minutes. Remove to wire rack to cool. **Yield:** 22 servings.

Approx Per Serving: Cal 224; Prot 3 g; Carbo 25 g; Fiber 1 g; T Fat 14 g; 53% Calories from Fat; Chol 25 mg; Sod 55 mg.

White Chocolate Brownies

"This one is for lovers of white chocolate."

10 ounces white chocolate
1 cup unsalted butter
1¼ cups sugar
4 large eggs, beaten
1 tablespoon vanilla extract
2 cups flour
½ teaspoon salt
1 cup coarsely chopped pecans

Line 9x11-inch baking pan with buttered foil, allowing 2-inch overhang at each end. Break white chocolate into small pieces. Heat white chocolate and butter in large saucepan over low heat until melted, stirring frequently. Remove from heat. Stir in sugar. Add eggs and vanilla; mix well. Mixture will look curdled. Stir in flour, salt and pecans quickly until just mixed. Pour batter into prepared baking pan. Bake at 325 degrees for 30 to 35 minutes or until top is golden brown and center is soft when pressed lightly. Cool in pan to room temperature. Chill in refrigerator for 3 hours. Lift brownies out of pan using foil overhang. Cut into servings. **Yield:** 20 servings.

Approx Per Serving: Cal 305; Prot 4 g; Carbo 31 g; Fiber 1 g; T Fat 19 g; 55% Calories from Fat; Chol 70 mg; Sod 54 mg.

White Chocolate Macadamia Nut Cookies

"They won't last long."

1 cup margarine, softened
1 cup packed light brown sugar
½ cup sugar
1 egg
2¼ cups flour
1 teaspoon baking soda
1 cup white chocolate chips
1 3½-ounce jar macadamia nuts

Cream margarine, brown sugar and sugar in mixer bowl until light and fluffy. Add egg; beat well. Add mixture of flour and baking soda; mix well. Dough will be stiff. Stir in white chocolate chips and macadamia nuts. Drop by heaping teaspoonfuls 1 inch apart onto ungreased cookie sheet. Bake at 375 degrees for 8 to 10 minutes or until light brown. Cool on cookie sheet for several minutes. Remove to wire rack to cool completely. **Yield:** 54 servings.

Approx Per Serving: Cal 101; Prot 1 g; Carbo 12 g; Fiber <1 g; T Fat 5 g; 48% Calories from Fat; Chol 4 mg; Sod 61 mg.

Lemon Nut Bars

1/2 cup butter
2 cups flour
1/4 cup packed brown sugar
3 eggs
2 cups packed brown sugar
1/4 teaspoon salt
1 cup shredded coconut
1/2 cup raisins
1/2 cup chopped walnuts
Grated rind of 1 lemon
2 tablespoons fresh lemon juice

Cut butter into flour and 1/4 cup brown sugar in bowl until crumbly. Press into greased 9x13-inch baking dish. Bake at 350 degrees for 10 minutes. Beat eggs, remaining 2 cups brown sugar and salt in mixer bowl until light and fluffy. Stir in coconut, raisins, walnuts, lemon rind and juice. Pour over baked layer. Bake at 350 degrees for 25 to 30 minutes. Cool in baking dish. Cut into bars. **Yield:** 15 servings.

Approx Per Serving: Cal 358; Prot 4 g; Carbo 61 g; Fiber 2 g; T Fat 12 g; 30% Calories from Fat; Chol 59 mg; Sod 137 mg.

Oatmeal-Date-Macadamia Nut Cookies

1/2 cup butter, softened
1/2 cup packed brown sugar
1/2 cup sugar
1 egg
1 teaspoon vanilla extract
1 teaspoon milk
1 cup quick-cooking oats
1 cup flour
1/2 teaspoon baking soda
1/2 cup baking powder
1/2 teaspoon salt
1 cup macadamia nuts, chopped
1 cup pitted dates, chopped

Cream butter, brown sugar and sugar in mixer bowl until light and fluffy. Add egg, vanilla and milk; beat well. Add oats; mix well. Sift flour, baking soda, baking powder and salt together. Add to batter; mix well. Stir in macadamia nuts and dates. Drop by teaspoonfuls 2 inches apart on cookie sheet. Bake at 350 degrees for 10 minutes or until golden brown. Cool on cookie sheet for several minutes. Remove to wire rack to cool completely. **Yield:** 40 servings.

Approx Per Serving: Cal 106; Prot 1 g; Carbo 15 g; Fiber 1 g; T Fat 5 g; 42% Calories from Fat; Chol 12 mg; Sod 257 mg.

Oatmeal Toffee Cookies

"You'll have to hide these."

1 1/2 cups oats
3/4 cup sugar
1/3 cup packed brown sugar
6 tablespoons butter, softened
1 teaspoon vanilla extract
3/4 cup flour
1/2 teaspoon baking soda
1/2 teaspoon baking powder
1/4 teaspoon salt
1 egg
5 1-ounce chocolate-covered toffee bars

Combine oats, sugar, brown sugar and butter in bowl; mix well. Add vanilla. Mix flour, baking soda, baking powder and salt together. Add flour mixture and egg to batter; mix well. Cut candy bars into 1/2-inch pieces. Stir into batter. Shape by tablespoonfuls into balls. Place 2 inches apart on ungreased cookie sheet; flatten slightly. Bake at 350 degrees for 12 minutes. Remove to wire rack to cool. Store in airtight container. **Yield:** 30 servings.

Approx Per Serving: Cal 113; Prot 1 g; Carbo 15 g; Fiber 1 g; T Fat 6 g; 44% Calories from Fat; Chol 13 mg; Sod 74 mg.

Butter Pecan Cookies*

"Easy all-time favorite"

1 1/2 cups butter or margarine
1 1/2 cups packed brown sugar
3 eggs
3 cups flour
1 1/2 teaspoons baking powder
2 cups chopped pecans
2 cups butterscotch chips

Cream butter and brown sugar in mixer bowl until light and fluffy. Add eggs; mix well. Mix flour and baking powder together. Add to batter; mix well. Stir in pecans and butterscotch chips. Drop by teaspoonfuls onto greased cookie sheet. Flatten slightly. Bake at 350 degrees for 8 to 10 minutes or until brown. Cool on cookie sheet for several minutes. Remove to wire rack to cool completely. **Yield:** 36 servings.

Approx Per Serving: Cal 247; Prot 3 g; Carbo 26 g; Fiber 1 g; T Fat 16 g; 56% Calories from Fat; Chol 39 mg; Sod 91 mg.

Microwave hardened brown sugar on Low for 2 minutes to soften and use immediately.

Devil Bars*

3 cups quick-cooking oats
1 15-ounce can Pillsbury coconut-pecan frosting
1 teaspoon vanilla extract
1 cup chocolate chips, melted
3/4 cup peanut butter

Combine oats, frosting and vanilla in bowl; mix well. Press into greased 9x13-inch baking dish. Bake at 325 degrees for 30 minutes. Cool for 20 minutes or to room temperature. Combine melted chocolate chips and peanut butter in bowl; mix well. Spread over baked layer. Let stand for 15 to 20 minutes. Cut into bars. **Yield:** 30 servings.

Approx Per Serving: Cal 157; Prot 4 g; Carbo 18 g; Fiber 1 g; T Fat 8 g; 45% Calories from Fat; Chol 0 mg; Sod 58 mg.

Raspberry Streusel Squares

1 1/2 cups flour
1 teaspoon baking powder
3/4 teaspoon salt
1/2 cup sugar
1/2 cup packed light brown sugar
3/4 cup butter, softened
1 1/2 cups oats
1 cup red raspberry preserves
1/4 cup chopped almonds
1 cup confectioners' sugar

Mix flour, baking powder, salt, sugar and brown sugar together in mixer bowl. Cut in butter until crumbly. Stir in oats. Press about 2/3 of the mixture into greased 8-inch square pan. Top with preserves. Stir almonds into remaining crumb mixture; sprinkle over preserves. Bake at 375 degrees for 30 to 35 minutes or until brown. Cool slightly. Sprinkle with confectioners' sugar. Cut into squares. **Yield:** 16 servings.

Approx Per Serving: Cal 293; Prot 3 g; Carbo 49 g; Fiber 2 g; T Fat 10 g; 31% Calories from Fat; Chol 23 mg; Sod 199 mg.

Ruffles*

2 cups unsalted margarine, softened
1 cup sugar
1 tablespoon vanilla extract
1 cup crushed potato chips
3 1/2 cups flour
1 cup chopped pecans
1 cup confectioners' sugar

Cream margarine and sugar in mixer bowl until light. Stir in next 4 ingredients. Drop by teaspoonfuls 2 inches apart onto ungreased cookie sheet. Bake at 350 degrees for 15 minutes. Sprinkle with confectioners' sugar while warm. Remove to wire rack to cool. **Yield:** 84 servings.

Approx Per Serving: Cal 85; Prot 1 g; Carbo 8 g; Fiber <1 g; T Fat 6 g; 64% Calories from Fat; Chol 0 mg; Sod 3 mg.

Special Shortbreads*

1 cup butter, softened
$1/2$ cup sugar
$1/2$ teaspoon almond extract
$1/2$ teaspoon nutmeg
2 cups flour

Cream butter and sugar in mixer bowl until light and fluffy. Add almond extract, nutmeg and flour gradually, beating well after each addition. Press into greased 11x14-inch baking pan. Bake at 350 degrees for 20 minutes. Cut into squares while hot. Remove to wire rack to cool. **Yield:** 24 servings.

Approx Per Serving: Cal 122; Prot 1 g; Carbo 12 g; Fiber <1 g; T Fat 8 g; 57% Calories from Fat; Chol 21 mg; Sod 65 mg.

Swiss Crisps

"These cookies will convince you never to make an ordinary sugar cookie again."

1 cup butter, softened
1 cup sugar
1 egg yolk
1 tablespoon grated semisweet chocolate
$1\frac{1}{4}$ teaspoons cinnamon
$1/4$ teaspoon nutmeg
$1\frac{1}{2}$ tablespoons Triple Sec or Cointreau
$2\frac{1}{2}$ cups flour
$1/2$ teaspoon baking powder
1 egg white
1 teaspoon water
3 tablespoons sugar
1 teaspoon cinnamon

Cream butter and 1 cup sugar in mixer bowl until light and fluffy. Add egg yolk, chocolate, $1\frac{1}{4}$ teaspoons cinnamon, nutmeg and liqueur; mix well. Add mixture of flour and baking powder; mix well. Shape into ball. Chill, covered, in refrigerator. Roll a small amount at a time very thin on floured surface. Cut with cookie cutters. Place $1/2$ inch apart on ungreased cookie sheet. Paint top of each cookie with mixture of egg white and water. Sprinkle with mixture of remaining 3 tablespoons sugar and 1 teaspoon cinnamon. Bake at 350 degrees for 10 to 12 minutes or until light brown. Cool on cookie sheet for several minutes. Remove to wire rack to cool completely. Store in airtight container. May substitute vanilla extract for liqueur. **Yield:** 96 servings.

Approx Per Serving: Cal 40; Prot <1 g; Carbo 5 g; Fiber <1 g; T Fat 2 g; 19% Calories from Fat; Chol 7 mg; Sod 19 mg.

Turtle Cookies

32 caramels
2/3 cup evaporated milk
1 cup flour
1/2 teaspoon baking soda
1/4 teaspoon salt
1 cup oats
1/2 cup packed brown sugar
3/4 cup margarine
1 cup chocolate chips
1 cup chopped pecans

Melt caramels in evaporated milk in saucepan over low heat, stirring frequently. Combine flour, baking soda, salt, oats and brown sugar in bowl. Cut in margarine until crumbly. Press mixture into greased 9x13-inch baking dish. Bake at 350 degrees for 12 minutes. Sprinkle with chocolate chips; drizzle with warm caramel mixture. Top with pecans. Bake at 350 degrees for 20 minutes. Cool slightly. Cut into bars. **Yield:** 24 servings.

Approx Per Serving: Cal 231; Prot 3 g; Carbo 27 g; Fiber 1 g; T Fat 14 g; 51% Calories from Fat; Chol 2 mg; Sod 144 mg.

Super Wheat Germ Cookies

3/4 cup sugar
1/2 cup oil
2 eggs
1 1/2 cups oats
3/4 cup unsweetened wheat germ
1/2 teaspoon salt
1 teaspoon cinnamon
1/4 teaspoon cloves
1/2 cup raisins
1/2 cup chopped pecans
Juice of 1 lemon
1 cup confectioners' sugar

Combine sugar, oil and eggs in mixer bowl; beat well. Mix oats, wheat germ, salt, cinnamon and cloves together. Add to egg mixture; beat well. Stir in raisins and pecans. Drop by teaspoonfuls onto parchment-lined or greased cookie sheet. Bake at 350 degrees for 10 to 12 minutes or until golden brown. Cool on cookie sheet for several minutes. Remove to wire rack to cool completely. Mix lemon juice with confectioners' sugar in bowl. Spread over cooled cookies. May top each cookie with 1/2 of a candied cherry for more color at holiday times. **Yield:** 30 servings.

Approx Per Serving: Cal 116; Prot 2 g; Carbo 15 g; Fiber 1 g; T Fat 6 g; 43% Calories from Fat; Chol 14 mg; Sod 41 mg.

Toast oats and wheat germ in 350-degree oven before using in cookies for a richer flavor.

Grand Marnier White Chocolate

1 tablespoon butter
1/2 cup whipping cream
8 ounces white chocolate, finely chopped
2 or 3 tablespoons Grand Marnier
4 ounces bittersweet chocolate, melted

Combine butter and whipping cream in saucepan. Cook over low heat until butter is melted. Remove from heat. Stir in white chocolate until melted. Pour into bowl. Whisk in Grand Marnier. Cool completely. Shape into tablespoon-sized balls. Place on baking sheet. Chill until firm. Dip into melted chocolate. Cool on waxed paper for several hours or until completely set. **Yield:** 12 servings.

Approx Per Serving: Cal 195; Prot 2 g; Carbo 18 g; Fiber 1 g; T Fat 14 g; 61% Calories from Fat; Chol 20 mg; Sod 28 mg.

Almond Roca

2 to 3 cups sliced almonds
2 cups each butter and sugar
1 8-ounce chocolate bar, melted
1 cup finely chopped walnuts

Layer sliced almonds in buttered 9x13-inch baking dish. Combine butter and sugar in saucepan. Cook over medium heat to 270 to 290 degrees on candy thermometer, soft-crack stage, stirring constantly. Watch carefully. Pour over almonds in baking dish. Spread half the chocolate on toffee; sprinkle with half the walnuts. Cool to room temperature. Turn out of baking dish. Drizzle with remaining chocolate; sprinkle with remaining walnuts. Break into pieces. Store in airtight container. **Yield:** 15 servings.

Approx Per Serving: Cal 559; Prot 6 g; Carbo 40 g; Fiber 3 g; T Fat 44 g; 68% Calories from Fat; Chol 70 mg; Sod 222 mg.

Chocolate Peanut Clusters*

2 7-ounce milk chocolate bars, broken
1 14-ounce can sweetened condensed milk
1 12-ounce can Spanish peanuts

Melt chocolate in double boiler over boiling water, stirring constantly. Blend in condensed milk. Stir in peanuts. Drop by teaspoonfuls onto foil-lined tray. Let stand until firm. **Yield:** 20 servings.

Approx Per Serving: Cal 264; Prot 8 g; Carbo 25 g; Fiber 2 g; T Fat 16 g; 53% Calories from Fat; Chol 11 mg; Sod 44 mg.

Conestoga Buckeyes

5 cups Special-K or Rice Krispies cereal
1 cup butter, softened
1 18-ounce jar chunky peanut butter
4 cups confectioners' sugar
2 tablespoons vanilla extract
2 cups chocolate chips
1/4 bar paraffin

Process cereal in blender container until reduced to 1 1/2 cups. Combine with next 4 ingredients in bowl; mix well. Shape into walnut-sized balls. Place on waxed paper-lined pan. Freeze, covered, for several hours. Melt chocolate chips and paraffin together in saucepan over low heat, stirring constantly. Coat 1/2 of each piece of candy with warm chocolate. Place on waxed paper to harden. Store in refrigerator. **Yield:** 80 servings.

Approx Per Serving: Cal 109; Prot 2 g; Carbo 11 g; Fiber <1 g; T Fat 7 g; 55% Calories from Fat; Chol 6 mg; Sod 64 mg.

Christmas Crunch*

1 pound Van Leer white summer coating or candy melts
1/3 pound red and green peppermint chips

Microwave white coating in glass bowl on Medium-High for 2 to 3 minutes or until melted, stirring 2 times. Beat by hand until glossy. Stir in peppermint chips. Spread on waxed paper. Let stand until firm. Break into servings. Store in airtight container. **Yield:** 20 servings.

Approx Per Serving: Cal 154; Prot 2 g; Carbo 17 g; Fiber 1 g; T Fat 10 g; 53% Calories from Fat; Chol 6 mg; Sod 24 mg.

Fool's Toffee

1 cup butter
1 cup sugar
36 2x2-inch saltine crackers
2 cups chocolate chips
1/2 cup chopped pecans

Combine butter and sugar in saucepan; mix well. Bring to a boil. Cook for 4 minutes. Place crackers in single layer in 10x15-inch baking pan lined with buttered foil. Spread cooked mixture over top. Bake at 375 degrees for 5 minutes. Sprinkle with chocolate chips. Let stand until chocolate melts. Spread over crackers. Sprinkle with pecans. Chill until cool. Break into pieces. Store in airtight container in refrigerator. **Yield:** 36 servings.

Approx Per Serving: Cal 138; Prot 1 g; Carbo 13 g; Fiber <1 g; T Fat 9 g; 61% Calories from Fat; Chol 15 mg; Sod 83 mg.

PIES

Apple-Cranberry Pie*

3/4 cup packed brown sugar
1/4 cup sugar
1/3 cup flour
1 teaspoon cinnamon
4 cups sliced tart apples
2 cups fresh cranberries
1 recipe 2-crust pie pastry
2 tablespoons butter

Mix first 4 ingredients in bowl. Add apple slices and cranberries, tossing to coat. Spoon into pastry-lined pie plate; dot with butter. Top with remaining pastry, fluting edge and cutting vents. Bake at 425 degrees for 40 to 50 minutes. Cool slightly before serving. **Yield:** 6 servings.

Approx Per Serving: Cal 548; Prot 4 g; Carbo 85 g; Fiber 4 g; T Fat 22 g; 36% Calories from Fat; Chol 10 mg; Sod 416 mg.

Country Apple Pie*

5 cups sliced cooking apples
1 unbaked 9-inch pie shell
1/4 cup flour
3/4 cup sugar
1/2 teaspoon cinnamon
1/2 teaspoon vanilla extract
1 cup light cream or half and half

Pile apples very high in pie shell. Combine flour, sugar and cinnamon in bowl. Sprinkle over apples. Pour mixture of vanilla and cream over apples. Bake at 400 degrees for 50 to 60 minutes or until apples are tender. Serve warm. **Yield:** 8 servings.

Approx Per Serving: Cal 279; Prot 3 g; Carbo 43 g; Fiber 2 g; T Fat 11 g; 36% Calories from Fat; Chol 11 mg; Sod 151 mg.

Sugarless Apple Pie

"Great healthy recipe for nearly everyone"

2 tablespoons cornstarch
1 teaspoon cinnamon
1 teaspoon nutmeg
1 12-ounce can frozen apple juice concentrate, thawed
6 apples, peeled, sliced
1/2 cup chopped walnuts
1/2 cup raisins
2 9-inch pie shells
1 tablespoon margarine

Combine cornstarch, cinnamon and nutmeg in saucepan; mix well. Stir in thawed apple juice concentrate. Cook over low heat until thickened, stirring constantly. Chop apples into bite-sized pieces in bowl. Add walnuts and raisins; mix well. Pour into pie shell. Add sauce. Dot with margarine. Cover with remaining pie shell, sealing edge and cutting vents. Place pie pan on baking sheet. Bake at 350 degrees for 40 minutes. Increase oven temperature to 425 degrees. Bake for 10 minutes longer. Cool slightly before serving. **Yield:** 6 servings.

Approx Per Serving: Cal 598; Prot 6 g; Carbo 84 g; Fiber 6 g; T Fat 29 g; 42% Calories from Fat; Chol 0 mg; Sod 406 mg.

Banana-Macadamia Nut Pie

1/4 cup butter
1 cup packed brown sugar
1 cup light corn syrup
4 large eggs
1 tablespoon vanilla extract
2 teaspoons banana extract
3/4 cup unsalted macadamia nuts
1 unbaked 9-inch pie shell
2 medium ripe bananas
1/2 cup ground macadamia nuts
1/2 cup flour
1/2 cup packed brown sugar
1/2 cup shortening, softened
1 teaspoon cinnamon

Combine butter, 1 cup brown sugar and corn syrup in saucepan. Cook over medium heat until mixture is smooth and hot, stirring constantly. Remove from heat. Cool to room temperature. Whisk in eggs, vanilla and banana extract. Arrange 3/4 cup macadamia nuts in pie shell. Cut bananas into 1/4 to 1/2-inch slices. Layer bananas over macadamia nuts; cover with filling. Combine ground macadamia nuts, flour, remaining 1/2 cup brown sugar, shortening and cinnamon in bowl; mix well. Sprinkle over pie. Bake at 325 degrees for 40 to 50 minutes. **Yield:** 6 servings.

Approx Per Serving: Cal 830; Prot 7 g; Carbo 107 g; Fiber 2 g; T Fat 44 g; 47% Calories from Fat; Chol 122 mg; Sod 263 mg.

Blueberry Cream Pie*

1 quart blueberries
1 unbaked 9-inch pie shell
2/3 cup sugar
1/4 cup flour
1/4 teaspoon salt
1/2 teaspoon nutmeg
1 cup whipping cream
1 teaspoon vanilla extract

Pour blueberries into pie shell. Combine sugar, flour, salt and nutmeg in bowl; mix well. Add cream and vanilla; mix well. Pour over blueberries. Bake at 400 degrees for 45 minutes. **Yield:** 8 servings.

Approx Per Serving: Cal 335; Prot 3 g; Carbo 41 g; Fiber 3 g; T Fat 19 g; 51% Calories from Fat; Chol 41 mg; Sod 220 mg.

Chocolate Amaretto Pie*

2 eggs
1/2 cup sugar
1/2 cup butter, softened
2 tablespoons Amaretto
1 cup chocolate chips
1 cup slivered almonds
1 unbaked 9-inch pie shell

Combine eggs, sugar, butter and liqueur in mixer bowl; beat well. Stir in chocolate chips and almonds. Pour into pie shell. Bake at 350 degrees for 30 minutes. Serve with ice cream or whipped cream. **Yield:** 6 servings.

Approx Per Serving: Cal 671; Prot 10 g; Carbo 53 g; Fiber 4 g; T Fat 49 g; 64% Calories from Fat; Chol 112 mg; Sod 343 mg.

Chocolate Ice Cream Pie*

18 Hydrox cookies, crushed
1/2 cup melted butter
1 quart coffee-flavored ice cream, softened
1/2 cup sugar
2 tablespoons butter
1 5-ounce can evaporated milk
2 squares unsweetened chocolate

Mix cookie crumbs and 1/2 cup melted butter in bowl. Press into greased 8-inch pie plate. Chill until firm. Spread softened ice cream in pie shell. Chill until firm. Combine sugar, 2 tablespoons butter and evaporated milk in bowl. Melt chocolate in double boiler over hot water. Add sugar mixture. Cook until thickened, stirring frequently. Cool to room temperature. Spread over ice cream. Freeze until firm. Garnish with whipped cream. **Yield:** 6 servings.

Approx Per Serving: Cal 763; Prot 13 g; Carbo 107 g; Fiber 4 g; T Fat 33 g; 38% Calories from Fat; Chol 59 mg; Sod 330 mg.

Graham Cracker Pie

"I have never seen this recipe anywhere but at my mother's. It is very old and comes from the mid-west. Very rich. Men seem to love it."

16 graham crackers, finely crushed
1/4 cup melted butter
1/4 cup sugar
1/2 cup flour
1 cup sugar
2 cups milk
3 egg yolks, beaten
2 tablespoons butter
1 teaspoon vanilla extract
3 egg whites
1/2 teaspoon vanilla extract
1/4 teaspoon cream of tartar
6 tablespoons sugar

Combine graham cracker crumbs, melted butter and 1/4 cup sugar in bowl; mix well. Press into pie plate. Combine flour, 1 cup sugar, milk and egg yolks in double boiler; mix well. Cook over low heat until thickened, stirring constantly. Add 2 tablespoons butter and 1 teaspoon vanilla; mix well. Pour into prepared pie plate. Beat egg whites with 1/2 teaspoon vanilla and cream of tartar in mixer bowl until soft peaks form. Add 6 tablespoons sugar gradually, beating until stiff peaks form. Spread over pie until meringue just touches edge. Bake at 350 degrees for 15 minutes or until meringue is brown. Chill overnight. **Yield:** 6 servings.

Approx Per Serving: Cal 521; Prot 8 g; Carbo 81 g; Fiber 1 g; T Fat 19 g; 33% Calories from Fat; Chol 149 mg; Sod 276 mg.

Kahlua Ice Cream Pie

"Grand Finale"

1 8 1/2-ounce package chocolate wafers, finely crushed
3 tablespoons sugar
5 tablespoons melted butter
8 ounces cream cheese, softened
1/4 cup dark rum
1 quart coffee ice cream, softened
1 cup whipping cream
2 tablespoons sugar
1 or 2 tablespoons Kahlua
1/2 ounce semisweet chocolate, grated

Combine cookie crumbs, 3 tablespoons sugar and melted butter in bowl; mix well. Press into 9-inch pie plate. Chill in refrigerator. Beat cream cheese with rum in large bowl until light and fluffy. Fold in ice cream. Pour into prepared pie plate. Freeze, covered, for 4 hours or longer. Whip cream in chilled mixer bowl, adding 2 tablespoons sugar and Kahlua gradually. Swirl onto pie. Sprinkle with grated chocolate. Freeze for 2 hours. Let stand at room temperature for 5 minutes before serving. **Yield:** 8 servings.

Approx Per Serving: Cal 609; Prot 7 g; Carbo 51 g; Fiber <1 g; T Fat 40 g; 61% Calories from Fat; Chol 121 mg; Sod 429 mg.

Lemon Volcano Pie

1/2 cup butter
2 tablespoons lemon rind
1/3 cup lemon juice
1/4 teaspoon salt
1 cup sugar
2 eggs
3 egg yolks
1 quart vanilla ice cream, softened
1 baked 9-inch pie shell
3 egg whites
1/2 cup sugar
1/2 egg shell
1/4 cup brandy, warmed

Melt butter in double boiler. Add lemon rind, lemon juice, salt and 1 cup sugar; mix well. Beat 2 eggs and 3 egg yolks in bowl. Add a small amount of hot mixture to eggs. Stir eggs into hot mixture. Cook over hot water until thickened and smooth, stirring constantly. Chill in refrigerator. Press half the softened ice cream into pie shell. Freeze until firm. Spread half the chilled lemon filling over ice cream. Freeze until firm. Repeat using remaining ice cream and lemon filling. Beat egg whites until soft peaks form. Add 1/2 cup sugar gradually, beating until stiff peaks form. Spread meringue over pie, sealing to edge. Insert empty egg shell into center of pie. Freeze until firm. Preheat oven to 475 degrees. Bake pie for 1 to 3 minutes or until meringue is brown. Fill egg shell with warm brandy; ignite. **Yield:** 6 servings.

Approx Per Serving: Cal 750; Prot 10 g; Carbo 90 g; Fiber 1 g; T Fat 40 g; 47% Calories from Fat; Chol 258 mg; Sod 532 mg.

Peaches and Cream Pie*

1 3-ounce can flaked coconut
1/2 cup finely chopped walnuts
2 tablespoons melted butter
1 quart peach ice cream, softened
1 pint vanilla ice cream, softened
1 12-ounce package frozen red raspberries, thawed
1/2 cup sugar
1 tablespoon cornstarch
2 cups sweetened sliced fresh peaches

Combine coconut, walnuts and melted butter in bowl; mix well. Press into 9-inch pie plate. Bake at 325 degrees for 10 to 15 minutes or until brown. Cool to room temperature. Spoon peach ice cream into cooled pie shell. Freeze, covered, until firm. Spoon vanilla ice cream over peach layer. Freeze, covered, until firm. Drain raspberries, reserving syrup. Combine reserved syrup, sugar and cornstarch in saucepan. Cook over medium heat until thickened, stirring constantly. Stir in berries. Cool to room temperature. Spoon peaches over frozen pie; top with raspberry syrup. **Yield:** 6 servings.

Approx Per Serving: Cal 635; Prot 8 g; Carbo 92 g; Fiber 5 g; T Fat 29 g; 40% Calories from Fat; Chol 69 mg; Sod 158 mg.

Bourbon Coconut-Pumpkin Pie*

1½ cups canned pumpkin
¾ cup flaked coconut
½ cup sugar
½ teaspoon ginger
¼ teaspoon nutmeg
¼ teaspoon allspice
1 cup milk
¾ cup whipping cream
¼ cup bourbon
3 eggs, lightly beaten
1 baked 10-inch pie shell
1 egg white, lightly beaten

Mix first 10 ingredients in bowl. Pour into pie shell brushed with egg white. Bake at 350 degrees for 30 minutes or until set. **Yield:** 8 servings.

Approx Per Serving: Cal 363; Prot 6 g; Carbo 32 g; Fiber 2 g; T Fat 22 g; 56% Calories from Fat; Chol 115 mg; Sod 208 mg.

Pumpkin Ice Cream Pie

¼ cup packed brown sugar
¼ cup honey
½ teaspoon cinnamon
¼ teaspoon ginger
¼ teaspoon nutmeg
¾ cup pumpkin
1 quart vanilla ice cream, softened
½ cup chopped pecans
1 9-inch graham cracker pie shell

Combine first 6 ingredients in saucepan. Bring to a boil over low heat; cool completely. Fold in softened ice cream. Sprinkle pecans in pie shell. Pour in ice cream mixture; freeze until firm. **Yield:** 8 servings.

Approx Per Serving: Cal 501; Prot 5 g; Carbo 63 g; Fiber 2 g; T Fat 27 g; 47% Calories from Fat; Chol 30 mg; Sod 302 mg.

Lancaster Raisin Crumb Pie

8 ounces raisins
¾ cup each water and sugar
Rind and juice of ½ lemon
1 unbaked 9-inch pie shell
1 cup flour
¾ cup sugar
2 tablespoons butter
1 teaspoon baking powder
½ cup milk
1 egg

Cook raisins, water, ¾ cup sugar, grated lemon rind and juice in saucepan for 5 minutes or until raisins are plump; cool. Pour into pie shell. Mix flour and ¾ cup sugar in bowl. Cut in butter until crumbly. Reserve half the mixture. Add baking powder to remaining mixture. Add milk and egg; mix well. Spoon in batter; sprinkle with reserved crumb mixture. Bake at 350 degrees for 30 to 35 minutes or until brown. **Yield:** 6 servings.

Approx Per Serving: Cal 593; Prot 7 g; Carbo 110 g; Fiber 3 g; T Fat 16 g; 23% Calories from Fat; Chol 49 mg; Sod 296 mg.

Rhubarb-Raspberry Custard Pie

"This pie is tart and incredible."

1¼ cups sugar
1 tablespoon flour
¼ teaspoon nutmeg
4 eggs, beaten
3 cups 1-inch chunks rhubarb
1 cup fresh or frozen raspberries
1 unbaked 9-inch pie shell
¼ cup flour
¼ cup sugar
½ teaspoon cinnamon
½ teaspoon nutmeg
2 tablespoons butter
¼ cup chopped almonds

Combine 1¼ cups sugar, 1 tablespoon flour and ¼ teaspoon nutmeg in bowl. Add eggs; beat well. Mix rhubarb and raspberries together in bowl. Pour into pie shell. Spoon in batter. Cover edge with foil. Bake at 375 degrees for 25 minutes. Remove foil. Bake for 15 minutes longer or until custard is set. Combine remaining ¼ cup flour, ¼ cup sugar, cinnamon and ½ teaspoon nutmeg in bowl; mix well. Cut in butter until crumbly. Stir in almonds. Sprinkle topping over baked pie. Bake at 375 degrees for 5 minutes longer or until topping is brown. Cool slightly before serving. **Yield:** 6 servings.

Approx Per Serving: Cal 508; Prot 8 g; Carbo 75 g; Fiber 4 g; T Fat 21 g; 36% Calories from Fat; Chol 152 mg; Sod 266 mg.

Strawberry-Coconut Pie

½ cup melted butter
2½ cups flaked coconut
2 pints fresh strawberries, sliced
¾ cup sugar
1 envelope unflavored gelatin
½ cup cold water
2 tablespoons lemon juice
1 cup whipping cream, whipped

Combine melted butter and coconut in bowl; mix well. Press into 9-inch pie plate. Bake at 350 degrees for 30 minutes or until golden brown. Cool to room temperature. Combine strawberries and sugar in bowl; mix gently. Soften gelatin in cold water in saucepan. Heat until gelatin is dissolved, stirring constantly. Add gelatin and lemon juice to strawberries; mix gently. Fold in whipped cream. Chill until mixture mounds when dropped from spoon. Spoon into baked coconut pie shell. Chill for 4 hours. Garnish with fresh strawberries. **Yield:** 6 servings.

Approx Per Serving: Cal 546; Prot 4 g; Carbo 47 g; Fiber 7 g; T Fat 41 g; 64% Calories from Fat; Chol 96 mg; Sod 153 mg.

Contributor List

Aceto, Kathleen
Alessandroni, Roxanne
Ammory, Julie
Andrews, Betty
Arms, LaVon
Arnold, Hazel E.
Arnold, Raymond
Ashton, Patricia
Babcock, Evie
Bafundo, Olympia
Bailey, Tania
Bain, Barbara M.
Bartola, Catherine
Baugh, Pauline S.
Baumgardner, Gerry
Benning, Jean
Bennyhoff, Judilee
Blankley, Charlotte
Bloss, Lois S.
Boehmler, Hazel
Bohlke, Genie
Bolger, Ann M.
Bollinger, Amy
Bollinger, James R.
Bollinger, Lucynda
Bollinger, Dr. James R.
Bonee, Terry L.
Borst, Barbara C.
Bowden, Phyllis
Bowen, Nancy
Bowes, Barbara
Boylon, Hildegarde
Brecht, Elizabeth
Brewer, Sue
Brooks, Marea
Brophy, Maripat
Brown, Debra
Brown, Debra K.
Brown, Eileen Cuff
Brown, Joy
Brown, Mary Frances
Brown, Pat
Brown, Peg
Brunner, Diane M.
Brunt, Kay
Bucher, Minnie
Bullen, Ann
Bunn, Sandy
Burton, Nancy
Cabot, Terry
Callahan, Barbara
Carlin, Bernice M.
Carmody, Esther
Carmody, Sharon
Carson, Joan Moller
Carter, Carolyn
Carter, Wanda
Carter, Yvonne S.
Cavanaugh, Therese E.
Cernonok, Trish
Chandler, Marjorie
Chulick, Carlyn H.
Claster, Ricki
Cleveland, Nancy M.
Cola, Cindy
Coleman, Cecelia
Colletta, Betty
Collins, Jeanne
Connus, Helen
Cooper, Bernice L.
Craig, Diane
Crawford, Victoria
Creamer, Mary Ellen
Cross, Jean
Crouse, Mary
Cuthbertson, Marie
Dahl, Phyllis
Dallman, Barbara
Daniels, Mrs. Spencer
Daves, Dottie
Davis, Mary C.
De Coux, Gail
DeHaven, Helen V.
Deisroth, Paddy
Dempsey, Kathleen
Dougherty, Gail

Drake, Diane M.
Drew-Larrabee, Jerri
Drill, Patricia A.
Dudt, Ruth
Dunn, Ann
Dunn, Julie
Easton, Joan S.
Eckert, Kathy
Egger, Helen M.
Eisler, Joyce
Endy, Pat
Engler, Sandy
Ernst, Thelma
Evans, Jeanne
Evans, June
Ewing, Eloise A.
Fabacher, Mary Helen
Facciolli, Betty
Fehr, Ann
Fell, Mary Ann
Feninger, Jill E.
Ficca, Christine M.
Finley, Justine S.
Flamini, Alice D.
Flynn, Betty Ann
Fogerty, Carolyn W.
Fonock, John
Forese, Rose
Forge, Joanne
Fosnocht, Mary L.
Fraidenburgh, Dot
Futer, Marie S.
Gallagher, Helene
Gamber, Carol
Gardner, Nita F.
Gardner, William R.
Garnett, Edith K.
Garrard, Anne T.
Gasho, Beth
Gates, Ann
Gilginas, Sophie
Gill, Millie
Gilliland, Carolyn
Gilpin, Betsy
Giordano, Linda
Goodrich, Lois
Gottier, Marty L.
Graham, Phyllis
Graybill, Elizabeth K.
Graybill, Martha
Graybill, Virginia
Gunnels, Joan
Haldeman, Edna L.
Hale, Elsie F.
Halstead, Virginia
Hancox, Judy
Hankin, Henrietta
Harnsberger, June H.
Hartshorn, Joy
Hashem, Laurice
Hatch, Mrs. C. B.
Helou, Mona
Henry, Gini
Herman, Ruth Anne
Hesch, Annetta
Hewitt, Pat
Hoffman, Peggy
Hollerbach, Ann
Holmes, Janet
Holmes, Phyllis
Hopkins, Karen P.
Horan, Eileen
Howard, Michele
Howley, Ginnie
Hughes, Gloria
Hughes, Marilyn
Hullett, Sandy
Hunsberger, Susan L.
Hutzler, Joan
Hyatt, Donna M.
Hynes, Peggy
Jackson, Joanne
Jefferys, Jane
Jenkins, JoAnn
Jennings, Pamela D.
Jensen, Pete

Jensen, Ruth
Johnson, Irene M.
Johnson, Linda
Johnson, Mary-Jo D.
Johnson, Mimi
Jommersbach, Dorothy J.
Just, Katheryn K.
Kadyszewski, Beth
Keeley, Julie A.
Kelly, Bernadette
Kendig, Karen
Kennedy, Louise
Kennedy, Suie
Kerr, M.D., Kim M.
Kerr, Natalie R.
Kinney, Ellen
Kinny, Ginger
Koegel, Marie
Koup, Shirley
Kovello, Mary Ann
Kukula, Marion
Kurtz, Jackie
Lamphear, Mary Lou
Landeck, Helen S.
Larrabee, Guy D.
Latshaw, LaRue S.
Laud, Sally
Lee, Rosemary M.
Lehman, Jeanne
Lehnert, Ruth
LeVan, Charlotte
Lief, Judy
Light, Mary S.
Linden, Angela
Listino, Olga
Livolsi, Anna Marie
Longaker, Dorothy
Lyon, Rosemary
Mack, Lynn
Mallon, Patricia A.
Malo, Joanne
Marano, Dorothy
Marcus, Linda
Maris, Barbara A.
Markle, Molly
Martin, Betty
Martin, Beverly
Martz, Fred
Mason, Peggy
Masters, Patricia K.
Maynard, Katherine
McAleer, Sandy
McCarthy, Bobbie
McCarthy, Lee
McCarthy, Toni
McCartney, Jim
McCartney, Joanne
McClenachan, Suzanne
McCoy, Eric
McCullough, Rose M.
McDonald, Athalia B.
McDonald, Louisa B.
McDonnell, Susan H.
McGroarty, Donna
McHugh, Patricia
McIntyre, Jo
McKeon, Carol L.
McOsker, Patricia
Mentzer, Mrs. Clyde S.
Meyers, Ann
Meyers, Lew
Meyers, Pamela Brown
Meyers, Rose W.
Miles, Jan
Miles, Nancy
Miller, Evangeline
Miller, Judith
Miller, Kay
Miller, Marilyn
Mitchell, Diane
Moller, Beth
Moller, Debbie
Moller, Lynne H.
Moller, Mary
Morehouse, Betty
Morelli, Ada

Moretzsohn, Marge
Moseley, Jan
Moser, Dottie
Mulhall, Maureen F.
Munday, Fran
Musikant, Shirley
Musslewhite, Elva
Nameth, Teny
Narcisi, Edie
Nasso, Kandy
Needham, Nancy G.
Nelson, Alice M.
Neumyer, Mary C.
Nicotera, Madeline P.
Nolan, Connie
Nolan, Kayo
Nyagwegwe, Cathy M.
O'Rourke, Debi
Omlor, Marie
Ourach, Linda M.
Ovelman, Grace S.
Overbeck, William M.
Page, Mrs. Wheeler
Palmer, Maud B.
Panitt, Marjorie
Papariello, Chris
Papariello, Kathleen
Partner, Katherine
Paskow, Carol C.
Perrone, Barbara
Pfleiger, Gloria
Phelps, Janet
Phiel, Louise
Phillips, Beverly
Pierce, Helen D.
Pierce, James A.
Piombino, Cindy
Portner, Kas
Post, Harriet
Potter, Roberta
Ranghelli, Anne
Rapoport, Brucie Roberts
Rebovich, Barbara
Recktenwald, Doris
Recktenwald, Fred
Reed, Ellie
Rehfuss, Lois G.
Reimann, Jean
Reinhard, Jane
Reynolds, Bette A.
Reynolds, Cynthia L.
Reynolds, Deedy
Riley, Ginny
Robinson, Jen
Robinson, Myra
Ross, Pat
Roth, Charlene D.
Roth, Sonja B.
Rouse, Patricia
Russell, Richard A.
Russo, Jo
Sacra, June
Sandquist, Rosellen
Saruk, M.D., Michael
Satterthwaite, Kay
Sausa, Deborah A.
Scharnberg, Patty
Scheifele, Alyce
Schoch, Ginny
Schopps, Jean
Schreiber, Nancy
Schwartz, Alicia
Schwartz, Kathy
Sempier, Mary C.
Severence, Evelyn N.
Shenk, Lori
Shimrack, Dede
Silverwood, Pat
Silvon, Kathy
Singmaster, Marj
Skillen, Marjorie
Skurla, Gloria
Smith, Karen
Smith, Mrs. Rayburn
Sobyak, Ardyth A.
Sobyak, Frank

Sommese, Terry
Sophocles, Annette
Spane, Mary Alice
Spigler, Janice
Staats, Louise
Stagnaro, Carol
Stalder, Janet G.
Stanton, Sharon
Steinbach, Gwen
Steinberg, Suzanne Spane
Steinmetz, Marie E.
Stephens, Mary L.
Stephenson, Bee
Stevens, Ella Parshall
Stine, Marti
Stoughton, Joanne
Stover, Pat
Swope, Joan
Taylor, Nancy
Telthorster, Audrey
Teti, Marguerite V.
Thayer, Charlotte
Thomas, Marge
Thompson, Barbara J.
Thompson, Diane
Thompson, Suzanne
Tily, Janet
Timberlake, Joy
Tinley, Betty
Tippy, Ann
Tozer, Cindy
Travis, Jane S.
Tully, Terri
Uhlenburg, Marjory S.
Van Gunten, Betty
Veronesi, Adelaide
Vitray, Mary E.
Waher, Barbara
Walsh, Connie
Ward, Constance J.
Watson, Ruth S.
Webb, Norma
Weber, Barbara
Werner, Barbara A.
White, C. S.
White, Florence A.
Whiting, Emma W.
Wigington, Alma K.
Wiley, Kay
Williams, Lannie
Wilson, Kathy
Wilson, Sally
Wilwol, John
Winner, Shirley
Yantis, Pat
Yarow, Carol Wells
Young, Linda
Zeager, Gertrude
Zentgraf, Mimi
Ziegler, Loretta S.
Ziegler, Ruth R.
Zimmer, Barbara S.
Zogg, Susan

Nutritional Analysis Guidelines

The editors have attempted to present these family recipes in a form that allows approximate nutritional values to be computed. Persons with dietary or health problems or whose diets require close monitoring should not rely solely on the nutritional information provided. They should consult their physicians or a registered dietitian for specific information.

Abbreviations for Nutritional Analysis

Cal — Calories	Dietary Fiber — Fiber	Sod — Sodium
Prot — Protein	T Fat — Total Fat	gr — gram
Carbo — Carbohydrates	Chol — Cholesterol	mg — milligrams

Nutritional information for these recipes is computed from information derived from many sources, including materials supplied by the United States Department of Agriculture, computer databanks and journals in which the information is assumed to be in the public domain. However, many specialty items, new products and processed foods may not be available from these sources or may vary from the average values used in these analyses. More information on new and/or specific products may be obtained by reading the nutrient labels. Unless otherwise specified, the nutritional analysis of these recipes is based on all measurements being level.

- **Artificial sweeteners** vary in use and strength so should be used "to taste," using the recipe ingredients as a guideline. Sweeteners using aspartame (NutraSweet and Equal) should not be used as a sweetener in recipes involving prolonged heating which reduces the sweet taste. For further information, refer to package information.
- **Alcoholic ingredients** have been analyzed for the basic ingredients, although cooking evaporates the alcohol thus decreasing caloric content.
- **Buttermilk, sour cream** and **yogurt** are the types available commercially.
- **Cake mixes** which are prepared using package directions include 3 eggs and 1/2 cup oil.
- **Chicken,** cooked for boning and chopping, has been roasted; this method yields the lowest caloric values.
- **Cottage cheese** is cream-style with 4.2% creaming mixture. Dry-curd cottage cheese has no creaming mixture.
- **Eggs** are all large. (To avoid raw eggs that may carry salmonella as in eggnog or 6-week muffin batter, use an equivalent amount of commercial egg substitute.)
- **Flour** is unsifted all-purpose flour.
- **Garnishes,** serving suggestions and other optional additions and variations are not included in the analysis.
- **Margarine** and **butter** are regular, not whipped or presoftened.
- **Milk** is whole milk, 3.5% butterfat. Lowfat milk is 1% butterfat. Evaporated milk is whole milk with 60% of the water removed.
- **Oil** is any type of vegetable cooking oil. Shortening is hydrogenated vegetable shortening.
- **Salt** and other ingredients to taste as noted in the ingredients have not been included in the nutritional analysis.
- If a choice of ingredients has been given, the nutritional analysis reflects the first option. If a choice of amounts has been given, the nutritional analysis reflects the greater amount.

Index

Quilted Quisine

Paoli Memorial Hospital Auxiliary
P. O. Box 115
Paoli, PA 19301

Please send me ______ copies of ***Quilted Quisine***

Quilted Quisine	@ $18.95 each $________
Postage and Handling	@ $ 3.00 each $________
Pennsylvania residents add sales tax	@ $ 1.14 each $________
	Total $________

Name ____

Address ____

City/State/Zip ____________________________________

Make check payable to ***Quilted Quisine***

Quilted Quisine

Paoli Memorial Hospital Auxiliary
P. O. Box 115
Paoli, PA 19301

Please send me ______ copies of ***Quilted Quisine***

Quilted Quisine	@ $18.95 each $________
Postage and Handling	@ $ 3.00 each $________
Pennsylvania residents add sales tax	@ $ 1.14 each $________
	Total $________

Name ____

Address ____

City/State/Zip ____________________________________

Make check payable to ***Quilted Quisine***